MIXED FEELINGS

Also by Francine Klagsbrun

The First Ms. Reader
(editor)

Free to Be . . . You and Me
(editor)

Too Young to Die:
Youth and Suicide

Voices of Wisdom:
Jewish Ideals and Ethics for Everyday Living

Married People:
Staying Together in the Age of Divorce

Books for Young Readers

Sigmund Freud:
A Biography

The Story of Moses

Psychiatry:
What It Is
What It Does

Freedom Now!
The Story of the Abolitionists

MIXED FEELINGS

Love, Hate, Rivalry, and Reconciliation Among Brothers and Sisters

FRANCINE KLAGSBRUN

BANTAM BOOKS
NEW YORK   TORONTO   LONDON   SYDNEY   AUCKLAND

MIXED FEELINGS

A Bantam Book / September 1992

BOOK DESIGN BY M 'N O PRODUCTION SERVICES, INC.

Library of Congress Cataloging-in-Publication Data

Klagsbrun, Francine.
     Mixed feelings : love, hate, rivalry, and reconciliation among brothers and sisters / by Francine Klagsbrun.
         p.   cm.
     Includes bibliographical references (p. 417) and index.
     ISBN 0-553-08841-6
     1. Brothers and sisters.   2. Brothers and sisters—Case studies.
     I. Title.
     BF723.S43K57   1992
     155.9′24—dc20   92-6769
                                                                          CIP

Published simultaneously in the United States and Canada

Bantam Books are published by Bantam Books, a division of Bantam Doubleday Dell Publishing Group, Inc. Its trademark, consisting of the words "Bantam Books" and the portrayal of a rooster, is Registered in U.S. Patent and Trademark Office and in other countries. Marca Registrada. Bantam Books, 666 Fifth Avenue, New York, New York 10103.

PRINTED IN THE UNITED STATES OF AMERICA

BVG   0 9 8 7 6 5 4 3 2

For Robert, with love
(mostly)

CONTENTS

PART II. PRESSURE POINTS

PART III. ENDINGS AND BEGINNINGS

ACKNOWLEDGMENTS

A great many people shared with me their thoughts and emotions about having siblings and being siblings. Because I promised them anonymity, I cannot thank them by name, but I am enormously grateful to all of them. Whether in personal interviews or in response to the survey, they were honest, open, and unstinting in allowing me into their lives. Without them this book would not have been possible.

Deep thanks go to Dr. Jerry F. Westermeyer for his scrupulous attention to all aspects of the survey and his unflagging enthusiasm throughout this project. For their invaluable aid in the research process, I thank also Cynthia Epstein Smith, who brought great sensitivity and intelligence to every task she undertook, and Cathy Markoff, whose unique ability to ferret out information and follow research leads has been of immeasurable help to me.

A number of therapists and social scientists generously met with me to discuss their ideas about siblings. My gratitude especially to Doctors Louise Kaplan, Alexander Levay, Peter Neubauer, and Arietta Slade and to Barbara Fields, Eileen Lefcourt, and Judith Stern Peck. I am grateful also to John Goodson and Theodore Cohn for their special expertise in the area of family businesses.

Three editors contributed to this project, each in her own way. Nessa Rapoport, in the early phases, helped me shape an amorphous mass of material into the structure of a real book. Linda Loewenthal, her successor, added clearheaded insights and ideas. Ann Harris, who became the book's main editor, read my manuscript with the critical eye of a superb professional. Her comments, suggestions, and uncompromising questions (always offered with grace and gentleness) inspired me toward new paths and greater depth in presenting this complex subject.

Finally, I thank my friend and agent, Charlotte Sheedy, for providing warm support when I most needed it, and my husband for giving me the gift of his expert psychiatric knowledge along with the gifts of his patience and love.

INTRODUCTION

"You'd better get the tissue box ready," the woman at the other end of the phone said. "It's going to be *that* kind of meeting."

The warning came toward the close of a conversation in which I had arranged to interview her about her relationships to her older sister and younger brother. But it wasn't necessary. I had already learned from experience that in interviewing siblings, tissues needed to be as much a part of my apparatus as a pad, pencil, and tape recorder, the emotions expressed were that strong, the meetings almost always of *"that* kind."

I have written books and articles about marriage and family ties, about religion, feminism, and a variety of other subjects that touch deep chords in people's psyches, but never have I experienced the overpowering emotional responsiveness that the subject of siblings evokes. Whether to a casual mention of the topic at a dinner party or to a formal lecture, the reactions are instant, visceral, almost urgent. "I think," said one woman, typical of many other people, "I feel compelled to be interviewed for this book."

That compelling interest should not be surprising. About 80 percent of people in the United States and Europe grow up with siblings. Beginning in the primeval days of childhood, even before language develops, the ties between brothers and sisters often stretch far into old age, enduring longer than any other attachment we have. Parents die, friends drift away, marriages dissolve. But brothers and sisters cannot be divorced: even if they do not speak to each other for twenty years, they remain forever connected by blood and history.

Given the intensity of the sibling bond, what *is* surprising is that so few people have actually examined its meaning in their own lives. Part of the powerful emotionalism I saw in interviews came from the difficulty siblings had and the pain many felt as they confronted thoughts and feelings they had rarely articulated before. We are all accustomed to analyzing (often incessantly) our relationships with parents. But when people try to analyze their attachments to their brothers and sisters, they may find themselves tripping over words as they struggle to reach into the depths of their being and their history.

That lack of experience in examining sibling ties parallels the lack of attention paid to the subject for years by professionals. Freud made the Oedipus complex—the longing of children for their opposite-sex parents and their fear of punishment because of it—the center of his theory of family life, relegating sibling connections to a subordinate place. His followers, perhaps even more than he, regarded sibling relations as spin-offs of parental ones, viewing sisters primarily as mother-substitutes and brothers as father-substitutes in the relationships among family members. As one woman explained, "I wanted to talk to my analyst about a problem I had with my brother. But he insisted that the real issue was my sexual fantasies about my parents."

Not until the 1970s, and more so in the 1980s, did psychologists, psychiatrists, and other social scientists begin to take a serious interest in the sibling relationship itself. Since then professional studies of siblings have multiplied, and many articles and several books on the subject have appeared. Even so, huge gaps remain in our knowledge of adult siblings and our understanding of how the childhood bond between sisters and brothers is carried over into their grown-up lives.

It was to help fill in some of those gaps that I undertook this exploration into adult sibling relationships. Judging from my own attachment to my older brother and the ties I witnessed between my parents and their siblings, I had always felt that this bond had profound significance in people's lives, not unlike the importance of parents themselves. I wanted to understand that significance, to delve beneath the layers of history that brothers and sisters have built over the years and reach the core of their connectedness, to know how they begin to shape one another in their earliest days and what they continue to mean to each other during their later ones.

Because this was an exploration, I let the material guide me in arriving at conclusions. I also realized early on that given the vastness of the subject, some specialized areas could not be covered in great depth. Twins, for example, are discussed at length, but mostly in the context of broader sibling matters—there are other books one can turn to devoted solely to this topic. Only children are also treated primarily in relation to sibling issues and not as a subject in itself.

As I proceeded I tracked down and read a wide array of studies from the different social sciences and integrated their findings into the overall themes of the book. But the heart of this exploration was my own investigation into the thoughts, feelings, problems, and pleasures of siblings themselves. That investigation took two forms: in-depth interviews with brothers and sisters, and a carefully designed survey of sibling attitudes and behaviors.

The interviews included people from many different regions of the United States and Canada and many walks of life. My intention was to write about a nonclinical population—"normal" people coping with the normal issues and challenges of family living—and I recruited them in several ways. In the course of lecturing around the country (often on my last book, *Married People*), I asked for volunteers to participate in this study and received more offers than I could handle. Other people responded to notices placed in community centers and organizational offices, and still others were recommended by participants themselves. Some thirty respondents to the survey questionnaire volunteered for interviews as well. Finally, Cynthia Epstein Smith and Cathy Markoff, who served as research associates on this project, recruited yet more subjects, and Cynthia—a talented social worker—interviewed a number of those.

After screening more than two hundred volunteers, I decided that simply examining the sibling experiences of a miscellany of people was not adequate to provide a full understanding of the *relationship*, the attachment, itself. So I undertook to interview every sibling in a family in which one member had been selected for the project, sometimes crisscrossing the country to meet with brothers and sisters, occasionally conducting extensive telephone interviews with those I could not travel to meet.

In all, the in-depth interviews included 122 people. The largest family interviewed had eight siblings, the majority had between two and five. Each interview lasted four to five hours, sometimes longer, and several were followed up with one or more shorter discussions. For the sake of confidentiality the names of all the people interviewed whose life stories appear in this book have been changed, as have geographic locations, occupations, and other identifying features.

In almost every instance, siblings were interviewed separately, although sometimes I would initially meet with them together. In those separate meetings each sib had an opportunity to speak freely, perhaps to say things to me that he or she had never said or dared to say to a brother or sister. For me, listening as siblings plumbed the depths of their feelings for each other provided insights into their relationships that often they themselves did not have. I might hear two brothers speak independently of their longing for greater intimacy, neither realizing that the other had the same longing. I might hear of hurts that stemmed back to childhood, of grudges that could not be put aside, of admiration and love that had never been expressed because of one sib's fear of looking foolish or being rejected by another.

What I heard in those interviews I have tried to convey in this book.

The survey questionnaire offered other valuable insights into sibling ties. Although statistics do not seem to me the prime path toward understanding human relationships, the survey was an important supplement to the interviews, adding another dimension to this investigation. It provided data on differences between siblings of the same sex and those of the opposite sex. It identified key factors that add to or interfere with closeness, and it turned up provocative evidence about the nature of parental favoritism. It confirmed some beliefs one is likely to hold intuitively, and produced surprises in other areas. (The data are presented and discussed in the text, and major findings are summarized in Appendix A.)

The survey questionnaires were sent out at the time the preliminary interviews were taking place. Dr. Jerry F. Westermeyer, who specializes in research on human development, worked closely with me in developing the questionnaire. An assistant professor in the Department of Psychiatry at the University of Illinois College of Medicine, Dr. Westermeyer also holds the position of senior psychologist at Humana Hospital Michael Reese Medical Center in Chicago. After the data from the forms were entered into a computer, he prepared all the statistical analyses. He also constructed the graphs found in Appendix A and rechecked for accuracy all survey findings and numbers in the book.

Although the sample in the survey was not random—meaning selected from a vast cross-section of society—it was substantial, and representative in many respects. But I would hope that this study becomes a source for future research and that others will replicate it with larger and broader samples.

The total survey sample consisted of 272 people recruited from three medium-sized business firms in large metropolitan areas, two in the Northeast and one in the Midwest. It included 64 men and 208 women who reported on their relationships with 610 brothers and sisters. That great preponderance of women respondents over men in part reflects the somewhat larger numbers of women employees, many of whom worked in the personnel, secretarial, and clerical departments. But it also reflects the greater interest women have traditionally demonstrated in relationship issues, and particularly in family matters. In spite of those uneven numbers, statistical analyses showed that most major findings were true for both men and women.

The subjects ranged in age from 19 to 71 years, with an average age of 37.1 years. Most (85 percent) were in their twenties, thirties, or forties. They came from all social classes and all business levels, ranging from chief executives to switchboard operators. They also came from all major religions. They were primarily white (95 percent)— unfortunately, only 5 percent of the respondents were black. As to marital status, 54 percent were married, 28 percent were single, 15 percent were divorced or separated, and 2 percent were widowed.

About 33 percent of the subjects had one sibling, 28 percent had two siblings, 18 percent had three siblings, and 21 percent had four or more sibs. The questionnaire allowed a respondent to report on his or her relationship with up to five siblings, and fewer than 5 percent of the subjects came from families with more than five sibs.

The questionnaire is included in Appendix B as "The Sibling Questionnaire." It consisted mainly of check-off questions that could be quickly and easily answered. (The technical term for these is "forced-choice" questions, because in answering, subjects must choose one option out of several.) But there were also several open-ended questions, as well as extra space for respondents to elaborate on their answers to a question or to write other thoughts they might have about their brothers or sisters.

And write they did. They filled up the extra spaces left after each open-ended question, and they filled up the blank page left at the end for additional thoughts, and then some of them added pages of their own. It was as though, having begun to think about their sisters and brothers, they could not stop now. They had stories to tell, and they needed to tell them.

They were not the only writers. I was amazed at how many letters I received from people I had interviewed, usually written a few days after an interview. They wrote to expand on some thought they were not sure they had conveyed to me clearly, or they wrote to reemphasize something they had said. Or—most usually—they wrote simply to continue the process of self-examination. Like the respondents to the questionnaire, in struggling to articulate their thoughts and emotions, they had tapped into an unknown part of themselves. Now they wanted to keep mining that part, to probe farther than they ever had before into the essence of this relationship.

The most satisfying letters and statements were those from people who said that in talking or writing about a brother or sister, they had realized how much that sibling meant to them. "This experience has been illuminating," wrote a man who had spoken at length about his differences with his younger sister but also his wish for her love and friendship. "I don't know what she said to you, and she doesn't know what I said, but we both know that we feel closer now and will try hard to remain that way."

It is my hope that this book will help other siblings draw closer and remain that way. We live at a time when divorce and shrinking family size have made family members more vital to each other than ever. This bond is powerful, complex, deep-seated, sometimes unfathomable. But for any person who has a sister or brother, it is a bond like no other in the world, and well worth the effort of examining and preserving. If the life stories presented here can spark a sense of recognition in readers, if the survey findings can trigger reflections on their own experiences, and if the discussions throughout on the nature of this profound and remarkable tie can shed light on their own sibling attachments, this exploration will have served its purpose.

MIXED FEELINGS

PROLOGUE

SIBLING IMPRINTS

One Sunday afternoon of my childhood stands out in sharp relief from all others. It's a grueling hot day in mid-July. We are on the way home—my father and mother, my brother Robert, and I—from a day at Jones Beach, about an hour's drive from our Brooklyn apartment. I am around six years old and my brother around ten.

We have been inching along, stuck in a massive traffic jam. Perspiring from the stifling heat (air conditioners in cars as yet unknown), our bodies raw from the mixture of sunburn and dried ocean salt and itching from the tiny grains of sand we have not bothered to wipe away with our towels, Robert and I fight constantly in the back seat. Irritated, my father finally pulls off the road and rearranges the seating, my brother in back with my mother, and I with my father up front. To quiet us, he also buys each a Dixie cup—those little round containers filled with equal amounts of chocolate and vanilla ice cream.

I begin nibbling at my ice cream with the flat wooden spoon that accompanies it, and in nibbling I hatch a delicious plan. I will eat slowly, so slowly that I will finish *last*. I'll have ice cream left after Robert has gulped down all of his, and just when he might be wishing for more, I'll produce mine. "Look," I'll say, "*I* still have ice cream to eat." What I will mean is that I have something he doesn't have, that this time I will have beaten him, this older brother whom I adore and idolize, but who has always bested me.

So I nibble slowly at my ice cream with my wooden spoon, and it begins to melt.

"Are you finished with your ice cream?" I call out every few minutes.

3

"No, not yet," he answers.

On we drive, and the heat becomes more intense, and the ice cream melts and melts until the chocolate runs into the vanilla, and the cup turns warm and sticky.

"Are you finished yet?" I turn around to try to see how much ice cream he has left, but he holds his cup close to his chest.

"Not yet." And my ice cream is now warm liquid, the chocolate and vanilla completely blended.

Then, finally, triumph.

"I'm finished," he says.

"Ha-ha," I shout in glorying delight just as I had imagined it. "*I* still have *my* ice cream." I hold up my cup, crushed and leaking now, to show him. "I scream, you scream, we all scream for ice cream," I chant, and in the next moment quickly gulp down the syrupy mixture. It bears little resemblance to the cool treat it had once been, yet nothing I have ever tasted is as pleasing to me as this victory.

"Ha-ha yourself." My brother's voice, rocking with laughter, rises from the back seat as I swallow the last drop. "I fooled you. I still have mine." Leaning forward, he shows me the leftover in his own cup, then proceeds to drink slowly, all the while bending close to my face so that my utter defeat will not for one second be lost on me.

Tricked! But worse. He has won again. I cannot make my mark. I cannot get a leg up on him, not even with a cup of ice cream soup. I bellow with the pain only a child knows who has been totally outwitted.

"It's not fair!" I scream. "He always gets what he wants. He always has more than I have. I can never win. I can never have anything of my own."

My brother roars with glee. "I scream, you scream, we all scream for ice cream," he mocks as I bawl uncontrollably. My parents laugh also, scolding me for acting like a baby. Why all this fuss? It's nothing more than ice cream, after all. What difference does it make who ate it first?

But I know what the fuss is about. It's about much more than ice cream. It's about coming out ahead for once. It's about establishing myself and holding my own. It's about being recognized.

Decades pass.

I am now a writer and my brother a businessman.

"You know, don't you," my husband says to me one evening when I'm describing to him some of my research and findings about adult siblings, "that I make a point of trying to avoid putting myself into situations with you that you would perceive as competitive?"

"What do you mean?" I ask cautiously.

Although my husband is a psychiatrist, there has long been an unspoken agreement between us that he not apply the tools of his profession to our family life. Little psychological jargon ever gets tossed around our home, and few of our discussions—or arguments—serve as sources for analytic interpretations. Now, however, I feel a worm of suspicion gnawing within. What is he trying to tell me?

"You've been talking about the influence of siblings," he says, "and I was thinking that I try to steer clear of situations that would stir up in you the old feelings of competition you have with Robert."

"First of all," I reply, "Robert and I get along just fine. Secondly, my old competitions with him have nothing to do with anything that goes on between us—you and me. Third of all . . ." I hesitate. "So what kinds of situations have you avoided that you think would make me feel competitive toward you?"

"Well," he says slowly, "I haven't written a book, even though I've thought about doing so from time to time."

"Written a book!" I explode. "Why should you write a book? *I'm* the writer in the family. You run a hospital, you hold academic appointments. You have everything you want. Why should you move in on my turf? Why can't I ever have anything of my own?" Echoing that long-forgotten wail of childhood, I add with fervor, "It's not fair!"

I stop, astonished at the vehemence of my reaction.

"Okay," I say, trying to laugh. "You made your point. Maybe I do repeat with you some of the competitive feelings I had with Robert. Let's drop this subject."

"Sure."

"Want some ice cream?"

I have never been unaware of the importance my brother holds in my life. That awareness, in fact, motivated this book, with its goal of exploring and unraveling the mysteries of sibling attachments. But it was not until I was well into my investigations, not until my conversation with my husband, that I became truly conscious of the lasting imprint my relationship with my brother has had on all aspects of my existence, including my marriage.

What I discovered in myself I have seen operating in others as well. The effects of our early experiences with brothers and sisters remain with us long after childhood has ended, long after the experiences themselves have faded into the past, influencing us as adults in ways we rarely recognize, from the intimate relationships we establish with lovers and spouses, to the attitudes we carry into the workplace, to our behavior toward our children.

The woman who, twice, married and divorced "exciting, dynamic—and irresponsible" men much like her younger brother is an example of the potency of that sibling influence. So is the corporate executive who time and again, without realizing it, stops himself from going after the top position in his company because somewhere within he believes that only his older brother and not he is capable of filling such a role. And so too—to take one more example—is the lawyer who describes growing up with a domineering older sister who physically and emotionally grabbed everything from her: clothes, toys, eventually even her friends.

"My sister dominates my life," the lawyer says, although they live miles apart and have little contact. She explains: "I still can't deal with any kind of rivalry. If I know someone else is competing with me for a client, I pull back. But at the same time, I feel despondent if the client doesn't come to me, as if I've lost out to my sister again. I have the same reaction to love triangles. I get into a terrible state if I think another woman is at all interested in a man I'm going out with. I don't want someone I care about to be taken away from me the way my sister took everything that meant something. But neither can I fight for what I want."

More aware of such inner conflicts, perhaps, than many people, she says, "In every relationship that I encounter, I reenact what I had with my sister."

We usually associate such reenactments with our parents, and certainly both professional and popular literature have made us conscious of the dominant and lasting impact of our parents on our lives. Yet the more closely one examines the sibling experience, the more evident it becomes that the bond between brothers and sisters leaves its own stamp, separate and apart from the mark parents make, and, in turn, demands scrutiny on its own.

Unlike the ties between parents and children, the connection among siblings is a horizontal one. That is, sibs exist on the same plane, as peers, more or less equals. Although one may be stronger or more dominant than others, brothers and sisters rarely exert the kind of power and authority over one another that parents hold over their children. Nor are there rules, codes of behavior for different stages of life or biblical commandments mandating siblings to respect and honor one another as they must respect and honor parents. As a result they are freer, more open, and generally more honest with each other, than they are with parents, and less fearful of punishment or rejection. As children, they say what is on their minds, without censoring their words or concerning themselves about the long-range effects of their emotions on one another. Even as adults, many sibs speak more bluntly to each other than they dare to friends or colleagues.

The freedom siblings enjoy with one another and the peer status they hold also allow them greater intimacy than they have with their mothers or fathers. In growing up, sisters and brothers often spend more time alone together than they do with parents, and they get to know each other in ways that their parents never know them. An older child reexperiences her own past in playing with a younger one. The younger learns from sharing the older's activities, and in the process comes to understand both his sib and himself.

Together, siblings become experts in penetrating each other's thoughts and feelings. Studies of empathy among young children have found that toddlers as young as two or three are able to interpret for their parents baby siblings' expressions and noises and explain a baby's wishes that a mother or father doesn't understand. "He wants to go out," an older child will say, or, "She's hungry," or, "Pick her up, Mommy," and usually the information will be correct.

Siblings have a compelling need to accumulate the knowledge they have of each other. Each *wants* to know what makes the other tick. Each *wants* to know which buttons to press to make the other cry or cringe. Each also wants to know how to make the other laugh and how to win the other's love and approval. In its intensity, their mutual knowledge becomes all-embracing—a naked understanding that encompasses the very essence of the other's being.

Once gained, that gut understanding remains a crucial part of the link between siblings for life. Even after years of separation, an adult brother or sister may quickly, intuitively, pick up on another's thoughts, sympathize with the other's needs, or zero in—unerringly—on the other's insecurities.

The intimate knowledge siblings hold is not limited to themselves; it also includes knowledge of their parents. Sibs are able to validate for one another realities about their parents. They may be the only ones who know, for instance, that beneath the wit and charm the world sees in their parents lies a cold, mutual anger that causes the family great suffering. More important, children often blame themselves for a parent's cruel or disturbed behavior. A brother or sister helps free the other from his guilt and blame, helps define family conditions for the other.

Discussing the pain of growing up with an abusive, alcoholic father, one man said, "My older sister was like an oasis I could escape to. I could bounce things off her and say, 'Hey, what's happening?' and she would reassure me that none of it was my fault, that it had nothing to do with me. I'll always be grateful to her for that."

But even in happy homes young siblings become allies. They may fight and scream at each other, but they also offer one another solace and safety in a world that appears overwhelmingly stacked in favor of adults. They share secrets parents never hear, and communicate with each other through signals and codes, private languages whose meanings only they know.

One of my sweetest recollections of the past is that of lying in bed late at night, speaking to my brother through the wall of our adjoining rooms. We speak loudly, oblivious of our parents in their bedroom down the hall. We imitate characters on the radio shows we listen to addictively, or we talk "silly talk," making up nonsense words and sounds that send us into peals of laughter and affirm for me that nobody is as clever and funny as my big brother.

"Shush," my mother quiets us angrily. "Go to sleep, both of you."

We snort as we try to squelch the waves of giggles that envelop us, dizzyingly conscious of our superiority to the parents we have excluded from our club.

"Are you asleep?" we continue to call out to each other in stage whispers until the voice down the hall sounds as though it means business, and one of us drifts off.

Through their clubby confidences and shared secrets, through the time they spend alone and the knowledge they gain, siblings learn to cooperate and get along together. They discover the meaning of loyalty, and master skills in defending one another against the outside even in the midst of their own angers or vicious battles. They cultivate their ability to have fun, to laugh and make jokes. They gain their first experiences in knowing themselves as individuals but also as persons connected to others. In short, they learn what it means to be "we" and not just "I."

Eventually what siblings learn with each other gets transferred to their dealings with the world beyond the family, to schoolmates and friends, later to adult peers.

With their learning and knowledge siblings also build a personal history that serves as a reference point through the years. That is not to say that brothers and sisters have identical histories. Each child in a family experiences life differently, relates differently to parents, and creates a different and unique environment for the other. Yet there is a family ethos and a pool of memories—of parental attitudes, of humor and expectations, of vacations and hard times—that transcend individual experiences and form a common past for siblings.

A Holocaust survivor whose parents were murdered in Auschwitz wrote on the questionnaire that although his sisters are much older than he and he lives far away from them, an "invisible thread" binds them to one another in a way they are not connected to anybody else. "When we see each other, we exchange memories," he wrote. "My sisters tell me about my childhood and what I was like as a baby. They're the only ones in the world who have that knowledge about me. Without them I would know nothing of those years. On the other hand, I have an excellent memory for details. I remember where the school was and what our house looked like, and that helps them recapture their past."

Other responses to the questionnaire also attested to the strength of that "invisible thread" that attaches siblings to each other. In answer to a question about problems with one or another sib, most respondents described current or earlier difficulties they had experienced, many indicating that a problem had not yet been resolved. Nevertheless, in response to a question about how close a subject felt to each sister or brother—"very close," "close," "somewhat close," or "not close at all"—only 17 percent of the sibling relationships were described as "not close at all." And to the question "Have there been periods of time when you and this sibling have not spoken to one another out of anger?" more than 75 percent of the respondents replied "No." The pull of memory and history and the rewards of sibling companionship draw adult brothers and sisters to each other in spite of their differences.

So highly regarded, in fact, are sibling ties by both individuals and society that since earliest times they have been idealized, turned into a metaphor for the very best of human relations. We speak of the "brotherhood of man" as a paradigm of love and loyalty, of an era in which people and nations will live together in equality and justice. "Sisterhood" triggers images of feminist strivings toward a new understanding by women of each other, a new joining with one another in friendship and cooperation.

The reality is, however, that such glorification denies the true complexity of the sibling condition by ignoring its other side, its darker side. That side appears among the earliest records of human history that we know of: the first murder that ever occurs in the Bible is fratricide—Cain's murder of his brother Abel. And that side continues

to dominate nations and peoples whose histories and lives are intertwined in siblinglike fashion: the various warring Moslem sects, for
example; Catholics and Protestants in Ireland; Arabs and Israelis.

In less global terms, the idealization of the sibling bond and the
denial of its complexity have taken a toll on groups and individuals.
Although I am devoted to feminism, for example, I know that the
women's movement has suffered from the disillusionment many
women felt in discovering that their "sisters" could be as envious and
competitive as any man and that struggles for power and position
were not uncommon among leaders of the movement.

Writing about women's friendships in their book *Between Women*,
feminist psychotherapists Luise Eichenbaum and Susie Orbach describe a workshop they ran in which women were allowed to talk
openly about "the pain of jealousy, the pain of envy, the pain of anger,
the pain of competition . . . when felt in relation to women." Although workshop participants were shocked to discover how many
negative feelings they harbored toward each other, in the end, "there
was a relief stemming from the honest realization that women *do* have
conflicting feelings for one another."

Similarly, within the sibling relationship itself, high-flown images
make it difficult for adult brothers and sisters to acknowledge—and
therefore deal with—ongoing feelings of jealousy and competition. Of
several surprises in the survey, one of the most astonishing did not
come from a response but from a lack of response. In a question
designed to gather information about competition, respondents were
asked to check for each of their siblings one or more areas in which
they compared themselves to that sibling, the areas given being "success or failure of children," "achievements," "finances," "education,"
and "occupation." An additional blank was left for anyone wishing to
check "I don't compare," a category in which I anticipated little response.

The results turned out to be just the opposite of what I expected.
Although brothers reported more frequently than sisters that they
compare themselves to each other, the majority of respondents—61
percent—checked "I don't compare." The numbers were even greater
in specific categories. In the area of finances, for example, 78 percent
said they did not compare themselves to their siblings, and 73 percent
said they did not compare themselves in terms of achievement, a
dimension that one might suppose would arouse the greatest competitiveness.

Results were also different from what I anticipated in response to
the question "Do you seek his/her approval?" It was a query planned

to touch on rivalry in a different way—through a sibling's desire for recognition and acceptance by another. The possible choices were "not at all," "some," or "very much." I expected few responses in the "not at all" category and a fair distribution between the "some" and "very much" possibilities. Instead, about 50 percent of the subjects indicated that they did not seek approval from their siblings at all.

How true is it that adult siblings do not measure their achievements against those of their brothers and sisters? That they do not look to one another for approval and affirmation? I would not have been surprised at the results of the survey had my interviews not told a different story.

In the privacy of an interview, in an atmosphere of trust and intimacy and with many hours in which to talk about and around a subject, individuals returned again and again to themes of competitiveness, comparisons, and longings for recognition and approval. When a forty-year-old man described driving home after visiting his older brother and crying into the emptiness of his car that he wished with all his heart that he could *be* that brother, and when a twenty-eight-year-old woman spoke of her unyielding bitterness at having squelched her own musical abilities because of her younger sister's talent as a pianist, he and she were speaking of comparisons and the pain of sibling jealousy, of lingering and deeply felt rivalries.

It was because of the competitive feelings that emerged in interviews that I was so surprised by the denial of rivalry on the questionnaire. But a review of transcripts and notes suggests a reason for this discrepancy. People rarely identified *themselves* as the source of rivalry. When they spoke of arguments and difficulties, or even of teasing and one-upmanship, many labeled a sibling, and not themselves, the competitive or envious one.

For many people, there is a kind of shame in seeing oneself as competitive, someone who compares personal achievements or finances with those of another and who by implication may feel envious of the other. The shame is compounded when the other is a sibling, whom we have been taught to love and protect. It's as though such comparisons—and the jealousy or resentment that may be embedded in them—are a violation, a betrayal in adult life of the idealized bond between brothers and sisters that has been built over the years. So people do not like to admit to, and in many cases may not even be aware of, rivalrous feelings in themselves, although they are quick to recognize them in their siblings.

Two psychologists, Helgola G. Ross and Joel I. Milgram, uncovered similar reactions in their research on rivalry among adult siblings.

Working with fifty-five volunteers, they met in small groups for several hours to discuss issues of rivalry. Almost three quarters (71 percent) of the subjects who took part in the groups spoke of having experienced rivalry with their siblings. But few saw themselves as ever initiating it, pointing their finger most frequently at a brother, less frequently at a sister, and "least often" at themselves.

Ross and Milgram also found that siblings rarely confess their own rivalrous feelings to each other. To bring such feelings into the open is to expose oneself, to become vulnerable—the same kind of vulnerability that comes with acknowledging longings for a sibling's approval. Admitting sibling rivalry, say Ross and Milgram, may also be "threatening and experienced as equivalent to admitting maladjustment," so powerful and so highly regarded is the primordial tie of sisters and brothers to one another.

Yet, as my interviews showed, feelings of rivalry exist along with bonds of closeness. Jealousy or competition among adults is usually (although not always) expressed more discreetly, less blatantly than it is among children, who as they grow up together spend much of their time with one another and fight openly about their differences. Rivalrous feelings may lie dormant for years when brothers and sisters do not live near each other or when their lives are not closely connected, then resurface full strength during times of change or crisis, such as the illness or death of a parent or wrangles over an inheritance. Or they may be played out in a larger arena, in a business, for example, in which siblings use financial issues as the terrain upon which to tear away at each other. They may take the form of teasing or friendly competition at sports, or they may take the form of bitter arguments, put-downs, and humiliations by one or another sib.

However it manifests itself, sibling competition in adult life, like the attachment itself, almost always has its origins in childhood. In children, rivalry develops on two levels, which run parallel to each other.

On one level—the most primitive, the most primal—siblings compete for parents' love and attention. The psychoanalyst Peter B. Neubauer links such rivalry to the root of the word itself: "A rival originally meant someone using the same river or stream as another person. It refers to fighting among early tribes for access to the river—who can go to the river and get the water, who will be the survivor, who has the advantage. In our terms the river is the mother who supplies our basic needs, and the children compete for access to her." For children, parents are the source of all nourishment; without them a child will starve both physically and emotionally. When children compete for parents, it is because each wants to hold on to the source exclusively, afraid that letting go of any part will mean losing out on all.

This rivalry for parents' recognition and affection takes its own form in adult life. Long after parents have grown old or even died, sibs may continue to vie through deeds and achievements to be the "best child." Typical of such open-ended rivalry is the woman who insists on personally ministering to her senile mother—although the thankless chore wears her out—because she is a "good daughter," as opposed to her sister, the "bad daughter," who has suggested that the family could and should hire nurses for their mother's care.

On another level, the rivalry between young siblings is a struggle not so much for parents' admiration and approval as for power and prestige in relation to each other. Using as their model the authority and control parents exert over them—but much more crudely—older sibs may try to dominate, to be always on top. Youngers may fight back, fiercely determined to gain the advantage themselves. Whatever their place in the family, sibs threaten, tease, cajole, shout, embarrass, or punch to acquire status or hold another in check.

In adulthood this type of rivalry can show itself in subtle, but stinging, ways. A brother may constantly hand out advice, usually unsolicited, often unwanted, always implying that the other cannot possibly get along without such counsel. Or a sister may consistently withhold any kind of praise and recognition, never commenting on another's achievement, or noticing a new hairdo, or complimenting on a dress.

Much of the pain and frustration people expressed in interviews came from such power struggles with siblings, and the worst part, they said, was that even calling attention to the techniques a sister or brother used to maintain control seemed to give that person the upper hand. As one man explained, "How does it make me look to tell my brother that the things I want most in the world are the things he won't give me—admiration, appreciation, to be seen and treated as an equal?"

From siblings' early days to later ones, both kinds of rivalry—the competition for parents' attentions and the competition for power over each other—remain intertwined with the devotion and loyalty of their attachment. To deny them is to limit understanding of that attachment, to shut out insight into one's sibling connections—and oneself.

Both the warmth of the sibling tie and the rivalry that accompanies it are highly subject, of course, to parental influences. Through their attitudes toward their own siblings and their behavior toward each other and their children, parents set examples that the children follow among themselves. Parents can also disrupt sibling attachments by appearing to show favoritism to one child or make undue demands on another. In fact, parental favoritism was a topic much in the minds of the people interviewed and those who responded to the questionnaire. So much so that, again, I was surprised at the survey findings—but this time by the enormous response to queries about favoritism. A whopping 84 percent of respondents—many more than I would have suspected—indicated that one or both of their parents had shown favoritism in the family. Only 16 percent said that neither had had a favorite.

The interviews supported these findings. As reluctant as people were to discuss their own competitiveness, they were more than willing to report on the favoritism they perceived in their parents. Perhaps it is because we are used to thinking only in terms of parents, or perhaps it is because sibling ties have been so rarely explored, even by siblings themselves, that people find it easier to examine their parents' behavior than to probe their own in relation to their brothers and sisters.

Because they affect sibling relations so strongly, parental influences are discussed throughout this book, with special attention given in the first section to gender favoritism and in the second to the effects of favoritism and its opposite, scapegoating.

But the dominant theme of the book is the sibling relationship itself, and each section is designed to focus on a different facet of that relationship. The first takes up various aspects of the bond—the roles siblings assume in their struggles for separateness, the influences of birth order and gender, the special situations of stepsibs and half-sibs. The second delves into sibling ties under pressure, whether they are the pressures of family disability, illness, or death, or of spats and fights that set sibs against each other. The last section explores the many shifts in the relationship from closeness to distance and back again as brothers and sisters journey together through the life cycle.

And through all the sections and chapters, whether about roles or favoritism, healthy families or disturbed ones, one common thread appears and reappears: the constant tension between the strength of the bond that sibs cherish and idealize and the strains of the rivalry that they find so difficult to acknowledge. The final chapter offers conclusions and suggestions for reconciling the strains and enjoying the richness and intimacy that this bond can provide.

But the last section also treats in depth another motif that wends its way throughout—probably the most hidden and least recognized aspect of the sibling connection. That is the indelible imprint the sibling experience leaves on all areas of life. What is examined through the words and memories and insights of family experts and siblings themselves is how the mixed feelings of love and hate, of warmth and resentment, that developed among sisters and brothers in childhood are reawakened again and again in adult life, in sex and marriage, at home and at work, in friendships and in family matters.

And in the way I balked at the idea of my husband's writing a book.

PART I

The Sibling
Seesaw

My relationship with my brother is lifelong, as if we
were forever to be at either end of a sibling seesaw,
one up, one down, now balanced, now left bouncing.
He is the one soul I shall sit across from all my life.

—**Peter, age 34**

CHAPTER ONE

"He's Mr. Serious and I'm the Clown"

SIBLINGS
IN DIFFERENT ROLES

It took Mark Platt two weeks to decide to allow himself to be interviewed. His name had been suggested by a friend of a friend as a
highly intelligent, articulate man who had a good relationship with his
younger brother, Jerry. The project, he told me when I called,
sounded challenging, but he was not sure he was the person for it. He
was not given to introspection. He had never been in analysis or any
kind of therapy and rarely revealed his thoughts or feelings to others.
It was hard to imagine what he could say that would be of any interest
to me. Still, at age thirty-two, he thought he might be ready to try new
things, expand his horizons and take some chances. But before decid-
ing, he would want to read other books I'd written, to determine
whether I was a writer he could trust.

When he finally set a date to meet with me at my home, I felt as
though I had passed a character test. Even then, he would not agree to
contacting or allowing me to contact Jerry to make an appointment
with him. That would have to wait until after our first interview.
Clearly, the test was not yet over. It was therefore with some appre-
hension that I opened the front door on a rainy Tuesday evening in
May and ushered Mark into my living room.

He was a nice-looking man, tall but slight, with thinning blond hair
and a hesitant smile that belied the intimidating presence he had projected by phone. When I took his raincoat, he suggested that I hang it
in the bathroom so that it not dampen the other clothes in my closet.

19

As a bachelor, he said, he had learned to be careful about things like that. Besides, although he earned a decent salary in his job as a research chemist with a large pharmaceutical company, he was in no position to squander money on clothes, and he made every effort to keep his coats and suits in good order.

Smiling somewhat stiffly, uncomfortable, and puzzled, it seemed to me, about what he was actually doing in my living room, he sat down in the corner of a love seat. It was straight sitting: back up, thighs at right angles to torso, feet flat on the floor.

"What I think you should know about my brother and me is that we're completely different from one another," he began. Then he stopped and looked at me quizzically as if to ask, "Did I do something wrong? Should I have waited for you to pose a question before speaking?"

"Please go on," I said. "In what ways are you different?"

"In every way. We look different, act different, have different interests. If you want to characterize us, I'd say that he's outgoing and I'm withdrawn. He reacts to crises by sharing them with the world and I keep things to myself. He likes to show off and I have excessive modesty." He blushed, as if suspecting that speaking of his own modesty was itself a form of immodesty. "He embroiders and exaggerates," he summarized. "I go the other way."

He stopped himself again. "It occurs to me that with all our differences we're probably the wrong people for you to be interviewing for your book," he said, sounding regretful. After finally venturing into this project, he was now disappointed to discover that he might not be right for it.

"Not at all. I'm extremely interested in the differences between siblings," I assured him.

I was not just being polite. Having interviewed a fair number of people before meeting Mark, I had been struck by how often a brother or sister would begin a discussion by warning me that I would have a *"Rashomon-*like" experience in speaking with other family members, so different was one from another and so different their views of family life. I was curious to explore these attributes of differences emphasized by siblings.

Moreover, in recent years the subject of differences among brothers and sisters has been investigated in some depth by a group of psychologists known as behavioral geneticists, and by the time I met Mark I had been immersed in many of their papers and articles. The main goal of these scientists has been to untangle genetic influences on human personality from environmental ones—the ancient and ongoing puzzle of nature versus nurture in human development. To do so, they have concentrated many of their studies on identical twins, whose genes are exactly alike, and adopted siblings, whose genes differ but who share the same home environment.

Through their research the behavioral geneticists have made some unexpected discoveries about the genetic base for traits once thought to be shaped almost entirely by home and family. Temperament is one such trait. In a dramatic investigation of identical twins who had been reared apart—in different homes and different communities—psychologist Thomas J. Bouchard, Jr., of the University of Minnesota, has found that on personality tests and questionnaires such twins give uncannily similar answers to questions concerning irritability, calmness, and other aspects of temperament. Their responses indicate that such traits are strongly influenced by the genes they share and less so by the environments in which they grew up.

What this means for siblings who are not identical twins is that many of the differences in temperament and disposition they exhibit ("He's outgoing and I'm withdrawn," said Mark), just like differences in hair color and eyes, may stem from hereditary dissimilarities. (Remember that every person has twenty-three pairs of chromosomes, and for each pair we inherit one chromosome from our mothers and one from our fathers. Siblings have about a fifty-fifty chance of inheriting the same chromosome from each parent, and on the average, they have similar genes for only about half their traits.)

More surprising than the effects of genetics in creating differences or similarities among siblings have been the behavioral geneticists' contentions that the home environment in which siblings grow up—usually thought to be a base of commonality among sisters and brothers—actually tends to make them *different from* rather than *similar to* one another, at least in terms of their personalities.

So different do sibs become, say some of these researchers, that two brothers who have spent all their growing up years together are likely to be no more similar in personality than any two people one might meet in the street. It's an exaggerated claim, in my opinion, a bit of hyperbole to make a point. Nevertheless, it is not an exaggeration to say that siblings *do* experience their home lives differently, or—to restate a truism—that no two siblings have the same parents or the same family backgrounds.

The differences begin with parents. A mother or father may be edgy and nervous with a first child and calmer and more relaxed with the next one. The child of the edgy parents may learn to be cautious, timid about venturing into anything new, afraid to take chances. His sister, the child of the relaxed parents, may learn to be curious and bold, secure in the knowledge that her parents have confidence in her judgment. Parents may be financially pressed and working long hours in the early years of their first children's lives, and economically more secure with more leisure time to spend with later children. A child of the financially pressed parents may acquire from them a healthy regard for money and hard work; his younger brother may always expect others to care for him as *his* parents did.

Other differences: One child in a family may be born to parents wed just a few years and still intensely in love; others to parents struggling with disillusion and marital problems. One may be born during an era of permissive childrearing, when demand feeding is all the rage and bedtime occurs whenever the child falls asleep; another may arrive during the next pendulum swing, when babies must conform to a strict schedule, with clear-cut feeding hours and inflexible bedtimes. One, compliant by nature, may have an easy compatibility with parents; another, more stubborn or strong-minded, may constantly arouse ire and disapproval. One may be a favored child; another disfavored.

In whatever ways parents respond to their children and whatever childrearing methods they use, they create different environments for each child, and those differences act on and help shape the different personalities and outlooks the children develop.

But siblings also help shape one another through the unique environment each creates for the next. If one sibling is assertive and another passive, the environment of the passive child may include a brother or sister who intimidates and demands, but who may also be protective, in that way increasing the other's passivity and dependence. The environment of the assertive child may include a sister or brother who cries at the drop of a hat and is afraid of anything new, but who may also depend on the other for strength, in that way increasing the other's assertiveness and confidence.

The effects of such sibling environments, of the microcosms sibs inhabit because of each other, can be as powerful as parental influences.

An example of just how powerful that impact can be comes from a study of shyness made by a group of psychologists at Yale and Harvard universities. An inclination toward shyness, the researchers found—like that toward other traits of temperament—is hereditary. Yet, whether that inborn tendency will continue into childhood and beyond depends to a great extent on a child's home environment, particularly the behavior of brothers and sisters toward the child.

In the study, infants who at birth were most easily startled by noise or unexpected changes were at twenty-one months still more likely than other toddlers to cling to their mothers and refuse to play with unfamiliar children, indicating shyness. But by the time they were seven, some children had stopped showing signs of shyness. Of those who continued to act shy, two thirds were found to have older siblings who may have bullied and belittled them. For these children, the environments created by their siblings exacerbated their innate tendency toward timidity, pushing them further into themselves.

The behavioral geneticists label the differences that exist within the home—both those created by parents and those created by siblings—the "nonshared environment." That environment, they hold, explains in large measure why siblings in a family may be so different from one another.

Because of Mark's determined view of himself as completely unlike his brother Jerry, he seemed a good person with whom to pursue the subject of differences among sibs.

Jerry, Mark told me, is three years younger than he and a successful jazz pianist who has received some fine notices. A funny, easy talker, he is often invited both as a performer and guest on late-night TV talk shows, and "loves every minute of it." Mark feels genuinely proud of the recognition Jerry has gained, and genuinely glad, he said, that it is Jerry and not he living that life.

"The way Jerry lives, always in the public eye, is not for me," he asserted. "I'm happy being who I am. A friend of mine told me that his brother became president of the family's multimillion-dollar business, and he said to me, 'I'm like Billy Carter. It's much more fun to be the President's brother.' That's how I feel. For the moment, I'd just as soon be a performer's brother as be the performer."

I made a mental note of the "for the moment," then asked about his family background.

The brothers grew up in Manhasset, a suburb about an hour's drive from New York City, where their father headed a successful accounting firm. Their mother, a "typical fifties mom," had devoted herself to her sons, shepherding them to Boy Scout groups, Little League, and such. Dedicated to giving them the best, she had launched Mark on piano lessons when he was seven. Occasionally four-year-old Jerry would sit in on the lessons and pick out little melodies himself. Later, when his turn for lessons came, he took to them like a sprout to sunlight, blossoming into an enthusiastic pianist.

Mark, meanwhile, hated the piano. More accurately, he hated having to practice it.

"Hated it," he said with conviction. "You know, if I write a report for my firm, I'll work on it forever, writing and rewriting, staying up into the night making sure to get it right. But I thought of piano practice as a form of torture. My brother was different. He may not have liked practicing, but he didn't rebel the way I did. He grew into it. He would sit at the piano for hours. It was as if his fingers were walking through their own world." (Later Jerry would tell me that "Mom was adamant about my playing. She would force me to practice, screaming and yelling. Now I'm grateful that she did.")

In fifth grade Mark finally convinced his parents to let him drop the piano lessons. Jerry continued his lessons through high school and college and spent most of his summers at music camp. Eventually he took singing and dancing lessons as well.

As Mark recounted the story, it seemed apparent that Jerry had an innate musical talent that Mark lacked. Mark's piano lessons, I supposed, had created an atmosphere that triggered Jerry's natural instincts toward music. Jerry's success at the piano had put into relief Mark's lack of ability, thereby convincing their parents to unleash him from the "torture" of practicing. Differences in both genetics and environment were at work here.

"So you were just not musical at all?" I asked, to drive home the point.

"Well, I wouldn't say I wasn't musical," Mark said unexpectedly. "I love music, it's terribly important in my life. In college I began playing the cello, and I still practice every day. On weekends I play in a small chamber music group. Of course we don't perform publicly or anything like that. For me music is just for fun. My brother Jerry became a musician. I became a serious music fan." (Later Jerry would also tell me that he was convinced that Mark regretted giving up the piano. "My mother says he was extremely talented," he said. "But once I started playing, they couldn't get him near the piano.")

"How do your parents feel about Jerry's career?" I asked. I have known parents who push their children to master a musical instrument, only to be shocked and dismayed when the child takes up the instrument professionally. "Did they encourage him to perform, or did they try to stop him?"

"Try to stop him?" Mark laughed out loud. He was beginning to relax and, I sensed, actually enjoy himself. "My mother was dying to be a backstage mom. God knows, she loved to show off her sons. I resisted her. I wouldn't give her the pleasure," he said. "Look, I'm a private person and I rebelled against that kind of display, but Jerry bought it all. He ate up the attention. He gave my mother exactly what she wanted."

Different temperaments, it would seem at first blush, propelled Mark and Jerry to different responses to their mother's ambitions, and she in turn became a different mother to each of them. Unable to force Mark into fulfilling her stagestruck dreams for her sons, she pulled back and allowed him to go his own way while she concentrated her efforts on Jerry. One son, as a result, followed his own inclinations toward privacy, the other toward the limelight.

Yet the more Mark opened up, the more I felt that the differences between these brothers did not stem only from the happenstances of genetics or the disparities in their nonshared environment. There was something purposeful in the path Mark chose to follow, a wish, a *need* to be different from his younger brother. It was a need that led him to direct his natural temperament and skills toward goals that set him apart from Jerry, and to close himself off to abilities they had in common. It was a need so strong that he felt it necessary to rebel against the very qualities in his mother that his brother most bought into.

"Was your father also gung ho for performance?" I asked.

"For my father, performance meant performance at school, 'bringing home the bacon,' as he called it. That became my department. Jerry is bright, but he never had time to study. He was too busy performing in concerts and acting in plays. Besides, my father was always holding me and my good school grades up as an example to him, and he hated that."

In defiance of his father, Jerry became the class clown in high school, neglecting his schoolwork and hanging out nights with his drama club friends. And the poorer his grades, the harder his father leaned on him. Just as their mother treated each son differently in regard to music practice, their father became, in regard to academics, an angry taskmaster to Jerry, an admirer of Mark, pitting the brothers against each other to some extent and reinforcing through his behavior the one's resentment of schoolwork, the other's successes at it.

"Jerry and my father had horrible confrontations," Mark recalled. "I never had anything like that. I was sort of the good boy in that sense. I did what was expected of me because I chose not to accept the consequences of not doing so."

"It sounds, also," I said, harking back in my mind to the findings of the geneticists, "as if you were more intellectually gifted than Jerry, so it was probably natural for you to do well in school."

"It's possible," Mark answered, looking down at his feet. "But he's very, very bright, even though you wouldn't know it at times. I'll tell you something I have rarely told anyone. When I was in elementary school, a new system was instituted of having an accelerated class for bright sixth-grade students. My parents just assumed I would be put into that class, but I wasn't. I remained in the regular classroom. When my brother's turn came three years later, he made it into the accelerated class. I'm not sure I realized right away how much that hurt, but it did become terribly important to me to do well in high school and college."

There was more emotion in his voice than one might expect about an event of so many years earlier. "But to answer your question," he continued, so softly I could barely hear him, "my brother was probably as gifted as I—or more so. He just chose a different path."

Again and again Mark returned to his original theme of differences, each time elaborating a bit more, like a painter constructing a canvas, one layer of pigment building on the next. He spoke of Jerry with great affection—"fabulous, a special person," and of the close friendship they have achieved in the years since both have left college and struck out on their separate paths. But he also sees Jerry as "immature—charming and immature," and it falls to Mark to be "stable," ready to calm his brother down when he is despondent over losing a job, or high over finding one.

An ongoing example of Jerry's immaturity is his attitude toward women. "Locker-room stuff," said Mark. "He judges himself in terms of conquests—sheer numbers. It's a score-keeping mentality, and that's something I really reject."

In fact the types of women the brothers date are as different as they. Jerry likes women who organize his life for him, the way his mother always had, even to picking out his clothes. Mark hates to have his independence encroached upon. He also knows, he said, that the kind of women he goes out with—"lawyers, intellectuals, high-powered"—are like "Martians" to Jerry, who prefers model types.

"What do you think when you see Jerry perform or catch him on television?" I asked toward the end of our interview. "Do you feel envious?"

It was a question I felt I could pose now that I could not have earlier in the evening. Mark had unwound considerably. His jacket was off, his tie loosened, his legs stretched out and arms spread around the back of the love seat. He was finding it fun to talk about himself after all.

"Years ago," he began, avoiding a direct answer, "when we were kids in school, it made me crazy to see him in the star role in a play. But that was when we were into the same kinds of things." He paused. "I guess I didn't tell you that I used to act in high-school plays sometimes also. I think performance was something we were both drawn toward."

I smiled. It had taken almost all evening for him to mention his own pull toward performance.

He smiled in return. "You know," he said somewhat sheepishly, as though confessing to something silly, "when I make a presentation to my company's sales force of a new product we've developed—the firm makes a big fuss about new products, and presentations are elaborate productions—I get a real charge out of it. It's gigantic. I love it. It's like being on stage."

He caught himself, recognizing that he had strayed from the subject. "Do I feel envious? No. In the beginning it was tough to accept. I felt confused. A lot of things that are attractive to him are attractive to me too. But ultimately they don't win out. I decided a long time ago that I wasn't interested in performing in that way. What draws someone to performing? I see it in his friends. Partly it's a wish to express something inside you, but the other side is materialistic, a need to be rich and famous. I'm more interested in the satisfaction of the work."

He was quiet and contemplative. Wondering, perhaps, I thought, whether his high moral road actually had led him to the satisfaction he sought to find in it.

After a moment he returned once more to the theme with which he had begun. "We're just two different people and two different ways of life," he said.

Mark prepared to leave, and to my delight, he gave me Jerry's phone number and suggested that I call him soon because he was about to embark on a tour.

I thought at length about Mark's continued emphasis on differences in light of the theories of the behavioral geneticists. While it seemed true, from what he had told me, that he and Jerry have innate differences in temperament and interests and that they have experienced their home environment in different ways, it also seemed true that they have—consciously and more often unconsciously—pushed aside many of their inborn similarities in order to take opposite stands in almost every area of their lives, from work, to music, to academics, to the women they date. As important as are the findings and theories of the scientists, they omit one crucial ingredient necessary to understanding differences among siblings. That is the need brothers and sisters have to *be* different, to distinguish themselves from one another, to establish their own identities.

Volumes have been written on the process by which children identify with their parents yet move on to form distinct and separate identities. The first steps in that process come at about five months, when infants discover that they exist as beings apart from their parents. From then on and into adult life we continue to struggle with the challenge of maintaining our psychological separateness from our parents even while incorporating many of their attitudes and values.

Far less has been written about identity formation in relation to siblings, yet it, too, is a complex and difficult process. Close in age and a different generation from their parents, siblings find it easy to identify with one another, to model themselves on, copy from, and see themselves in each other. They have a parallel challenge to the task of separating from parents, and one that also begins early in life and extends into adulthood. It is the challenge of carving out a self that is both distinct from that of a brother or sister and strong enough to maintain connectedness without being riddled with envy or longing to be that brother or sister.

For many siblings, asserting differences is a path toward finding that self. It is a path that sets up demarcation lines, as if to say, "Here you are and here I am, so we do not need to get in each other's way." It is also a path through which envy and competition may be held at bay.

Two researchers, Frances Fuchs Schachter and Richard K. Stone, have advanced some important theories about the way siblings limit competition by emphasizing their differences and maintaining separate identities.

Curious about hearing their college students constantly describe themselves as entirely unlike their brothers and sisters, and listening to parents characterize their children as "different as day and night," these theorists decided to find out why that was so. They began by asking students with only one sibling if they were alike or different from that sib in overall personality. They found that these students reported themselves to be different from their siblings almost twice as frequently as they reported themselves to be alike. Using more sophisticated tests, they then studied siblings in three-child families, and discovered that firstborn and secondborn siblings, especially those of the same sex, emphasized their differences far more often than did first and third or second and third sibs in relation to each other.

From these results the researchers hypothesized that siblings who tend most to compare themselves and hence to feel most rivalrous are apt to be those who feel the greatest need to define themselves as totally different from one another. These include the only two children in a family; the first two in larger families (who begin comparing and competing before there is a third to serve as a buffer); and siblings of the same sex, who share more attributes and interests than sibs of the opposite sex. By drawing on the field of study called social comparison theory, Schachter and Stone explained how forging separate spheres as opposites can help siblings cut down comparisons and competition.

One of the ways we learn about ourselves, social comparison theory teaches, is by comparing ourselves to others. But, necessary as they are, those comparisons can be painful and difficult when they lead us to recognize that someone else may be smarter, prettier, more successful, or more athletic than we. They can become less painful and damaging if we can establish to ourselves and others how different we are from the smarter, prettier, more successful, etc., person. In one study, for instance, men spurned by a woman they liked in favor of another man felt less hurt and angry if they thought the chosen man was completely unlike them. "It has nothing to do with me; clearly she wanted someone altogether different," went the reasoning.

In the same way, siblings can be less jealous and less competitive with one another if they see themselves, and present themselves to others, in contrasting images. When Mark and Jerry were young and "into the same kinds of things" in terms of piano or performing, it made Mark "crazy" when Jerry had a lead part in a school play. Once Mark established his own direction and firmed up his identity as a person who did not want to perform in a public way ("I'd rather be a performer's brother," he said), he could feel proud of Jerry.

Does affirming differences eliminate all rivalry between siblings? Not really. Since emphasizing differences is in part a response to rivalry, edges of that rivalry are certain to push through. Still, dividing up the turf and creating clear boundaries between sibs can temper jealousy and competitiveness. (Using the phrase "Cain complex," Schachter and Stone argue that dwelling on differences can at least hold back the most murderous of sibling thoughts).

Paradoxically, establishing differences may not only control rivalry, but may also serve as an acceptable means of expressing rivalry. Ensconced in their separate domains, siblings can feel superior about their own choices even while appreciating those of others. In that sense, seeing themselves as opposites allows them some of the satisfactions of competition while containing the most threatening comparisons and conflicts. Having given up the performer's life, for instance, Mark can admire Jerry's accomplishments, yet secretly look down on the "materialistic" drives of Jerry and his friends. The real enjoyments, he holds, are the kind he gets—from work itself.

Schachter and Stone have applied a ponderous term to their theory about differences: "de-identification," which simply means not identifying. The term I prefer to use is "role assumption." Siblings take on separate roles within their families through which they define and differentiate themselves and in the process box off some of the competition between them.

Jerry had no doubts about the roles he and Mark had chosen for themselves in life. "When we were in high school," he told me when I called, "he became Mr. Serious and I became the clown. He was the genius and I was the playboy. We're still that way." A second later he added, "You sure you want to interview me?"

I was indeed.

We arranged to meet on the morning before he left for an extended concert tour. I could see a physical resemblance to Mark when I greeted Jerry, but it was well hidden behind longish hair, bushy mustache, and a warm, gregarious manner. Jerry sprawled on the love seat upon which Mark had sat straight and serious. Within moments he had his shoes off ("Who invented shoes anyway?") and his shirtsleeves rolled up.

"What can I tell you that Mark hasn't already revealed?" he asked, winking, then continued, "Mark's a genius, as I told you on the phone. Boy, I really admire him. He's my idol—always has been. He's so modest. Did you know he heads up a research lab in his firm? He's one of the most respected and highly paid people there." (I didn't know that—Mark had made such a point about frugality.)

"What made you become a musician?" I asked, curious to hear his version.

Like Mark, he described the early piano lessons and the struggles over practicing. Unlike Mark, he found nothing to criticize in his mother's unrelenting insistence on his playing. What Mark regarded as pushiness in their mother became in Jerry's version "warm encouragement," in spite of the "screaming and yelling" that accompanied it. Through her persistence, his mother had made him feel talented, he said, and he has thanked her many times for leading him to the success he now enjoys.

Jerry's easy acceptance of his mother and his openness about his own achievements contrasted sharply with Mark's guardedness in all areas of his life. A more placid disposition, I supposed, yet one styled also, I became convinced, by a determination to keep out of his brother's shadow.

In fact, Jerry appeared to me even more intent than Mark on seeing the brothers in opposition and glossing over similarities between them. Two themes crossed and crisscrossed our discussion.

One centered on competition, the other on Mark's brilliance.

The competition theme was essentially one of denial: "We never competed," he stated time and again, a phrase that acquired several modifications as we went along.

"We never competed," he said early in the interview. "Oh, we fought as kids; he once smashed my middle finger to the floor and broke the nail off so that I couldn't play the piano for weeks, but that was kid's horseplay. As I said, once we got to high school, he became Mr. Serious. Me, I was always a clown, a kid. I couldn't have competed with him."

"We never competed," he reiterated a little later. "I guess I wanted my father to spend more time with me than with him. And I guess when we played baseball, I always tried to be better. I was better in tennis too. But we never competed. Mark wouldn't have thought about competition. He would have been thinking about Aristotle or something like that."

"I'm a very competitive guy," he allowed after some time. "Even with girlfriends. I once competed with a girl I was going with in high school in terms of music. But I never competed with my brother. I did *not* compete," he insisted, although I had not once challenged him. "Mark's so smart. He's my idol."

Along with noncompetition, the theme of Mark's intelligence emerged so emphatically that I questioned whether it had been hard for Jerry in school to follow a brother regarded as so smart. He responded by retelling the incident of his being placed in the accelerated class that had been denied Mark back in sixth grade. The criterion for acceptance to that class had been IQ, he related (Mark had omitted that piece of information). Mark had been "devastated" by Jerry's acceptance (Mark had omitted that, too, admitting only that he had not realized how hurt he was at being rejected), and Mark's pain had upset Jerry. Still, he had been proud of the honor. So proud, I noticed, that he found a way to bring it into the conversation at least two more times.

Clearly, Jerry wanted me to know that he was no slouch in the intellectual realm. Having established that, he was able to return repeatedly to the refrain of Mark's academic prowess, presenting his brother as an almost superhuman being.

"He read a lot, I never read. . . . I was good at math, he was better; I was okay in science, but he was really great. . . . I'm a procrastinator, he does everything right on time. . . . He is just supremely bright. . . ."

Occasionally Jerry would, unawares, drop a few hints of what—if he hadn't assured me of his lack of competitiveness with Mark— might have sounded like competition. "I think he always wanted to have the social life I had," he said once. "I have gone out with a lot more women than he has, and they were all beautiful. He's had girlfriends few and far between. . . . He didn't screw around as much as I did, and I think he wanted to." Another time he described a friendship that had grown between Mark and one of his—Jerry's—best friends. "I was jealous," he admitted, "especially when I found out they were double-dating and doing things together that they had never even told me about."

But such open lapses were minor. For the most part, Jerry worked hard at maintaining his stance as the perfect fan of a perfect brother. If his constant denial of jealousy and rivalrous feelings belied what I sensed to be the reality—the actual existence and force—of those feelings, his admiration for his brother was nevertheless real. In good social-comparison style, Jerry could control his envy by placing Mark on a pedestal, lauding his brilliance to such an extent that there was no point in competing openly. He might secretly compare himself to Mark and gain satisfaction in knowing that he had once bested Mark in the academic arena. But, having ceded that arena to his brother, he did not need to live in a state of competition and conflict. Like Mark, Jerry had, early in life, determined his own style of being, his own role within the family and outside it. In that role, he did not intrude on his brother's domain, nor did his brother intrude on his.

The roles these brothers have assumed may have had their origins in different temperaments and nonshared environments. But they are also an expression of the need of each to be different from the other, to have an identity and space of his own.

For many siblings, like the Platt brothers, roles become a way to establish differences that ensure distinct identities. The roles, and the distinctions they represent, usually take form by the time children have reached school age, and often last a lifetime.

In large families, there may be a variety of roles and slots that siblings fall into. One sib (usually the eldest or the oldest daughter) may be the responsible one, another the popular one, another the studious, still another the dreamer in the family. There may also be in the family one who takes on the role of the wild one or the "crazy," who gets attention by inspiring worry in everyone else. (A young woman who had suffered a serious bout of anorexia explained that "everyone in my family was smart and achieving. I had to do something different. So I became anorectic.") As each role gets preempted by one child, say sociologists James Bossard and Eleanor Boll, who studied a hundred large families, the next child seeks recognition by finding a distinctive and unoccupied place.

In smaller families, where the possibilities for comparison and competition may be more intense, the roles may become more polarized, built around clear-cut differences: Mr. Serious and the Clown, the knight and the jester, Snow White and Rose Red. One college student I speak with is the campus nerd, thoroughly immersed in researching the classical origins of medieval poetry; his sister is the cutup, the party animal who can't remember the name of the last book she read. One sister, Bianca, in Shakespeare's *The Taming of the Shrew*, is all softness and purity, adored by her father, sought after by many suitors; Kate, the other, is spirited, angry, stubborn, and independent. One brother, a newspaper article reports, is a state senator in Boston, a man who wields formidable power in political circles. The other is a criminal, wielding his power among drug dealers and racketeers.

And I am a writer and my brother a businessman, not only by profession but in our personas, our identities. My friends are authors and artists. His friends are bankers and brokers. I studied literature and art history. He studied accounting and law. I am careless about money and uninterested in either financial or political power. He is meticulous about money and fascinated with the politics of power. When I describe our family life, growing up, what I see as most influential was our parents' emphasis on religion and education, on culture and community life. When he describes our family life, growing up, what he sees as most influential was our parents' anxiety about money, their worries about financial security and lessons in thrift. We cut out different paths for ourselves, shaped in part by heredity, in part by the differences we experienced as a male and female in a traditional household, but shaped as much by the need we had to be different selves in relation to each other.

The roles my brother and I adopted for ourselves, the roles Mark and Jerry and other siblings adopt, provide unique identities and separate self-images. In doing so, they also help curtail competitiveness and sweeten comparisons by allowing each of us our own turf on which to win.

. . .

In many families, long before siblings begin to take stock of each other, parents have begun to compare them. The first baby was easy, the second more difficult; the second is placid, the first was active. Although advice books admonish parents not to compare their children, but to view each only as an individual, most parents find it almost impossible not to make some comparisons. After all, everything they know about a baby's eating and sleeping habits, about kindergarten or college, they learn from their first child, and they apply that knowledge in gauging the development of the next.

It is when the comparisons turn into labels used to define and slot children that they may become problematic; that is, when the difficult baby is seen and treated as the difficult child and the placid one is labeled and regarded as "slow." For those labels, stuck on in early childhood, become part of the internal image children have of themselves, later to be incorporated into the roles they assume with each other and in the world outside the family.

In many cases, the labels parents give their children, like the differences children emphasize among themselves, may be applied with the best of intentions: to underline the strengths of each child and restrain rivalries and jealousies. If one child is praised for being the "caring one," another for being the "funny one," one seen as "the athlete," another as "the artist," each has a special place in the sun, and none need feel less worthy than another.

But often, and usually unwittingly on the part of parents, labels may also become deterministic and self-fulfilling prophecies. In a family I know, a soft-spoken, sensitive child was constantly referred to as vulnerable and weak by the parents, in contrast to another who was regarded as strong and independent. The "weak" child, as an adult, continues to need and depend on the attentions and protection that weakness requires. The "strong" one, in adulthood, feels burdened by having to live up to that role in the family and resentful of being expected, always, to cater to the other, more needy sib.

Furthermore, although the labels may truly reflect differences in temperament or personalities among children, they may also reflect parents' own conflicts and desires, their needs and aspirations. In fact, children's roles may become formed in their parents' minds even before birth. A mother may respond to the way she feels during pregnancy by thinking of her unborn child as "gentle" or "a terror." A father may project onto the forthcoming baby goals he could never achieve himself, his dreams of glory and greatness. Or both parents, struggling with a failing marriage, may fantasize that this child will be its savior. With birth, the child begins to be treated according to the mother's or father's internal script.

Certainly the roles Mark and Jerry staked out for themselves were primed and reinforced by their parents' hopes and wishes. Mrs. Platt relished being a "backstage mom." Regretful that she had allowed Mark to drop piano lessons, she directed her energies and longings toward her younger son. Her ambitions fed into Jerry's own talents and his needs to separate from his brother, and the combination helped turn him into the family performer. But Jerry's acquiescence to his mother's desires and her delight in him may also have aroused resentment and jealousy in Mark (Jerry "ate up the attention," he said). And those feelings probably strengthened both his determination not to give his mother the "pleasure" of realizing her show-biz fantasies and his drive to find his own niche, as far as possible from Jerry's. At the same time, Mark lived out his father's expectations of "bringing home the bacon" and excelling as a serious student, probably arousing Jerry's envy and helping to send him to the opposite side of the room as a clown and playboy.

Parental labeling and slotting were among the problems most often described by people responding to the questionnaire, with descriptions also of feeling shortchanged and cheated as a result. Here are the words of a thirty-six-year-old woman:

"My sister acted as my father's son. He expected great things of her, and pushed her to do well in school. I was treated more as a princess. I was warm and pretty and caring, he said, so I would make a good nurse.

"He died when I was sixteen and my sister was fourteen. She excelled in school, has only a few friends, and has never been comfortable in large groups. I felt attractive and supportive, but not until much later did I realize my own intellectual capacities, convinced that my sister had all the brains.

"My mother feels we both bear the scars, twenty years after his death, of my sister not feeling 'pretty enough' and me not feeling 'smart enough.' My sister would have liked him to be less critical; I would have liked him to have expected more of me."

Even more problematic and more devastating to siblings as individuals and in relation to each other were the value judgments many felt went along with parental labels. It's one thing to see oneself as the pretty child and the other as the smart one, as this woman did; quite another to have it made clear that the smart one is the best one.

Wrote a fifty-five-year-old woman:

"When we were children my brother was assigned the terrain of the 'brain' by parents who thought there was nothing more important in the world than being smart. I was seen as the 'creative one' because I had some ability at drawing. My parents kept my brother on a pedestal, and the more they bragged about him, the worse I did in school.

"It wasn't until college that I discovered that I wasn't so stupid after all, and I became compulsive about getting A's and competing with my brother. It took me a long time (maybe thirty years) to realize that I'm not only smart but also human, with many parts to my character. All those wasted years!"

The worst scenario occurs when one child is cast as the bad one, the devil, as opposed to another's angel. ("To this day," said a man, "my parents still see us as Dan the good—that's me—and Joey the bad—that's my brother. He barely talks to any of us because of that.") Such typecasting by parents and the reasons for it are discussed in Chapter Eight, "The Scapegoat."

The labels parents apply and the way they treat their children in response to those labels are another aspect of the nonshared environment siblings experience within their homes. At their best the labels and the traits parents assign bolster their children's separate identities. But even then they bear the danger of tipping over into narrow and constricting categories from which the children may never escape.

Whether generated by parents or initiated by sibs themselves, or a combination of both, the roles siblings assume may extend far beyond childhood, serving as defenses against the worst rivalries and assuring sibs their own places in life. They may also, however, like parental labeling and typecasting, narrow and limit the self, fencing in identities, flattening out the contradictions and oppositions that exist *within* each person. Although Mark gets satisfaction from being Mr. Serious, the brainy chemist, he has forfeited the satisfaction of publicly performing music (an accomplished cellist, he has confined himself to being a "serious music fan"). Jerry denies the intellectual side of himself, yet the unrealized importance of that side makes itself known every time he finds it necessary to mention the IQ score that got him into the fast track back in sixth grade.

The other limitation of role assumption comes within the sibling relationship itself. It is the limitation of masking the similarities siblings share by highlighting their differences, and in that way narrowing each sib's connection with the other. The great emphasis placed by parents, professionals, and sibs themselves on sibling differences pushes underground the base of sameness within them, that center of shared heredity and shared experiences, of family values and ideals and history. Mark turns away from performing as a reaction to his mother's pushiness. Jerry becomes a performer in response to the very same thing. Each started at a center and moved in opposite directions, but the opposite poles they claimed are actually two ends of the same center.

(The newspaper story about the Boston brothers, the senator and the criminal, goes on to say that the criminal, "Whitey," controls most of the area's small-time rackets. As a drug trafficker and bank robber, he always lives on the edge of danger. His brother, the senator, is known for the tight control he holds over the state's upper house. Although the dangers he skirts are political ones, his work is exciting, he says, because "there's something exhilarating about being almost on the high wire every day.")

So profound and deep are the likenesses among siblings, although few recognize them, that there exists in all sisters and brothers the potential for reversing roles, for—in a sense—turning into each other. In an extraordinary play, *True West*, Sam Shepard probes that potential.

The play presents two brothers, as polarized as any could be. Austin, an educated and successful screenwriter, speaks in cultured tones. Lee, a drifter and two-bit thief, uses ungrammatical, sloppy language. As the play develops, each brother takes over the characteristics of the other, so that eventually Austin drinks too much and steals all the neighbors' toasters, and Lee negotiates a script for himself with his brother's Hollywood producer. "We just sorta' echo each other," Austin says, as he begins to sound more and more like his coarse, uneducated brother.

The point Shepard is making is that in spite of all the differences in the world, neither brother is everything the other is not: neither is totally good or bad, totally conforming or nonconforming, totally intellectual or anti-intellectual. There is a commonality between them that allows each to slip into the other's role.

For some siblings, away from their parental home and over time, the need to be opposites becomes less pressing, echoes of the other's voice become stronger, and roles begin—if not to reverse themselves —to meld into each other, allowing each sib a fuller identity and a fuller understanding of the other.

I have seen some of that melding in my own life. As I have become more established in my profession and more economically secure, I have become less closed off to the financial matters I had always regarded as my brother's turf. I sit on boards of museums and libraries where I help make far-reaching budgetary decisions. And I have begun to count among my friends (I, who refused ever to date a businessman) bankers and businesspeople who are also my brother's friends. As my brother has become well established in his field, he (who had once relegated all community matters to my domain) has taken on major leadership positions in community organizations. And he has begun to count among his friends artists and journalists who are also my friends. Our differences will always exist, but we are also able to call up and acknowledge our samenesses.

Some brothers and sisters cling tightly throughout life to the roles they cut out for themselves years earlier, in that way holding off competition or incursions into their separate territories. Mark and Jerry seem be doing this still. Yet in a follow-up interview with Mark, after Jerry had left on tour, I heard some softening of defenses.

I had noticed, I told him, that he had qualified his decision to be a performer's brother rather than a performer by using the phrase "at the moment." Was he, I wondered, ever planning to pursue his own musical interests further?

Unknowingly, I had timed the question well. Friends of his had recently asked him to join their string quartet, their cellist having moved out of town. Theirs was a seriously committed group that had performed professionally and hoped to do more.

"I haven't decided yet," Mark said. "If my brother weren't a professional musician, would I grab this opportunity? I've always wanted to do more with my music. Sometimes I've even dreamed of changing careers in that direction, in spite of my reservations about performers' lives. Am I holding myself back because of my brother? Am I afraid of competing with him, or am I afraid he would feel competitive toward me?"

Leaving his thoughts hanging, he launched into an anecdote about twin brothers he knew. They were both talented cartoon artists, and, while holding a variety of jobs, both would make up and illustrate comic strips that never saw the light of day. Then one of them decided to pursue his talent as a full-time career. After struggling for several years, he created a comic strip that took off and is now syndicated in a slew of newspapers. His twin continues to draw cartoons on the side while he works at odd jobs, unable to "take the risk" of a full-time commitment.

"Now, has he not taken the step," Mark asked, "because his brother is out there doing it successfully and he's afraid to test himself on his brother's ground? Or is this the way he wants it to be?" Turning to me, he said, "There's a parallel here to Jerry and me, although it's not exactly the same because I'm in a completely different field of work and the music I'm interested in is so different from Jerry's. Still, what would happen between us if I became more professional about my music? I'm not sure."

The question was left unanswered. Mark and Jerry have established a careful balance of rivalry and closeness by meticulously maintaining their differences. How much of those differences they can give up while still keeping that balance and their individual identities is hard to know. But if I were asked to guess, I would say that as they get older, Mr. Serious will find his way toward more public performance, and the Clown will become more serious about himself and his work.

Differences in heredity and in home environments help shape differences among brothers and sisters. The roles they assume go a step further, firming identities and assuring individuality, so that no sibling has to wrestle another for the same piece of pie. Later, more secure in their own skins, some sibs find that they can relax their roles and identify more closely with each other without fear of losing their own identities.

There are other roles siblings hold among themselves that are not assumed but simply exist as part of sibling life. And these roles, changed as they may be in adulthood, remain at the core of each sibling's being. They are the roles of older or younger in the family, and they grow from the positions sibs occupy as firstborns or seconds, middle children or lasts.

CHAPTER TWO

*"You're Forty-five Years Old—How Much
Longer Will You Go On Testing Me?"*

TO BE AN
OLDER SIBLING

*M*y friend Lucinda and I have rented a video of *The Fabulous Baker Boys*, a movie about two brothers. We thought it would be fun to watch the movie together because she *has* a younger sister and I *am* a younger sister. She has written a novel about two sisters and I have been writing a book about sibling relationships.

The film story is not terribly original, but the characters are beautifully and subtly developed. The brothers earn their living playing trite piano music together in half-empty supper clubs. The elder, a family man with wife and children, arranges the pair's bookings and manages their money. Single, better-looking, and more creative, the younger has a woman in every town the brothers play. When they decide to hire a female singer to beef up their act, he becomes romantically involved with her, eventually leading to the breakup of the act and a split between the "boys." After an emotional fight and then reconciliation, the younger decides to launch a career of his own, while the elder digs deeper into conventionality.

Lucinda and I watch transfixed as the small drama of these two brothers' lives unfolds.

"Much as I disliked the older brother," she says, as the video ends, "I liked him so much more than the younger one. I couldn't stand that

40

younger one. Complaining that he got a raw deal, as if the world owes him a living. What did he ever do? He was a two-bit piano player waiting for his brother to do everything for him."

"I sympathize with the older brother," I reply cautiously. "He tried so hard. But the young one sacrificed himself playing in those clubs when he really had so much more talent."

"Sacrificed himself? If he'd had any real talent, he would have gotten a good job years earlier. He just liked to blame his brother for his own inadequacies. Typical younger sibling. It's always someone else's fault."

She stops short, wondering—I think to myself—whether she has cut too close to home in generalizing to me about the faults of younger siblings.

"I will say," she hurries to add, "that what I hated most about that older brother is what I like least about all of us older siblings. We always have to be on top—the jolly ones, mobilizing everybody, assuring everybody that things will work out. You know, we're the 'you can do it' type people."

"What I hated most about that older brother," I state, stepping around the self-criticism, "was his need to be in control all the time. He just assumed that any decision his brother made was wrong because he himself had not made it. He always had to dominate, be the big boss."

"Okay, Fran," Lucinda needles, "own up. You really liked that younger brother, didn't you?"

"Well," I respond, avoiding a direct answer, "he was loyal. He put his brother's needs ahead of his own. He squelched his own career for years to help his brother and keep the act going . . ."

"Oh sure," she jumps in. "As if he would have had a career without his brother. And how about that fight toward the end when he tried to break his brother's finger? Didn't you hate him? I cringed. I wanted to kill him. How could he?"

"But he wouldn't have done it," I snap, "if he weren't in a rage at always being told what to do by an older brother who thinks he knows best."

"*I* think," Lucinda says, "that we'll never agree. What comes through in this movie is that one brother is stronger and one is weaker, but you can't tell which is which. We're reacting to them from our own perspectives as older and younger sisters."

It was true, and the reaction was natural for both of us. Although the roles siblings assume and the differences they stress help them fashion separate identities, their identities also grow from an even deeper and more primal base: birth order positions and the roles that accompany them. From that base siblings get their earliest perspectives of themselves in relation to parents and each other, and eventually to people outside the family. Which perspective and which position offers the greatest strength or weakness, satisfaction or dissatisfaction, is a question that nobody has yet answered definitively.

That is not to say nobody has tried. Of all the areas surrounding siblings, the one most studied and argued about by social scientists—inordinately studied and argued about—has been the area of birth order and its effects. Hundreds of professional papers have been published comparing intelligence, achievements, personalities, even marital success of groups of first, second, or laterborn children, and dozens of popular books and articles have spread the results of those studies.

The theme that appears most often in the professional studies, beginning as early as the 1870s, emphasizes the accomplishments of firstborns, particularly men (women were not even included in the earliest studies). Firstborns have been shown to have higher IQ and SAT scores than those who come later, to be listed more often in *Who's Who*, to stand out among the eminent leaders of society. Some of the most gifted scientists in history, such as Isaac Newton and Albert Einstein, were firstborns, as were such statesmen as Julius Caesar, Alexander Hamilton, and Winston Churchill. Some of the greatest poets and writers of world literature were also firstborns, including Robert Browning, Johann Wolfgang von Goethe, and Robert Frost. Firstborns have been found to be overrepresented among senators and Supreme Court justices, among jet pilots and Rhodes scholars.

Theorists have been less kind in analyzing the firstborn personality. They have portrayed the eldest in a family as overcautious and perfectionistic, motivated by both anxiety and aggression. At work, in committees, in any area that requires cooperation, they say, firstborns often become bossy and critical. The firsts may also be "conforming," "conscientious," and "conservative."

The explanations given for all these traits, from prominence to personal aggressiveness, center on the closeness of firstborn children to their parents in the early years of their lives. Because firstborns start out alone with parents, they tend to identify more directly with them than do laterborn children, and therefore to be more prone to please, more eager to fulfill expectations, and more likely to strive for high achievement. Through their parents, the theory goes, firstborns also identify with all forms of authority, becoming conformists rather than rebels, defenders of the social order rather than challengers.

In all these characteristics, firstborns have often been compared to only children, who also have strong ties to parents. But firstborns appear to do better on tests and intellectual tasks, and the reason given is that they sharpen their abilities by teaching younger siblings, a benefit onlies do not enjoy.

Moving beyond its original focus on firstborns, over the years birth order theory has expanded to include analyses of laterborn children and adults as well: Seconds have been described as "manipulative" in working their way around their more powerful older sibs; middles are labeled "negotiators," making peace between those above and below them; and youngests, the most pampered, are seen also as most "charming." (These and other laterborn labels are discussed further in the next chapter.)

But how accurate are the birth order stereotypes?

Two Swiss researchers with the intriguing names of Ernst and Angst conducted a painstakingly systematic review of dozens of birth order studies, from the 1940s to the 1980s, and found little evidence for the sweeping generalizations about birth positions that have come to be accepted as truths. Many factors, they said, such as a family's social class and income level as well as the number and spacing of children in it, need to be taken into consideration in any assessment of birth order differences. For example, the higher intelligence and greater achievement ascribed to firstborns in large-scale comparisons with laterborns may actually be a result of family size. The laterborns tested and measured may have come from larger families in which parents did not have the means to give them the kind of education and training firstborns of smaller families received. If researchers were to compare the IQ scores of firstborns and secondborns within these small families, rather than across family lines, they might find little difference between them.

When we consider the wide range of variables in family life, argue Ernst and Angst, blanket statements about differences according to birth order positions do not hold up—or at least not to the extent to which they have been touted. What does come through as valid in affecting siblings, however, are what these researchers call the "power interactions" between older and younger children in a family—aggressiveness, competition, attempts to dominate, but also power to help one another and to intervene for each other with adults when necessary.

I agree. I would not write off birth order effects completely (even Ernst and Angst accept, for example, the idea that firstborns identify more readily with parental authority and are more influenced by parental values and behavior than are laterborns). But when we look at actual siblings in actual families, and not just at large statistical comparisons, it becomes clear that the emotional, intricate, ambivalent interplays among them—their "power interactions"—have a much greater and more lasting impact on their personalities and attitudes than does the simple fact of birth order.

The sibling interactions in a family get underway when a firstborn child is called on to move aside and give up forever the position of "onlyborn." (Although much of the discussion that follows concerns the oldest child in a family, it is not confined only to firstborns. Much can be applied as well to others who hold similar roles in relation to their siblings. The first daughter after one or two sons, for instance, may be seen as a "firstborn" in regard to daughters born later. Equally important, in families of more than two children, every child, except for the youngest, is an "older" to another, and may function that way in their relationship.)

It was Freud who first described the displacement a child feels when a second is born. (Later writers used the more loaded term "dethronement" for the firstborn's predicament.) Freud could well understand displacement and the anger and rivalry that accompany it, because of his own position as eldest in his family. True, he enjoyed the status of an indulged and favored eldest. Lovingly called "my golden Sigi" by his mother, he commanded so much respect at home that his sisters had to give up piano playing because the music disturbed their brilliant brother's studies. Still, as an adult he could recall the "ill wishes and genuine childhood jealousy" with which he welcomed his baby brother Julius, born just a year after him, and the guilt he suffered because of those feelings when Julius died. He could also recall the misery he felt upon discovering after the birth of the next baby, his sister Anna, that she had grown inside his mother—another form of rejection to young Sigmund. He disliked that sister all his life.

From personal experience and observations of his patients, Freud wrote with passion about the hostility of siblings. "A small child does not necessarily love his brothers and sisters," he said. "Often he obviously does not. There is no doubt that he hates them as his competitors, and it is a familiar fact that this attitude often persists for long years, till maturity is reached or even later, without interruption."

So disturbing can be the presence of siblings, especially from the perspective of the elder, Freud held, that the appearance of small animals or vermin in adult dreams are actually symbols of a person's brothers and sisters. Furthermore, he stated, "if one comes upon a wish for the death of a brother or sister behind a dream . . . one can trace its prototype without any trouble in early childhood and often enough in later years of companionship as well."

Freud attributed part of the rage and rivalry a firstborn experiences to what he called the "family complex," an extension of his famous Oedipus complex. Portraying early childhood as a time of hopeless love for a parent of the opposite sex combined with jealousy and fear of the same-sex parent because of that love, he regarded siblings either as competitors or replacements for parents. A boy might view his baby brother as one more rival, in addition to his father, for his beloved mother, but a rival more easily subdued (and more safely disliked). In his mind, his baby sister might become a substitute for the mother he could not have. He might then turn his disappointment at not being able to marry his mother against her. Or he might love her as he does his mother, but also resent her because like his mother, she, too, is forbidden to him. Or he might simply love her in place of his mother.

In Freud's theory, a girl might view her younger sister as a rival for her father's love. But the sister—or a younger brother—might also arouse maternal feelings in the older girl, becoming a "substitute for the baby she has vainly wished for from her father." A girl might see her brother as a competitor or as a substitute himself for her adored but unattainable father.

And then, regardless of gender, the simple fact of the birth of a baby, in Freudian thinking, reawakens dashed hopes and resentments in an older child. The baby serves as a symbol to the child of something that went on between the beloved and longed-for parents, some profound intimacy that excluded the child and that resulted in the creation of a new being.

Freud's Oedipal theories have been argued and reargued for decades, and his focus on rivalry as the linchpin of sibling relationships has been rightly criticized as overemphasizing the negatives. Yet Freud described as nobody had before him the visceral pain and the fearful void a child enters (at least in fantasy) when another arrives on the scene.

More recent researchers have been less pessimistic about the reactions of the firstborn. Observing young siblings at home and in laboratories, they have noted what every parent has observed: that along with anger and jealousy, children have warm, loving feelings toward their new sisters or brothers. Psychologists Judy Dunn and Carol Kendrick, for example, watched children as young as three years old comfort baby sibs, adjusting their speech, repeating their words, and raising the pitch of their voices to speak in soft, motherly tones that the baby could understand and assimilate.

As months and years go by, this mixture of empathy and anger takes on a life of its own. Modeling themselves on the way their parents treat them and their younger siblings, the elders become teachers and trailblazers. They learn how to make their sibs smile and laugh, how to show tenderness toward them, how to imitate, and in turn be imitated by them. Because parents often caution them not to hurt their sibs, olders learn to protect and shelter the youngers—at first, perhaps, only to please parents, but eventually out of their own sense of responsibility.

Actually, that sense of responsibility toward younger sisters and brothers becomes so vital a part of the elders' self-view that as children they often go out of their way to foster dependency in younger ones. The elder sisters in one study of young children rewarded their younger sisters with warmth and love if the sisters accepted their help on a project but bossed and bullied them if the sisters rejected their help. The olders liked seeing themselves as teachers, in charge, like their parents.

Less rewarding to older children is their discovery that a younger sibling can be an expert at making parents laugh and smile and a genius at hogging adult time and attention. "Younger children think older ones have everything," says psychoanalyst Louise J. Kaplan. "What they don't understand is how painful it is to an older to go off to school and leave the baby at home having Mother all to itself." Older brothers and sisters also discover that younger ones have no compunction about grabbing toys, interfering with games, and using any means they can to move in on what their elders have and do.

(Says a six-year-old girl to a child-development counselor: "Did you ever wish and wish very hard for something, and then when you got it you wished you didn't have it?"

"Sure," replies the counselor. "What did you wish for that you're sorry about?"

"A little sister.")

By school age, along with loyalty and support, the power interactions Ernst and Angst allude to—the struggles for parents and possessions, for dominance and control, for space—begin to solidify. For many siblings those pulls for power become part of a lifelong pattern of relating.

Eager to find out how power plays among siblings work, two investigators, Brian Sutton-Smith and B. G. Rosenberg, studied both schoolchildren and college students, using written questionnaires and face-to-face meetings.

"How does your brother (sister) get you to do what he (she) wants?" the investigators asked.

"He wanted to play baseball," said a boy of his older brother, "and I didn't want to, so he started teasing me, like saying, 'What's the matter? Can't you pitch? Can't you catch?' "

"If I want her to do something for me, I'll tell her that I'll play house with her," said a girl of her younger sister.

"I wanted to stay up and clean the bedroom and she didn't want to, so I told her she'd turn into a hog and would turn brown. . . ." related another girl of her dealings with her younger sister.

The findings for schoolchildren and college students turned out to be fairly consistent: firstborns perceive themselves and are perceived by their siblings as exerting the most power, using in the process "high" power tactics. That is, they command, boss, and scold. They also bribe, give and take away rewards and privileges, and—especially among younger children—use physical force. Laterborns "counterreact" with lower power techniques. They cry, shout, sulk, and pester their older sibs to get what they want.

As traditional birth order studies claim and common sense acknowledges, firstborn children, the study found, have greater need for parental approval and allow themselves to be swayed more often by parental pressures. The firstborns tend to apologize or give in if parents get angry at them; the laterborns to get defensive and angry in return.

In relation to their siblings, the olders, identifying with their parents and imitating them, behave in a less openly confrontational style than the youngers. They internalize or restrain their most competitive and angry feelings, and express their aggression in subtler, more adult ways. They tease and criticize, ridicule and disparage younger ones, unerringly hurling their most stinging sarcasm toward the younger's area of greatest vulnerability. When necessary, they also know how to cover their tracks with alibis and excuses.

In sum, from Freud to the developmental psychologists, the data collected on firstborn children in their relations with laterborns adds up to a potpourri of contradictory sentiments and behavior. Older children in a family feel empathy and they feel resentment toward their younger brothers and sisters. They protect and they belittle. They lead and they push away.

"My sister is seven years younger than I," a woman, a television writer, said. "I always saw myself as her protector, a kind of second mother, and I never thought of myself as jealous of her. But thinking back, I realize how jealous I was.

"I loved to tell stories, even as a kid," she explained, "and my sister loved listening to my stories. I remember how, when she had her appendix out, I sat on the edge of her bed and regaled her with silly tales. I kept making her laugh, and she kept saying, 'Don't tell me any more, it hurts so much when I laugh.' But I wouldn't stop. I knew I was making her hurt, and I wanted to keep on making her hurt, and the best part was I could do it under the guise of entertaining her."

And what about adult siblings? Do the power tactics of the elder and the patterns of interacting with youngers carry over into adult life?

To a great extent they do, although with more subtlety (and sometimes more effectiveness) than in childhood. More to the point, what carries over is the image older siblings have of themselves in regard to younger ones.

In adult life, to be an older sibling means to continue to see oneself, still, always, as leader of the family, a parentlike figure on whom others rely and to whom they look for advice. When asked on the questionnaire whether they had sought advice from a sibling in the past year, most respondents, both olders and youngers, indicated that they had not. But when asked whether a sibling had sought their advice, a significantly larger number of older siblings (58 percent) responded that their younger sibs had come to them for advice than did youngers (47 percent) indicate that elders had come to them. Because older siblings expect to be consulted, they perceive their youngers as turning to them for counsel.

To be an older sibling is to feel *entitled* to offer advice, to receive respect, and to have authority in the family. ("Being older," writes a forty-one-year-old clerk of her forty-six-year-old sister, "she expects more respect from my children than she thinks I am entitled to from hers.") That the respect and authority may originally have come from having greater strength and greater knowledge than younger sibs is not the issue. The expectation of receiving these rights persists because in the eyes of the eldests the rights have been well earned. They have been earned by years of being on top and years of doing things first, of guiding and setting an example.

The eldest in a family of six explained it this way: "I was always out there testing the waters that a lot of the family later ventured into, and

I'll always keep the authority that comes with having been there before them. I was the one who experimented, and they followed—from traveling to having affairs." (Indeed, research indicates that having been shown the way, younger siblings become more sexually active during adolescence than their elders had been at the same age.)

But to be first, the family leader, also means to bear responsibility for those who come later, to look out for them and be available to them. Both Mark and Jerry Platt, in the previous chapter, spoke of a time when Jerry, flat broke as he began his career as a jazz pianist, turned to Mark for money to tide him over. He could not bring himself to ask his parents for help when he should have been self-supporting, Jerry said, but he knew he could count on his older brother. Many other olders described being called on to lend money to younger sibs and doing so, although with less than enthusiasm.

The sense of responsibility for younger siblings can be especially pressing in large families. It was not unusual in the large families studied by Bossard and Boll for the oldest, or several older children, to sacrifice themselves for younger ones. They worked to pay for the others' college tuitions, cared for sick parents, and in some cases gave up marriage or personal careers to provide security for their younger sisters and brothers. Some of these sacrificial elders felt bitter about the burden that had befallen them. For others, the heartfelt gratitude of younger siblings made up for personal losses.

With their assumptions of leadership and responsibility, elders often find themselves—like all leaders—somewhat isolated and lonely, leaned on but with no one to lean upon. A researcher examining families of four children asked college-age siblings to list the names of the sibs in whom they most often confided. Younger siblings almost always listed the firstborn's name; the firstborn rarely listed any names.

By the same token, for many people, to be an older sibling is to recognize your importance in the life of younger brothers and sisters, but to give less importance to their place in your life. "I love you and care very much about your happiness," my brother said to me, "but I never thought I had the same strong feelings you have about our relationship. When I think of that relationship I see it through your eyes. It looms larger in your life than it does in mine." Probably he is right, for studies have shown that younger siblings feel themselves to be more affected by older ones than olders do by youngers. (Or at least they admit more readily to being affected.)

Older siblings, also, tend to recognize the jealousy or competitiveness of a younger sister or brother but to downplay competitive or jealous urges within themselves. Although many people in my study denied comparing themselves to siblings, younger siblings more often than older ones admitted making those comparisons.

"If displacement by a second child is such a traumatic experience for a firstborn," I asked psychoanalyst Peter Neubauer, "why don't firstborns regard themselves as competitive with those who have displaced them?"

"Think of it this way," he replied. "The younger says, 'I like you, I admire you, I want to be like you, I want to share what you have.' The older says, 'Why should I? It's my turf. This is all mine, and you came in and want me to share it with you.' The eldest just pushes the younger one away. 'You don't exist,' he says. 'You are an intruder. Go away. Don't exist.' For the older the competition is hidden. He doesn't see it as competition. It all belongs to him."

(My brother continued: "I was there. I wasn't trying to compete. You reacted to my being there as something you had to deal with. I didn't have to deal with it.")

Another explanation, from the woman who had made her sister laugh so hard it hurt: "The older can't admit to feeling jealous or competitive. It's unseemly. You are the caretaker of the younger one. How can you be jealous or resentful of that beautiful little baby? And in fact you do feel loving and caring. You also feel jealous and resentful, but it's not nice to say so."

To be older, even in middle age, is to see yourself as more mature than younger siblings, mature enough not to be jealous, mature enough to restrain open aggressiveness as you had learned to restrain it in childhood. Older siblings in adult life still use the power techniques they perfected in youth—verbal put-downs or simple dismissiveness of the younger—but if they can, they try to suppress direct expressions of anger, because they believe the power is on their side, and with it the obligation to keep their strength bridled. A political leader has maintained a running conversation with me about his younger brother, who never phones or writes but accuses the older of neglecting *him*.

"Look," he concludes after each report of another blow from his brother, "I'm the older brother, the understanding one, the more responsible one. I don't shout. I don't scream. I just take it out on my insides."

To keep anger bridled does not mean, as this man points out, that the anger is nonexistent. What angers and irritates older siblings most about younger ones is their tendency to complain about their lot in life, as if they have lost out on something the older has received. Equally irritating, say elders, is the attitude underlying those complaints, a belief that the olders somehow owe them something and must pay back for having come first. Because of this attitude, olders often feel that youngers, like the politician's brother, take them for granted, expecting them to behave like all-forgiving parents no matter how much abuse the younger dishes out.

When Freud described small animals and vermin as dream symbols of brothers and sisters, he captured the quality of older siblings' annoyance at youngers who are constantly—in the words of one woman —"yapping at your feet, wanting to deny you your very existence." When my friend Lucinda characterized the second brother in *The Fabulous Baker Boys* as a typical younger who always held someone else responsible for his problems, she expressed the vexation of many an older sibling who feels blamed for having been born first.

That sense of being unfairly blamed that elders have can carry over into many relations aside from those with siblings. "I think having a younger brother who envied and resented me affected my personality in a profound way," said an education consultant. "I know that I have no tolerance for people who always find reasons to be unhappy and are always bitching about their hard luck, the kind who try to make you feel guilty for things you didn't do and were not your fault."

Yet, for many people, to be an older sibling is to feel on some level that it *is* your fault. I sensed in a number of firstborns that some of the anger at being made to feel guilty stemmed from actually *feeling* guilty. In psychoanalytic terms, on the most primitive level, that guilt comes from the earliest fantasy of childhood, the wish to get rid of the intrusive new sibling. The wish disappears or gets converted into kinder feelings with time, but the guilt may remain deep within the unconscious mind of the elder.

The guilt an older sibling feels may also be due to the elder's real physical or verbal abuse of a younger sibling in childhood. A man who owns a business in partnership with his younger brother complained about the younger's irresponsible behavior at work and the burden that fell on his own shoulders because of it.

"Still," he said, "I make excuses for him today—even to myself— because of the things I did to him as a child."

"What kinds of things?" I asked, supposing from his pained expression that he had inflicted permanent damage.

"They sound like little things, and they *are* little things," he said, "but they stay in my mind. I remember babysitting for him—I was six years older—and he wouldn't go to sleep, so I rapped him around, real hard. And I can remember walking him home from school, and he wouldn't hold my hand crossing the street, so I yanked his arm so forcefully that he cried all the way."

Little things (a sister recalls with anguish mocking a younger one because of a scar on her face caused by a dog bite) hound some older siblings, giving them an amorphous sense of guilt even while they take offense at the attempts of younger siblings to make them feel guilty.

That burden of guilt helps give truth to Lucinda's observation that in *The Fabulous Baker Boys* one of the brothers is strong and one weak, but you never know which is which. For even though older siblings excel at power plays and domination, younger siblings gain power through the guilt those power plays provoke in the elder and the protectiveness that goes along with the guilt.

Not that all protective impulses on the part of elders stem from guilt. Protectiveness toward a younger sister or brother, like responsibility for them, comes with the territory of being older. Born in those earliest days of childhood, it lasts far into adult life. Even with disagreements and vast changes in relationships, olders continue to regard youngers as dependent on them and themselves as the youngers' protectors. When, in Philip Roth's novel *The Counterlife*, the older brother, Nathan, gets a call to help the younger, Henry, the call evokes in him what it would in many an older sibling, "the need to be responsible, not so much to the disapproving brother with whom I'd already come to blows but to the little boy in the flannel pajamas who was known to sleepwalk when he was overexcited."

Finally, for many people, to be an older sibling in a good relationship with a younger is to take pride in the younger's accomplishments despite envies or irritations. To be an older is to identify with the younger, just as the younger identifies with you, and therefore to see the other's success, achievement, or good fortune as reflecting well on you, the family, and your attachment to each other.

Eddy Deveau is proud of his brother Roy. He's also annoyed at what he regards as Roy's immaturity, guilty about the inequities in the upbringing he shared with Roy, and always very much aware of his position and responsibilities as elder by five years.

At my first meeting with Eddy, annoyance and anger were the qualities that most colored his conversation with me about Roy. With subsequent meetings I began to understand the depth of the other feelings he has and the interplay of those feelings with one another.

I became acquainted with Eddy during a trip to Dallas, and our interview took place in the downtown office he occupies in one of the city's tallest buildings. His stature as vice president of a leading oil company is clearly delineated by the large, bright corner room he occupies. From a window of that room, he pointed out to me an older, more historic part of town where Roy runs an elegant and highly popular restaurant.

"I wrote him this letter and I said," Eddy began, picking up the thread of a story he had told me when we first met, "you're forty-five years old. How much longer will you go on testing me?" His voice sounded strong with anger, but his eyes had what I can best describe as a quizzical look, as if to say, "Why do I continually put up with this?"

The letter had been sparked by the latest in a series of incidents that had occurred since Roy had publicly declared himself gay about four years earlier. During that time he had moved from coming out of the closet, to allowing his restaurant to be used for AIDS fundraising events, to becoming an active member of the local chapter of the Gay Men's Health Crisis (GMHC).

None of those moves in themselves perturbed Eddy. He had known of his brother's homosexuality for years and had long ago accepted it as a fact of their lives. Although he had worried about the effect of Roy's activism on the restaurant, business had actually picked up rather than declined. Many of the restaurant's regular clients were well-known local actors and models who had themselves become involved in battling AIDS, and their presence attracted the well-heeled business community and curious tourists.

The problem Eddy had was that Roy's increasing anger and frustration with AIDS issues were spilling over into his dealings with Eddy. He'd bawled out Eddy's wife Sue about the amount of money she spent on clothes that should have gone to gay causes. At a party in Eddy's home, he had been less than polite to guests who he thought had not shown sufficient sympathy for those causes. And most recently—the fight Eddy was fuming about—he'd interfered in Eddy's business.

Roy had recommended a friend for a job with Eddy's company. Deemed insufficiently qualified, the friend had been turned down. Enraged at what he considered discrimination against a gay man, Roy had urged his friend to institute a discrimination lawsuit against the company. Roy himself had sent a vitriolic letter to the personnel director, hinting that if the decision was not reversed, the man would find himself in trouble with Eddy, the powerful vice president.

Eddy blew up when told of his brother's actions. He quickly apologized to the personnel manager, making it clear that he had no vested

interest in hiring the man, and promising that he would in the future
put "a lid" on his brother's impulsive behavior. Still, word of the incident had spread through the company, embarrassing Eddy and, he
believed, undermining his position.

Another executive to whom Eddy had introduced me told me that
people in the company considered Eddy something of an enigma.
Many staff members turned to him for counsel on either business or
personal matters because they regarded him as both wise and empathetic. In fact, he encouraged junior executives to seek his advice
(so much so that behind his back some had taken to calling him
"Pop," in recognition not only of his fatherly role but of how much he
enjoyed playing that role). Yet nobody could be harder on those young
executives than he when he sensed any challenge from them to his
authority.

"He squelches opposition quickly," Eddy's colleague told me. "But
he lets his own younger brother get away with the devil. I sometimes
wonder whether the reason he's able to tolerate Roy's shenanigans is
because he shifts his anger away from Roy and onto the staff here."

Certainly I could see, even in our first meeting, that Eddy tolerated
a great deal from his younger brother. Although he felt himself
wronged by the personnel incident, he made it clear that somehow he
would make the first move toward reconciliation.

"I always do," he said, resignedly. "I'm the grown-up in this relationship. I know he needs me, and I can never turn my back on him."

That knowledge and the determination to be at (if not on) his
brother's side had begun decades earlier, its origins rooted in family
history and makeup.

"My father didn't want a second child and never liked Roy," he
explained. "Everything about them was incompatible. Father owned a
cattle ranch, where Roy and I were born. It had been his father's
ranch—*his* father, my great-grandfather, had come here from France
—but my father couldn't make a go of it. The Depression had knocked
him out, and he was never able to recoup. He sold the ranch and
moved us here to Dallas, where he went to work for a company that
manufactures airplane parts. There was a period of time when he
made so little money that my mother had to work as a cook for some
well-to-do families. My father hated having to depend on her and
hated himself even more for being in that position. Eventually he
became a foreman at the plant, but he always saw himself as a failure.
The more unhappy he became, the more he directed his unhappiness
toward Roy."

Eddy told his story dispassionately, as if he were speaking about mere acquaintances, but as he spoke he kept tugging on a rubber band, pulling the band with one hand tightly across the fingers of the other. He is a large man, tall and muscular, with big hands and fingers. The nervous rubber-band gesture seemed not only to release energy, but also to symbolically contain energy that might otherwise burst out of control.

His father, too, he related, was tall and strapping. Feeling stifled on the airplane assembly line, he eased some of his frustration by playing football or baseball with his sons on weekends. Roy, slighter in build than either his father or older brother, hated those ball games and usually ended up crying or feigning illness to get out of them.

As Roy got older he became interested in art and theater, pastimes, Eddy explained, that the elder Deveau didn't understand and therefore hated. With each passing year, tensions between the two mounted, leaving Eddy and his mother caught in the middle. "I would find excuses to stay in school late, or play ball after school until it got dark," Eddy recalled. "I had the kind of interests and abilities my father appreciated, so I didn't get much flak about anything I did."

When he was home, Eddy tried to intervene, to protect his brother. "I was grateful I wasn't the butt of my father's unhappiness," he said, "but I felt sorry for Roy. I also felt guilty for not being the butt." Still, as he moved deeper into the role of his brother's protector, Eddy resented becoming the boy's custodian, resented admonitions from his mother (who loved her younger son and tried in her own way to shelter him) to take care of his little brother.

"I remember once taking him out behind our house—this was after we had moved to Dallas—to show him how to tackle at football. He didn't want to learn and was being stubborn, so I decided to teach him a lesson."

For the first time, the dispassion disappeared from Eddy's voice. He paused between words, breathing with difficulty. His fingers turned white where the rubber band pulled against them.

"I beat him up," he said softly. "I beat him real bad. I'll never forget my feelings. I *had* to be on top. He *had* to know I was boss." He lowered his eyes, watching his hands pull at the rubber band.

"Sometimes," he said, almost to himself, "when I play tennis with my son, I have this same sense that I have to win out, to be in control. It's reminiscent of that time when I beat up on Roy."

We were both quiet. Regaining his composure, Eddy looked at his watch and suggested we continue at our next meeting. That meeting, he decided with a grin, would take place at Roy's restaurant.

It was a beautiful place for an interview, all pastels and soft lighting. Roy greeted us at the door, cold and formal with Eddy, polite but guarded with me. He must know, I thought, that I know about the tiff because of the personnel incident. It had occurred to me to try to talk Eddy out of this meeting place, but I had thought better of that idea. As angry as he was with Roy, I sensed that he wanted to make contact, and our meeting would provide an excuse to do so.

Slighter in build, as Eddy had described him, Roy has sharper and more defined features than his brother. Unlike the restrained energy I had seen in Eddy, in Roy energy seemed to hover close to the surface, ready to burst out at the slightest provocation. He seated us and moved away, never looking back at his brother.

"Where do things stand in terms of your quarrel?" I began.

"Roy sent me a one-line note in response to my letter, saying he's ashamed of me," Eddy whispered. "Nothing new, I've had such 'love notes' from him before."

"How will this end?"

"It'll blow over. His friend has already dropped the lawsuit, and I guess I'm ready to forgive and forget."

"But he doesn't seem ready," I pressed.

"He will be." Eddy smiled confidently. "He needs me. I take care of him in all sorts of practical ways. I watch over every one of his financial dealings, including the restaurant. But it's more than that. Look," he said, leaning over the table to make his point. "You're writing this book, so you'll understand. He and I, we play out scenarios of childhood over and over. He *wants* me to take care of hmm. He poses all sorts of horseshit dilemmas so he can have a problem that I can help him with."

"What do you mean?"

"For example, he's been thinking of expanding the restaurant. We've reviewed the pros and cons a thousand times, but he keeps asking everybody else's advice. Then he comes to me again and we start all over. It bothers me. Why doesn't he just accept what I say in the first place?"

"When did you realize he was gay?" I asked after we had ordered.

"I didn't realize it. In this part of the world you don't think in those terms. We all see ourselves in the old cowboy tradition—real men and all that. I didn't know Roy was gay until he told me."

Roy told Eddy—and, for some years, only Eddy—soon after he'd graduated from college (Eddy had supported himself and then helped put Roy through school). He'd been studying drama, hoping to become an actor—the restaurant business came later—when he had his first homosexual affair, with a well-known veteran actor. It had ended badly, and, frightened, he had turned to Eddy. Eddy's first reaction, he told me, was to "go right to the analyst's couch." This was the late sixties, and while the world may have been changing drastically, in Dallas, Texas, Eddy knew no one who was gay; in fact, the word "gay" did not exist in his vocabulary then.

"I worried about whether I had contributed to it. I worried even more about what it signified about my own sexuality. I know, as the older, I had influenced him in many ways. But how had he influenced me? Besides, I was engaged to be married then, and Roy's news was very unsettling."

Along with his own treatment, Eddy urged Roy to get psychiatric help, too, under the assumption that it would "cure" him of his homosexuality and make him "normal" again. Today he is embarrassed that he had once viewed the matter so simplistically. He has come to accept Roy as he is, and expects the same acceptance from his friends. In fact, even in the midst of their fight, Eddy acknowledged that he takes pride in Roy's activism. He's even a little "jealous" of the publicity Roy has received.

"Sometimes I feel," he said, with more warmth than he had previously displayed, "that I missed out on things, on being all that I could have been. I think to myself that if I had not worked for a large company and had gone off on my own instead, or had taken up some cause, I could have done it all better than Roy has."

It was the only openly competitive thing he had said in regard to Roy, and he quickly pulled back, sitting up straight and changing his tone to a businesslike one. "But I didn't do it and he has, and he's to be admired for standing up for what he believes in."

On any objective test Eddy would rank as a highly accomplished and successful person. In birth order parlance, he would be considered a typical example of the achieving firstborn. Yet, in taking on the responsibility of caring for his younger brother, he had restrained a part of himself that the younger brother had let emerge—anger, flamboyance, a devil-may-care attitude. Eddy, I thought, must get great pleasure out of being "Pop" in his company, and probably does rid himself of some of his irritations with Roy by keeping young executives in line. Still, in some part of himself, I suspected, he felt himself less free than he may have wanted to be.

None of this did I say to him. As we left the restaurant Roy nodded an icy good-bye, and Eddy turned away angrily.

"Why do you keep this relationship going?" I asked.

"Because it's incumbent on me to do so, as the older brother," he replied dryly.

"Is that really all?"

"And because he's my brother for better or for worse. He needs me, and it's good to be needed," he added.

"And," he went on with feeling now, "when we're not into one of these fights, I trust him. I trust him deeply. In some part of me I have no doubt that if I had to, I would put my fate into his hands."

He laughed out loud. "And I do like him, I love him in spite of all this shit."

CHAPTER THREE

"Maybe You're Afraid to Compete with Big Brother or Sister Because They'll Kill You"

TO BE BORN LATER: SECONDS, MIDDLES, OR LASTS

I didn't get to meet Roy Deveau alone until some months after I had interviewed his older brother Eddy at Roy's restaurant in Dallas. By that time the brothers had ended their quarrel. Roy's anger at the fact that Eddy's company had not hired one of his gay friends had subsided, and Eddy's anger at Roy's attempt to blackmail the personnel director into hiring the man had dissipated. Eddy and I had continued our discussions by phone after I left Dallas. He called one day to tell me that Roy was coming to New York to gather ideas to use in the expansion of his restaurant and had agreed to be interviewed. Roy, he said, was on his "best behavior" now that the two had settled their differences.

"So many of Roy's friends have died of AIDS," Eddy explained, "he's beginning to value the family more than he ever did before. And I value him. I also worry about his contracting AIDS. He seems to be fine, though, and he's looking forward to seeing you."

He neglected to tell me how the feud had been resolved. I suspected, from the indications I had in Dallas, that Eddy had brought it to an end. Roy confirmed that suspicion.

"He always makes the first move," he said. "Sometimes I think it's easier for him to apologize than to really deal with the issue."

I wasn't sure whether "the issue" meant the specifics of their arguments or the overall issue of Roy's homosexuality. Roy answered somewhat vaguely that they were interconnected. Although Eddy accepted Roy's homosexuality, he still explained it in classic Freudian terms: rejection by his father and overprotection by his mother had led him to identify closely with her and consequently to seek the love of men. Roy is convinced—and has become militant about that conviction—that homosexuality is genetically predetermined, a result of nature, not nurture. Those differences in attitude, he believes, lie at the base of all disagreements between the brothers.

"But I no longer press it," Roy said, following up on what Eddy had told me. "I've seen too many friends die to remain angry at my brother." He was subdued but far more relaxed now than he had been when I saw him in Dallas, and unwilling to reopen the history of the Great Fight—as he called it—with Eddy.

We had met in a new restaurant in New York's SoHo district, and Roy eagerly inspected everything before we sat down to a serious discussion. I watched him scrutinize the china, silver, glasses, and other accoutrements of the business with the kind of attentiveness to detail that had helped make his restaurant in Dallas so popular.

"Eddy was stunned at the success of my restaurant," he said, after we settled into our meal. "I had been struggling to get into the theater after college, and he didn't know what would become of me. I worried myself that I might have inherited my father's failure genes. It was a terribly low point in my life."

As Roy recalled his early years of struggle, seeking a professional life and trying to come to grips with his homosexuality, the petulant image of him I had carried with me from Dallas faded. He spoke with intelligence and sensitivity.

The idea for the restaurant had come from a friend, another would-be actor. The two traveled to Europe to study with the finest chefs. When Roy returned, his brother helped him raise money to get started, even though, Roy is sure, "Eddy didn't really expect this to work."

But work it did, and beautifully. Through contacts, careful planning, and good luck, the restaurant quickly received rave reviews. Still, Roy will never forget opening night when Eddy and his wife, Sue, came for dinner.

"I was walking around, greeting clients. I sat down with Eddy and Sue for a while, and they just kept eating, never saying a word about the restaurant or the food. I was beside myself with fear. I care more about pleasing Eddy than anyone in the world, and there they were, sitting in silence. Later Eddy claimed that they were just bowled over by the whole thing, and especially by the fact that little Roy had pulled this off so well."

Roy smiled with delight. He relished in memory his older brother's awe at his achievement. "It took Eddy a long time to take me seriously in anything," he said. "But nowadays, the world's taking me seriously has led him to take me seriously."

Being taken seriously by Eddy became a refrain that would come up repeatedly in our meeting. In spite of many friends in both the gay and straight worlds, a slew of loyal restaurant clients, and a kind of celebrity that has grown from the restaurant's reputation and his own as a gay activist, Eddy's appreciation is what counts most for Roy.

Certainly it ranks as far more important than any recognition or lack of it by his parents. Roy speaks about his mother with some affection ("I remember thinking, 'He's Daddy's favorite; I'm going to be Mommy's,' and she and I did have a closeness he didn't have with her"). Nevertheless, he and Eddy both view her as possessive and controlling. He has far more negative feelings toward the father who had belittled him all his life. It is Eddy on whom his emotions center, Eddy who became his protector, Eddy about whom he says, "In some core place, he felt sorry for me."

Not, he hastens to add, that Eddy had always acted on his behalf. "When Daddy would yell at me," Roy related with some bitterness, "Eddy wouldn't just step in and take my side. After all, he got something out of *my* being the one yelled at." His tone softened. "I know he feels guilty that he didn't look after me better when we were kids, so when we got older and he was able to help me, he's done so in spades."

One of the most important things Eddy did for Roy was help him understand that their father's unhappiness stemmed from within himself and not from anything Roy had done. "My father," Roy said, filling in some family history Eddy had omitted, "was a mama's boy, weak and dependent." Throughout life, that father had idolized his own older brother, a charismatic, highly successful oil tycoon, but had been rewarded only with disdain and disparagement. Even when the Depression forced him to give up the family ranch, he got little help from his brother. In fact, as an adult, and after psychoanalysis, Roy had wondered whether his father's dislike of him, his second son, had been a projection of the older man's dislike of himself, the despised second son in his own family.

"I'm so glad," Roy said only half jokingly, "that Eddy has a son and daughter—he broke the chain of the second-son curse."

But if Roy sees himself as the cursed second son in his family, he also sees himself as freer and less constrained than the first son, precisely because he is less connected to the family. He took risks—experimenting with acting and later opening his own restaurant—that Eddy would never have dared to take. Eddy, Roy stated with an unmistakable touch of superiority, is far more conventional than he.

As an example of Eddy's conventionality, Roy described, with some distaste, a passion his brother has developed for collecting Americana. Although Eddy's growing collection of antiques and paintings of the colonial period has received some notice in the art world, to Roy, it is nothing more than a "tangible manifestation of having achieved," unrelated to any special sensibility.

"Do you feel competitive with Eddy?" I ventured, aware that Roy took great pride in his own refined artistic taste.

"I have never thought of myself as competitive with Eddy," he responded testily. "This collecting thing bugs me because it's like a statement, a symbol: Eddy saying to the world, 'Look at me. I can afford the best.' "

"Do you ever feel he's achieved more than you have?"

"In obvious ways I suppose he has. But I've always had it in my head that I was going to surpass him, and I think I'm getting there. In fact, in some ways I've achieved more than he has, through the restaurant, through my own activities . . ."

He broke off, recognizing, perhaps, that he had revealed more rivalry than he may have wanted to. Looking directly at me, he said, in a voice that sounded as if he needed to clear his throat, "It's hard for me to gauge my achievement in terms of his. After my restaurant opened and it was clear that I had a winner, I suffered an enormous anxiety attack. I went back into therapy, and what came out was that I had done something prideful, and it was almost too much for me to handle after all the years of being put down by my father and looking up to Eddy." He turned his eyes away from me to stare straight ahead.

"Maybe I don't look upon myself as competitive," he said, returning to my original question as though to free himself of that label, "because I'm afraid to compete." He stopped again, toying with that idea. "Maybe you're afraid to compete with big brother or big sister because they'll be jealous. Or maybe you're afraid to compete because they'll kill you." He looked at me again, startled by his own thought. "I've not let myself examine all that, and maybe I should."

Suddenly Roy burst out laughing. "Look at this restaurant," he said out loud, happy, I thought, to be able to change the subject. "We're the only ones left, and they're beginning to set up for dinner. We'd better get out before they throw us out."

As he signaled for the check, insisting on paying it although I had invited him to lunch, he spoke of the closeness he and Eddy share. It is a closeness unlike anything either of them has with anyone else, and it more than outweighs their recurring spats. "He was the first person I told I was gay," he said, "the most important revelation of my life. But it's not just one-sided. There are things both of us would discuss with each other that we would not discuss with anyone else, things Eddy tells me that he would not even tell Sue."

He had relaxed again, more comfortable speaking of closeness than of achievement or competition. I knew from conversations with Eddy after their fight ended that what Roy said was true. As good as Eddy's marriage is—and I had the impression that it is very good—a piece of him belongs only to Roy and to no one else. They remain now, these grown men, what they have always been: Eddy, the protective father-brother, sometimes angered and annoyed, occasionally envious, but always loyal, always dependable, trusting of his younger brother and, in turn, unconditionally trusted by him; Roy, idolizing and dependent, at times resentful and competitive, dreaming—in some far corner—of surpassing his older brother, but wanting more than anything to be taken seriously, appreciated, and admired by that brother.

"In all my relationships, with friends or colleagues," Roy told me early in our meeting. "I feel like the younger person, the kid brother, even when I'm older." As we shook hands to say good-bye, he thanked me for listening. Then he said, "Here's something to ponder. I'm forty-five years old, and I still think of myself as a kid. Is that true of all younger ones?"

The condition of being a younger sibling, with its dreams and limitations, its ambitions and fears, has occupied people's thoughts since earliest times. Historically, from ancient societies to modern ones, the rule of primogeniture reigned, giving firstborns (sons, usually) the family inheritance and key position. Yet in religion and mythology laterborns have been the ones celebrated.

Younger siblings in the Bible invariably succeed in overtaking their elders: Isaac wins out over his older brother Ishmael; Jacob takes the birthright, and with it his father's blessing, from his firstborn twin Esau; Rachel, rather than her older sister Leah, gains and retains Jacob's love; Joseph, sold by his older brothers into slavery, becomes a powerful Egyptian prime minister; Moses, not his older brother Aaron, leads the Israelites out of Egypt.

"It is as if to say," declares Dr. Neubauer, "that the firstborn has privileges by birth. Seconds and later children earn privileges by their deeds." The Bible may also be teaching a lesson in showing the triumph of younger over older siblings—nothing in this world is fixed or unchangeable; even the natural order can be reversed.

In myths and fairy tales, youngest children also walk off with the prize, be it a princess or a sack of gold. One analysis of more than a hundred Grimms' fairy tales discovered that in stories about three children, the third child "wins" 92 percent of the time, and in stories of seven children, the seventh child comes out ahead 66 percent of the time. In many of these fairy tales, the youngest child starts out as the slowest, a simpleton whom others look down upon, and grows to become a hero.

That portrayal reflects the feelings of younger children in a family, wrote psychologist Bruno Bettelheim, who studied myths and fairy tales from a psychoanalytic point of view. No matter how bright they may be, they see themselves as stupid or inadequate in relation to their older siblings and their parents. The "happy endings" offer young children the hope not only of catching up, but of outdoing the others. (Another explanation: Maybe all the myths and fairy tales were written by younger siblings dreaming of revenge.)

How do the Bible and mythology connect to real life? What is it like to be a younger sibling in childhood? As an adult?

Although there are many different birth positions younger children hold—secondborn in families of two children and secondborn in families of more than two, middle children and youngests in families of varying sizes—many younger siblings interact with older ones in similar ways, irrespective of the specific places they occupy in their families. This discussion will focus first on those common ways of interacting and afterward explore some of the unique characteristics of individual birth positions.

Birth order theory sometimes labels laterborn children "friendly" and "diplomatic," their ability to get along with others stemming from the skills they develop in getting along with their dominating older sibs. Sometimes it labels them "manipulative" and "pragmatic" (Niccolò Machiavelli, one of the great pragmatists of all times, was a laterborn son), able to work their way around difficulties and adapt more readily to change than firstborns, who hold on tightly to their positions and beliefs.

Along these lines, Frank J. Sulloway, an historian of science, has argued that laterborns are most likely to attack accepted scientific theories and firstborns to defend them. Analyzing the participants in major scientific controversies over the last four hundred years, Sulloway found that a large number of laterborns led revolutions in thought, whereas onlies and firstborns staunchly supported the status quo. Copernicus, for instance, second of four children, fought a bitter battle to prove that the earth revolved around the sun and not the sun around the earth, the accepted theory in his time. His chief opponent, Tycho Brahe, was an only child. Charles Darwin, also a laterborn, challenged forever traditional views of creation with his theories of evolution and natural selection. Many of his severest critics were firstborns. Sulloway argues that laterborns feel freer than firstborns to rebel against convention because they grow up less tied to parental authority and, at the same time, have gained experience resisting the authority of their older siblings.

Like theories about firstborns, broad generalizations about the effects of birth order on laterborn children have not stood up to careful scrutiny, and other factors—such as family size and social class—have been found to be more important. As for Sulloway's arguments, further investigation by other researchers needs to be done before anyone can state definitively that laterborns make up the rebels of society. But as in theories about firstborns, what comes through as valid in Sulloway's studies and others is that laterborns do tend to identify less than their older siblings with parental authority and to depend less on parental approval, separated as they are from their parents by the children who came before them. That separation may give them a certain degree of freedom and independence that older siblings do not have.

More important, what comes through as valid in birth order studies is the strong connectedness of later children to earlier ones. Laterborns never know a world that does not include siblings, and those siblings become a standard against which they measure themselves—idolizing their older brothers and sisters, imitating them, and trying to break loose from them. And just as the power interactions with younger sibs help shape the images olders have of themselves, those interactions help form the self-views youngers will carry within them, views of themselves very different from those olders hold.

One of the few modern researchers to pay serious attention to the self-views and inner life of laterborn children in a family was Alfred Adler, an early follower of Freud who later broke with the master to advance his own theories of the human psyche. If Freud gazed out at the world from the perspective of an eldest child, Adler peered at it from the vantage point of a second son among four boys and two girls. Freud wrote about children in relation to parents; Adler about children in relation to children. Freud emphasized Oedipal conflicts in shaping personality; Adler struggles for power and dominance. Freud expected conformity from those he taught, brooking no criticism. Adler longed to strike out on his own.

"Do you think it gives me such great pleasure to stand in your shadow my whole life long?" Adler once exclaimed to Freud, sounding much like a younger brother straining against the elder who refuses to budge from his seat of dominance. And Freud, angered by what he called Adler's "striving . . . for a place in the sun," denounced the younger man and had him expelled as a disciple.

Adler portrayed the plight of all children as a struggle to overcome feelings of inferiority and helplessness in the overwhelming adult world. "Sooner or later," he wrote, in *Understanding Human Nature*, "every child becomes conscious of his inability to cope single-handed with the challenges of existence. This feeling of inferiority is the driving force, the starting point from which every childish striving originates." Younger children especially, Adler said, suffer pangs of inferiority and inadequacy, confronted as they are with the greater strength of older siblings. Secondborns may be filled with envy and feel slighted and neglected, while the youngest child in a large family faces special difficulty, being not only younger than others "but also usually the smallest, and by consequence, the most in need of help."

Older children in a family, Adler taught, take power for granted; youngers must strive to attain it. Even as they strive—and even when they succeed in overtaking older siblings—youngers continue to carry within them feelings of inferiority. It is true, said Adler, that "what a child *feels* need not actually be the case," yet "it does not matter what really has happened, whether an individual is really inferior or not. What is important is his *interpretation* of his situation." Younger children often interpret their situation as being inferior to that of olders and view themselves as being at a disadvantage.

That view, at least in childhood, has been documented more recently by psychologists observing young children with their families. Laterborn children, they have found, may tend toward lower self-esteem than their older brothers and sisters, and the reasons are twofold. As Adler emphasized, the youngers must constantly face the fact that their elders are larger and more capable than they are. But be-yond size—and far more devastating—younger siblings also suffer the criticisms, disparagements, and patronizing dismissals with which many older sibs greet their ideas and efforts.

Here is Stanislaus Joyce, younger brother of James Joyce, on whom James relied for everything—from money to story ideas—writ-ing in his diary at the age of eighteen:

"It is terrible to have a cleverer older brother. . . . I perceive that he regards me as quite commonplace and uninteresting—he makes no attempt at disguise—and though I follow him fully in this matter of opinion I cannot be expected to like it. It is a matter beyond the power of either of us to help."

Sometimes parents unintentionally contribute to younger chil-dren's self-denigrations by encouraging olders to feel and act superior to them. Guilty about having produced another child to intrude on the happy world of the first, they minimize the child's importance by con-stantly referring to it as "the baby" instead of by name, or by pointing out the older's greater ability or intelligence compared to the younger, who "can't do anything alone." The parents' goal may be to diminish the threat the elder sees in the younger; the results for the younger may be to feel diminished by the elder.

Reinforcing the self-doubts of laterborns, also, is the recognition that their very existence can be a source of irritation, jealousy, and anger to their older siblings. Without fully understanding why, younger sibs know that the older brothers or sisters whom they adore often see them as being in the way. Roy, not Eddy, recounted an anecdote about his own birth, which had become part of family lore. Soon after he was born, his grandfather told Eddy about the beautiful new baby in the family. Eddy ran all the way to the hospital to see for himself. He took one look at his baby brother and said, "Boy, is Grandpa a liar."

After telling the story, Roy added ruefully, "I guess he could have lived without me; I could never have lived without him."

Along with the elders' exercise of strength, that gut knowledge younger siblings have that their older siblings could have lived with-out them—did, indeed, have a life without them—contributes to their feelings of inadequacy.

But to speak of low self-esteem among younger children in a fam-ily, or the disparagements of older ones, is to tell only a small part of the story of young siblings' interactions with their elders. For along with the insecurities they may suffer because of their older siblings, younger ones also bask in the security of the older's presence and protection. Babies placed in playrooms away from their mothers have been observed to cry less and smile more when their older siblings are present, even if the elders are just a few years old themselves. With their siblings present, also, young toddlers fearlessly wander off to explore the world farther away from their mothers than they do without their siblings.

From the earliest years of childhood, older siblings appear to younger ones as demigods, not far behind the parental gods themselves. The youngers look up to their big brothers and sisters, imitate them, follow them around, long to play with them, crave their recognition, and want—in every way possible—to be like them.

And there's the rub. For in that "wanting to be like" lies the essence of what may be the most crucial aspect of younger siblings' interactions with older ones. That is their striving to catch up to—or get ahead of—older siblings, the corollary, in Adler's terms, to their feelings of inferiority or inadequacy. There comes a time—about the second or third year of life—when the "wanting to be like" their elders turns into a compelling passion among younger sibs, and they are no longer content only to gaze in awe at the all-powerful other. At this point they want to have what the older has, go where the older goes, be what the older is—and more.

Jennifer, at the age of nine months, remains calm and unperturbed when her brother John, twenty-two months her senior, acts aggressive and rivalrous toward her. At age three, notes the psychologist observing her, she instigates almost as many fights as John does, competes with him for possessions, and reacts with fury when he takes something of hers. Competition has become for Jennifer more than rivalry for parental attention, and she is less interested in impressing her parents than in impressing her brother. Most of all, she is consumed with measuring herself against him. Her greatest despair grows from not being able to match his age and achievements or his predominance over her because of them.

With their newfound strivings to equal their elder sibs, laterborns begin to disrupt the social order in the family. Comparing the relationship among siblings in childhood to those among members of any social group, psychologists Sutton-Smith and Rosenberg point out that the sibling system stays balanced, with little conflict, as long as the members keep their places. Keeping their places means that the older maintains authority and the younger accepts that authority. As soon as youngers become less willing to accept their elder's domination, they move toward unbalancing the system. Now—and even as they continue admiring, depending on, and seeking the approval of their elders—the youngers struggle in whatever ways they can to make their own mark.

The techniques the youngers use in their struggle differ from those of their more powerful older sibs. The youngers may be overtly competitive, showing their feelings by yelling, fighting, or sulking, as opposed to the more restrained and subtler skills of the olders. And like weaker members of any social group, when they feel themselves outdone, they turn to outsiders for aid—in their case, parents. They complain and cry to parents, seeking their help. Sometimes they even intentionally provoke their elders into an all-out fight guaranteed to send parents running in to protect the younger.

Like younger siblings in the Bible and in fairy tales, then, younger sibs in real life may counter their own sense of weakness by learning early how to fight back and defy the established order. (A case can be made, as Sulloway does—without going overboard into broad birth order generalizations—that this early defiance of sibs by laterborns contributes in some to a spirit of rebellion and innovation in adult life.)

By adolescence, and more so by adulthood, most of the overt battles have ended, as siblings find their own places and make their own way in life. Some laterborns, content within themselves, stop measuring their abilities against those of older sibs. Others, like Roy, continue to be inspired by dreams of making their mark, of forging paths of their own that will one day surpass those of their sibs. Still others, giving up finally on trying to keep pace with their elders, may make no attempt to reach for what another has achieved. One woman, a file clerk, wrote on the questionnaire, "Hard to live up to my older brothers—the 'A' students. They became engineers. I became the 'black sheep' and married a 'black sheep' like me. Oh well."

But whether they've given up the race or are still striving to win out, whether eighteen or eighty, younger siblings in adult life retain a special sensitivity to attempts at domination by older ones, a special rage at reminders of the inequities that marked earlier years. To them the sounds of power plays are like the sounds of an old record, grooves worn thin, pitch a bit lower, but words and melody easily recognizable.

Of all the complaints I heard from laterborns, the most consistent concerned older siblings' maneuverings for control, their assumptions that they are still entitled, by dint of their position, to be in charge.

There are many variations on the theme.

"My oldest sister," said a woman, third in a family of four, "surrounds me like a blanket. It's her way of competing with me. By worrying about me, fussing over me, smothering me, she tries to hold me under her thumb. I handle it by trying to keep my distance as much as possible."

"A few months ago my older sister and I were playing bridge together," said another woman, second of three sisters, "and I made a mistake. She lashed out at me, humiliating me in front of everyone. Later she apologized privately. Then she added, 'But you really were stupid.' It still makes me cry when I think of it, because it's typical of the way she acts toward me." The speaker is seventy-three years old; her sister seventy-eight.

"If my husband and I take a vacation," explained a third woman, this one aged forty-six, "my older brother calls several times to suggest we go to the same hotel he had stayed at. If we decide to buy a new car, he insists that the only good car to buy is the same one he has. If my son is applying to college, my brother tells me in a hundred different ways which school *he* thinks is best. If I don't take his suggestions, he makes a point of letting me know how much better his choice would have been. If I do take his suggestions, I'm never sure it's because I really agree with him or because I don't have the guts to stand up to him on every issue."

"I insisted a year or so ago that my brother not call me 'Brother' anymore," a twenty-eight-year-old man named Thomas said during a highly emotional interview.

"What's wrong with calling you 'Brother'?" I asked.

"You don't understand. He never called me Tom, the way everybody else does. He started calling me 'Brother' when we were very young. I decided, finally, that it was a terrible put-down for him not to call me by my name. It was very hard for me to assert myself, but finally I did."

"How did he react?"

"He was in shock. At first, when he said my name it really came out stilted. But he got used to it; he doesn't call me 'Brother' anymore."

Firstborn and older siblings interpret youngers' complaints as emanating from envy and resentment of their very being, and to some extent they are right. But in adult life these complaints are also about assumptions of superiority long after the reasons for that superiority have disappeared, and about a sense of entitlement long after status should have been equalized. "Give it up," the youngers cry. "Stop bossing; stop orchestrating; stop expecting to rule the roost. You are no longer bigger and wiser."

But then the man whose brother finally calls him by name says to me, "I really miss it."

"What do you miss?"

"I miss being called 'Brother.' There was a fondness in that title. We have two younger sisters, and I was the only person in the world he could call 'Brother.' It was part of his caring about me."

And I discover (but of course I have known it all along) that mixed with the laterborns' complaints, there exists a contradictory impulse *toward* seeking the elders' authority, toward dependency, toward wanting to be taken under their wing. For if being an older sib means feeling protective toward younger siblings, no matter how old, being a younger sib, no matter how old, means wanting, in some part of one's being, to continue to be protected by the older one.

For some younger siblings the dependencies can be extreme. Roy Deveau borders on the edge of that extreme, counting on Eddy to handle all his finances, expecting Eddy to be understanding and forgiving no matter how badly Roy treats him. Others go further, some to the point of becoming deeply depressed, even suicidal, when their older sibs marry or move away, so fearful are they of losing the elder's support.

In a different mode of dependency, other youngers almost blindly idolize their older siblings throughout life. Daniel, a gifted thirty-nine-year-old college professor, devoted hours of interview time to describing his brother Richard's superior traits. He portrayed Richard, five years older than he, as a "giant," a "golden boy," a "war hero." "Anything he ever did, I would try to do, but he would always be better at it, and it's still that way," he said. Daniel admitted that while he was well aware of some failings on his brother's part, his "clay feet," he continued to look up to Richard. "When I'm with him," he explained, "I feel I'm being taken care of, just because I'm there. When I'm with him, I get a relaxed feeling."

The real Richard I met bore little resemblance to the hero Daniel worshiped. Shortish, roundish, red-faced, boasting of his own abilities and successes, he didn't hold a candle—in my mind—to his better-looking, modest younger brother. But with his bluster and the advantage of age, he had long ago convinced Daniel of his superiority, and those convictions continue to govern their relationship.

In any form it takes, the impulse toward dependency in younger siblings includes also a wish for approval, and the wish for approval includes the urgent need to be taken seriously by older sibs. The need has its source in those early years when olders so blithely dismissed their younger siblings' ideas and opinions. It becomes all the more pressing in adult life when olders consciously or unconsciously withhold recognition. Roy Deveau rationalizes his brother's silence on the opening night of his restaurant as stemming from Eddy's awe at his achievement, and that may or may not be the case. But Roy found that silence devastating precisely because he needed to hear his older brother's voice articulate the approval that would validate Roy's accomplishment.

So greatly do many younger siblings hunger for this recognition and approval that they sometimes turn a blind eye to an opposite truth: their elders' wish for *their* recognition and approval. I had not expected to find, among those respondents to the questionnaire who said they seek their siblings' approval, almost as many older sibs seeking the approval of younger ones as the other way around. And in interviews quite a few laterborns spoke of being taken aback by the impact their words or advice had on an older brother or sister. After an argument with her older sister, one woman said she simply didn't realize she could hurt her sister so much. "I didn't know I had such power," she explained.

In truth, regardless of their dependencies and longing for approval, younger siblings *do* have considerable power, and regardless of blind spots about that power, on some level many are aware of it. In adult life much of that power comes from permitting the olders to maintain their identity as olders, meaning their authority, their leadership, their position and postures. In part younger siblings allow this because it is comforting and natural to them; in part they do so out of an ancient and primitive fear of the elder's retaliation—as Roy said, "because they'll kill you." But with the naked understanding siblings have of one another, laterborns also see that older ones have a continued *need* for the status and deference that have always defined them, and a vulnerability that grows from that need. So when they continue to hold on to their role as youngers, they do so in large measure as their way of satisfying the needs of the older, of offering their brand of protection to that image the older ones hold of themselves.

Tom, the man who reclaimed his name, elaborated on his reservations about having done so: "I felt I was being squashed and I had to assert myself, but it has made me feel bad to see him suffer. He's more insecure in a lot of ways than I am, and his needs are greater. He needs to dominate. Even as a child he was that way, which made it hard for him to have friends. I felt sorry for him then, and I wanted to protect him. I still feel that way."

Who, then, was the stronger in the movie *The Fabulous Baker Boys*? Was it the older brother, who made the decisions, arranged the pair's bookings, and maintained a stance of confidence and certainty? Or was it the younger brother, who allowed him to do this, knowing that by pulling away he could destroy the stance of certainty and possibly also his brother? Who is the stronger, Eddy, the fatherly, concerned sibling who tolerates the antics of his younger brother, or Roy, who reads Eddy's heart and understands his motives even while he continues to test him?

The most potent of the power pulls between younger and older in childhood as well as adult life occur in families of two siblings or, when there are more than two, between the second and first, especially if they are close in age. Why this intensity? Because with no other children around—or before others arrive—the competition and anger as well as the protectiveness and loyalty the first two share are undiluted, concentrated only on each other.

When dilution does set in, when a third child arrives—or a fourth or fifth—the intensity between the first two, well established as it is, usually continues. At the same time, new rivalries develop, not only for the attention of parents, but for the attention of siblings themselves. And new configurations form, as the secondborn becomes a middle child (or, with more children, a third or fourth becomes a middle), and a new youngest steps into place.

A few thoughts about middle children aside from what has already been said about all laterborns: Children in the middle hold unique positions in their families in that they take on the roles of both older and younger siblings. According to birth order theory, those dual roles turn them into good compromisers and negotiators, able to find their way between those above and those below them. But they may also have to find their way alone, neglected by parents busily involved with the achieving eldest or dependent youngest. Theorists cite Richard Nixon, second of five brothers, as a classic middle child—complaining to reporters about being "kicked around," but also able to negotiate breakthrough talks between the United States and China.

In real life, middle positions in a family can be more complicated. For many, the result of being sandwiched in the middle is to see themselves as having no particular role, the "eternal outsider," as one man put it. Or, in the words of a twenty-one-year-old woman, third in a family of four, "my older sister was firstborn in the family, my older brother the first boy, and my younger brother the youngest. Me, I had nothing special, no unique place, and I hated that." Supporting such complaints is the finding on the survey that middle children in families of three tend less frequently than the oldest or youngest to perceive themselves or be perceived by others as the favorite of their mother or father.

Nevertheless, plenty of middles view their world as the best of all possible ones. In Bossard and Boll's study of very large families, other children in the family coveted the middle places. They regarded oldests as having too much responsibility and youngests too little, while those in the middle were "just right," comfortable and secure in their positions. Even in smaller families, seconds or thirds often enjoy their roles as both youngers and olders. Dominated by their older brothers or sisters, they can in turn dominate those below them in the pecking order. But because they know what it feels like to be the low-powered member of a sibling system, they may also show special sensitivity to younger siblings and establish special friendships with them.

The most satisfying middle position in small families or large ones comes from being of a different sex than other siblings around. The first boy after one or two girls, even if followed by another boy, may enjoy special status in the family; the same holds true for the first girl. When siblings are of the same sex, those in the middle need to work hardest to distinguish themselves from the oldest and youngest. Sometimes such children become the most achieving or most competitive in the family, and sometimes they assume roles as unlike the others as possible, keeping themselves different and apart through adulthood.

A question that deserves some attention is whether in becoming middles, children suffer a form of "dethronement" comparable to the dethronement of a firstborn. When a second is forced to give up the position of youngest to become a middle child or a third moves aside to make room for a fourth, do they experience the anger and sense of intrusion a firstborn is said to feel when a second arrives? I am convinced they do, although little in this area has been documented.

One piece of evidence can be found in studies made back in the 1930s by David Levy, a psychiatrist known for his research into sibling rivalry. Levy conducted experiments among Indian tribes of South America to see whether, regardless of cultural background, children show jealousy and hostility at the birth of a new baby. He found that they did. He also found that middle children could be as jealous as firstborns. In an experiment in which children played with dolls representing parents and siblings, a seven-year-old named Marta, next-to-the-last of ten children, looked at a mother doll with a baby doll and stated, "When the sister sees the little one, the sister is unhappy because the mother is nursing her." Soon afterward she amputated the arm the mother doll used to hold the baby.

Another fragment of evidence comes from a nutritionist, second in a family of four, who said that her younger sister's entire personality —and even her appearance—changed after a baby brother was born. The sister, Tara, had been a beautiful child, "all curls and dimples, the kind of baby people would stop to look at in the carriage . . . always smiling and laughing." After their mother gave birth to the new baby, Luke, the older children were sent to an uncle's farm while she regained her strength. When they returned, Tara, aged four, found her new brother ensconced in her mother's arms and her older sisters enlisted to help with the baby.

"Poor Tara was pushed aside, as if she didn't exist," said the nutritionist. "She became the saddest child I have ever seen. Nobody looked at her anymore and nobody became her friend. She even stopped being pretty. A real sourpuss, crying all the time. And she never stopped crying until the day she was married."

Tara doesn't remember becoming the "saddest child" in the world after Luke's birth. She can say only "I was four years old. That was a long time to be the baby, and then suddenly here comes Mother with another baby, smaller and cuter than me. On top of that, he was a boy, and I was the third girl in the family—a meaningless position. So there were a lot of reasons for me to resent him."

Her siblings describe Tara now as someone they all trust, but someone also secretive, a little aloof from the others and never confiding in any of them—a result, perhaps, of becoming isolated from them after her baby brother's birth. They also describe her as the one most in need, still, of her mother's approval, although she is in her fifties and her mother in her eighties. That, too, may be an outgrowth of her brother's birth, when her mother turned her attention away from Tara toward Luke.

The point is—without trying to psychoanalyze Tara—that although the displacement a younger sibling experiences may not be as charged as that of a firstborn, who had been the sole star in the parental universe, it can be charged enough. After all, a firstborn holds the title of "first" no matter how greatly a family expands. But when a second or third child relinquishes the position of youngest to the nextborn, that position disappears forever. For Tara, even acquiring the status of being older than her brother, with all that it implies, could not compensate for the loss of having been the family baby, with all that *it* implied.

(There's a moral here for parents as well as siblings: Middle children often do feel neglected and may need some extra attention, especially in giving up their place as youngest.)

The one child in a family whose position never gets displaced is the lastborn; nor, however, does that child ever experience the rewards of being bigger, stronger, or wiser than another. That combination of circumstances makes the situation of lastborns, especially in large families, unique, and calls—as the middleborn position does—for some specific comment.

Birth order proponents almost invariably describe the youngest child in a family as "charming" and "outgoing," sometimes also "spoiled," and "irresponsible"—all consequences of having been doted on by parents and cared for by older sisters and brothers. Those older siblings tend to concur on the "spoiled" and "irresponsible" labels, and to complain about them, as did a woman who wrote of her youngest sister, "As a child she was a pampered brat who always got to do things that we three older children were not allowed to do. For example, I resent the fact that my parents paid for her college education and did not do so for any of the rest of us. I guess I *still* see her as a spoiled, pampered child, even though she's thirty-five years old now."

The youngests have different things to say. They speak of unremitting hand-me-downs, with rarely a toy or piece of clothing acquired explicitly for them. They speak, sometimes with a shrug or even a smile, of family photograph albums stuffed with pictures of the oldest and a good sampling of some of the youngers, but barely a trace of them. Some speak, with pain or sadness, of feeling neglected by parents who'd had their fill of childrearing by the time the last one was born; others of being ignored or left out of dinnertime conversation and of the more grown-up world of the others, as in the woman who wrote, "My three older sisters seemed bigger than life to me. I was always in the way and needed a bath. Their prom dresses were more important than the frog I caught."

Most pressingly, when lastborns complain about their lot in relation to older sibs, they speak of feeling overwhelmed by the concentration of authority and capability above them, sometimes almost to the point of being crushed. "I hated being the youngest," a man wrote. "I always felt I was being compared to my brothers and sister, and thereby robbed of my own identity. I'm still always comparing myself to other people and struggling to find out who I am." Moreover, with a hierarchy of olders up front, the youngests often remain slotted as the babies in their families long after they have babies of their own. Witness the fifty-nine-year-old physician whose sibs continue to call him "Junior," and whose older sister confided that she is still unable to think of him as a "real" doctor.

In their relations to parents, lastborns also carry a burden of their own. Indulged and protected as the baby in the family, they often have the hardest time of all breaking free and establishing independence. That independence may be hampered even further by parental needs and demands, so that the lastborn becomes what family therapists call "the sacrificed child." Some youngests, picking up tensions between their parents, live at home long after they should have left, hoping to keep their parents' marriage intact by their sheer presence. Others devote themselves to nurturing one or the other parent when a marriage does break up or a parent dies. And there are still parents who inculcate in their youngests the expectation that they will be the parents' caretakers in old age, and still lastborns who take that expectation as a commandment. Giving up their time and family life—if they have a family of their own—they sacrifice themselves on the altar of parental duty, sometimes receiving little thanks from either parents or siblings.

But there can be another side of the coin for lastborns: feelings of chosenness that stem from the protection and pampering received. These feelings are not unlike the confidence and sense of themselves enjoyed by only children who know their parents adore them in spite of pressures the parents might exert. Such feelings give some lastborns the strength and initiative to strike out in directions unexplored by others in the family.

One of the most contented lastborns I met was an ebullient woman of thirty-two who considered her position in a family of seven perfect. Not only had her parents been more relaxed and financially secure with her than with their older children, and not only had she not been spoiled by all the good that came her way, and not only did her parents favor her, but—she felt sure—she was the favorite of each of her siblings.

"Ask them," she prodded before we parted, "I'm sure they'll all say I'm their favorite."

I did, and while her assessment was not absolutely accurate—some regarded her as overindulged—her brothers and sisters did admire her. They most admired, one brother said, her ease in getting along with friends and colleagues, a knack she had of incorporating people she liked into a large family structure, as if all the world were her siblings and she their delight.

In my interview with Roy Deveau, he spoke of his anxiety attack after the successful opening of his restaurant, and he touched on the fear a younger sibling has of overtaking an older. "You're afraid to compete with big brother or sister," he had said, "because they'll kill you." Roy did not pursue the concept further, but it is one that cannot be over-looked. For it sometimes happens in families that youngers do compete ferociously, or, even without determined competition, simply outstrip their elder sibs. When they do, when the younger, as in Bible stories of old, steals the older's "birthright," the result can be devastating for both younger and older.

No mystery surrounds the cause of devastation for an older surpassed by a younger. In childhood, the simple reality of having been born first bears with it every expectation of remaining first. Because so much of the identity of the older gets built around this expectation of superiority, a reversal of positions can threaten the very foundation of the older's self-view.

"I always felt I was stupid, because my sister was so brilliant," a woman said. "We entered college at the same time—she was fifteen and I was eighteen—and I felt driven to graduate in three years so that once in my life things would be normal and I could be ahead of her. Nobody understood the need I had to do it, but I had to get out before her."

The pain and disappointment can be even sharper when the reversals occur in adulthood, and what was once had is now lost, leaving the elder feeling cheated of his or her due.

For a younger who has triumphed over an older, the pain can be more convoluted and ambiguous, as the younger tries to integrate the wish to win with the guilt and fear that accompany winning. The guilt comes of having hurt the older by disrupting the natural order, of pricking the other's pride and piercing the armor that shields the other's vulnerability. The fear is fear of the other's wrath and revenge, but also of being alone, too far up front, out of the protective embrace of the older sib.

The great German writer Thomas Mann fought bitter literary wars with his older brother Heinrich, brilliant also but not equal to the younger. Having won, especially with his masterpiece *The Magic Mountain*, Thomas then denied to himself and the world that he wanted to win. He went out of his way to portray himself and his brother as equals, even refusing the high honor of election to the Berlin Academy of Arts unless the academy also elected Heinrich. In a letter written shortly before his death in 1955, Thomas described a dedication Heinrich had made to him in one of his last books. "To my great brother, who wrote *Doctor Faustus*," the dedication read. And Thomas added, "What? How? *He* had always been the great, the big brother. . . ."

Thomas Mann found it too difficult to face up to his own wish to outshine his brother (although that wish may have been the motivating force in his life), and even more difficult to accept wholeheartedly the fact that his wish had come true.

The tensions between wanting and not wanting to outstrip an older sibling can be so conflicting that some younger sibs respond to them by going the other way, unconsciously preventing themselves from achieving more than the elder. Therapists see people who hold—and hate—jobs unworthy of their abilities but who cannot bring themselves to move to a higher level for fear of moving beyond an older sister or brother. Other youngers, like Mann, hold on to the image of the older as more successful long after the reality behind that image has been reversed.

Do all younger ones go through life thinking of themselves as kids? Roy had asked me.

Not necessarily. Often they assume roles of authority outside their family that offset the powerlessness they may have felt within it. But even when they don't think of themselves as kids, many younger siblings continue throughout life to admire elder brothers and sisters and resent them, seek their protection and reject it, strive to outstrip them and fear outstripping them. In short, no matter how they behave toward others, in relation to their older brothers and sisters, they continue to behave as younger siblings.

One more key factor influences the behavior of younger siblings as well as older ones: the gender of each. When sibs are of the same sex, a special kind of identification takes place between them, and a special struggle goes on against that identification.

CHAPTER FOUR

"Dear Santa: My Turtle Died. I Hope My Sister's Turtle Dies Too"

SISTERS AND SISTERS AND BROTHERS AND BROTHERS

*I*n the novel *His Little Women,* Judith Rossner's character Louisa tells a lawyer about herself and her half sisters.

"I can see you're beginning to get it," she says.

"But what is it I'm beginning to get?" he asks.

"That all sisters are half sisters."

"And so?"

"And so . . . well, let's just say that when I was growing up in the Bronx, I was an only child. Then my father left us and had another daughter. . . . So now I had a father. And I had a baby sister. Half sister. Sister, half sister, what difference did it make what anyone called her? The fucking little brat had *my father,* and I hated her!"

In Louisa May Alcott's *Little Women,* the take-off point for Rossner's novel, Jo, every girl's heroine and tomboy of the March family, cries at the thought of her older sister Meg marrying. "I just wish I could marry Meg myself, and keep her safe in the family," she says. "She'll go and fall in love, and there's an end of peace and fun, and cozy times together."

Rossner's "little woman" is expressing the Freudian view of sisters as Oedipal rivals for their father's affection, a view that permeates this contemporary novel. Jo March is expressing the warmth sisters can enjoy among themselves, undisturbed by the world beyond the family. Rivalry and warmth, competition and intimacy characterize all combinations of siblings in any permutation of age and order. Yet as Rossner and Alcott show, and many siblings would agree, there can be a special dimension to the qualities of closeness or competition when sibs are of the same sex.

Central to that specialness is the issue of identity. I spoke earlier of the process of finding our own identities in relation to parents and to siblings, and of the challenge among siblings of forming independent selves, crippled neither by envy nor the desire to be the other. As peers, siblings identify with each other naturally, easily taking on one another's characteristics. This identification is closest in siblings of the same sex because they are most alike. So for them, the challenge of forming distinct identities is greatest.

The most intense and most challenging of same-sex sib situations is that of twins of the same sex, especially identical twins, and by examining some of the identity issues in the lives of twins, it becomes possible to understand similar issues in the lives of other siblings of the same sex. (Identical twins are born of a single fertilized egg that has split in two in the mother's uterus, giving the fetuses identical genetic makeups. Fraternal twins are born of two separate fertilized eggs and have about as much chance of sharing genes and being alike as any two siblings. But because they are exactly the same age, they usually spend much more time together than do other siblings, making separation that much more difficult.)

Buried within all of us, say those who study the human psyche, lies a longing to be a twin, to have someone else in the world who is just like us. At the beginning of time, the philosopher Plato suggested, humans were created with two identical faces turned in opposite directions, and with two bodies formed into one unit, one side male and the other female. But the gods changed their minds and split us into two beings, ever aspiring to wholeness again. Sexual love is a reaching toward that wholeness. So is the fantasy of having a twin, of being made complete by a duplicate who perfectly understands our innermost selves. But what is it really like to have such a duplicate?

Here is Doug, aged twenty-two, talking about having an identical twin brother, Mike: "Sometimes we think it would be a lot easier if there was only one of us. But I don't think we wish the other one never existed, because we've learned so much from each other and had so much fun together. Maybe sometimes we wish there was just one of us."

And here is Mike, talking about Doug: "I remember thinking that. Feeling like killing him. No way would I ever do it, but, in the heat of anger, just thinking, 'He should be dead. I should kill him.' "

Doug again: "I've heard people talk about being alone in the world —that ultimately you're alone . . . I never really knew what they were talking about. We don't know what it's like to be lonely."

And Mike: "Having an identical twin follow you around is like having a mirror follow you around. You always know what you look like."

Twins see themselves mirrored in each other, sometimes liking what they see and sometimes not. In the liking department can be listed the companionship, the security, the empathy (some say also the telepathy), and the support each shares with the other. "Our most important goal," a forty-year-old twin told me, speaking about herself and her sister, "is to spur each other on, to do for one another and to make sure the other is happy."

Into the not-liking department go the obverse sides of the same qualities: feeling overly dependent on each other, being fearful of separation, and having a sense of confusion about where one leaves off and the other begins. The mirror image is continuous, as if they are not individuals but the same person twice. "Most mothers of identical twins assert that they have never mistaken one for the other," says the narrator in the Jane Smiley novella *Ordinary Love*. "I assert it, too. But, inevitably, one twin is the theme and one is the variation." Echoes Mike: "I always wanted Doug to know I'm me, I'm not some double."

For some identical twins (and this belongs firmly in the not-liking category), the struggle not to be a double, to be the theme rather than the variation, becomes a source of frustration and friction. These twins may cultivate their differences and overemphasize them in order to create boundaries between them. But because they so closely resemble each other, they may also become highly competitive, demanding to be treated exactly alike, equals in every respect. Each keeps a sharp eye on the other's attainments and attentions received, jealous of even the slightest sign of advantage. Although in their imagination, say psychiatrists, many twins see themselves as two halves of a whole, when twins focus on comparisons, they often do so because each feels like less than half and perceives the other as having received more than an equal share.

Years ago parents fed into the competition and identity difficulties of their twin children by treating them as doubles. People took it for granted that twins should have cute, rhyming names and be dressed exactly alike, down to matching socks and hair ribbons. And because everyone fussed over their cuteness, the twins usually conspired to remain duplicates as long as they could.

The forty-year-old twin mentioned previously, whose goal is to ensure her sister's happiness, described being dressed like her twin and continuing to dress like her through their teenage years. When they were about twelve, she related, they read a magazine article advising parents to treat their twins as distinct individuals, not dressing them alike or buying them the same possessions. So invested were these twins in their style of twinship that together they wrote the editor a heated letter defending their upbringing. Not until several years later, attending separate colleges, did each begin to realize how important it had become for her to be her own person, apart from her sister.

"Living separately saved us," said this woman. "Otherwise we would never have developed our individuality." Laughing, she added that in spite of that individuality and each sister's long and happy marriage, "our husbands don't realize that we'd still rather be with each other than with either of them."

Today many parents of twins, aware of the importance of encouraging their children's separate identities, make a point of regarding them as individuals from the moment of birth. They dress the children differently, have them placed in different classes, and even send them to different schools when possible. Such practices can be crucial in helping twins along their journey toward individuation. It's not uncommon, also, for parents to designate one twin as the older and the other the younger even if the age gap between them can be counted in minutes. Both may go through life then seeing themselves and each other in the roles of older and younger, another form of differentiation.

Yet for all the pains parents may take to create distinctions, twins *are* alike and have shared their life spaces from the earliest moments of existence, beginning in their mother's womb. Forming separate selves is a task they need to cope with themselves, regardless of parental behavior. It is a task that involves giving up some of the security of their twinship in order to stand alone as individuals. It also involves becoming independent enough to transfer some of the intimacy they share with each other to the outside—to friendships in childhood and to the intimate partnerships of adult life. When twins ignore that task, particularly by the time they reach adolescence or young adulthood, they run the danger of remaining forever themes and variations of each other, repeated mirror images that never stand out in clear relief one from the next.

For siblings of the same sex who are not twins, being together is "like looking into a mirror that does not reproduce the exact image," in the words of a photographer who has photographed many sisters. Nevertheless, although not exact, the image is familiar, resonant, easy to recognize and therefore sometimes difficult to distinguish from one's own. In that sense, while same-sex sibs may offer each other deep companionship, like twins they face the formidable task of individuating, of giving up some of their dependencies in order to forge unique selves. And as it is with twins, parents can aid in the process of separation by regarding sibs as individuals, or they can hinder it by grouping the siblings into units, as in "our girls," or "the boys."

A thirty-one-year-old woman named Rita is a good example. As children, she and her sister, two years younger, attended the same schools, were given similar gifts, and were always dressed alike in the same "adorable little outfits," as though they were twins. She described their situation as "almost a forced intimacy. The same clothes, the same toys—maybe in different colors—well, there was not supposed to be any rivalry because we both had the same things. But that actually exaggerated the rivalry, because if one thing broke or one liked the other's color, there would be trouble."

She illustrated with an anecdote: "We each had one of those horrible little green turtles that develop those dreadful eye diseases, and mine died just before Christmas. I wrote a long letter to Santa Claus and said that I had been particularly good that year and felt I was quite deserving. I ended with, 'I look forward to seeing you.' Then I added, 'P.S. My turtle died two days ago. I hope my sister's turtle dies too.' "

Even their different talents did not temper the rivalry between the sisters. "I was very studious and my sister athletic," Rita said. "You might have thought, 'Now isn't it nice? They have different territories.' But actually, because we thought of ourselves almost as one person, we were each jealous of the other's territory. I used to think, 'Why can't I be more athletically inclined?' And she, 'Why is Rita always getting credit for being such a good student?' "

The sisters married within six months of each other, and now "there seems to be a lot of competition" between their husbands, who work in related fields of government service. As for the women themselves, they have found that the best way to maintain their separate identities and contain their competition is to see little of each other. If there were a family problem, Rita says, they would help one another, but on a day-to-day basis, "in terms of support and emotional involvement, it's a very arid landscape."

Although Rita and her sister are not twins, the entanglement of their lives in childhood can be put under the heading of what psychologists call "twinning," meaning a fierce attachment not unlike that of twins. So knotted together were these sisters, and so intense their rivalry, that now the only way they can keep their apartness is by being physically apart and deliberately staying that way.

It is precisely to avoid the powerful rivalry and the "arid landscape" that may result from twinning that many siblings of the same sex "de-identify," making a point of taking on opposite roles in life. Mark and Jerry Platt—"Mr. Serious" and the "Clown"—have maintained good relations since childhood by not overstepping each other's boundaries. So in their own way have Eddy and Roy Deveau, one the conservative fatherly figure, the other the brash gay activist.

Schachter and Stone, who coined the term "de-identification," found the process to be most common among children of the same sex and especially the first two in a family, who usually experience the most burning rivalry. As with twins, that rivalry may exist side by side with the closeness same-sex sibs feel, and it also may be the result of that closeness. And both the rivalry and the closeness may be fueled by the same thing—alikeness.

Schachter also argues that two siblings of the same sex tend to "split" their parents between them so that one takes after the mother and the other the father, again as a mechanism to keep rivalry checked. Presumably such splitting would occur even if parents are divorced and living apart.

It's a theory that rings true most clearly in regard to sisters. Jo March of *Little Women* was the "boy" in her family, barely tolerant of her sisters' preoccupations with hairdos and parties. Similarly, quite a few women told me that they or their sisters filled the role of their father's "son" when there were no boys in the family, moving closer to his interests than to those of their mother. Fathers often bolster such splitting among their daughters. Unconsciously feeling cheated of a son, they encourage one daughter—usually the youngest—to play out their own dreams and ideals. Mothers may collude in that encouragement, disappointed themselves at not having a male child.

The splitting, if it occurs, takes place less overtly among brothers. Though some men may view themselves as resembling their mother more than their father in personality, none that I have spoken to characterized himself as his mother's "daughter" as opposed to his more masculine brother. Nor do mothers or fathers encourage sons to see themselves in that way. Such a self-image would be far too threatening to a young boy or a grown man, in part because of a fear of homosexuality. In part, also—and despite the many gains of the women's movement—society still holds it preferable for a woman, like Jo March, to "think like a man" (to use an old cliché) than for a man to identify with a woman.

Even when siblings of the same sex choose up parents or create opposing identities to establish their separateness, they often continue in dozens of ways to influence each other and to measure themselves one against the other. An area of particular influence and particular measurement is the area of sexuality. I am not speaking of sexual preference, of whether one sib is straight and the other gay, like the Deveau brothers. Nobody has definitively determined the causes for those differences. (Freud, who viewed homosexuality as a psychological entity, suggested that extreme hostility toward a brother, in competition for a mother, can contribute to it; many others argue for genetic, not psychological, causes.) I'm speaking of sexual understanding and behavior, of the awareness of one's body, of selecting clothes and cosmetics, of going out or making love or choosing a marriage partner.

Sisters of sisters or brothers of brothers often complain of being deprived of the experience of learning about the opposite sex at home via siblings. It is a legitimate complaint, and some experts have suggested that same-sex siblings have a more difficult time than those of the opposite sex in adjusting to sexual relationships and marriage. But what these siblings have instead is a better understanding of their sexual selves, of their innermost yearnings and feelings, of their bodies. A woman described the "sensual" pleasure she experienced in bathing her younger sister when she was eleven and her sister five. Poised at the edge of puberty, she found her sister's body a textbook of her own body. "With a brother," she said, "you have to suppress any erotic sensations. But with a sister you can let it come out a bit because she's also you."

As children, same-sex sibs usually have their own version of "playing doctor," looking, examining, and touching each other. Later, during adolescence, an older might guide a younger through sexual terrains, showing the way with more honesty and less self-consciousness than parents usually have in these matters. A social worker remembered experimenting with her sister, a year younger than she, in kissing on the lips, preparing themselves for their first kiss with a boy (and stealthily enjoying, like the woman above, the erotic sensations of the moment). Several men recalled learning to accept their own sexual impulses by seeing their older brothers masturbate. Many sibs of the same sex spoke of sharing sexual confidences with each other, and some could still sense the irrevocable loss they felt when a sister or brother's marriage shut them out of the most intimate secrets of that sibling's sexual life.

If siblings are close in age, it may happen that the younger becomes more sexually active or knowledgeable, less inhibited, perhaps, and more willing to break new ground. In that case, the younger might serve as the pioneer, showing the way to the older, instead of the other way around. Or a younger's precocity might push an older sibling into a more conservative stance as a sign of disapproval. When Mark Platt speaks with derision of his younger brother Jerry's "score-keeping mentality" in regard to women, he knows that his own attitude of respect for women and cautious selectivity has been constructed in direct opposition to his brother's.

In this realm of sexuality, also, lie the subtle, unconscious influences that reach into the choices siblings make of friends, lovers, and spouses. The effects of opposite-sex siblings on such choices are more obvious, and it may not be difficult to recognize that a woman's husband resembles her brother. Yet a sister too can be the hidden model of choice for her sister's lover; a man's wife can be reminiscent of the man's brother.

Not unusually, siblings may find themselves attracted to the same person, a testimony to mutual tastes and the appeal of a man or woman who resembles someone in their past, usually a parent or other relative. Sometimes such attractions lead two sisters to marry two brothers, an arrangement that may create exceptional closeness between the two families, or exceptional rivalry, or both. And sometimes siblings will become rivals for the same lovers or marriage partners. In Freudian terms such rivalry has strong Oedipal overtones: two brothers competing for the love of a woman, as they once competed for the love of their mother. But the rivalry of brothers or sisters for the same lover may also reflect highly charged feelings between siblings still powerfully entwined, still competing as they did in childhood, still unclear about boundary lines between them.

"Kiss her, most passionately, in all my private places—neck—and arm, and eye, and eyeball . . . ," wrote Virginia Woolf to her lover, Clive Bell, husband of her sister Vanessa. Although the sisters had divided their world—Virginia to be a writer, Vanessa an artist—they remained profoundly tied to each other emotionally, with Virginia feeling desolate after Vanessa married. In her mind, loving Vanessa's husband was like loving Vanessa, and she never recognized that she had betrayed her sister through her flirtation with Clive.

.   .   .

There have been no such betrayals among the four Ginetti sisters I interviewed. But there is a husband who psychologically resembles a sister and a sister who wanted to marry a clone of another sister's husband. There have been arguments about dresses that were really arguments about identity, and struggles with identity that revolved around clothes and calories, spouses and parents. There have been rivalries and loyalties, distancing and closeness, and four sisters who, although married with children of their own, still think of themselves as the "Ginetti girls."

I met with the sisters initially as a group at the Connecticut home of the secondborn, Nancy. The family had gathered to welcome the eldest, Mary Ann, who was visiting from Seattle. The guests included the two younger sisters, Kate and Lisa, and their families, and the women's elderly mother, their father having died some ten years earlier. The first thing that struck me about the sisters was their ease with one another and with Mary Ann, although they had not seen her in almost a year.

"Mary Ann called to say she was coming to town, and the next words out of her mouth were 'How much do you weigh?' " Nancy said soon after she introduced me to the others. She gave her sister a hug, and added, "So, are you satisfied? I'm no thinner than you."

"That's not for lack of trying," Lisa jumped in. "The minute Nancy hears that Mary Ann is coming to town, she runs to Weight Watchers."

The bantering was comfortable and the women were so inherently knowledgeable about one another that nobody dared dissemble for a moment.

The second impression I had, and it was not hard to pick up, is that the "heat" in the family hovers around Mary Ann and Nancy, the two eldest. As I would learn, just a year apart in age, they had always had the strongest, and most problematic, relationship.

My third impression had more to do with me than with the Ginettis. Although many women with brothers had told me that as children they had longed for a sister, I had never felt that way myself. I had regarded it as an advantage to have a brother rather than a sister, who might offer more direct competition. But observing these sisters gave me a tug of wistfulness. I had never known the kind of sharing they have, and for a moment hankered after it.

The sisters themselves were pleased with their connectedness.

"Like all sisters, I guess," Nancy said, "we thought of ourselves as the real Little Women." Then, glancing round: "Of course I was Jo, the best."

"Oh sure," Mary Ann jumped in. "You never cared about boys and such girl things, did you? Why, you were going with Tony before I even met Ken, and you married about two minutes after I did. Some Jo!"

"So what?" Nancy would not let go. "I'm still different. I don't even look like the rest of you."

She wasn't wrong about that. She is the only one of the women who has the light hair and skin of her mother's Polish-German ancestry. The others, dark-haired and brown-eyed, resemble, they told me, their father's Italian-American family. Ranging in age when I met them from Mary Ann's forty-four to Lisa's thirty-five, the sisters are of average height—with Lisa the tallest—and average build, although, they insist, all have a tendency toward plumpness that sets them on constant rounds of dieting and weight matching.

Having grown up in modest circumstances in Norwich, Connecticut, the women had, after marriage, all made their homes in locations not far from their parents or one another. Mary Ann's move to the Northwest about five years ago—her husband's company transferred him—marked the first major geographic separation among them, and the family still feels sad about it. Nancy felt most saddened by the move, but may also have benefited most from it.

"I cried every night for a year after Mary Ann moved away," she told me when we met alone the day after the reunion party. "I was thirty-eight years old, I had my own family, and I still felt like a baby deserted by its mother. Finally, Tony, my husband, said, 'Why don't you go visit her?' She had been in Seattle for three months by then. So I bought a plane ticket and I called her up, and I said 'I'm coming out to visit.' "

Nancy paused, tears dripping from her eyes. "And she said," she continued, " 'Don't come. We're not settled in yet, the painters are still here.' Don't come! I couldn't understand it. I had my ticket and everything."

Hurt by that rejection and needing to fill the time she had always spent with Mary Ann, Nancy enrolled in a course in home design. She worked diligently, earned her license, and has since been steadily building a business of her own as an interior decorator.

"It never would have happened," she said, "if Mary Ann had not moved away, because we did so many things together."

We were seated in the den, where I faced directly a picture of her and Mary Ann, aged about eight and seven, in which Mary Ann is grinning broadly and Nancy looking straight into the camera with tongue stuck out.

"I was the dizzy blonde—that's what my father called me and it's how I thought of myself—and Mary Ann was the beauty," she said, slipping into memories without being asked. "She was the oldest, the prettiest, and the smartest of us all. I would lend her everything and she would never lend me anything, but it was an honor to have her borrow my clothes. Oh, I wanted so much to be like her. I wanted dark hair like hers and brown eyes. When Tony gave me my engagement ring, I felt miserable because it had a round diamond in a square setting and hers had been set simply with only prongs. Can you imagine what it's like to wish more than anything in the world to be like your sister and know that you can't?"

The words jumped out, a far cry from the lighthearted bantering I had heard the day before.

"Then there's the famous story of the dresses," she continued. "The others all know it because we've talked about it. What they don't know is the lasting pain of it."

The story was actually two stories. The first took place when Nancy was fifteen and Mary Ann sixteen. The sisters had been invited along with their parents to the black-tie wedding of a wealthy family member. Although money was tight, the Ginettis had decided that the occasion warranted long dresses—their first—for both girls. Mary Ann shopped with her mother in a local discount store, but because Nancy had a babysitting job that afternoon, she and her father went to a department store on the following Saturday.

"It was the best day of my life," she recalled. "Just my father and me in that fancy store. We picked out an absolutely gorgeous dress. I still see it in my dreams—black taffeta, with a pink sash. I was the happiest girl in the world. But when I came home, Mary Ann took one look and said, 'You can't wear that. You're too young for black. That dress is much better for me.' "

Before Nancy knew what had happened, her mother agreed with Mary Ann. The two of them returned Mary Ann's original dress, buying, instead, a "fluffy baby-blue" number for Nancy. "They told me *this* was my dream gown, not the other," Nancy said. "I hated it but I wore it, and Mary Ann wore my black one. Oh, how I cried. I couldn't get over the unfairness of it."

The tears streamed forth. "But would you believe," she continued, regaining composure, "that the same thing happened again years later after we were both married? The same damned thing."

Another wedding. Both sisters invited. Nancy sees a dress she loves that costs two hundred dollars, more than she has ever spent. She calls Mary Ann from the dress shop for a consultation and—she hopes—approval. "Two hundred dollars!" scolds Mary Ann. "Where do you come off spending that kind of money?" Nancy settles for a lesser garment. At the wedding, Mary Ann appears in the very dress Nancy had ached for, explaining that she had gone to the dress shop after Nancy's phone call and fallen in love with the dress, which was, in terms of price, "more appropriate" for her. This time, as appeasement, Mary Ann exchanges dresses with Nancy in the middle of the wedding. "It was fun," says Nancy, "except that she got to keep the dress."

Mary Ann, when we spoke, acknowledged Nancy's feelings about both dress stories, but without great sympathy. "Okay," she said, "so I wore Nancy's black dress before she did when we were kids. There were many things my mother didn't understand about raising kids, and that was one of them. She shouldn't have let me wear the dress. But was that so terrible? And the second time, we switched during the wedding. That was a lot of money for a dress in those days. I didn't think she could afford it."

Mary Ann looks straight at you when she speaks. No embellishments, no nonsense, just concentrated intelligence.

"Look," she said early in our meeting, which occurred the day after I met with Nancy, "there are many things I feel guilty about in my behavior toward Nancy. The dress business takes low priority."

What she feels guilty about is what she perceives as her own favored status in relation to Nancy. "They always told me I was older and smarter, and I had to take care of my sister. My father called Nancy the dumb blonde. Really, I thought she was retarded or something the way they made me feel so responsible for her."

I noted that in Nancy's version the label had been "dizzy" blonde— not much better, but of a slightly higher order than "dumb." Feeling burdened by this sister, Mary Ann went on, she treated Nancy badly. She hated to lend her clothes because Nancy was so "sloppy," and she refused to allow Nancy into her group of friends, although the younger girl would have done anything to be included. Worst of all, determined to keep her status as the favored, "grown-up" sister, she let Nancy take the blame for mischievous things they both did.

Measured against these "crimes," for which Mary Ann has apologized to Nancy many times, she told me, the dress incidents seem fairly trivial. Yet I think they have more meaning to her than her dismissiveness suggests. For Mary Ann, taking a stand on the dresses served as a way of taking a stand on her own identity, of warding off incursions by the younger sister who wanted to be her. Only *she* could wear black, she was telling Nancy as a teenager, and only *she* could afford an expensive dress during their early married years. And only she was the older sister, with both the burdens and privileges that position engendered. No matter what Nancy wore or did, she could not be *her*, Mary Ann. Nor would Mary Ann brook any competition that would threaten her self-image.

So determined is Mary Ann to keep the lines clear between her and the sister closest to her in age that she downplays any suggestion of need for Nancy on her part. Some years before her move to Seattle, she and her husband had bought a home in New London, near Nancy's neighborhood. There Mary Ann made a point of cultivating her own friends and living her own life, she said. Although eventually she began spending more time with Nancy, she remained scrupulous about keeping some distance, staying "out of Nancy's pots."

Nancy's version of those years, described toward the end of our interview, was that Mary Ann had "followed" her to New London, and even though Mary Ann made her own friends, the "bottom line was the two of us." Nancy cherishes the closeness of those years and is convinced that Mary Ann does also but is not able to admit to even the slightest sign of dependence.

"Mary Ann is very much like my husband Tony in that way—in a lot of ways," Nancy said. "In fact, when we were first married, I would slip sometimes and call him Mary Ann by mistake. I see things in him that I see in Mary Ann in terms of their own insecurities and needs."

When I asked her to elaborate on those insecurities and needs, she felt unsure about articulating her feelings. "They both use cover-ups," she said. "They both cover up for things they can't do or for feelings of inadequacy they have that they don't want anyone to know. They always act as if they're on top—they have to be on top. But inside— well, sometimes I feel stronger than either of them."

I had heard such words about elders' weak points from other younger siblings, but I found something touching in Nancy's comparison of her sister to her husband and in her willingness to protect the vulnerabilities of both. Nevertheless, at least in terms of her sister, her protection goes just so far.

"I still accept a lot of things from Mary Ann because I admire her so much, and I still wish I could be like her," she told me in summing up. "But I've won. We both have wonderful marriages and wonderful children, but I also have a career and she works part-time as a secretary. Maybe I've accomplished a lot because I wanted to show that I'm better than she is. Whatever you want to make of it, it's there."

Mary Ann, like many elder siblings, remains aloof from open competition, just as she remains aloof from feeling responsible in the dress incidents. "She has a right to feel proud, she has done very well," she said when I asked about her response to Nancy's career achievement. "Here is someone who had to wear my hand-me-downs and who thought of herself as a dumb blonde." She hesitated.

"I suppose," she added with some irritation, "if anything bothers me, it's the fact that she has to flaunt everything she does. I left college to help support the family, and I've never had a chance to go back. Doesn't she realize her showing off hurts me?"

Nancy does realize it. Yet the part of her that never freed herself from Mary Ann can't seem to help drawing attention to her achievements, seeking again and again the recognition she still craves from the older sister she still idolizes. Mary Ann, for her part, has held back, setting up barriers to keep Nancy from moving too near and swallowing up her being, her person. So close in age, these two sisters might have taken on opposite roles, as other siblings of the same sex have. Instead they have remained locked together, their closeness and their competitiveness intertwined.

The sister who *has* set herself apart—not so much physically but emotionally—is Kate (who says, "I'm number three, I don't try at all"). If it can be said that there is one "boy" in every family of sisters, she is he. Her sisters speak of her as the "jock" in the group, the one who loved fishing or pitching balls with their father. An avid hiker, she frequently camps out with her family, far away from the pain and suffering that have become part of her life as a nurse on the cancer ward of a large hospital.

Perhaps it is the work that has given Kate an air of self-sufficiency and a pragmatic sense of what she regards as important in life. Or perhaps Kate chose the kind of work she does because of her self-reliant outlook. Certainly something about her position in the family gave her a feeling of separateness.

"There was always a tightness between Mary Ann and Nancy," she said when we met in her apartment not far from the hospital, where her husband also works—he in the administrative department. "And Lisa came so much later; she's six years younger than I. I kind of had to fend for myself, especially since Mary Ann and Nancy loved to gang up on me."

As an example of the "ganging up," she cited the trauma she had suffered in learning about menstruation. "When I was about eight or so, my sisters told me—and I was terrified—that one day blood would come gushing out of me. Imagine telling that to an eight-year-old. They scared the hell out of me. In fact it was so scary that when I did get my period, I didn't associate it with what they had told me. But then, I didn't know what was happening to me because nobody had explained it. Here I was in a family with two older sisters and nobody ever told me anything real."

Kate draws up such recollections with a kind of resignation, having adjusted long ago to being the outsider. In their book on large families, Bossard and Boll list as one of the sibling roles in such families "the isolate," the person who is more alone and closed off than others, and Kate seems to fit that category. Paradoxically, because she is outside, she is also the sister in whom each of the others confides most, although when asked to whom they felt closest, none designated her (Nancy and Mary Ann named each other and Lisa chose Mary Ann). She, in turn, saw herself as equally close to each of the three, confiding in none, but able to keep their secrets without betraying any of them—a leveler in the family, or, some might say, a true middle child adept at negotiating both ends.

"Negotiator" is hardly a word anyone would think to apply to Lisa, at the youngest end of the Ginetti clan. As opposed to Kate's calm steadfastness, Lisa bubbles, her words hopscotching over one another, so that she manages to reach the finish line of a thought just as you are grabbing on to its beginnings. Many of the thoughts concern her sisters, whom she finds endlessly fascinating.

"I like my sisters as people," she said after insisting that I have iced tea and cookies on the back porch of her Victorian home in the suburb of Mohegan. Married to a businessman fifteen years her senior, Lisa lives a comfortable domestic life, unconflicted about not having pursued work outside her home. She dabbles in gardening and local politics but devotes most of her energies to her three daughters, the youngest of whom is six. She hopes her daughters grow up to be "separate, interesting people" like her sisters, but also free and self-confident like her.

"There was enough distance between the others and me that even though I admired them, I remained the most independent," she said with conviction.

She had not always been as independent as she now felt, she admitted. During her teen years she had become greatly dependent on Kate and particularly on her husband, Chris, to the extent that she almost married a man much like him.

Chris, an only child, had been delighted to acquire upon marriage a large and warm family. Almost instantly, he took on the role of big brother to Lisa, driving her to parties and calling for her afterward so that she would not have to take a bus or train home late at night. He advised her on clothes and boyfriends, and when she toyed with the idea of dropping out of college, he convinced her to stay. For her part,

Lisa developed a mad crush on Chris, viewing him as the most important person in her life—even more so than her parents or sisters in those years.

"Did Kate resent your closeness to Chris?" I asked. Kate had never mentioned a word about her husband's relationship with her younger sister. When I later inquired about it, she shrugged it off.

"She should have, but she didn't. He was the be-all and end-all of my existence. But I guess she felt sure of her marriage. During the first two years of *my* marriage, however, my husband, Sal, was very jealous. 'It's Chris this and Chris that. I'm going to beat him up,' he would say."

"Did you compare your husband to Chris?" I had met both husbands at the family gathering but had no basis for judging them.

"It's interesting that you ask that. When I was going out with Sal, I also had another boyfriend named Frank, and Frank was very much like Chris. I couldn't decide between the two men, and I spoke to Kate about it. She's so smart. She said, 'Do you really want a husband just like mine?' I thought about that a lot. Was I competing with Kate for her husband? Would there have been something almost incestuous about marrying a man so much like my brother-in-law? And I knew that a husband like Chris would have been no challenge for me. He would be accepting of me, the way Chris is, sweet, nice, uncomplicated acceptance.

"I guess I didn't want that. It's okay for a big-brother type, but in a husband I would have found it boring. In our family you don't get bored. We're firm Catholics, and with us you marry and stay married. As my mother always says, we're not Macy's; we don't accept returns. So I married Sal and it's been a difficult marriage. He's so much older than I and a complicated, tough person. Sometimes I think about what it might have been like to have a husband so similar to my sister's husband. In the end, I think the man I married is more like my father than my brother-in-law."

She stopped, finally, for breath, then went on, "You know, I think I've never openly said that about my father before. I wonder if Kate's known it all along though. I wonder if they all knew that I was my father's favorite."

And off she launched into another subject, as loaded as any we had discussed. During the course of our interviews, all the sisters spoke frequently about their mother, portraying her as the force in the family who made the decisions that had most affected them. Now in her seventies, she lives with Nancy, but the others in the area visit regularly. Although occasionally the women get huffy with each other about who has done most for their mother, they seem to cooperate better than many siblings I have met in their attentiveness to her.

They've reached far less agreement in regard to their father. Until his death he had worked hard, first as a laborer, later as an owner of a construction business, leaving himself little time for the everyday activities of his daughters. Consequently, each daughter lays claim to the time he did make available for the family.

Mary Ann regards herself as her father's "princess," in a category so superior to the others that she felt no need to discuss it at length. Nancy, in contrast, found every opportunity to speak of her father's respect for her work and his frequent phone calls—"more than to anybody in the family"—to see how she was doing. Kate, with quiet confidence, informed me that because she had shared so many interests with her father, he loved to be with her. "He chose me," she said, "and none of the others had anything like that with him." And Lisa, probably most attached to her father, stated definitively, "He gave me the most time, and loved me best. When I was in fifth grade and big and fat and taller than the other kids, he would tell me I was his 'long-stemmed rose.' To this day, I stand straight, with pride, and try to think of myself as my father's long-stemmed rose."

His little women, as Judith Rossner might say, competing, through memory, for first place in their father's affections.

But rivalry for their father makes up only one part of the complex connections among these sisters. The issue of finding their own identity has been with them since their earliest days, and remains with them, to some extent, today. Nancy continues to idolize her older sister Mary Ann even while she speaks with pride of her own accomplishments. Mary Ann still holds her sister a bit at bay, tightly guarding her standing as eldest. Kate has been able to create herself as a separate entity by shutting out the others to some degree. And Lisa, still seen as the "baby" by her older sisters, sees herself—and may be right—as most independent of all, near enough in age to appreciate the others but distant enough to be a distinct person. These four women differ from one another in myriad ways, but none can imagine her own being without relating it in some fashion to her sisters.

Like the Ginetti sisters, many siblings of the same sex continue in adult life to define and redefine themselves in relation to one another. But do relationships among sisters differ from those among brothers? That is one of the questions I set out to explore in conducting both the survey and interviews.

In terms of the survey, the answer was a resounding *yes*. Sisters differ in their relationships with each other from brothers in their relationships in one major area: their closeness to one another. On almost every measure of closeness on the questionnaire—and it included nearly a dozen measures—women reported themselves closer to their sisters in significantly greater numbers than did men to their brothers or did brothers and sisters to one another.

Here are some examples. To a broad, general question about how close respondents feel toward their siblings, 61 percent of the women reported feeling "close" or "very close" to their sisters. In contrast, less than half the men (48 percent) reported feeling "close" or "very close" to their brothers, and less than half the men and women (46 percent) reported feeling "close" or "very close" to their opposite-sex sibs. To a question about how often they see or speak to their sibs by phone, more than two thirds of the women (67 percent) saw or spoke to their sisters monthly or more. But less than half the men (48 percent) had such contact with their brothers monthly or more, and only about half the men and women (52 percent) were in contact with their opposite-sex sibs monthly or more.

Along the same lines, women tended to live somewhat closer to their sisters than brothers did to their brothers or opposite-sex siblings to each other. But even among those men and women who lived approximately the same geographic distance from each other, sisters had more frequent contact than did brothers or opposite-sex siblings.

Even more revealing were responses to specific questions designed to measure closeness. For example, to the question "How much do you share your inner feelings?" with a sibling, sisters responded "some" or "very much" 77 percent of the time in relation to their sisters, whereas men answered "some" or "very much" only 61 percent of the time in relation to their brothers. Similarly women reported telling their sisters about their successes and failures, giving and accepting advice from them, and looking to them for approval to a significantly greater degree than did men in regard to their brothers.

The categories on the questionnaire in which brothers responded in greater numbers than sisters were those involving comparisons and competition. Although many people claimed they did not compare themselves to their siblings, those who did were more likely to be men comparing themselves to brothers than women comparing themselves to sisters. For instance, a third of the men (33 percent) said they compare their finances with their brothers' finances, but fewer than a quarter of the women (23 percent) compare their finances with those of their sisters. The same is true of other kinds of comparisons, such as achievements, education, and occupations.

In interviews, where people had more time to reflect, themes of rivalry and comparison, of slights and wounds suffered, arose in the conversations of both sexes. But men did tend to refer more overtly to areas of competition, as in Roy Deveau's declaration that he would one day surpass his brother in achievement. Even Jerry Platt, who dealt with his competitive feelings by denying them, denied them so often and so loudly that they formed the undercurrent of his entire discussion about his brother.

Now these findings about women and their sisters and men and their brothers fit directly into the gender stereotypes of society. Women (as a group—there are great variations among individuals), it is often said, are more concerned about relationships, more involved with understanding others, more open to intimacy and expressiveness. Men (again as a group) are more aggressive and competitive, especially with one another, less prone to "talk about talking," or to be as linked to one another or as curious as women about those linkages.

All the changes—the vast changes—the women's movement has wrought seem not to have vastly changed these differences between women and men, and psychologists, biologists, sociologists, anthropologists, and other learned people are wondering why not. The answers may lie in the basic biological makeup of men and women or in the stubbornness of society and the individuals in it to adopt changes, or most likely in both.

One of the more far-reaching theories about emotional differences between women and men comes from Nancy J. Chodorow, professor of sociology at Berkeley. She suggests that in growing up, girls identify closely with their mother, including their mother's nurturing and care-giving attributes, and—through those attributes—her connectedness to others. Boys, who as infants also identify with their mother, must turn away eventually and establish their own identity by defining themselves as different from her. In so doing, they repress the powerful mother-ties, and with them, many of their mother's nurturing and empathetic aspects.

Chodorow emphasizes individuals and not siblings, but it may be that in the sibling arena brothers reinforce each other as they pull away from the maternal care-giving role. An older brother may become a model for a younger in being a "man," like his father able to hold back emotion and stand tall and straight. The older might also test his own strength against a younger, aggressively making sure the other knows who is boss. The younger, in turn, learns to fight back and resist the other's authority, honing his own skills in the realms of aggression and power.

"When a man has a brother," writes essayist John Bowers, "he is forced from the start into a deep rivalry. . . ." Bowers learned early that his brother, twelve years older than he, was "someone whose sole purpose was to keep me ever smaller and whipped back." As for him, his greatest triumph came on the day he threw his brother—then a naval officer—to the floor in a hand-wrestling match.

If there are no sisters in the family, the brothers have little opportunity to temper their identification with each other and with their father. Even if they do have sisters, brothers may support each other in rejecting their sisters' interests in emotions and connection, exaggerating, in contrast, their masculine identities.

Following this line of thinking to its conclusion, we might say that in repressing their identification with their mothers, brothers lose some of the ease that sisters have in forming relationships, not only outside the family but also with each other. Certainly the overwhelming indications of closeness among sisters in my study and others attest to their ability to understand and cooperate with each other more freely than do brothers, and to sustain their ties more firmly through adult life. Mary Ann described becoming "very emotional" one year after receiving an admittedly "corny" birthday card from Nancy that said, "Words can't describe how I feel about you. I love you, Sis." The card confirmed Mary Ann's own feelings that no matter how often she and Nancy fought, "deep down we're sisters, and we'd do anything for each other."

There are, however, two caveats. One is that the closeness sisters enjoy does not necessarily eliminate aggressiveness. To the questionnaire query "Have there been periods of time when you and this sibling have not spoken to one another out of anger?" it was women in relation to their sisters who more frequently than any other sibling combination responded "yes." And again: asked "Do habits or behavior of this sibling that annoyed you in childhood still bother you today?" women were more likely to answer "yes" in writing about their sisters.

Aggressiveness among sisters does not usually take the form of whipping one another back or wrestling to the floor. More often it appears as pulls and tugs about beauty and body images, weight, clothes, and family matters—the stuff of women's identities assigned to them by society and instilled in them by family early in life. Much of the competition between Nancy and Mary Ann, as well as their struggles to keep their separateness, got played out in their fights about dresses, about who would wear what and when. And rivalry among all the Ginetti sisters continues to revolve around dieting and comparing weight.

The closeness sisters share may at times actually exacerbate their competitive and aggressive feelings. Because they are so close, they become entwined in the details of each other's lives, and the details may lead to jealousies and fights. Also, because sisters remain close and involved in adult life, the habits they carry over from childhood may continue to irritate, leading them on occasion to pull away from each other. "I gave my older sister some advice about how to handle her adolescent son," wrote a thirty-five-year-old woman about her forty-year-old sister. "She accused me of 'butting in' the way I always did, and stopped phoning me for some time."

The other caveat about the closeness of sisters concerns brothers in relation to one another. To say that men are less close to their brothers than women are to their sisters and are more competitive or aggressive is not to say that men are not close at all to their brothers or operate only—or even mainly—on the level of competition and aggression. ("No one can make me madder," John Bowers writes of his brother. He also writes, "No one makes me laugh the way he does.")

Although many people, including some experts, believe that the relationship between brothers is the least close of any, that was not my finding on the survey, where brothers rated themselves as close to their brothers as they were to their sisters or as sisters rated themselves in regard to their brothers. Only the sister-sister combination stood out as being closer and more intimate than that of brothers.

The feelings brothers have for each other can be powerful and complicated. Older brothers, especially, may be deeply conflicted about their behavior and feelings, according to a study of college students conducted at the University of Michigan. Both older and younger brothers in the study regarded the older as more dominant in their relationship. But the older brothers appeared to suffer internally for the dominance and aggression they directed toward their younger brothers. They believed the younger ones to be more unhappy than they actually were, and often blamed themselves for the perceived unhappiness. They also struggled within themselves, torn with self-accusations, wishing to command and control their younger brothers but also wishing to contain their dominance, to master their feelings and support the youngers.

"I know how he saw me," said one college man sadly of his younger brother, "conceited, self-centered, fake . . . not really caring about him or anybody else. . . . I wasn't fair to him, and I resented him, and he knew it."

Many of the brothers I interviewed had given less thought to their relationships with each other than had many of the sisters, and seemed not to have the language available to express emotions as openly and freely as did the women. To that extent, the gender stereotype about the inability of men to "talk about talking" holds up among brothers. (Supporting it also is the fact that there exist any number of books by women exploring the meaning of sisterhood through their ties to their sisters; I have found no similar books by men exploring the meaning of brotherhood.)

Yet the stereotype breaks down when it comes to the emotions brothers feel. These emotions are very much there, in many cases more profoundly experienced than the men themselves realize. For example, one man whose brother lived miles away spoke with moderate regret of not corresponding more frequently. "But if anything ever happened to him, I . . . ," he started saying, then broke off, amazed to find himself choked with tears.

Roy Deveau suggested that the deep-felt closeness he and Eddy enjoy has been stoked by his understanding of Eddy's feelings, even though Eddy has trouble expressing those feelings. As an example of that understanding and the help he has given Eddy in opening up, he told of an incident in Eddy's family (confirmed by Eddy) that took place a few years earlier. Eddy's daughter, Kelly, then sixteen, had been feeling herself less favored than her older brother. At dinner one evening, a slight reprimand by Eddy had sent Kelly running to her room in tears, accusing her father of not loving her.

"Eddy just sat there, taken aback," Roy said. "He keeps his emotions so controlled, he didn't know what to do. I shouted, 'What are you sitting there for? Go to her!' He did, and they had a good long talk that has helped matters ever since."

Because of Roy's ability to understand his older brother, he said, Eddy has been able to confide in him and even to admit to fears and self-doubts he would reveal to no one else. "We are able to pour out our hearts to each other," he said. "I don't think many brothers have that, and it's too bad, because many of them really care very deeply about each other."

Overall, compared to attachments among sisters, those among brothers may be less intimate and more directly competitive. But without trying to romanticize brotherly ties, I do want to emphasize that they often include a great deal of intimacy, affection, and empathy, and far more than is openly acknowledged and recognized.

When siblings are of the opposite sex, the chemical makeup between expressiveness and distance, between nurturing and aggression, changes, and a different equation gets formed. Parents, some authorities say, pay more attention to a second or later child if the child is of a different gender than the one or those before it, which may lead to greater jealousy by the older child or greater respect for the next one. More important, opposite-sex siblings themselves cope with issues those of the same sex don't face in the same way—about family names and ambitions, about being "mama's boys" and "daddy's girls," about sexual understanding and sexual desire.

CHAPTER FIVE

"As the Boy I Felt Handsome, Smart, and Sweet—My Sister Felt Shortchanged"

BROTHERS AND SISTERS AND SISTERS AND BROTHERS

*I*t's mid-December, temperatures have dipped down into the low teens, and I'm at an outdoor phone booth speaking to my mother. The wind howling about me is at its fiercest on this corner of Madison Avenue and Eighty-ninth Street in Manhattan, where the configuration of buildings creates a funnellike effect. I have stopped here on my way to a meeting and on my way back from having interviewed my brother.

"I have a few minutes before my meeting," I say into the phone, "and I wanted to ask you about something Robert said."

This is ridiculous, I think to myself as I hug the collar of my coat tight around my neck. I could have waited until I got home. But then, I answer myself, I do have the time now, and I might as well check this out.

"Robert says he was always the favorite in the family. He said all the years he was growing up, he felt—and I'm quoting—'adored, admired, and encouraged, the hope of the future,' and other things like that. Is this true?"

I hear my mother laughing. Ridiculous, I tell myself again. I can't believe I'm actually making this phone call. I sound like my six-year-old self whining about her big brother's teasing. *Ridiculous.* Who cares at this point in life who the favorite was or whether there even was one?

"He says," I go on without waiting for her to reply, "that to this day he feels—and I'm quoting again—that his 'presence on the scene is like a blessing,' that he still holds a kind of 'godlike position' in your eyes and Daddy's." The hell with it. No stopping myself now. Let it all come out. It had been, after all, quite an interview.

We had met at my brother's midtown office, with its custom-designed furniture and expensive paintings, to talk about ourselves in relation to my research. We'd spoken pleasantly about the close feelings our parents had to their brothers and sisters and the positive effects of that closeness on us. Then I tried to push deeper into our own connections, and he began to fidget.

"It makes me uncomfortable to talk about us," he had said.

"Why?" I'd asked in foolish innocence.

"I guess," he had replied, not altogether unhappily, "because I was so clearly the favorite."

"You were the *favorite?*" I'd repeated, astonished to feel my face flushing. (Was it rage? Embarrassment? I wasn't sure.)

"Of course I was," he'd responded, now warming to the subject himself. "You perceived me as the favorite, the folks perceived me as the favorite, and I perceived myself as the favorite, so it must have been so."

"I'm not sure I perceived you as the favorite," I had managed to say. "I may have been jealous because you were older and got more privileges than I did. That's not the same as thinking they loved you more."

I meant what I said. I had not felt unfavored growing up, although I had done a good bit of complaining about my brother's privileges. It was then that he began elaborating on his "godlike" status and on the many ways in which he was loved and "adored." He was clearly enjoying himself. "Look," he'd insisted, "you speak of jealousy or competition, but I never had any of those feelings toward you. I never had to compete with you for Mom and Dad's affection because I had it. I had everything from them."

Noticing, I suppose, my flushed face, he'd finally stopped and asked, "Is something wrong? You look upset."

"You just told me you were our parents' pet. How do you expect me to look?" I'd answered.

"Honey," he'd said, laughing, "the folks are very old and we're middle-aged, with wonderful families of our own. What difference does it make anymore?"

Of course he was right. I'd adjusted my tape recorder and swiftly moved on to other topics I wanted to cover. When we'd finished, we kissed good-bye amicably and I headed uptown to my meeting—but before that to the phone booth.

"So what do you say to all this?" I shout into the phone to my mother. The wind is so strong, I can hardly hear my own words.

"I always told you," she states cautiously, "that you were *both* more important to me than anything in the world."

"I know, but that doesn't really answer the question. He's convinced he was most important, the absolute favorite, your 'source of pride and joy,' to use his words."

"You have to understand," she says, and I'm glad I'm not looking at her, "he was a boy. Boys are special. Every parent wants a son. It's not a matter of favoritism."

"Oh," I answer, say a quick good-bye, and hang up the receiver, my eyes tearing in the icy gusts of wind blowing my way.

Every parent wants a son. That has been a truism since the beginnings of recorded history, expressed with simple passion by the biblical Rachel crying to her husband Jacob, "Give me sons or I shall die." To understand your relationship to your brother, my mother was saying, to understand any relationship between opposite-sex siblings, one has to start with a recognition of the position of sons, and brothers, in society throughout time.

I need not belabor what is well-known: In most cultures sons have been valued over daughters and have been—especially firstborn sons —the inheritors and guardians of family property.

In Asian families the eldest son holds a position of such high respect that others learn at a young age to bow to his will without question. At the other extreme, the youngest daughter takes on the burden of caring for her elderly parents, putting their needs ahead of her own. In China, Korea, and India parents so prefer sons that they often abort pregnancies if fetal tests reveal that a woman is carrying a female child. And in rural areas of those countries, when food is scarce, daughters are more likely to suffer from malnutrition than sons.

In Greek society the birth of a son brings a mother great prestige, and daughters grow up knowing that they must obey their brothers, although they may also turn to them for help when needed.

In Jewish culture special laws and rituals welcome a son into the community; only recently have ceremonies for baby girls been created, and they do not carry the weight of law.

Although women often take a dominant role in African-American families, parents still look to their sons for achievement and expect their daughters to be sympathetic toward male struggles. (Supreme Court Justice Clarence Thomas enjoyed the advantages of college and law school educations, while his sister, Emma Mae Martin, stayed home to help her mother—deserted by their father—and later to care for an elderly aunt who had suffered a stroke. With no source of income and three children to support, she had to go on welfare, for which her successful brother publicly criticized her.)

And in white Anglo-Saxon Protestant families—the dominant culture in the United States—traditional roles based on gender have always held sway. (Witness the bitter, public family battle waged by Sallie Bingham against her brothers, the adored male heirs of a great newspaper empire in Louisville, Kentucky.)

No doubt this overwhelming emphasis on the importance of sons has diminished in Western society in the past few decades under the impact of the women's movement. Surveys that once showed parents preferring to have sons over daughters indicate a narrowing of the gap, with a desire on the part of many parents for a child of each sex, although usually for a boy first. Certainly the great numbers of women in professional and vocational schools once restricted to men reflect the fact that parents are more willing to support their daughters' career goals as well as those of their sons—and sometimes instead of a son if the daughter shows more ability. Those numbers also speak, of course, to daughters' determination not to play second best to their brothers or other men.

Still, the old attitudes linger on, and even if (God willing!) the future holds visions of a society in which daughters are esteemed, encouraged, educated, and endorsed equally with sons, many of today's adults, young adults, and even adolescents have experienced a different reality. (In fact, the reality continues to be that by high school, girls' self-esteem plummets in comparison with that of boys, according to studies by Carol Gilligan, professor of education at Harvard, and others. Nobody can say precisely why this happens, but surely girls pick up many of the views they hold of themselves in their homes.)

For some women the reality of growing up with a brother, or several, has meant seeing themselves as less important than the boys in the family. "I was born on April first," a thirty-eight-year-old dental technician reported. "When they told my father it was a girl, he said,

'This is an April Fool's Day joke, isn't it? It's really a boy, right?' " A forty-six-year-old bookkeeper with an older brother and a younger one was more bitter in recounting a conversation she'd had with her mother, who described a childhood scene of walking down the street holding each son's hand in one of her own while the little girl cried her heart out.

"Why was I crying so much?" asked the daughter.

"Because," said the mother nonchalantly, "I didn't have a hand for you."

"That," said this woman after telling her story, "did it for me— Mom, you just gave me the answer to my problems today."

For other women the issue has been less a matter of importance than of feeling that they somehow missed out on what their brothers received. When these women look back to childhood, they often point to greater opportunities and a broader arena within which their brothers could stretch and grow. In some cases that arena is defined most clearly by the kind of toys their brothers had: the stereotypical "boys' " games involving action or experimentation as opposed to girls' dolls or makeup kits. "The boys had a chemistry set," a twenty-nine-year-old librarian said of her two older brothers. "I assumed I would inherit it. I thought this was related to age, not sex. It was a wonderful chemistry set, but I didn't get it. My parents gave it away without thinking of me."

Although many brothers acknowledged having the status their sisters so bitterly complained about, few had ever dreamed of it as a cause for complaint. "I never questioned my special treatment," said my brother, voicing the thoughts of others. "I assumed that's how the world should be." A few men did express admiration for sisters who tolerated their second-place standing with grace. An even smaller number spoke regretfully of their sister's situation in comparison with their own.

One of the most sympathetic was fifty-four-year-old Philip, a pediatrician who has become an ardent feminist because of the differences in the ways he and his sister Regina, eleven months older than he, were raised. "As the boy," he said, "I felt handsome, smart, and sweet. My sister felt shortchanged. I was paraded out and shown off. Nobody singled her out."

The most glaring proof of this difference in treatment came during their college years. As a child Philip had lost a year of school because of a car accident. Regina, keeping her own pace, entered college two years before him. When Philip's turn came, their father announced that he could not support two college students, and Regina would have to drop out and get a job. Eventually, after marriage, she returned and earned a college degree, but too late to pursue the archaeology career she had planned.

Philip hasn't completely made his peace with the guilt he feels about his sister's life, but he has channeled the sense of unfairness it gave him into support for the women's movement. What he has not been able to do is erase the heritage of hard feelings that has impeded the closeness he would like to have with his sister (who did not wish to be interviewed). "Our relationship is cordial but not really friendly," he said, "friendly but not really loving, and maybe loving underneath but covered over by the things I got that she didn't."

So many women and men reported variations on the kind of preferential treatment Philip received that I assumed my survey would provide overwhelming statistical confirmation. The results, as it turned out, were less clear-cut—and more interesting.

"Were you your father's favorite child?" was one question asked, followed by "If not, which brother or sister was your father's favorite?" The questions were then repeated for the mother's favorite.

The answers showed that in significantly greater numbers, respondents perceive that *mothers* do indeed favor sons. *Fathers*, on the other hand, are perceived as favoring their daughters.

In statistical terms, among those people who reported favoritism in their families, 66 percent of the men regarded themselves as their mother's favorite, compared to only 27 percent of the women. In contrast, 62 percent of the women chose themselves as their father's favorite, compared to 49 percent of the men. Furthermore, when they did not choose themselves, respondents tended to choose a brother over a sister as their mother's favorite and a sister over a brother as their father's favorite.

These results are not really startling. Parents, said Freud, as well as their children, obey "the pull of sexual attraction, and . . . where there are several children the father will give the plainest evidence of his greater affection for his little daughter and the mother for her son." Or, in the words of a woman from a large Irish-American family, "We girls all knew that Mom liked her boys a whole lot. They were kind of good-looking and they could make her smile and laugh in a way we never could. It still feels as though she likes them best."

But if mothers alone, and not both parents, favor sons, what of the constant claims about the overall preferential treatment of sons? And what does it mean, in terms of everyday living, to say that mothers favor sons and fathers favor daughters?

To begin to answer these questions, we need to return for a moment to the basic role of sons within a family. In most societies, sons have been the bearers of the family name and with it the family line; daughters have married out, usually taking their husband's name and carrying, through their children, his line. (Though increasingly more women today have been keeping their family names after marriage, their children still usually assume their father's name.) On some level, and often it is an unconscious one, parents still long for sons to perpetuate their name, and in that sense, themselves—as my mother had said, every parent wants a son.

Fathers, in particular, view sons as their ticket to immortality, their alter ego who will follow in their footsteps and carry their name and bloodline into the future. The father who thought the news of his daughter's birth was an April Fool's joke may have been crude and cruel in reacting as he did. But his wish for a son echoed the wishes of fathers through the ages, and of many a father today.

Under these circumstances, and aware of the elevated places their brothers hold in their fathers' hearts, even women who regard themselves as having been favored by their fathers often see their brothers as chosen in the family as a whole.

That view of their brothers' chosenness by fathers as well as mothers also gives many women the overall perception of having received less than their brothers, no matter how loved they felt. In one of his most disputed theories, Freud argued that many of the self-views women hold come from their envy of the male penis. Little girls, he said, seeing the penis of their brother or a playmate, feel inferior about their own, visually simpler sexual anatomy, and from that feeling of inferiority may grow later sexual problems (as well as a wish to have children, as substitutes for the missing penis). Many people, including many psychoanalysts, have repudiated Freud's theory of penis envy. And many people, including many psychoanalysts, recognize, instead, that when women speak of feeling shortchanged in relation to their brothers, what they feel cheated of are the privileges and positions that go with maleness in the family and society.

But there is more to be said on the matter of cross-favoritism by parents.

It often happens, a number of therapists to whom I broached this subject pointed out, that even though fathers long for sons and identify with them, they also make greater demands of them. So a father may place a family business under the control of his son and not his daughter, but he may also expect more of the son and—potentially— be more disappointed in him. A father may also be more competitive with a son, encouraging the son to outdo him, yet not really wanting

to be outdone. In those respects, a daughter may have a less complicated or problematic relationship with her father and feel herself to
be closer and more favored.

Then again, proposed Louise Kaplan, *both* perceptions—that fathers favor daughters and mothers favor sons—may be further extensions of the social order, with its tilt toward male privilege. Girls, she
explained, often fantasize that they are their father's favorite, even
when that may not be the case. They take on the role of "Daddy's
girls," identifying with their father's achievements and values as opposed to their mother's and in that sense feeling themselves superior
to their mothers (and victorious, perhaps, in the everlasting Oedipal
competition for Daddy). On the boy's side, a mother may invest in a
male child her own thwarted ambitions (some say, also, the qualities
she had sought—and found lacking—in her husband). Her favoritism
of her son may be real, spurring him to higher goals and accomplishments.

From this point of view, daughters' beliefs that their brothers are
favored may not be off the mark, for even when they think of their
fathers as favoring them and their mothers as favoring their brothers,
maleness somehow wins out.

Finally, and probably most accurately: For many women, to be
father's favorite, Daddy's girl, may mean to have been cuddled and
cared for by Daddy when young, even admired when older, but not
taken as seriously as their brothers. Women may see themselves or
their sisters as Daddy's girl and still perceive of their brothers as all-
around winner, because on some level they recognize that Daddy
loves them always as his *little* girl and not as full-grown sexual and
independent beings.

(And yet. On the porch of my parents' home of an early autumn
evening, I tell about my research and findings on cross-favoritism. As I
prepare to leave, my father, aged ninety-something, as sharp as ever
he was, whispers, "I don't know whether mothers favor sons or fathers favor daughters, but I favor you." Oh joy! Oh relief! Oh sweet
revenge: Daddy's girl or not, wait until I tell Robert!)

If it exists, and especially if strongly felt, the predominant position
given sons over daughters may leave lifelong strains in the relationships between sisters and brothers, with the sisters feeling angry at
parents for what they did and resentful of brothers for what they got.
It may leave some sons, like Philip, feeling guilty and others happy to
accept their lot in life. When less pronounced or intrusive, the preferential treatment of males in a family may be taken for granted by
everyone as simply part of the culture. The woman whose mother

"liked her boys" explained that "my sisters and I talk about it to each other, but we have always just accepted it." (For a discussion of the effects of many kinds of parental favoritism on siblings, see Chapter Seven.)

Gender favoritism is a subject much on the minds of women, and some men. But it is only one of many issues that affect relationships between brothers and sisters. Not least among others is the sexuality that is an intrinsic part of the bond between siblings of the opposite sex. Just as siblings of the same sex identify with each other, opposite-sex sibs also identify, gleaning knowledge from one other about the meanings of maleness and femaleness.

From their earliest days, sisters and brothers gain that knowledge as they bathe together, play together, fight, touch, and examine one another—all part of normal childhood curiosity and exploration. Freud may have been wrong in his theory of penis envy, but he was right about the fact that at a young age—about sixteen to eighteen months—girls begin to notice their brothers' more elaborate sexual equipment and wonder about it, and boys begin to wonder why their sisters do not have what they do. From their curiosity grows the germ of sexual understanding. Children without opposite-sex siblings gain that understanding from playmates, but for those with such sibs, the learning is a continuous and natural part of everyday living.

Sexual learning expands for brothers and sisters during adolescence as they observe (while seeming not to notice) one another's changing bodies and changing voices, as a brother struts around in his underwear and a sister leaves an open tampon box in the bathroom, as they share secrets and offer each other advice about dates and clothes, pimples and prophylactics.

Sometimes, of course, the learning process contains heat as well as light. Sibs of the opposite sex may feel sexually attracted to each other simply by virtue of *being* of the opposite sex. They are a miniature couple, mother and father in abridged form. So when they dance or fight, hug or wrestle, that attraction can spark sensations of excitement. There's an excitement also for a brother in trying to assert mastery over a sister, and for a sister in resisting but secretly admiring a brother's strength and manhood. There's an excitement, too, in having, as one man told me, a "mad, mad crush" on an older sister, "hidden fantasies about her" and an "insane jealousy" of her boyfriends.

The excitement includes guilt, particularly during adolescence. The guilt comes of feeling sexually drawn to a forbidden person whom one also loves as a sibling, and of knowing that no matter how strong that magnetism, it must be suppressed. A girl who had long been her brother's "buddy" may suddenly, as a teenager, begin to pull away and shut him out of her life as she—unconsciously—tries to keep a tight grip on the erotic attraction she has begun to feel for him. A boy who had always been close to his sister may begin to taunt and insult her when puberty sets in, incessantly poking fun at her hair, her body, or her behavior as a way of repressing the unacceptable desires and sexual urges he now has toward her. (Unrepressed desires in the form of sibling incest and exploitation are discussed in Chapter Nine.)

In some cases the attractions between opposite sex siblings remain powerful undercurrents in their later love lives, leading a sister to be jealous, for example, of all her brother's girlfriends or to view his wife as her adversary. Occasionally, also, the strong taboos siblings maintain against incest interfere with their sexual life outside the family. But, for the most part, the normal underlying attractions between siblings get channeled into mature sexual experiences with boyfriends and girlfriends, lovers and spouses, just as yearnings for opposite-sex parents get directed toward acceptable love partners.

There's a reason, says psychiatrist Alexander Levay, for why husbands and wives so often seem to look alike, aside from their having picked up facial expressions from each other. It is that women and men frequently marry people who resemble their cross-sex sibs (as well as their same-sex sibs), and who therefore resemble *them* in some way. We also marry people who look like our parents, but siblings are not necessarily stand-ins for parents as our love ideals. Often they *are* the ideals themselves, and they become in many cases the unconscious models upon whom we base our choices of sexual partners.

Influencing the way in which early sibling sexuality gets redefined in later life, and influencing in even larger measure the lifelong connections between siblings of the opposite sex, is their order of birth. Although the survey turned up little difference between the degree of closeness brothers feel for sisters and sisters feel for brothers, the nature of the relationship between brother and sister differs greatly depending on who came first.

An older brother and younger sister mirror the traditional—patriarchal—social order: the older husband, younger wife; older father, younger mother; male as dominating, woman as nurturing; and so on. That mirroring adds a twist of its own to the usual pulls among older and younger siblings between protectiveness and power, devotion and aggression.

Certainly the positives of protectiveness and devotion have been major themes between brothers and their younger sisters through history. For sisters in many lands, older brothers were (and still are) considered, like fathers, defenders and guardians, treated with great respect and an admiration that may border on adulation. In one of the unforgettable scenes of ancient Greek drama, Antigone, heroine of Sophocles' tragedy, decides to sacrifice her life to give her brother Polyneices a proper burial. It is a burial that Creon, ruler of Thebes, has denied him, and for which Antigone will be punished with death, because Polyneices fought against the state.

"What law, you ask, is my warrant . . . ?" she begins, in defending her decision to defy Creon's ruling and go to her death. She answers with impassioned words: "The husband lost, another might have been found, and child from another to replace the firstborn; but . . . no brother's life could ever bloom for me again." A woman can find a substitute for any other love, says Antigone, but not for the love of a brother, one's own blood and flesh.

Long before Antigone, tradition has it, a woman forced by the cruel Persian king Darius to choose between the life of her husband, children, and brother chose to save her brother, using the same reasoning: husband and children are replaceable; a brother is not.

Long after Antigone, in Russia of the late 1800s, Maria Chekhov, sister of the brilliant writer Anton Chekhov, lovingly devoted her life to promoting his career and watching over his writings. Although he eventually married, she turned down a marriage proposal because she believed he disapproved. "To be happy," wrote his biographer Henri Troyat, "he needed discreet, industrious, loving Maria at his side; he needed to be assured that no suitor would distract her from her sisterly vocation." To be happy, Maria needed to be at her brother's side, helping and supporting him.

It's likely that the sisterly devotion of Maria Chekhov—and Antigone as well—included a strong, unconscious sexual component in its excessive self-sacrifice and adoration of an older brother. But even if in exaggerated form, these women represent the great value sisters have always placed on their older brothers, whom they could trust and turn to in a world they often perceived as unsafe for them.

For their part, older brothers returned that trust (and still do) by sheltering and protecting their sisters. One of the more bloody incidents of brotherly protectiveness is the biblical account of how two of

Jacob's sons slaughtered the entire male population of a town because the son of its leader had raped their sister Dinah. A far gentler form of protection is the practice still in force in India and parts of South Asia wherein a brother helps assemble the dowry his sisters will use in marriage. In this system older brothers often have to defer their own weddings for years while they work and save money for their sisters' marriages.

And then there is the twenty-two-year-old secretary who wrote sweetly on the questionnaire that she loved having an older brother on whom she could count for care and guidance, although sometimes he was a bit overdiligent. In summer camp a few years earlier, for example, he had made his presence so well known that "guys were afraid to come near" her. Still, she adored him.

There exists, however, at least in childhood, another, darker aspect to the older brother–younger sister relationship. In that aspect, greater physical strength along with the authority of being male in a male-oriented society can lead to an intensification of the older's desire for mastery and control. The result for the sister may be an increase in the feelings many youngers experience—hero worship mixed with rage and frustration. Myths and legends rarely describe this side of the relationship, but many sisters, and some brothers, speak about it often.

In fact, people so frequently recalled the power aspects of older brother–younger sister relations that in listening to tapes of adult siblings and rereading transcripts, I began to lose track of whose life I was examining. It was as though interviews I had conducted at different times and in different places were all of the same person—and of me.

"I used to think of my brother as a god," a woman in California said of a brother two years older than she, then went on to describe a scene she had recently witnessed in an old family home movie. In it, she and her brother, aged ten and twelve, are playing in the backyard, and he begins to pull a barrette "out of my hair, and out of my hair, and out of my hair, and I try to get him to stop and he's getting a lot of pleasure in doing that and hurting me, and my parents are standing by and laughing. Boys will be boys and that kind of thing. . . ."

Her words sound just like those of a woman in Mississippi, six years younger than her brother, who began by saying, "As a child, I adored my brother," then went on, "he was alternately loving and cruel to me. He could be caring when I suffered from allergies, but he never thought twice about inflicting mild shocks on me with a 'shocking machine' he had made. He would ask me to be his 'experiment,' and I was so eager to play with him that I would volunteer."

She, in turn, sounds like the Boston woman who had felt as a child that her brother, three years older, "could do no wrong," but had also always felt belittled by him. One example she gives is of the time she helped him walk to school after he broke his ankle, and he reciprocated by hooking his cane around her neck.

And echoes of all three stories came through in that of a brother, aged thirty, who wants very much to be close to his twenty-seven-year-old sister and cannot understand the distance she places between them. He does recognize that some of the "innocent little pranks" he played on her as a child seem to "linger for her," making her a somewhat "fearful adult." What kinds of things? "Oh, you know, it's a Saturday night, the babysitter's taking care of you, you go down to the basement and your sister's down there and you lock the door and turn out the light on your way up the stairs so she's alone and locked into the dark—more or less the kind of thing that every brother has done. . . ."

The man's sister remembers this too. She also remembers being afraid of the crabs her brother invariably threw at her at the beach. None of that, however, does she profess to hold against him. "We love each other as brother and sister," she says, and adds, "I would just rather not see much of him." Nor does she plan to invite him to the home she has set up since her recent marriage.

It's not news, of course, that older brothers or sisters tease and torment younger ones. But there does appear to be—at least from the perspective of the women interviewed—a particular quality of cruelty, and sometimes even sadism, to the type of behavior inflicted when the older is a boy and the younger a girl. Older brothers seem to use their greater physical strength to take special advantage of younger sisters, who may not be as capable of fighting back as a younger brother is. It's possible that the undercurrent of sexuality in a brother's exertion of power, and the terror (mixed with excitement) a younger sister might have felt in response, may make such experiences particularly indelible for women. It's also possible that younger sisters speak more openly than younger brothers about an older brother's domination. Men may be embarrassed to portray themselves as submissive or weaker than others, even as children.

In their recollections, women with older brothers also have the impression that they were not protected enough by parents, even very good parents. They complain that parents did not take the older boy's hostile "teasing" seriously, either because the parents were not present when it occurred or because they maintained that "boys will be boys" attitude. As a result, the sisters felt "trivialized," in the words of one woman—"in a double bind in which you know you have been put down, but your feelings of being put down are never acknowledged so you think there's something wrong with you for feeling that way."

What does all this mean in terms of adult life, this feeling of having been trivialized as a young girl (and often well into adolescence), of having been put down by someone much stronger, who you know can hurt you physically, but whom you still revere and whose love and approval you want?

For some women, like the sister quoted above, it means having little to do as adults with that childhood source of power and put-down, maintaining only the most minimal sibling ties. For others, the positives—the protectiveness and devotion of an older brother and the attachment and admiration of the younger—can overshadow childhood aggression and lead to warm, or at least cordial, adult ties.

But regardless of what form their adult relationship with their brother takes, for many women, the denigrations of an older brother early on can turn into feelings of insecurity and shaky self-esteem later in life.

Claire Morris, from Buffalo, New York, was most articulate about these long-term effects, not only on her image of herself but on her first, disastrous marriage. If some of the things she says are more extreme than what I heard from other younger sisters, through her intensity she conveys the flavor of feelings and attitudes many of them expressed.

"There is a yearning that goes around with me, and it's everywhere I go," Claire said during a meeting at her home, where she lives with her second husband and her two sons from her former marriage. "It's a wish I have to be treated well and loved and admired, and all the things that I always felt were missing with my brother."

Fortyish, with salt-and-pepper hair and a roundish figure, Claire has a soft, glowing complexion that gives her a girlish, almost innocent look. Her voice, too, is soft and musical, but her words pulsate with emotion. What I discovered within moments of speaking with her is that she loves to play with language, never content to use one adjective when she can find five that have slightly different shades of meaning. The repetitions form a cadence that gives added emphasis to her words.

The yearning she describes began in childhood when she and her brother Turner, some four years older, shared a room in the family flat in Toronto. In her recollection, Turner resented her presence in his room and his life from the very beginning.

"He competed with me on all levels," she said. "He would push and hit me, and of course I could never win. I was so much smaller and weaker. The thing I remember most, though, and it went on for years, is the wrestling. We were constantly wrestling, fighting, rolling, and climbing all over each other."

If that wrestling and rolling had sexual overtones—as it surely must have—Turner expressed no warmth or affection to counter the aggressiveness. For Claire, the end result was an affirmation of her own weakness: "Do you know what it's like, time and again, to have your shoulders pinned down, and you are angry, enraged, weak, help-less, and most of all humiliated all at the same time? That's how I felt, and that, in many ways, is how I continue to feel."

Claire's parents worked together managing a small art gallery they owned on the lakefront. Busy with their work, they had little time to focus on their children's schedules, sending Claire off to play with Turner to keep her occupied. Yet, when he complained that she inter-fered with his schoolwork and his friendships, they scolded her for bothering him. Consequently, says Claire, "in childhood, and even more in adolescence, and even up to right now this very moment, I have always tried to win approval from my brother, have never gotten that approval, and somehow, in some sort of reversal, have been blamed for trying to get the approval in the first place."

When Turner reached thirteen and Claire was about nine, the fam-ily moved to a larger apartment, allowing each child a separate bed-room. But instead of easing Turner's antagonism, the separation made him more distant and disapproving of Claire. He may have been re-sponding, unconsciously, to his own increasing adolescent attraction to his sister, especially as she became more unavailable, but from her perspective her brother became dismissive and more critical than ever.

It also seemed to her that her parents made few demands on him. A brilliant student, he decided at an early age to study law (and is today a corporate attorney in great demand). A fine student herself, Claire received double messages: achieve, but not more than your brother; succeed, but not so much that you will move away from home and family. Dutifully, she studied art history in college and worked briefly afterward in her parents' gallery, fulfilling expectations that she would be a "good daughter" in every respect. Her brother, on the other hand, was "off the hook" in terms of any kind of family responsibility.

In a twist of fate that nobody expected, Claire has ended up leaving her family and Turner has remained behind. At the age of twenty-five, about seventeen years ago, she married a man she had met in college and moved with him to his hometown of Buffalo. She remained in Buffalo after her divorce, working in a museum, and, now remarried, plans to stay there. Meanwhile, after finishing his training, Turner married and settled into work at a Toronto law firm.

Her move, Claire feels, has balanced the responsibility scales and in that sense "saved" her life by allowing her to separate from her parents. Yet for a long time family influences, and specifically the influence of her brother, continued to dominate that life. As she sees it now, her first husband was an emotional duplicate of Turner, although that is far from what she took him to be at the beginning.

"John, too, had a younger sister," she said, "but he didn't seem to me to be anything like Turner. I felt at first that he acknowledged me as a peer, and I was so pleased with that. In looking back, I really think I had such low expectations about what a man and woman should be to each other that I just felt grateful for every crumb of recognition he gave me."

Soon Claire discovered that her husband had many of the characteristics of her brother. "Like Turner," she said, "he couldn't talk about anything that was on his mind. I never knew why he was angry at me or even whether he was angry. He also competed with me about achievements, and even about our physical appearances—he was heavy and kind of embarrassed about that—so that there developed an underlying hostility between us."

As the relationship progressed, or, as Claire said, "didn't progress," she found herself "replicating" her sibling experience. "Just as I had been all my life," she recalled, "I was flooded again with that yearning to get some kind of approval and recognition and to be loved in a basic way." Even sexually, she and John had become "brotherly and sisterly" in a marriage that lacked passion. "Being a sexual person and expecting the other to be a sexual person with no holds barred somehow became taboo for us," she said.

The marriage ended after nine years, and Claire began therapy, which she feels has helped her make a good second marriage that does not replay her attachment to her brother. Nevertheless, with Turner himself the old patterns remain. Although both she and he have many friends of their own and are "respected both socially and professionally," and although they visit and keep in touch with each other, when they are together they quickly revert to type. He becomes "dismissive and critical." She, as always, tries to impress him, yet remains for him, she is convinced, "exactly as he has always known me to be—sort of bumbling, angry, impatient, edgy, but mostly incompetent. Always somehow fucking up."

Even beyond Turner, that sense of "fucking up" hounds Claire. In spite of success in her work, she still sees herself as a "fraud—the if-only-you-knew-what-I'm-really-like syndrome." And she reenacts the basic dilemma of her relations with Turner in a dozen different ways: "At work, with friends, it happens all the time. I want to assert myself, to say what I believe or wish, but I'm frightened, I'm intimidated, I'm nervous. Growing up with Turner cast a continuous doubt on my whole image of myself, on any feeling of accomplishment or capacity to have an opinion. With my brother I was always wrestled to the ground, shoulders pinned back, unable to get up."

When I asked Claire whether I might interview her brother, she was skeptical. She would be "shocked" if he were to consent to speak with me. She would also be frightened of his anger at her for agreeing to reveal anything about him to a stranger. Not until shortly before my arrival in Buffalo did she inform me that Turner and his family were coming to town for a weekend. She gave me his phone number reluctantly and was dumbfounded when he agreed to see me briefly at his hotel during our joint stay in Buffalo.

Having met Claire, I recognized Turner immediately; the same salt-and-pepper hair, the same glowing complexion. His manner, though, bore no resemblance to hers. Where she amplifies thoughts and phrases, he pares down ideas, responding to questions with concise, direct answers, volunteering little of his own. He was not at all unpleasant; he was simply not given to "wasting" words or time.

In any event, even if he were as "loquacious" as his sister, he explained within minutes after meeting me, he had little to say about the early years, because he had no recollection whatsoever of sharing his childhood or adolescence with Claire.

None at all? What about childhood fights and such?

Well, Claire was so much younger and they had such different interests, it was unlikely he would have fought with her.

Didn't they share a room until he became a teenager?

Yes, but he had his own schoolwork and friends. And later, he went off to college while she was a teenager, so they had little contact.

Did he think she had any influence on him—his view of himself or attitude toward others?

Not at all.

Did he have any influence on Claire?

He would think not, although one would have to ask her.

Did he feel close to Claire today?

It was difficult to be close when they lived in different localities.
Did he wish they could be closer?

It would be nice for his two sons to know her two sons better. But
she had chosen to settle out of town.

Were his sons close to each other?

Very.

But aren't they about as far apart in age as he and Claire?

About. But it may be easier for boys to be close to one another. He
and Claire had so little in common.

And that was about it. Except that, Turner offered as we were
winding up, it would have been easier for him had Claire not moved to
Buffalo. As it was, he had carried the major burden of responsibility
for their mother, who had died recently of Alzheimer's disease and
had been deteriorating for years. The burden had been made heavier
by Claire's incessant phone calls.

Claire and I had spoken of her mother's illness and death. She had
been torn with guilt, she told me, at not being able to spend more of
her time at her mother's bedside. But she had also known that if she
moved back to Canada, things would be the way they had always
been, with her brother free of care and the full responsibility resting
on her shoulders. She had compromised by arranging to have a caretaker for her mother and, since she did not live very far, flying home
every other week to check on the situation. In between, she phoned
Turner. She persisted in her phone calls despite the annoyance she
knew he felt, determined to be involved although not inundated. Toward the end, the two agreed to place their mother in a nursing home,
where she died soon afterward.

Their mother's death, Claire said, had led to a very "brief respite"
from the kind of competitiveness she and Turner had always experienced. The sadness they both felt brought them closer than they had
ever been, and Claire relished that closeness.

Turner said nothing of the sadness or closeness and, after mentioning his own feeling of being overburdened, showed little interest in
discussing the subject further. His reaction is indicative of his entire
relationship with his sister: For her it was and continues to be the
most significant one of her life. In his eyes it had no influence at all on
his life.

Although Turner's personality certainly does not typify older brothers in general, and many men with younger sisters are far more loving
and affectionate than he, many do share with him two traits: their
denial—true of older siblings in general—of having been influenced
by their younger sibs, and an amnesia toward the kinds of physical

and psychological denigrations of which so many younger sisters complain.

Other researchers have also noted these traits. The study of college-aged brothers at the University of Michigan, mentioned earlier, found that older brothers of sisters have fewer inner conflicts over their wishes to dominate than do older brothers of brothers. With sisters, these brothers expect to be in charge, so they struggle less with self-reproach or self-doubts about their exertion of power. But because they take for granted that they will be "top dog" in the relationship, they also tend more to deny their aggressiveness and active attempts to keep a sister in her place. Like Turner, they emphasize their differences from their sisters (and in many cases their disappointment at not having a younger brother instead of a sister), in that way bolstering their denial of envy or competitive feelings.

But what many older brothers deny as they look back to childhood, many younger sisters see as pivotal forces in their adult lives.

How pivotal are the influences of older sisters on the lives of younger brothers and vice versa? Profound also, but in different ways.

The relationship between an older sister and a younger brother is the most contradictory of all sibling combinations in the sense that it reverses the conventional order of society, in which men are seen as dominant and women as more submissive. By being there first, a sister rather than a brother, a female rather than a male, has the advantage in the sibling seesaw. But the advantage is not complete. For whereas an older sister starts out physically stronger than a baby brother, unless they are separated by a great age difference, "baby" has a good chance of overtaking her in physical size and strength, thus limiting the head start. And women's frequent perception that boys have an edge over girls in the eyes of parents can further skew the power equation.

"Troublesome" is the word Carol Holden, a researcher, uses to describe the feelings older sisters often have in relation to their younger brothers.

Holden conducted a study among college students at the University of Michigan on what it means to be a sister that parallels the study on being a brother. She found older sisters of brothers to feel more guilt about their treatment of their younger sibs than do older sisters of sisters. She also found—and this is the source of much of their guilt—that in greater numbers and with more intensity than other sisters, these sisters remember wanting to hurt or get rid of their younger brothers. Significantly more of them (as opposed to older sisters of sisters) view themselves as having tried to dominate and control their younger brothers, and in doing so making those brothers extremely unhappy. The parallel study of brothers did not find younger brothers of sisters to be significantly more unhappy than other brothers, but older sisters perceive them that way.

Holden's findings point up some of the underlying conflicts faced by sisters in their contradictory connections to younger brothers. As elder children they expect and want the "perks" that go with being first: control, authority, leadership. Because younger brothers may resist that control and authority and fight back more fiercely than do younger sisters, the older sisters may strive harder to gain and keep the upper hand. In the process they may impose their own brand of psychological dominance that corresponds to the physical dominance of older brothers.

("I'm the big sister and you're the little brother! That's the way it's always going to be," says Lucy to Linus in the cartoon strip "Peanuts."

"It's going to be that way today, tomorrow, next week and forever!" she continues.

[Sigh], responds Linus.

"Ha! I knew that'd get a rise out of you!" says Lucy gleefully.)*

But as eldests, and as females, sisters know that they are expected to protect and care for their younger sibs. So they feel conflicted about their extra attempts at domination, feelings that may turn into guilt as they get older and reflect back on their relationship. (One woman now in her fifties recalled with excruciating anguish having humiliated her brother when he was about six and she nine by telling his friends that he still wet his bed. "I can never forgive myself for the shame I caused him," she said.)

The conflict and guilt become still greater when older sisters perceive their brothers to be preferred, and therefore even more threatening. During childhood, the sister, like most older siblings, may harbor secret wishes to harm or destroy the younger brother who displaced her, and those wishes may be especially strong because he is a boy and different from her. At the same time, she may herself buy into the social system that values boys over girls. Regarding her brother as superior, she may envy and resent him, but also suffer an extra dose of guilt for her wishes and fantasies.

Not a bad word, "troublesome," for these sisterly emotions.

Yet, troubles notwithstanding, older sisters have always managed somehow to be protective and caring of their younger brothers. Iden-

* "Peanuts" reprinted by permission of UFS, Inc.

tifying with their mothers (and not having to reject mothering qualities to assert their difference, as boys often do), girls pick up their mother's nurturing behavior at an early age. In spite of internal conflicts, they learn to feel responsible for younger sibs. It is also possible that in reaction to their inner conflicts, older sisters turn their jealous, negative feelings about younger brothers into the more positive ones of tenderness and caring.

On the whole, the brothers benefit from their sisters' care. They do their own share of fighting and teasing, but they may even find it easier to draw closer to a sister than to their mother. In Freudian terms, the brother does not have to compete with his father for his sister's love, or fear that his father will destroy him as he might if he tries to steal his mother away from the older man. Theory aside, in everyday practicalities, an older sister's love and support may come with fewer strings attached than a mother's, both in childhood and adult life.

This is how Matt Elliot, age thirty-six, described himself and his sister, Debra, age forty: "My sister and I have always been extremely close. Even though I'm close to my brother George—he's two years older than I—I'm much closer to her. When she introduces me to her friends, she says, 'Oh, this is my baby brother.' It's wonderful. I love it."

Because of his sister, Matt says, he has been able to study for a career in music: "My sister is a professional musician. My mother had been a housewife but had urged her to have a career and seek out as many opportunities as possible. My father was more rigid. It's okay for a girl, but boys don't do music, according to him. My sister intervened for me. She convinced him to let me do what I really wanted—study opera."

The best thing about Debra, says Matt, is the way she gives advice: "Before I got married to the woman from whom I'm now divorced, Deb told me she thought I was making a mistake. She wasn't bossy or anything. She said, 'Matt, I don't see the two of you together. You're made of different kinds of wood—you're mahogany and she's oak.' Once I married, she never said another negative word and was really nice to my wife. When I told her I was getting divorced, she didn't go into this motherly thing of 'Why didn't you listen to me; why didn't you take my advice?' It's natural to say, 'I told you so,' but she never did. She just said, 'I'm sorry.' "

When problems arise in this comfortable arrangement, it is often because an older sister pushes her role to extremes, overprotecting, overcontrolling or overbabying her brother, and in some cases, competing on an unconscious level with her mother in caring for him. These sisters enjoy their brother's dependency, which gives them a sense of power and control.

Some younger brothers who feel themselves dominated in this way make a point of asserting their maleness by acting aggressive and superior toward their sisters. Some pull away during adolescence and continue to keep their distance as adults. Those boys who remain overinvolved with older sisters may grow up dependent and needy, looking to others to take care of them. This is especially true if the father in the family is absent, weak, or unengaged with his son. In therapy, reports Louise Kaplan, such men often relate to her as if she were an older sister, and actively try to get her to watch over them.

Sometimes these babied younger brothers don't marry at all, feeling a lack of ability—or of permission from their sisters—to be grown, mature men with families of their own. Even if they do marry, they often devote themselves to their sisters, remaining responsible for them throughout life. That responsibility allows them to be rewarded with their sister's love and gratitude even while they stay forever attached to her.

In balanced measure, as Matt described it with his sister Debra, the closeness between an older sister and younger brother can remain satisfactory throughout life. And benefit others as well, for word is out among young women that the best kind of man to marry is a man who has had an older sister. Why? Because he is attuned to women's interests and feelings, having been sensitized to these things over the years by his big sister.

Actually, becoming sensitive to the opposite sex is one of the great pluses of having a sibling of a different gender than you. Just how sensitive is open to some dispute.

Some authorities hold that growing up with a sib of the opposite sex makes a person more like that sib in interests and behavior. A girl with an older brother (youngers being more influenced by olders) will tend to have more "masculine" interests, according to this theory, having used her brother as her model. Others contend that because sibs seek separate identities, a girl with an older brother will emphasize her "feminine" interests to set herself apart from her brother. Some theorists suggest that real differences arise not when there is one opposite-sex sib but when there are several. A boy with two older sisters, they say, is more likely to behave in opposition to them, determinedly cultivating "masculine" values and interests.

In my interviews I found that men who grew up with several sisters and no brothers or women who grew up with several brothers and no sisters almost always described themselves as being isolated in their families, but for different reasons. The men, as the theorists suggest, spoke of wanting to separate themselves from their sisters, of "looking for boys outside the family before you'd set up a ball game with your sisters," in the words of one man. The women, however, spoke of wanting very much to be included by their brothers, but of being ignored and disregarded (again, maleness seems to win out).

One woman, aged twenty-three, had this to say about having two older brothers and one younger:

"My friends always think it must have been so great being the only girl with all these brothers. The truth is, I was terribly alone in those years, and it's only recently that we've become close. My brothers always felt they had nothing in common with me, even though I was a tomboy and tried so hard to be like them."

Yet despite their isolation, these women—as well as the men who had pulled away from their sisters—are convinced that the reality of growing up in a household with siblings of the opposite sex prepared them for the real world of sexual differences. In fact, the woman just quoted wrote me a note after our interviews to be sure she had made that point.

"Three of my best friends and I were together recently," she wrote, "and I mentioned that I considered one of them (who grew up in a family of five sisters) to be the biggest flirt in the group. They all flatly disagreed! They said that I and another friend who grew up with male siblings were the real flirts. We were the ones who knew how to 'charm' the men, because we were more aware of what made them tick. I guess they're right. I've always been pretty confident around guys. Even in my work now I feel sure of myself in dealing with men."

Not every sister is that sure of herself, but most sisters of brothers and brothers of sisters do learn at home much about what makes the opposite sex "tick." Aside from sexual understanding, they build up a storehouse of knowledge about how the other thinks and what the other feels, about what it is like to be that male or female other. Moreover, they learn to trust members of the opposite sex, to recognize that they have fears and vulnerabilities not too different from one's own. From getting to know each other's friends in the safe atmosphere of their homes, brothers and sisters also learn to feel comfortable with members of the opposite sex, to make easy talk, to understand the secret languages and the inside jokes of the others.

It is true that opposite-sex siblings often struggle with issues of gender favoritism and gender roles that siblings of the same sex do not have. It is also true that children who have only a sib of the opposite sex may feel cheated of a sibling like themselves and fantasize about what it would be like to have one. But it is also true that from their first lessons at home, brothers and sisters discover—in ways that same-sex sibs do not—what is pleasing both in the opposite sex and to the opposite sex, gaining a good start toward finding satisfaction later in love and marriage.

CHAPTER SIX

"Stepsiblings Have to Choose One Another, Blood Relatives Don't"

STEPSIBS, HALF-SIBS, AND OTHERS

*T*hrough the first part of my interview with the stepbrothers Bill Craine and Jared Larson, neither man looked at the other, each directing most of his comments to me even when they were intended for his brother. Through the latter part of the interview, neither man looked much at me, both directing almost all their comments, agreements, and disagreements toward each other even when they were intended for me.

These two men were among the very few siblings or stepsiblings whom I interviewed at length together rather than apart. Earlier I had spoken to each separately, but it seemed important that I meet with both together, not informally, as I had with the Ginetti sisters or the Deveau brothers, but in a structured interview setting. Their styles had been so different in our separate talks—Bill brimming with admiration and praise for Jared; Jared more distant, speaking of his own experience with fewer sympathetic references to Bill—that I wanted to see them together, interacting with each other and with me.

At forty-four, Bill, the elder by a year, has almost no hair, a slight paunch, and a full, round face punctuated by a dimple in his right cheek. The total impression is of a cherub, and one with an easy and inviting smile. Jared, hair graying at the temples, is short and wiry, with the lithe walk of an athlete and the focused attention of a perfectionist determined to do things right. In fact, he is both. An inveterate jogger, he hasn't missed a day of running since he began some seven years ago. An independent filmmaker, he is known for the meticulousness of his work and his careful attention to detail.

The men live in different suburbs of Los Angeles, but our meeting took place in Bill's office in Burbank, where he works as a producer in a middle-sized television production company owned by his father. We sat in a triangle, the two men parallel to each other and facing me.

"As I told you," Jared said, referring to the conversation we'd had alone, "I had a blood brother, Chip, two years younger than I, who died when he was twenty. My parents were divorced when I was five and Chip three, and my mother married Bill's father two years later. Until the marriage, Chip and I were together all the time and I was very, very involved with him. Afterward, I began hanging out more with Bill. Chip had a congenital muscular disease and was always sickly. It was more fun for me to play with Bill, and I have the feeling that I didn't pay a lot of attention to Chip again. But I was devastated by his death. I've increasingly realized how terribly important he was to me, and how sad I've been to have lost him."

He was determined from the start to distinguish between siblings and stepsiblings. He'd made a point in our earlier discussion of telling me that his feelings toward Chip "get to the essence of what brothers are" and are therefore very different from his feelings for Bill. Now he was reconfirming those visceral brotherly emotions.

"How did *you* feel about Chip?" I asked Bill, somewhat surprised to hear myself pursuing Jared's line of thought instead of my own. Yet I was doing so because I sensed that it was easier for them to begin by speaking about Chip than about themselves.

"I never really bonded to Chip," Bill said, smiling at using the kind of jargony word he might poke fun at in one of his films. "There's nothing negative there; I have a sweet feeling about him, and I was very sad when he died. But nó, he hasn't been a major figure for me the way he was for Jared." He glanced at Jared, then looked back at me.

"Why do you suppose that is?" I asked. I knew that Bill had been an only child and had lived with his mother immediately after his parents' divorce. But two years after his father remarried, his mother moved out of town and Bill moved in with his father and new stepfamily. One might have supposed that he'd have stronger feelings for the littlest brother, just three years younger than he.

"Because, Francine," he said, as if explaining the obvious, "stepsiblings are not the same as blood siblings. Nothing is taken for granted. There are no automatic expectations of closeness among steps as there are with blood sibs. Stepsiblings have to choose one another and keep choosing if they want to make something of their relationship. Blood relatives don't have to do that. I didn't choose Chip when we were children—it was Jared I became close to. And I couldn't choose him as an adult because he died so young that I didn't get a chance to."

It was well said, also picking up the more indirect sentiments of Jared and summarizing them simply. With the cards thus on the table, I found it easier to lead the brothers toward a frank discussion of their relationship and the subject of stepsiblings in general, a subject shrouded in mystery even in our divorce-prone society.

The term "stepparent" originally referred to a person who replaced a dead parent ("step" from the Middle English *steop*, meaning orphaned or bereaved). Historically, more remarriages resulted from the death of a spouse than from divorce, because death rates were much higher than they are today and divorce rates much lower. In the 1970s divorce began, for the first time, to outstrip death as the cause for remarriage, and since then "step" terms have become most commonly associated with divorce situations. According to the Census Bureau, there were 5.3 million stepfamilies containing 7.3 million children under the age of eighteen in the United States in 1990. Based on the high rates of divorce and remarriage, the Stepfamily Association of America predicts that this will be the most common form of family life in the twenty-first century.

The association publishes an extensive bibliography that includes hundreds of articles and dozens of books dealing with the problems and challenges of stepfamilies. Almost all the listings concern stepparents in relation to one another and their children. Close to forgotten is the fact that stepsiblings, like biological siblings, form ties of their own that influence them as individuals and affect the family as a whole. Experts say, for example, that the children each partner brings to a remarriage often become the major source of conflict between the couple. It follows, then, that relations among stepsibs can shape the overall tone of a remarriage, yet the vast stepfamily literature pays little attention to this.

I met with Bill and Jared and others like them to fill in some of the blanks, on the assumption that as different as stepsibling relationships may be from those of blood siblings, they are still a form of brother or sister attachment that needs to be explored. What I found is that yes, of course, as Bill informed me, great differences do exist, and the relationship cannot be understood unless those differences are openly acknowledged. Nonetheless, I also found that stepsiblings and blood siblings share some basic traits, most importantly the struggle for power and position, and the search for balance on the sibling seesaws of love and rivalry, closeness and distance.

But that is getting ahead of the story. For where stepsiblings begin, when they tell about themselves, is with their histories apart and together, and when that history involves the divorce of parents, as it does for Bill and Jared, the divorce becomes the center of the telling. To children of divorce, either young or adult, the breakup of their parents' marriage is a watershed event, a divider between the before, when the world was tight and secure, and the after, when nothing was or ever would be the same again. In fact, say family experts, for some children looking back, the divorce of parents, the remarriage of one or both, and the acquisition of stepsiblings are all compressed into a single time frame, blurred together and often streaked with lines of pain.

This is how Jared dates the beginning of his history with Bill, viewing "the whole time, leading up to the divorce and subsequent to it" as "unhappy."

Until then, he and his family had lived in the heart of San Francisco, where his father worked as a hotel manager. Afterward, when his mother married Bennett Craine—Bill's father—Jared, Chip, and their mother moved to Bennett's big house in the Los Angeles suburb of Burbank.

"It was a big change," Jared said. "My mother had never been a very present mother to begin with, and now my stepfather demanded a lot of her attention, so that my little brother and I were kind of left out in the cold. He was so confused by everything that had happened, and I tried to comfort him, but it was very hard for me too."

The situation was made more difficult by the fact that the brothers were separated in their new home. "I had a room to myself on the third floor," Jared recalled, "and Chip had a room near my mother and Bennett on the floor below because he wasn't supposed to climb a lot of stairs."

"It was my childhood room, my cherished place," Bill interrupted, in a flat, unemotional voice, eyes determinedly away from Jared. "I never begrudged Chip the space, but there was a lot of dislocation."

For Bill, that dislocation was part of a larger one begun even before his parents' divorce. By second grade he had become a "major behavioral problem" in school, his misbehavior, he believes in retrospect, a result of years of marital tension between his parents. Consequently, he was "kicked out of second grade," and sent to a boarding school for the next year. "When I went off to boarding school, my parents were living under the same roof," he said. "When I came back, my father had left and they were in the midst of divorce."

With the same blurred memory as Jared's, Bill is not quite sure when he and his mother moved out of the big house in which he had been born to a small apartment and his father moved back in with his new wife and stepsons. He does remember having to sleep in a tiny bedroom, the "size of a closet," in the new apartment while his mother slept on a couch in an equally small living room. And he remembers the day his mother informed him of her decision to leave California for New York. "I can't deal with you," she told her son. "You're just like your father, so go live with him."

Later he understood how little his father had provided for his mother and how hard her life had been. But at the time he felt abandoned, "bewildered and starved for love." He was ten, Jared nine, and Chip seven when he went back to his father's house to live with them, sharing Jared's room.

Almost immediately, though Bill was the elder of the two, Jared took on the role of older brother. He was the good boy; Bill the bad. He was the responsible one; Bill, as he sees himself then, "blind, just groping for anything that would feel like it could take care of me." For Jared, the role reversal added to the burden of his own parents' divorce.

"I did a lot of taking care of Chip, and then Bill came along," he said with some bitterness. "There I was, looking out for two brothers now and trying to watch out for myself in what still felt like alien territory."

As alien as that territory may have been to Jared, Bill's father regarded it as his family grounds. True, the boys were not permitted to eat with the parents except on Saturday nights, when they all roasted hot dogs around the fireplace. Still, Bennett saw himself as head of a family of three sons and avoided as much as possible the fact that Jared and Chip had a father of their own.

The family image was so important to him that when Jared, at age thirteen, wanted to leave the household and return to San Francisco to be with his father, Bennett convinced his wife that such a move would not be in her son's best interest.

"My father had remarried and had two new sons," Jared said, "and I was always aware that we had a blood connection, even though I didn't see much of them. When I did see them, we got along well. It felt like a much more normal family to me. I think my father really wanted me to live with him, but my mother insisted that it would be better for me not to move. Bill is sure Bennett influenced her in that decision."

"I think my father, whose ego knows no bounds, felt he could better provide for Jared and Chip than their own father could, as if he knew best how to raise sons," Bill moved in to explain.

"That could be true," Jared responded. "It could also be, looking at it ungenerously, that it was a lot easier for him to have the three of us, in terms of my taking care of you and his not having to worry, than it would be to have just you and Chip at home."

"And generously speaking," Bill replied quickly, as he looked at me and addressed Jared, "he may have felt—and I think rightly—that it would have been a tremendous loss to me again. By now Jared was my closest friend. We did a lot together, and I don't know how I would have dealt with his moving away."

"We did a lot together," Jared echoed softly, turning for the first time to look at Bill. "I enjoyed it, too, and there's sadness in that because the memory of the good times is somehow entangled with the feeling of all the difficulties of those years."

Bill returned his look and nodded, and the men fell silent, staring at each other while they dug through their own thoughts.

I reflected on the pattern I saw emerging. Both stepbrothers clearly felt deep anger at their own parents: at the basic act of divorce and at the household structure that had kept each separated from the adult who had been "his." Nevertheless, each man also felt a loyalty to his own parent that led him to jump to that parent's defense in the face of criticism. Asserting that his father *really* wanted him back although he did not say so, Jared was quick to attribute selfish motives to his stepfather for preventing this. Bill, disapproving as he might be of his father's boundless ego, still found a loving aspect to Bennett's behavior, both in wanting to do what was right for his stepsons and in protecting his own son from another loss.

The same mixed messages characterized the men's attitudes toward each other. Both remembered with warmth the good times they had shared, but their inability to speak directly to each other while telling their life stories to me reflected the wariness that still exists between them. Only after Jared had broken the ice with a tender reminiscence were the two able to relax and look at each other while they spoke of their joint history. Even then, they shifted back and forth from appreciation of one another to suspicion, from unity against stepparents to each man's defensive support of his own parent.

"I always saw Jared as my older brother," Bill said, breaking the silence in the room. He had turned his chair at an angle so that he could more easily face Jared, even when he was speaking to me. "I knew he was younger, and I bullied him the way older brothers bully younger ones, but on some level I knew that he held and was asked to hold a certain 'keep your eye on Bill' role, which he did very well."

"Didn't you resent that?" I asked.

"Well, I suppose so," he said, adding after a pause, "I suppose I resented it profoundly."

"You must have resented it," Jared cut in sharply, turning his chair so that the two were almost face to face, "and I must have, too, *greatly*, in fact."

"But my resentment was balanced," said Bill, with a friendly smile, "by my innate sense that you were a good person who made life tolerable for me."

"And I got a lot out of playing with you," Jared said softly. Then his tone turned bitter again. "But what you speak of as bullying I remember as a kind of trickiness and treachery. I knew I had to be careful around you."

"In what way careful?" I asked.

"The incident I remember," he said, speaking to Bill as if I didn't exist, "was when we were in the same prep school. I was a sophomore and you a junior. You said the soccer coach had told you that I was one of the best players on the team, and that made you wonder why I was never put into a major game. You said it so straightforwardly that I believed you, and I agonized through the whole season about why I wasn't in a game. But then I realized there was no way he could have said that. You were zapping me."

Bill appeared pained. "I don't think I would have done that purposely," he said. "Maybe I just meant to encourage you when you were worried that you wouldn't make the team, or something."

"Maybe," said Jared.

Back and forth, back and forth they went.

Bill played the role of appeaser. He had chosen, as he said, to be Jared's friend, and he was determined to win Jared's approval with words of admiration. He praised Jared for being married to the same woman for more than twenty years, while he himself had been divorced and remarried, just like his father. He spoke of placing Jared on a pedestal and feeling unworthy in comparison.

Jared maintained the role of injured party. "For me," he said coolly, "what goes on between us is kind of clouded over by the struggles of those years when we lived together, then went to prep school and college together." Still, in the midst of complaints about Bill, he felt he had to acknowledge his own untrustworthiness. "I used to befriend Bill's girlfriends," he said, "and while I was too ethical to actually get into a romantic involvement with them, I was very capable of inciting them to feel romantic toward me." His purpose, he explained, looking at Bill, was to "get back at you, but even more so, to get back—by hurting you—at Bennett."

Back and forth, back and forth they went.

Both agreed that Bennett had been a roadblock to closeness between them, pitting them against each other in schoolwork and athletic prowess. "It was a way for Bennett to prevent us from loving each other so he could have control over both of us," Jared said. "Yes," Bill concurred with a laugh, "but here was the real kicker—the purpose of the competition was for me, his natural son, to win, and I didn't win. Jared did. Jared is more athletic than I am and he's more intellectual than I am, more of what my father admires. So the competitiveness was a waste!"

But Bill had his own grievances against his stepmother, Jared's mother Phyllis, that spilled over to Jared, and Jared could not refrain, time and again, from equating Bill with Bennett.

After his own divorce and remarriage, Bill had been eager to keep close ties to his two daughters from his first marriage, and it seemed natural to him to ask Phyllis to share some of her insights about stepmothering with his second wife. To his amazement she refused. She had always tried to be a mother to him, she said, and she resented being seen as the personification of stepmother. To his even greater amazement, Jared defended his mother, arguing that Bill had made an unfair request.

"I said 'Fuck you' to her and I said 'Fuck you' to Jared," Bill related, with more passion than I'd seen in all the hours we'd been together. He shifted his gaze briefly toward me, then back to Jared. "I was totally pissed, and I wrote them both off. That was probably the coldest time in my history with Jared."

There was silence until Jared volunteered that they had long since put that cold time behind them. But he made a point of saying that he still finds himself on guard and has difficulty feeling close because of the "extent to which Bill has been like Bennett over the years." Seeing Bill's look of unhappiness, he added quickly, "I know you've struggled valiantly to find your own identity. But it's inevitable that some of Bennett would rub off on you."

"I know you're right," Bill answered. "It's strange that no matter how I try, I'm still unconsciously a chip off the old block."

Ironically, in spite of their many differences, the stepbrothers have ended up in related fields and in Bennett's shadow. Jared became fascinated with the process of TV and film production after working for Bennett one summer. Steadfastly refusing repeated offers to join his stepfather's production company, he set himself up as an independent filmmaker. Bill had planned on a career in journalism after college but finally gave in to Bennett's pressure to enter the business. He could do so, he said, because knowing his father as he did, he felt strong enough to hold his own even while working with him.

True to form, the men maintain that being in the same field has both exacerbated the competitiveness between them and brought them closer. Jared envies the economic security Bill has in working for a corporation, while he feels himself "vulnerable" in making a living through his own wits. Yet he feels comfortable in the knowledge that each man has his own "niche" from which he can help the other. Bill envies Jared's independence and freedom to create. Yet he feels that through their work they have "moved toward each other," almost as if it were "preordained" that they end up in the same field as friends and not competitors.

By the end of the interview, smiling and relaxed, the stepbrothers assured me that although, as Jared put it, they might "still be capable of doing something unfriendly" toward each other, they were truly beyond that. Then each man returned to where he had begun.

Jared spoke again of his powerful blood connection with his deceased younger brother that still outweighs any other attachment he has. Expanding on that theme, he described his two half-brothers from his father's second marriage. He has little in common with them, yet when he "gets in a room with them, something starts to happen." It's a feeling that comes over him, "different" from what he has with Bill, although he knows that his ties to Bill are much stronger.

Bill returned to his theme of choosing among stepsiblings. "We were brought together circumstantially," he said, "but I keep choosing to make more of our relationship. I don't know how many times I've *chosen* to move toward Jared, *chosen* to keep our connection going. I think for me, the stepsibling relationship is more like a marriage than a sibling situation. It's not as cool as a friendship, or as happenstance, and it's not a 'given,' like blood. It's something more *made*, the way a marriage is made, and like a marriage, you have to keep working at it."

Countless permutations and combinations go into the "making" of stepsiblings who, like Bill and Jared, come together as the result of their parents' divorces and remarriages. In some families, children from the previous marriages of both a husband and wife live together under one roof. In others, the most common, the children of a remarried woman live with her and her new husband—their stepfather—while *his* children live with his former wife and visit with him and his new family. In a smaller number of cases, a remarried woman's children remain with their father, becoming visitors in her home, where she serves as stepmother to her husband's children. And in smaller numbers still, children move back and forth between parents who have joint custody over them.

Regardless of these many configurations of stepfamilies formed by divorce, the themes that emerged from Bill and Jared are themes that came up again and again in meetings with stepsiblings: of divorce and dislocation, of the pressures of instant intimacy, of power struggles and rivalry, and above all of ambivalence and ambiguity as stepsibs try to decide whether and how and when to "choose" one another.

The divorce of their parents remains the dominant and recurring undercurrent of their lives. In her humorous, touching book, *Funny Sauce*, about being a stepparent, Delia Ephron describes the relentless dream of children of divorce that somehow, magically, against all logic, their parents will get together again. With tongue in cheek, she offers schoolchildren some advice: "Go to the school Science Fair. Your mom is there with your stepfather. Your dad is there with his girlfriend. Notice how different your mom and dad are. They don't like to do the same things. They don't like the same music. They don't like the same movies. . . . Think, I used to wish they would get back together, but now I know that's impossible. Have a fantasy: Your mom changes to be like your dad (or your dad changes to be like your mom). They get back together."

Both the fantasy and the painful knowledge that it can never be haunt stepfamilies and stepsiblings long after Science Fair days. A woman in her thirties who feels that both her parents' remarriages have been successful, who liked the stepmother with whom she went to live during her teen years, and who developed strong, positive ties to her stepsiblings, says she can still feel the unhappiness she experienced in both her mother's house and her father's house simply because they were separate homes.

"The most difficult thing," she recalls, "was that my father wasn't married to my mother. He was married to my stepmother, and as well as we got along, that was always there. I just wanted my parents to be married, and I guess that's why I moved from one house to another. I wanted the stability of a real family, but I never found what I was looking for. In one place it was my dad but it wasn't my mom, and in the other it was my mom but it wasn't my dad."

Psychologist Judith Wallerstein, who has studied a group of divorced parents and their children over the course of ten to fifteen years, says that the sorrow of parental divorce and the unfulfilled fantasy that they will reunite can continue for years, in some cases causing depression in adult children of divorce. Much of the sorrow comes from the double loss the children suffer. The first is the loss of the sense of protection that intact families simply take for granted. The second is the loss—in many cases—of the everyday presence of their father in the children's lives. (Occasionally that loss is of the mother, but about 90 percent of children live in the custody of their mothers after a divorce.)

Those losses bring with them feelings of rejection and the unending wish to undo the divorce in order to feel whole and loved again. Moving from one parent's home to another, as this woman did and as Jared wanted to, may be a way of seeking wholeness by being in close contact with both parents. Many children also idealize their absent father, seeing in him and his home the answer to whatever they believe to be lacking in their mother's home. Thus Jared saw his father's family as "more normal" than his mother's, and asked to live there. All these years later, he still believes that his father "really wanted" him, and that his stepfather, Bennett, stood in the way of his move. It is not unusual, by the way, for adolescents to actually move from a mother's to a father's home, at least for a few years. Teenage boys, especially, identifying with their fathers, often have a pressing need to be with them during adolescence.

Siblings may react differently to the breakup of their parents' marriage, depending on their ages. Very young children, like Chip, tend to suffer most immediately following the divorce. Because they don't really understand their parents' behavior and motives, they often blame themselves, viewing their "badness" as the cause for Daddy's anger or Mommy's tears. Their older siblings, although suffering great pain, still have enough understanding to avoid self-blame and enough independence to turn to friends or other family members for help and comfort.

Ten years after a divorce, it is the younger children who are usually faring better than the older ones. As youngers, they have generally been more sheltered by their mothers, while the olders have borne the brunt of their parents' unhappiness. Youngers also have fewer memories of either intact family life or parental fights, so they are able to move on with their lives with less nostalgia and fewer bad feelings than the olders.

Their parents' divorce may also intensify all the emotions siblings have for one another. Angry at their parents, brothers and sisters may lash out at each other, easier and more available targets. They may also compete more than ever for parents who, preoccupied with their own troubles, become less available. In some cases, brothers and sisters parrot their father and mother's quarrels, some taking the side of one parent, some of the other, bitterly fighting over their conflicting loyalties. Occasionally siblings move to separate homes, following the parent for whom they feel greatest loyalty. "After the divorce my brother and I split up according to gender: mother-daughter, father-son," wrote a thirty-year-old woman on the questionnaire. "We haven't seen each other much since then."

But their parents' divorce can also awaken in siblings sympathy and concern for one another. Many adult children of divorce expressed feelings similar to those of a twenty-three-year-old file clerk who wrote, "I think it would be safe to say that until my parents' divorce, when I was thirteen and my sister ten, we tolerated each other, as most siblings do at those ages. But when my father moved out, we found solace and support in each other, and we continue to do so." And more than a few people said that their sisters or brothers were the only persons with whom they could talk about their anguish during a divorce without feeling like traitors to their parents.

Older siblings often lead the way for younger ones, serving as buffers against the sharpest pains and disillusionments divorce brings. That role may weigh the olders down with responsibility, but it can also bolster them with the knowledge that they are needed and important. Even though Jared complained of the tremendous burden he felt in looking after Chip, his position as his brother's caretaker gave him a solid base in a world that was otherwise rapidly slipping out from under him. Bill lacked that base. He found himself alone and isolated while his parents fought and then broke up.

On a slightly more optimistic note than Wallerstein, University of Virginia psychologist E. Mavis Hetherington holds that family members usually adapt to a divorce within two or three years. With the worst traumas behind them, children as well as parents accept the breakup of the family and begin to adjust to a new way of living.

For most children that new way means living alone with their mother and becoming visitors to their father. In such single-parent homes, sibs often become protective and supportive of one another and of their mother as they begin to pick up the pieces of their lives together. With their mother usually working, all the siblings pitch in to help, and an informal and egalitarian atmosphere may take hold.

When sibs do have difficulties in single-parent homes, these usually stem from their rivalries for a mother who is herself overworked and emotionally drained (although rivalries for the noncustodial parent can also develop, with children vying for time alone, for gifts and special notice). One divorced mother sought psychiatric help because her eight-year-old son had become viciously hostile toward her five-year-old daughter and she feared leaving them alone in the house. She recognized after a while that in her own need for comfort and love, she had turned toward her cuddly, affectionate little daughter and away from her more independent and less accessible older son. Feeling himself neglected and less loved, the son vented his rage on his sister.

As they do in other difficult family situations, Hetherington has found, girls often shoulder the major responsibilities in these homes, looking out for the other children and becoming companions to their mothers. Boys seem to have more difficulty living with single mothers, and show more behavior problems at home and at school, even two or three years after their parents' divorce. It may be that boys, longing for the authority and companionship of their fathers, consciously or unconsciously blame their mothers for this deprivation. Girls, who identify more closely with their mothers, generally have more sympathy for the difficulties of their lives. The girls' closeness to their mothers may further exacerbate their brothers' difficulties, leading to tensions between sisters and brothers.

Once parents remarry, the boy-girl responses reverse themselves. In general, school-age boys adjust better to stepfathers than do their sisters, and may also fare better with stepmothers when their fathers remarry. A loving stepfather can offer boys the male presence, support, and friendship they lacked when living alone with their mothers, but girls tend to view a stepfather as an interference in their position as mother's best friend and main support. Also, girls may bridle at any physical show of affection by a stepfather, in that sense building roadblocks to intimacy. "I shouted, 'Don't you ever touch me like that again!' " recalled a court stenographer of the first time her stepfather hugged her. "He had put his arm around me and it was completely innocent, but I was a teenager and into personal safety and the women's movement and stuff. We still joke about that line today. He's turned out to be a terrific dad."

When a father remarries, a girl might see his new wife as a rival for her own special status as "Daddy's girl," especially if she has been in her father's custody. But her brother may welcome the presence of a woman in the household. (Sometimes adolescent girls do build strong friendships with stepmothers, with whom they share confidences about sexuality and other subjects they feel they cannot discuss with their mothers.)

For siblings in relation to each other, a parent's remarriage raises new situations with which to cope. Most remarriages take place within three to five years after a divorce (and most divorced parents *do* remarry: 75 percent of women and 80 percent of men take new spouses, according to Hetherington). Now the adjustment is not to loss, as it is with divorce, but to additions—in the form of stepparents and, in many cases, stepsibs.

Looking back, many adult siblings remember clinging to each other in the early years of their parents' remarriage (the consensus of experts is that children have even more difficulty adjusting to remarriage than to divorce). Years later, even if they had become close to their stepsiblings, those early sibling loyalties still overshadow all others. Jared's insistence that his feelings for Chip—long after Chip's death—transcend even his warmest emotions toward Bill is typical of almost every child in a stepfamily who has a blood brother or sister.

In fact, the strength of those blood ties accounts for an unexpected finding in the interviews. When a parent remarries and a child acquires one or more stepsiblings, birth order positions within the extended stepfamily often get rejuggled. A boy who had been the elder of two may find himself with an older stepbrother who expects the respect due an elder. A girl who had been the darling youngest child in her original family may discover that a younger, cuter stepsister has pushed her aside. One would expect such changes to upset and confuse children trying to cope with a situation that is upsetting and confusing enough to begin with.

Yet adults give such birth order changes low priority in their recollections of life with siblings and stepsiblings. A few did mention resentment of older stepsiblings who tried to boss them around. But for the most part, people seemed almost puzzled by questions about birth order reversals. Because they continued to view themselves in relation to their blood siblings and not their stepsiblings, they still saw themselves in the positions they had always held, no matter how many stepsibs now ranked before or after them in birth order.

"It's strange," said a saleswoman, representative of other people, "you ask how it felt for me to become a middle child when I had always been the eldest, and I guess I was a middle sister after my mother remarried and I got an older stepsister. But I never felt that way at all. From day one I have been the older sister and my sister has been the younger one. We never thought of ourselves in any other way, even though we were both close to our older stepsister."

None of this means that stepsiblings do not have strong feelings for each other. In spite of the tight ties among blood brothers and sisters, both men and women speak of times in their lives when they found it more important, or more enjoyable, to move closer to stepsiblings— sometimes guilt-ridden that they had betrayed their own siblings in doing so. Jared had more fun hanging out with Bill than caring for Chip, and he still suffers the sadness of feeling he neglected his brother. The saleswoman who sees herself as an older sister although she has a stepsister older than she is remembers leaving her younger sister behind when she moved from her mother's home to her father's during her high school years. "I would go home in the afternoon with my stepsister," she said, "and I'm sure that was very hard for my sister. I didn't understand this then. I was thinking more about me than about her. We talk about a lot of things now, but I've never been able to ask her about that."

Others feel less guilt and greater gratitude for the important roles stepsiblings filled for them. A woman with three brothers who had wished as a young child for a sister was "excited and delighted" to get one in the form of a stepsister when she was eleven years old, and has remained good friends with that step. Another woman regarded her stepbrother and stepsister as "lifesavers" in the years after her mother married their father. She was fourteen at the time, and her own older brothers had gone off to college. "I was so alone," she said. "My parents were still fighting and my brothers were gone. Who wouldn't have been receptive to stepsiblings? I was thrilled."

(Complaint made by a fifth grader to his happily married biological parents: "How come everyone else in school has a stepbrother or stepsister, and I can't have one?")

From the positive side of the stepsibling ledger came many descriptions of aid and kindness by stepsisters and stepbrothers, as in "I shared my stepbrother's room whenever I came to visit my father, and he never once made me feel I was invading his space," or "My stepsister looked out for me, and it was because of her that I survived all the turmoil," or, in a simple statement of fact, "I got along fine with my stepbrothers and stepsisters. It wasn't them I was mad at, it was my parents."

Some people also felt they were able to become friends with their stepsiblings, particularly during adolescence and adult life, because these relationships did not carry the emotional baggage blood sibs are burdened with: the "old stuff and old patterns and history" that "get in the way," as one man put it, in relations among siblings.

Yet that very strength of the stepsib connection—its freedom from the old baggage—is also its greatest weakness: a dearth of history, a lack of emotional depth, an absence of those visceral feelings and unspoken knowledge of one another that originate in sibling prehistory. The instantaneousness of stepsib relations makes them harder to sustain than sibling attachments. Instant family life, instant expectations of love and loyalty, and the converse, instant rivalries, create hindrances to closeness.

Soon after a remarriage, for instance, one parent's children must suddenly share bedrooms and bathrooms, clothing, toys, and dinner-table conversation with the other parent's children, with whom they may have little in common and whom they might never have chosen as friends, let alone housemates. If both parents' children live together under the same roof, the sharing becomes permanent, and it can lead to overblown versions of ordinary sibling fights over territory and possessions. Even in the more usual cases, in which a stepfather lives with his wife and her children while his children visit regularly, the sharing can be a source of tension and resentment.

For visiting stepsibs in this situation, the resentment grows from feeling that they have been displaced in their father's house by his stepchildren. And often they are right. Bill saw his own "cherished" bedroom given to his youngest stepbrother, Chip, while he had to sleep in a closet-sized room in his mother's apartment. He insists he didn't begrudge Chip that space, but he also admits that he never established any connectedness to Chip, even after he moved into his father's house and joined his stepbrothers.

Bill's cramped living arrangement with his mother speaks to another form of displacement and a major source of resentment among stepsibs. After a divorce, women's living standards usually slip downward, whereas men—who customarily earn more, and may have been the main breadwinners in their first marriages—maintain the same standards or better them. Children of divorce who live with mothers who have not remarried often find themselves, like Bill, in tight quarters, with few of the comforts they may have enjoyed before the divorce. If they perceive that because of their father their stepsiblings live better than they do, or that their father shows more generosity to his stepchildren than to them, they're not likely to harbor many good feelings for those children.

For their part, children living with their mother and stepfather have their own angers about visiting stepsiblings. At a time when they feel vulnerable and in need of her special attentions, a mother's well-intentioned attempts at evenhandedness can provoke deep resentments. Girls who became their mother's confidante after her divorce may suffer the most intense jealousy and bitterness, feelings that can extend far beyond childhood. "She's my mom, and I shouldn't have to share her!" exclaimed a thirty-three-year-old woman, still unhappy that her mother treats her no differently than her stepsisters.

Children may also feel out of place when they move with their mother into her husband's home. Chip may have been too young to realize that he had taken over Bill's cherished room, but older children can be so aware of dispossessing a stepsibling that they feel not only guilty but homeless themselves. A man told of occupying his stepsister's bedroom after the stepsister left to live with her own mother. In an attempt to make the room comfortable for her son, his mother had redecorated it and moved all the stepsister's belongings to the basement. But when the stepsister came to visit her father, she was enraged to find everything she owned packed away. "I hated being in that room after that," the man said, "and because of it I never really felt I had a home after my mother's remarriage. But whatever my feelings, imagine how crappy my stepsister must have felt. There was no way we could ever become friends."

Underlying the many obstacles to stepsibling closeness is both the simplest and most difficult of all: the ambiguity of the relationship itself. How should stepsiblings treat each other? Should they pretend they are really sisters and brothers, or should they try to establish as much friendship as possible and let it go at that? Are they "The Brady Bunch" or simply a bunch of people thrown together by circumstances?

And small things (but often not considered small): How should stepparents be addressed—"Mom" and "Dad"? But stepchildren have their own moms and dads. By their first names? But doesn't that create yet one more difference with stepsibs who do not address their parents this way? How do you introduce a stepparent—as "my stepmother" or as "my father's wife"? What do you call your stepsiblings' grandparents—"Grandma and Grandpa"? "Grandma and Grandpa Blake"? And myriad other questions.

Stepsiblings may struggle for years to sort out their unclear relationships and feelings, swinging, like Bill and Jared, back and forth in their attitudes toward each other.

"They're really like brothers and sister to me. There's no difference," said a woman of her two stepbrothers and one stepsister in the course of an interview. "Well, of course," she added moments later, "they're not really my brothers and sister. It's never the same." A few minutes later came the assurance that "I include them in thinking of my family. We're really one big family," which was qualified almost immediately with, "Well, I wouldn't say I love them as much as my own sister and brother. It's different with them. I don't feel we have to maintain contact in the same way."

High on the list of ambiguities are the sexual confusions that can arise in stepfamilies. Bill said at one point that as an adolescent he had sensed an "erotic element" in his stepmother's attitude toward him, although as an adult he's not sure he wasn't reading something that didn't exist into the situation. Often, however, that element does exist in stepfamilies. Incest between stepfathers and stepdaughters, for example, is a common form of father-daughter incest, first because the taboo between these partners is less strict than between blood relatives, and second because stepfathers who did not raise their stepdaughters may not have acquired the protective and paternal feelings of natural fathers.

The incest taboo can become somewhat blurred for stepsiblings as well: they are siblings but they are not blood relatives. How do they respond to the normal sexual pulls that occur between all sisters and brothers, particularly during adolescence? Most families would consider sexual relations among stepsibs—especially if they have grown up together—to be incestuous, or at the least inappropriate, but feelings and fantasies do exist. And the obvious sexual components of their parents' remarriage intensify these feelings for children, who under ordinary circumstances prefer to think of their parents as asexual. (That obvious sexuality between stepparents is one reason why children between the ages of nine and fifteen—when their own sexuality is burgeoning—have the hardest time adjusting to a remarriage.)

Opposite-sex stepsibs may counter their sexual longings by fighting fiercely with each other or becoming cold and withdrawn. In well-functioning homes, they eventually put their attractions aside, but strains may remain. "Sometimes my oldest stepbrother will put his arm around me," a twenty-five-year-old woman said, "and it's still kind of awkward. I think, 'You can't be my boyfriend, you're my stepbrother,' but I don't know how to say that to him, and I'm not sure I really believe it."

Nuclear families have centuries of history and tradition on which to model themselves. Stepfamilies have few models and even fewer happy traditions—visions of the wicked stepmothers of fairy-tale land haunt the memory of many a child of remarriage. These families need to find their own way through often unmarked terrains.

Part of the challenge for stepsiblings trying to find their way, as Bill said, is deliberately having to choose one another in a manner that siblings do not. That choosing may be easier in adult life if in childhood stepparents do not labor to re-create their first families through their later ones but allow stepbrothers and stepsisters to acknowledge the ambiguities. Stepfamilies become true families when they build their own histories and traditions. For that they need time—for stepparents and children to grow accustomed to one another and for stepsiblings to form their own attachments apart from attitudes toward parents or stepparents.

An example of a stepfamily that became a "real" family in this sense came from an executive who attached a three-page letter to the questionnaire, detailing all the "right" things his mother and stepfather had done. Among them was a Halloween tradition they invented. After the kids went trick-or-treating, the stepfather's children from his first marriage would join his new family for a "ghost party." Everybody would sit in a circle with the lights out, and the children—there were five in the blended family—would take turns at making up a story and then talking about anything they wanted to. In the dark, not having to face each other, the children were able to pour out some of their deepest hurts and angers and get to know each other at the same time.

"Halloween was as special to us as a stepfamily as Thanksgiving or Christmas had been in our original families," the man wrote. "We still all get together with our children every year for our own version of the ghost party." He added, in a P.S.: "My sister and I feel so close to the sisters and brother in our mother's remarriage that we never use the term 'step' in referring to them. We don't use the term 'step' for our father's second wife or children either, but for the opposite reason. No one helped us to know them, and we feel no connection to them at all."

Sadly, for stepsiblings, the connections that develop can collapse if a parent and stepparent divorce, and with the rate of divorce among the remarried as high or possibly even higher than among the first-married, such an event is not unusual.

For blood siblings, a parent's second (or later) divorce can reawaken all the pain and confusion of the first. Children may blame a stepparent for the marital failure and feel, as Valerie, an office manager, said, that "you can't count on anyone but your blood relatives."

Struggling to get her bearings after her father's second divorce, Valerie spoke bitterly of having invested herself emotionally in her stepfamily. "You can't win," she said. "You can choose not to become involved with your stepfamily and not look at them as your family, and that makes it really hard to adjust to having them. Or you can become involved with them, as my sister and I did, and look at them as your family, and then your parents get divorced again and you're left with nothing."

For children and adults who had become close to their stepsiblings, the dissolution of a remarriage may lead to even greater loss than the breakup of the original marriage, for it is not uncommon for them to lose all contact with their stepfamily. Even if they attempt to stay in touch, the ties often become fragile with time. Valerie described a meeting of all the stepsiblings, "shattered" by their parents' divorce, in which they vowed to remain close. But she was not optimistic. "It's not just a regular sibling where no matter what happens you're brother or sister," she said. "When your stepsiblings become just like friends, and if you don't live near each other, maintaining contact is an effort, and people don't always make that effort."

Much that has been said about stepfamilies formed as the result of divorce applies as well to families formed as the result of the death of one parent and the remarriage of another. If bereaved children acquire stepsiblings through a parent's remarriage, the same hurdles toward—and opportunities for—closeness and friendship exist among them. Nevertheless, there are some special circumstances that hold for children who have been orphaned that do not apply when divorce has broken up a home.

One, of course, is that death is final, and a deceased parent, unlike a divorced one, does not remain part of children's lives. That means that bereaved children are more likely to see themselves as an integral part of their stepfamilies than are children whose lives are linked to two parents who live apart. The finality of death also prevents bereaved children from fantasizing—as so many children of divorce do —that their parents still love each other and will get together again; and in that sense orphaned children may find it easier to accept stepfamily life in spite of their grief.

The other side of the coin is that children and adults tend to idealize their deceased parents, seeing them as the all-loving unblemished parents they would have liked to have. The fairy-tale image of the wicked stepmother is the obverse of the image of the good mother, the one dead and lost to the child, but the one who may return in fantasy as the fairy godmother who rescues the child from the stepmother's evils. Real-life stepmothers and stepfathers often find themselves pitted against the ghost of such a "perfect" parent as they attempt to create new family lives with partners whose spouses have died. If, also, a child perceives a stepparent as trying to replace a dead parent—in the child's mind, as if that parent had never existed—there can be a resentment so profound that it permanently interferes with all stepfamily relationships.

Such resentment poured out of a forty-two-year-old woman named Sophie, who loves her two younger half sisters and is loved by them, but whose anger at her father and stepmother has remained an unresolved irritant among the siblings. Sophie had such strong feelings on this subject that even after a long and emotional interview, she felt the need to write her thoughts down.

"Although my sisters are not 'full' sisters, they are terribly important to me," she wrote in a letter to me, "and their importance has been enhanced by my history of loneliness. I have come to realize that after my mother died (I was six years old), my father became emotionally unavailable to me, and he continues to keep his distance as his way of handling his unthinkable loss. Instead of grieving adequately or allowing me time to grieve, he found a 'perfect' replacement, the 'ideal' wife and mother who would pick right up where her predecessor left off. He married her three years after my mother's death, and my two sisters were born within four years after that.

"Since then, the unspoken myth in our family has been that Dad's first wife never really died because his second wife replaced her 'perfectly.' Because I have never accepted that myth, the dilemma for my sisters has been something like, 'Why doesn't our big sister love our mother the same way we do?' The dilemma for me, as a child and an adult, has been that neither of my sisters can be empathic with me around this matter that means so much to me. Now my task has become to accept what I can't change, to quietly grieve for what might have been, and to hope that my sisters and I will continue to strengthen the bonds we have in spite of this major difference."

Actually, her sisters *were* empathic to her feelings, but they were also torn between their loyalty to her and their loyalty to their mother. "I've always felt sad for Sophie because her mother died," said the older one, "and I've felt close to her. But what makes me mad is that whenever there's a problem in the family, she distances herself and speaks of 'your mother,' as if Mom hadn't raised her for most of her life. This bothers me deeply. I feel protective of my mother, and I also feel this anger is a crutch. She uses Mother as an easy target for blame."

The second sister went a step further in her reactions. Angry at Sophie's attacks on their mother, she reported that she had once blurted out, "Listen, if you're looking to me to side with you against Mom, you've got it wrong, because she's more important to me than you are." She has regretted the hurtfulness of that outburst but has not regretted confronting Sophie. "She needs to know," the sister said, "how upsetting her anger and bitterness are. Deep down I'm scared that she'll dislike me the way she dislikes Mother, because, after all, I'm my mom's daughter and she's not."

Sophie's pain and the tensions in the family might have been avoided, at least somewhat, had her father and stepmother openly recognized the enormous loss she had suffered when her mother died. For as with divorce, when a parent dies, children and adults need to have the ties to their biological parent recognized and validated before they are able to stretch those ties to embrace substitute parents and new siblings.

Technically speaking, Sophie's sisters were not stepsiblings but half-siblings, and that relationship raises another issue of stepfamily life, whether the remarriage results from the death of a parent or a divorce. Half-siblings share one biological parent; in Sophie's case, she and her sisters were the children of one father and different mothers. Frequently a remarried couple want to have a child of their own, not only as the offspring of their new union but as a symbol of their commitment to each other. What effect that new child has on the siblings and stepsiblings in the family and how they will relate to him or her is a question to which nobody has a conclusive answer.

Sociologist Lucille Duberman, one of the first researchers to focus on remarried families, reported from her studies that a new baby is a boon to stepfamily relationships. Since all the stepsiblings are related to the new child, all feel more closely connected to one another because of that child. But Duberman's conclusions drew on the comments of stepparents only; they did not include the reactions of the children involved. Those reactions can be mixed. Stepchildren may see the new child as "belonging" to a remarried couple while they themselves have become outsiders. ("My daughter from my first marriage looks at the son my second husband and I have had and wonders, 'Am I in this family?' 'What is my role?' " observed a woman who is concerned that her daughter has felt rejected because of the baby.)

And jealousy and resentment can be exacerbated if the baby comes relatively soon after the remarriage, before the stepchildren have had time to adjust to their new family arrangements.

Adult children also may be disturbed when a parent who has remarried has a baby (no longer an unusual event with the rise in divorce rates for couples married twenty years or more and the tendency for men to remarry younger women who want to have families of their own). They may be embarrassed by the birth of a half-sib at a time when they are planning children of their own. They may also resent sharing future inheritances or family possessions with a child with whom they feel no connection.

Despite these problems, with time, both children and adults usually find ways to adapt to the brothers or sisters born to a remarried mother or father. Many come to feel, as Jared does, an instinctive "blood connection" with these half-siblings that dissipates resentments and may lead to closeness.

The new arrivals themselves may have no problems at all; like youngers in nuclear families, they usually look up to and identify with older brothers and sisters. Difficulties can develop when the identification is so strong that the younger siblings grow up unaware that they have a different mother or father than an elder one. This is most likely to happen if the elder has little contact with a noncustodial parent or had lost a parent before the remarriage. Finding out the truth can be a shocking experience for a younger sibling.

In one such case a woman did not learn until she was ten years old that the older brother whom she adored, fifteen years her senior, was a half brother, with a different mother than she.

"I remember the moment with absolute clarity," she said. "My mother and I were in the kitchen, talking. She asked me to tell her how old she was. I answered, 'Thirty-six.' She then asked how old my brother was. I said, 'Twenty-five.' She asked me what the age difference was. For as long as I could count, I knew my mother and brother's ages, but it had never occurred to me to find something wrong with those numbers. Now for the first time the arithmetic hit me. In my mind I knew the answer was eleven, but I couldn't deal with it. I asked my mother for a piece of paper and a pencil, and slowly and confusedly wrote down the correct answer. Then I looked at my mother, and the tears rolled down my eyes. It was almost as if she had given me news of a death, like, oh my God, my whole reality had changed."

When I asked whether the information had altered her attitude toward her brother, she thought for a while, then said, "No, at first I believed it would, but it never changed my love for him." She thought again, and said, "When you grow up together as we did, the connection is very strong, even if it's not biological." She laughed and added, "Besides, my mother told me many times after that moment that there is no such thing as a half a brother. There are only whole brothers."

Wholeness is the underlying motif of one other nonbiological form of sibship that occurs in stepfamilies as well as nuclear ones, and that is adoption. A stepparent who adopts a stepchild creates binding legal ties to that child, similar to the bonds of parents to their biological children. (Without adoption, stepparents have no legal obligations for their stepchildren.) Most adoptions by stepparents are of stepchildren who have lost a birth parent; a few are of children who have little or no contact with a noncustodial parent.

When a man adopts his wife's children (the most common form of stepparent adoption), legally they assume the same last name as his biological children or of any half-siblings born to the marriage. In that sense, the family becomes more unified, more whole. Yet such name changes can also become the most sensitive and troublesome areas of stepfamily adoptions. Children who have lost a father may see themselves as traitors to their own parent or their own heritage if they drop their father's name, even if that change brings them closer to stepparents and siblings. Blood siblings may also differ among themselves about whether they want to be adopted—older ones wishing to keep their original family ties and names, youngers longing for a more secure connection to a stepparent, yet reluctant to separate themselves from their older sibs.

When the parent of adult siblings remarries and wants to adopt a stepchild, his or her adult children sometimes object, as they might to a new half-sibling, because of the effect of the adoption on wills and future inheritances. Or feeling themselves unrelated to a much younger child, they may simply disapprove of sharing the same name and family connections.

These many ramifications make the adoption of stepchildren a volatile subject. All parties involved need to think through carefully the consequences of such an adoption so that all the children in a family —biological sibs, half-sibs and stepsibs—may benefit, and no individual will feel deprived of a rightful place.

Adoptions in nuclear families have an altogether different meaning and different ramifications. Couples usually adopt children because of infertility problems and raise those children no differently than they would biological ones. In some families two or more adopted children grow up together as siblings; in others, a biological child, or children, might be raised alongside an adopted child, or children, all regarding themselves as brothers and sisters.

Of the many unexplored areas of sibling life, the area of adopted siblings may be the least understood. Behavioral geneticists have conducted the most widescale adoption studies for the purpose of sorting out the differing effects of heredity and environment on siblings within the same family, as discussed in Chapter One. Their findings that adopted siblings reared together may differ greatly from one another have supported their theory that the home environment creates differences rather than similarities among siblings.

But these scientists have not been interested in investigating the effects of adoption itself on individuals or siblings. Much of the information we have about that subject comes from case studies and reports on adopted children and adults seen by psychologists and psychiatrists in their clinical practices. These reports present the problems for which adoptees have sought help, such as questions about their own identity, cut off as most are from their biological parents; fantasies about parents or about half-siblings the adoptees may have; feelings of having been rejected by birth parents.

This information sheds light on the special issues adopted children face, but it tells little about the adjustments of the majority of adopted children and adults who have not sought psychiatric help, and almost nothing about relationships among adopted and nonadopted siblings in a family. Do adopted siblings feel as closely tied to each other as do biological sibs? Do difficulties arise among siblings when one is adopted and another is not? Are adopted children more likely to undertake a search for their biological parents when they have siblings who are not adopted?

One of the few investigations to deal with some of these questions and with a nonclinical population is a long-term project known as the Delaware Family Study, begun in 1962 and conducted by two psychologists, first among elementary and then among high school students drawn from the Pennsylvania, New Jersey, and Delaware areas. Fifty adopted and forty-one nonadopted students participated in the high school study, the more interesting of the two because it dealt with basic questions of identity among adopted children.

Based on extensive interviews and questionnaires, the researchers found little difference between adopted adolescents and nonadopted ones in terms of their views of themselves or their adjustment to their home, school, or social environment. When they examined sibling influences, they also found no significant differences in the identity formation or adjustment of adopted teenagers who had siblings and nonadopted ones with siblings. Nor did they find differences among adopted teenagers whose brothers or sisters were also adopted and those whose siblings were not adopted.

These last results surprised the researchers because in their earlier study of many of the same subjects as young schoolchildren, the adopted children with nonadopted siblings appeared to be under greater emotional stress and have more adjustment problems than those from "nonmixed" families. That stress may come from the teasing nonadopted children use as weapons against adopted ones, as in "I'm their real child; you're not." (Therapists report that nonadopted children with adopted siblings often feel themselves to be their parents' "real" and favored children but may also feel jealous that parents actually "chose" the other through adoption.)

As they move into adolescence, nonadopted siblings may put aside their teasing or find it no longer effective. It's also possible that by adolescence adopted children who feel secure in their home life are no longer bothered by differences with nonadopted ones. Some of the adopted subjects in this study reported, in fact, that having a nonadopted brother or sister confirmed their own sense of self-worth because they had never been treated differently or felt less loved than their sibs.

The Delaware study did not find that adopted teenagers were more likely to want to search for their birth parents if they had nonadopted siblings, but it did show that the teenagers most eager to make that search were generally those most dissatisfied with their adoptive families. Presumably, a search undertaken by one adopted child in a family and not another might indicate the dissatisfaction of the one or differences in treatment of the children by parents, but the study did not explore such matters.

The children in the Delaware study had all been adopted before they were two years old. The implication of the findings is that adopted children who from an early age grow up together or with nonadopted sisters and brothers feel as connected to one another as do biological siblings. Results might have been different if the investigation had focused on children adopted when they were older and had already formed attachments to birth parents and siblings or to foster families, but we do not know.

The numbers of children in this study were small, and dozens of questions about adoption, and adopted siblings, remain unanswered. Needed here, as in so many other aspects of the sibling bond, is good research, hard data, and a willingness to put aside myths in order to better understand the realities.

People can become siblings in many ways—through birth or blood, through parents' remarriages, through adoption into a stepfamily or adoption into a nuclear family. Blood ties may be, as Bill said, the most "given" of all, but given the many choices people make in life, "choosing" a stepsib or half-sib or adopted sib may be one of the best choices an adult can make.

PART II

Pressure Points

Sophia was surprised to detect tears in her sister's voice.

"Now, my dear Constance," she remonstrated. . . .

"Well," Constance interrupted her despairingly. "I wish you wouldn't try to domineer over me!"

"Domineer!" exclaimed Sophia, aghast. "Well, Constance, I do think—"

She got up and went to her bedroom. . . . She was shaking with emotion. This was what came of trying to help other people! . . . And Sophia encouraged in her breast the feeling of injustice suffered. . . .

"Domineer!"

—**Arnold Bennett,** *The Old Wives' Tale*

CHAPTER SEVEN

The Chosen

FAVORITISM AND ITS EFFECTS

"*M*om always liked you best," Tommy Smothers would say in a whiny, little-boy voice to his older brother Dick, and no matter how often he repeated that line, he always got a laugh. Parents watching "The Smothers Brothers Show" on television laughed with recognition—and sometimes guilt—as they recalled accusations their children had made to them dozens of times about being unfair, or giving one child more than another, or allowing one privileges the next didn't have. Children, both young and adult, laughed with recognition —and sometimes sadness—as they recalled accusations they had made to get their own way with parents or to manipulate a sibling, or because they had genuinely felt less loved or important than another.

Everybody laughed because everybody could identify with Tommy, the grown-up brother with the childlike feelings that somehow touched on everybody's life.

That the subject of parental favoritism touches on the lives of a great many people was borne out by my survey, in which an overwhelming 84 percent of respondents indicated that their parents had shown favoritism in the family. The gender preferences discussed in Chapter Five made up only one form of the favoritism people pointed to, and even when profoundly felt, such preferences were often linked to social norms and traditions. Just as pressing, or more so, respondents wrote and spoke of personal favoritism parents displayed, a feeling that, for whatever reason, a mother or father had chosen one child over another for special treatment or singled that child out to "like best."

Both those who saw themselves as favored and those who did not felt affected by their parents' preferences. People blamed parental favoritism for ongoing jealousies and competition with their siblings or for angry clashes that flared up from time to time. In the most extreme cases favoritism had created so much acrimony that it had destroyed all relationship among siblings. Even when far less pernicious, it often created pressure points in the family that radiated throughout the sibling connection.

With all that, favoritism remains a subject that is difficult to explore and murky with contradictions. Siblings may talk about it (and talk and talk about it) as a major factor in shaping their lives separately and together, but parents regard it as taboo, a topic they wish to avoid. Rarely does a mother or father say, "I favored Susan over Sally," and even less frequently will a parent state that both Susan and Sally suffered because of preferences shown.

Why this discrepancy between adult children and their parents?

First, because parents regard favoritism as something shameful—a failure on their part. "It's terrifying to think about," said a mother of four. "How can you acknowledge that you might not love all your children in the same way?"

More to the point, parents deny playing favorites in their families because often they truly are not aware of doing so. Few, if any, parents consciously and deliberately choose one child over another. Most do the best they can to deal well and fairly with their children and treat them according to their individual personalities and needs. But it is in the very context of that individual treatment that favoritism may rear its head, unrecognized by parents.

Of necessity parents behave differently toward each of their children. A six-month-old baby may require a great deal more of a mother's attention than does an eight-year-old child, and it would be appropriate for the mother to provide that attention. A colicky infant may demand more time and care than did his calmer older sister, and providing that time and care would also be appropriate.

Moreover, parents—all parents—react to children from within their own experiences. Their ages, financial resources, marital happiness, and other life circumstances shape their attitudes toward their children at any particular time, as discussed earlier. Their own natures also determine their responses to each child. A father may shy away from diapering and tending a young baby but fall head over heels in love with his three-year-old. Another father may become less demonstrative and more uncomfortable with a teenage daughter who has suddenly emerged into womanhood than he is with the ten-year-old who is still a happy-go-lucky little girl.

At different times in the history of any family, most parents feel closer to one child than to another or give one more attention than another. At different times they react more warmly to the traits of one child than to those of the next. The colicky baby turned adorable eleven-year-old, for instance, may find his parents more responsive than does his once-placid sister turned rebellious adolescent. The teenage daughter turned mature young adult may establish closer ties to her father than her younger sister who has now become the more threatening adolescent.

It is perfectly normal, natural, and appropriate for parents to have different feelings toward each of their children and to treat those children differently. The challenge they always face is to appreciate what is unique about each child, and to show that appreciation in a balanced way so that over the course of years all children feel equally loved and valued.

Parents fail in that challenge when the line between different treatment and preferential treatment becomes muddied, and without ever realizing it, they begin to slip from the one to the other.

Unintentionally on their part, the most achieving child, the most affectionate one, the firstborn or the last (some people say the one conceived during a session of great sex), the one most like or unlike a parent or relative can move from a position of equality with other children to one of receiving or seeming to receive special attention.

A successful surgeon says his success has come because he was named for an uncle—his grandmother's favorite son and also a surgeon—and was therefore treated as special from the moment of birth. Although his sister and brother have done well in life, neither, he maintains, has achieved as much as he because of the benefits accrued him on his uncle's account.

More usual as a key source of favoritism was the explanation given by a father, a warm, gregarious man, who more readily admitted showing his preferences than do most parents. "I tried hard to be evenhanded but I failed," he said apologetically. "It was a matter of temperament and compatibility. My younger daughter and I were so much more compatible. We just reacted well to each other. My older daughter played into all the things I don't approve of: negative feelings about herself, denigrations of others. Maybe those attitudes threaten my own positive views of myself and others, so I don't want to hear them. The result is I've never been able to get close to the older one, and I'm very sad about that."

The compatibility this man speaks of does not necessarily come from similarities between a parent and child. More significant is what psychiatrists Stella Chess and Alexander Thomas call the "goodness of fit" between them. That means that in temperament and personality the child is able to satisfy the parent's demands and expectations and the parent is able to react with empathy and understanding to the child. A high-strung child, for example, may have a better fit with a low-key parent who can calm the child down than with an excitable one. If, as in this man's family, the fit between one child and a parent is particularly good while another child seems always to rub the parent the wrong way, the "well-fitted" child may be headed toward the favoritism track.

This father raises another matter that can lead to partiality: the image parents have of themselves. Through her responses to her father the younger daughter reinforced the confident, warm image he likes to project of himself, whereas his older daughter's negative attitudes may have churned up self-doubts and insecurities that lie beneath that surface confidence and warmth. For other parents the child who differs most from them may become the best-loved because that child represents a hidden part of their identity, a secret longing that the parents have not been able to express: the staid, reserved parents who admire their wild, mischievous son best of all because he acts out their own deep-seated wishes to let go and run free—wishes they don't dare act on themselves.

Perhaps the most concealed source of favoritism for parents is their tendency to reenact their own childhood histories. A mother, eldest in her family, may identify closely with her eldest son. Because she may have hated having to care for her younger siblings, she may go out of her way to pamper her son and free him of all family responsibilities. Or, guilt-ridden because as eldest she had mistreated her younger sibs, she may baby and protect her youngest child and make greater demands on the eldest.

Often, too, a parent will repeat a pattern of favoritism that was ingrained in his or her own family life. A brilliant nuclear physicist described with sorrow how his parents had "shamelessly" favored him, causing enormous resentment in his younger brother and a dreadful relationship between the two men. The physicist had promised himself that he would never treat his own children in the same way. Yet now he finds himself doing the "exact same thing"—favoring his eldest son over his daughter.

"I can't seem to help myself," he said. "My son is me. I identify with him in every way, and I act toward him the way they acted toward me. I don't know how to behave differently."

While the preferred treatment of one child usually begins in childhood and may last through a parent's lifetime, it is not always that way. Some parents don't show preferences until their children reach adolescence, writes Terri Apter, author of a book about mothers and daughters. Because a mother usually considers an adolescent less vulnerable than a young child, she may become less careful at this time about suppressing her biases and less guilty about revealing them. In their study of adult siblings, Ross and Milgram found that some parental favoritism starts even later, in adult life, when one sibling overtakes another in achievement—getting a better job, a higher academic degree, or more recognition from the outside.

Along these lines, people describe changes in their parents' attitudes toward them or their siblings as they reach maturity. A woman who had always been the family favorite lost that status when she married a man her parents disapproved of. A man who decided to enter law school suddenly found himself showered with attention from his mother, who had little regard for the acting professions of his two older brothers. Often, one study showed, daughters rather than sons become preferred children in their parents' later years because they stay in closer touch and provide the most care and comfort (a change from earlier days, when the favoritism scales tend to tip toward sons).

Parents may not be aware of slipping from a normal course of treating children differently to giving one preferential treatment. But siblings —whether children, adolescents, or adults—are highly sensitive to such slips. And the more so because they pick up signals of favoritism not only from the way parents behave toward them but also from parental behavior toward their brothers and sisters. Young children monitor their parents' treatment of their siblings just as they monitor their own treatment, and that relationship of parent to sibs becomes as important as the relationship of parent to self. So even if a child feels admired and loved, the perception that another is admired and loved more can be devastating.

Sometimes those perceptions grow from concrete evidence: the daughter who, sorting out the belongings of a mother who has entered a nursing home, finds photos of her brother at different stages of life tucked into every purse; she finds no pictures of herself, although she had been devoted to her mother. ("It was," she says, "the most shocking thing that ever happened to me.") Or the son who overhears his mother respond to a question about how many children she has by saying, "I have a daughter. And then there's the boy." Despite her protests to the contrary, the response confirms for him forever, he says, his mother's preference for his sister.

More often, charges that parents favored one or another child grow from an accumulation of perceptions that have piled up over time rather than from specific incidents.

But how accurate are those perceptions? Shouldn't a distinction be made between what siblings *perceive* as favoritism and what parents *really* feel?

It is certainly true that what young children label favoritism may be far from the real thing. Children are quick to accuse parents of being unfair or playing favorites when they don't get what they want or are jealous of a brother or sister, and much of that kind of harassing can be dismissed out of hand.

Adult perceptions, however, can be another matter.

The questionnaire asked people who thought one or both parents had a favorite to identify that favorite. I wondered whether most respondents would choose a sibling as favorite, carrying over in that way their childhood jealousies and accusations against parents. Or would most choose themselves instead of another, as a kind of wishful thinking that they had won out no matter what? (I had seen that wishfulness in a woman who spent hours describing tearfully all the privileges her older sister had received, all the attention, all the praise from parents, and who ended almost pleadingly, "But underneath, I'm sure they liked me best. They must have. I'm so easy to get along with.")

Neither extreme occurred. The answers were remarkably balanced: nearly half the respondents who perceived favoritism in their families chose themselves and not a sib as the favorite of one or both their parents, and a slightly larger number regarded a sister or brother as the favorite.

Those balanced results and extensive conversations with siblings have led me to accept adult reports about favoritism. As I see it, when adult children, in looking back, speak of feeling favored or not favored in relation to brothers or sisters, or receiving or not receiving special attention, they are speaking not of momentary envy or anger but of perceptions that have existed over many years. Whatever the real feelings of parents, from their children's perspective, long-standing perceptions represent reality as the children experienced it. In terms of that reality, perceived favoritism and true favoritism cannot be teased apart.

Listen to the taped interview of a seventy-year-old mother and her forty-four-year-old daughter. During part of the interview the women speak about a second daughter, Tina, five years younger than her sister, who became, according to her mother, a "drifter" during the late sixties, and is still a "flower child," barely earning a living. As they discuss Tina, the mother's voice swells with feeling.

"Tina never got the warmth from you that she wanted," the mother says reproachfully. "She worshiped you, she imitated you, she followed you, and she didn't get warmth from you."

"Well, she certainly got it from *you*," the daughter answers sarcastically.

"She could never do things right," the mother continues. "You, you excelled at everything. You could go to the sky if you decided you wanted to. But she was shy and clumsy. She wasn't happy in school. She couldn't focus on things . . ."

"Are you still supporting her?" the daughter cuts in.

"We send her some money, and she picks up odd jobs here and there. She lives from hand to mouth. She has no relationships."

"She has a million people in her life. Did it ever occur to you that she wants to live the way she does? She has no responsibilities. She just has to say one word, and you're there with the money and food."

"Daddy grieves about her so much," the mother pushes on, ignoring the bitterness in her daughter's words. "She's so wounded. He cares about her more than about anything."

"Yeah," the daughter replies. "And where do I fit into this picture? I have no sense from either of you of your ever caring about anything *I've* done."

"Oh," the mother answers hurriedly, "but you don't know what I say to others."

"I don't care what you say to others!" The daughter is shouting now. "I have never experienced from you a sense of anything but criticism. I never get a feeling that you have any pride in what I do or who I am. All you ever do is sigh about Tina and tell me I should have been warmer to her."

Her mother sighs audibly. "I know," she says. Pause. Then, "But her life has been so hard."

From the mother's point of view, she has been protecting, not favoring, her younger, weaker daughter, knowing that the elder can take care of herself. From the elder's point of view, whatever her mother's motives, she has been given short shrift, has been less cared for, attended to, appreciated, favored. Her perceptions make up her reality. (Which leads to the thought, also, that if children repeatedly complain about favoritism or point with intensity to unfairness in the family, parents would do well not to dismiss those charges easily. Such persistent perceptions become psychological truths to children, part of the overall image of childhood they carry with them to adult life.)

Occasionally siblings in a family seem to have different perceptions of who is the favorite. I have interviewed brothers and sisters who each claimed to be the same parent's favorite, or who each maintained that the same parent favored the other. Such cases may truly reflect the sibs' different perceptions. They may also reflect a reluctance—usually because of guilt—to see oneself as favored, or a reluctance—usually because of rivalry—to concede that another had been chosen. All four Ginetti sisters, for example, declared themselves to be their father's favorite, each one proud to present herself as dearer to him than her sisters.

In some families, also, parents make a practice of telling each child individually that he or she is the favorite, hoping in that way to make each feel special. Sometimes that system works, but often when sibs compare notes later as adults, all feel they have been betrayed by parents who led them on but never meant what they said.

For Christina and Vivian, two sisters from Chicago, perceptions of having been favored or not have led to tortured accusations and counteraccusations, to denials, fights, and an inability to overcome barriers to friendship erected between them by parents now dead.

I met Christina first, after a lecture I gave in which I mentioned my research about adult siblings. She introduced herself, saying that she found the subject "fascinating" and would love to be part of my study. She was forty-seven years old, she told me, and her sister Vivian was four years younger. She hoped Vivian would agree to participate, but she couldn't be sure. She never knew how her sister would respond to any suggestions she made.

Next morning, Christina phoned to inform me that to her amazement Vivian had accepted the idea of being interviewed, but only on condition that what the sisters say be held in strictest confidence. I assured her that confidentiality was a basic premise of all interviews.

"But what Vivian wants," Christina persisted, "is your promise that we not even recognize each other in your book."

That condition, I told her, was more difficult to guarantee. Although I would disguise identities, both women would probably recognize elements in their life stories. But I would certainly not betray Vivian's trust if there were things she did not want me to reveal.

"I don't know what secrets she has," Christina said with a laugh. "A friend of mine thinks that it's not so much that Vivian doesn't want me to know what she says about me, but that she's afraid to know what I say about her."

With that beginning, I arranged to spend additional time in Chicago, and scheduled a series of separate meetings with Christina and Vivian, who consented, after all, to go ahead with the project.

As I rode up the elevator to Christina's twelfth-floor apartment in a high-rise building off Michigan Avenue, I reviewed in my mind—as I always do—the questions I would ask to get the interview moving. As I rode down two and a half hours later, I could not remember asking a single question I had planned. Christina had prepared herself thoroughly with family histories, genealogies, and interpretations of the sisters' ties to each other.

"My sister will tell you that I had an unnatural attachment to my mother and she to me," she began, almost as soon as we sat down, "but it's not true."

It was an opening worthy of her position as copywriter for a large advertising agency. She knew how to catch my attention and get to the heart of a message without wasting time. In fact everything about Christina suggested efficiency. Divorced more than ten years earlier, she lived alone in a meticulous modern apartment, where the pristine whiteness of the walls was relieved only by rays of sunlight flowing through glass terrace doors and tall windows. Dressed in a honey-colored tweed skirt and matching silk shirt, she managed to look stylish without being overly fashionable. She spoke quickly, her thoughts and words organized and precise.

Only one small flaw marred the overall picture of strength and control Christina projected: She had a slight lisp, a thickening of the letter *s*, noticeable especially because she referred often to Vivian not by name but as "my sister." The lisp made her somehow vulnerable— a chink in her armor—and somehow endearing.

"My parents were both Greek immigrants," she continued. "They went to live in a poor neighborhood on the South Side of Chicago because my father had some relatives there. But my mother was miserable. She came from a well-to-do family and had been highly educated and now she was living with my father's working-class relatives. Eventually my father developed a successful export business and their life improved, but I think Mother never really got over those years of poverty.

"I'm telling you this to explain Mother's feelings about me," Christina said, interrupting herself. She was not one to burden a narrative with extraneous thoughts. "When I was born I was the first thing in this strange country that she considered really hers, the only thing of her own that she could attach herself to separate from Father's family. It was four more years before my sister was born, and in those four years my mother became very close to me and I to her. My sister refuses to understand that. She's always resented and blamed me for being Mother's favorite."

Christina wanted to make absolutely clear to me that she had done nothing to win her mother away from her sister. She had simply been available to a lonely woman who needed her.

That said, she went into the kitchen to fetch the coffee and cookies she had prepared earlier. I glanced around the living room while I waited. On a light oak bookcase in one corner, I spotted several neatly arranged framed photos. One was of a man and woman and two others of the same woman taken at different times.

"That's a picture of my parents," Christina said, following my gaze as she entered the room. "My father died seven years ago, my mother" —her voice cracked slightly—"just nine months ago. Those two pictures are of her."

She put down the tray and carried the photos of her mother over to me. I was struck by how alike mother and daughter looked, both with straight, blunt-cut hair and dark, intelligent eyes.

"My sister has her own theory about why my mother was closer to me, or, in her terms, why Mother was not close to her," Christina said. "She thinks I don't know this, but she's hinted at it often enough that I know it very well." She sounded annoyed, both at the theory and at Vivian's failure to recognize how much Christina knew.

Vivian's theory was that their mother had favored Christina because of the strong resemblance between the two. She had felt cool toward Vivian because *she* resembled a sister whom the mother disliked. The sister, who had curly black hair and blue eyes—something of a rarity in a Greek family—had been regarded as the family beauty. Although pretty enough and an outstanding student, their mother had suffered by comparison.

"The truth is," said Christina forcefully, "the only similarity Vivian has to my aunt is the color of her eyes. God knows, she makes such a fuss over those blue eyes, but other than that she does *not* look like my aunt. It's ridiculous to think that her looks affected my mother's feelings for her."

Actually, Christina believed, Vivian greatly exaggerated her difficulties with their mother. The mother had been truly proud of Vivian, an architect, and had always urged friends to recommend her for design projects. But Vivian got little satisfaction out of that. All she ever noticed were her mother's criticisms.

"My mother would say, 'Vivian, I liked your hair better before you had it cut.' Or, 'I think you should buy a new coat; the one you're wearing looks draggy,' and Vivian would get hurt and angry. What she didn't recognize is that my mother used to say the same kinds of things to me. I just didn't let them bother me."

She didn't let them bother her, Christina explained, because she sympathized with the difficulties of her mother's life, something Vivian did not understand. To a great extent, their father caused those difficulties by being withdrawn and "closed off," interested only in his business. Old-world in his attitudes, he had not permitted Christina even to wear lipstick until the age of fifteen. Nor would he allow his wife to work when they were pressed for money. Later, when their situation improved and she longed to go to school and prepare for a career, he would not hear of it.

Ironically, after her husband died, Christina's mother took over his business and made it far more lucrative than he had ever dreamed possible. "She was a brilliant woman," Christina said, again with a catch in her voice. "My father didn't appreciate her and that's why she turned to me. I was her eldest daughter, so she confided in me." And she reiterated, "My sister is jealous of the closeness Mother and I had."

As we were ending our first meeting, Christina told me that her mother had left both daughters an equal and substantial amount of money in her will. They were cooperating in investing the money so that both could have financial security. Christina felt good about that cooperation. Yet, she said, her sister remains bitter. "She's still waiting for Mother to give her the love she wanted—the love she says I got, but that she will never get now that Mother is gone."

On my way to Vivian's brownstone apartment in Old Town, I reviewed in my mind what I had learned from Christina. She had given me a great deal of information about her parents and her sister and had presented herself as a victim of Vivian's jealousy and hurt feelings. But except for the quaver in her voice when she referred to her mother, she had revealed little of her own inner feelings. I determined to be more astute in questioning Vivian.

It was a concern I need not have had. If Christina had appeared all capability with just a touch of softness, Vivian wore her vulnerability on her brow, a mark of sensitivity and need. Cool and cautious at first, as our meeting progressed she spoke freely and cried openly, conveying the depth of hurt she felt. Oddly, she also conveyed a sense of inner strength she seemed unaware of herself.

If Vivian was vain about her eyes, as Christina had said, she had good reason to be. They were a remarkable iridescent, shimmery blue-green made even more prominent by the halo of curly gray hair that framed her face. Christina had not mentioned the prematurely gray hair, which I later learned was characteristic of their father's family. As she greeted me, Vivian showed me around her apartment, a third-floor walk-up, barely big enough for her and the husband she had married just a year before we met, after remaining single until the age of forty-two. An architect's table stood in a corner of the living room facing a cabinet covered with photos.

"Christina was quite artistic as a child," she said as I admired a picture of the sisters as young girls. "She used to draw beautifully, but she dropped it when I became interested."

Later she explained that from her vantage point, while her sister may have been afraid to compete with her in artistic skills, actually neither Christina nor their mother really valued anything Vivian did. True, her mother had promoted her work to family friends, but that was because she didn't believe Vivian could get clients on her own. She never regarded Vivian as really capable.

"In my mother's eyes," she said, "I was the lightweight, the feather-head who didn't know anything."

As she dug into her subject her voice became stringy with emotion. "I wasn't planning to tell you any of these things," she whispered at one point, "but it's all coming out."

What came out was a description, from childhood on, of a union between Christina and their mother that Vivian regarded as so tight that she could never squeeze through: "I felt my mother should never have had a second child. She was completely fulfilled with Christina; they had a totality and there was no room for me."

The "totality" showed itself in the mother's praise of Christina— " 'You look wonderful,' she would say to my sister, or 'What a delicious meal you cooked,' but I never heard from her in my whole life that I looked pretty, that my hair was nice, etc., etc."

It showed itself when, as youngsters, the girls accompanied their mother to the theater and "Christina talked and talked during intermission and Mother listened and listened and listened, and I would sit there completely ignored."

It showed itself, also, in the lack of seriousness with which mother and older daughter regarded Vivian—a complaint returned to again and again. "If I spoke about wanting to study literature or history, they laughed at me. I was the baby. Christina was the smart one, the funny one. Nothing I could do would impress them. I have carried that feeling of inadequacy with me all my life. I can sit with a prominent client and act professional, but inside I still feel like the baby, out of my depth, not good enough. I was like a Chinese woman whose feet had been bound—I had a mind that I was never encouraged to use."

Vivian's pain floated in the air like particles of dust, silently coating all her words. She described her mother as "tremendously needy" and demanding constant attention, a result not of her husband's neglect but of being outshone by her own sister. Christina provided that attention. She "adored" their mother and told her so, while Vivian, who also loved and needed her, did not know how to express her feelings so openly.

Vivian had not the slightest doubt either that her resemblance to her aunt influenced her mother's attitude toward her. "I'm not beautiful like my aunt, but I remind people of her and I reminded my mother of her," she said, as if the conclusions were obvious. "The way she treated me reflected that."

Her father, she claimed, balanced that treatment somewhat. Her description of him took me by surprise. Far from the distant, withdrawn man Christina had depicted, in Vivian's portrayal he was warm and affectionate, never too busy to give his daughter the praise she lacked from her mother. "When he saw that I felt left out because of my mother and sister, he would lean over and touch my arm," she said, smiling wistfully. "It meant so much to me."

During adolescence, Vivian admitted, she too found her father difficult and rigid. Nevertheless, in adult life they became close again. "I used to ask him to tell me about himself," she recalled. "We would stay up late into the night and talk about his dreams and plans. He never talked to anybody the way he talked to me."

I pointed out at that meeting and the next that when she spoke of her father, she often sobbed softly. Her tears, Vivian explained, were of a different order from the tears she shed in remembering her mother—"I'm sad, but I don't have pain when I think of him."

Vivian's pain at their mother's preference for Christina was palpable. I wondered how Christina felt about Vivian's closeness to their father. She had said nothing of that. Without revealing Vivian's description, I turned the conversation around to their father at my next meeting with Christina.

"I'm sure Vivian told you that she was our father's favorite child," she said, moments after we began speaking about him. "I meant to mention that to you." Again, I thought, here is Christina telling me what Vivian thinks. But what does Christina think?

"It's all nonsense, of course," she answered my unasked question. "Vivian was *not* my father's favorite child. My father *did not* have a favorite child. My sister has idealized that relationship. It's true she was close to him for a while in the years before he died, but she had a terrible time with him during her adolescence. I remember."

Christina was speaking more quickly than usual. For the first time I knew the heat of her feelings. Her lisp became more pronounced. She looked like a child in need of comfort.

"When I was very young," she said, "before Vivian was born and until she was just a few years old, my father adored me, indulged me, played with me all the time. I found a letter I wrote him when I was about six and he was away on business in which I said I couldn't wait to see him to tell him all the 'bad things Mommy did.' *He* was my love, not Mommy. A year later I was traumatized because he turned completely to my sister. My mother never made me feel rejected in that way, and maybe that's why I remained so attached to her."

She was crying now. "But you have to understand," she said. "Later he dropped Vivian also. My father was a man who enjoyed little children. As soon as we got older, he lost interest. Vivian doesn't want to face that, and, to be honest, it was harder for her. By the time he stopped paying attention to her, I was in a tight relationship with my mother. There was no room for her, and she had no place to turn. That's why she dwells on the little that she had with him."

Feeling sorry for herself for the loss of her father to her sister, Christina also felt sorry for her sister. Gradually the sympathy for Vivian turned again to frustrated anger:

"One of the biggest fights my sister and I have ever had was after our father died. I was broken up, and she said something to the effect of, 'Why are you crying so much; you weren't close to Daddy anyway.' I went crazy. I started yelling at her. I wanted to hit her, and almost did before our mother intervened."

I would not have thought Christina capable of losing so much control, but now I could see it. The touch of softness, the vulnerability I had sensed at our first meeting had broken through to expose the emotions beneath the cool exterior. As her anger faded she became sad and contemplative.

"Sometimes I think Vivian truly hates me," she said softly. "Her eyes, when she gets angry at me—it's like looking into a dragon's cave. I always feel guilty, although I didn't intentionally do anything bad to her, and I can't become the mother she feels I had but she didn't. Yet I'm not able to talk to her about any of it. As soon as we talk about the past, we begin fighting. After our last fight I made a rule. I said we have to stick to the present. It's a shame. She means a great deal to me, and we're cutting ourselves off from each other in a very important way."

Vivian expressed some of the same feelings at our next meeting. "My sister," she said, "is the only person who has been a continuum in my life, and we share a lot. But there are so many things we can't talk about." Later, trying to sum up her feelings, she said, "I love my sister and feel protective of her. If anyone hurt her or treated her rudely, I would be terribly upset. Still, I have tremendous resentment toward her about the past."

For both Christina and Vivian, perceptions of favoritism in the past continue to dominate the present. Whether their mother *really* favored Christina or their father *truly* favored Vivian matters little. Their reality has been formed around their perceptions, and that reality determines their views of themselves and each other. Vivian resents and suffers from what she sees as her own deprivation in the face of Christina's chosenness by their mother. Christina remains hurt and defensive, frustrated at being blamed for her favored status yet still basking in the special closeness she had with her mother. At the same time, although outraged at Vivian's claim to a preferred place in their father's heart, she suffers her own jealousy because deep within her she suspects that her sister may be right.

The reactions of Vivian and Christina exemplify those of many siblings who perceive favoritism in their families, even if their perceptions differ from those of their parents.

"If you think your father had a favorite son or daughter, or you were the favorite, how does this make you feel?" asked my survey, and the question was repeated for mother's favorite. The choices of response—and respondents could choose as many as they wished—were "resentful," "secure," "jealous," "guilty," "independent," "capable," "no effect."

The most important response for people who felt favored was "secure," checked by almost half the subjects (43 percent) who saw themselves as their father's favorite, and over a third (36 percent) who saw themselves as their mother's favorite. By contrast, only a minuscule number of people who viewed a brother or sister as favored indicated that they felt secure (4 percent in regard to fathers, 3 percent in regard to mothers).

Such a reaction is not unexpected. To feel favored by parents is to feel prized, protected, wrapped in a mantle of approval. The Bible—that sourcebook of sibling sagas—describes Joseph as the best loved of all Jacob's sons, the recipient from his father of a wonderful coat of many colors. In the security of his special position, Joseph has fantastic dreams of standing at the center of the universe with the sun, moon, and stars all bowing down to him. And that confidence continues throughout his life. Despite slavery, imprisonment, and other hardships, Joseph rises to become one of the great ministers of Egypt.

Of course, when favoritism is extreme, security can be accompanied by arrogance and feelings of entitlement. Joseph flaunted his dreams of glory before his brothers, insensitive to how furious that made them. Much later, as an Egyptian prince, he humiliated and punished them before revealing his true identity.

But the security of chosenness can also become a source of strength. From his position of favor in his family Freud once wrote, "A man who has been the indisputable favorite of his mother keeps for life the feeling of a conqueror, that confidence of success that often induces real success."

To feel that another has been chosen, however, can lead to insecurity and a sense of unworthiness, and these feelings, too, can spill over into many areas of life. Alfred Adler, who was *not* his mother's favorite, described that state of being. "Almost every discouragement in childhood," he wrote, "springs from the feeling that someone else is preferred. . . . It is not possible for a human being to bear without disgust and irritation the position of being put on a lower level than someone else."

Vivian fits Adler's description. An accomplished architect, she still sees herself as a "baby" when she meets with clients. No amount of success can erase her memories of being less favored than Christina or her resultant feeling of being "inadequate," not as good as her sister in her mother's eyes—and therefore her own.

Even more significant, to see someone else as a parent's favorite is to feel resentment—a deep, gnawing, and bitter anger at inequities suffered.

On the questionnaire, over a third of the respondents (36 percent) who perceived a brother or sister as their mother's favorite and a little less than a third (32 percent) who were not preferred by their fathers checked "resentful" as their reaction to their position.

Here is how one woman elaborated on "resentful":

"I resent my brother because my parents paid for his college education ('He has to support a family eventually'), while I had to work two jobs some summers and get a loan to pay for mine.

"I resent it that when he works around his house, my parents say, 'He's so smart, he can do anything.' When my husband and I installed a new hot water heater in our house, my father's reaction was, 'It's crazy to do those things yourself. Couldn't you afford to hire someone to do it?'

"I resent him because my mother is always telling my fourteen-year-old daughter and eleven-year-old son about *his* children and how great they are. . . .

"I don't know what kind of relationship my brother and I would have had if my parents hadn't favored him so much, but I'm sure it would have been a lot better."

This woman, like Christina and Vivian and many other people who feel a sibling has been favored over them, directs part of her resentment toward the parents who chose her brother, and an even larger measure toward the favored brother.

When I asked Vivian why she resented Christina for their mother's favoritism when, after all, Christina didn't make her mother choose her, she said simply, "She was in league with my mother." When I probed Christina's feelings about her father's closeness to Vivian, she said, "She was always ingratiating herself with him. She would pick up Greek phrases from him and repeat them, or walk around singing Greek ditties he had taught her."

It is far less threatening and more acceptable to one's security and self-image to accuse a sibling of currying favor or playing up to a parent than to face the idea that the parent simply selected that sibling, perhaps out of greater love or admiration. The blame comes also because by winning the parent, the sib has won the competition—the underlying, primitive, primal rivalry that goes back to the beginnings of sibling relationships. The price the winner pays for such triumph is the loser's resentment.

The practice of transferring anger from parents to siblings can be the most destructive part of the favoritism game, creating, as it has with Christina and Vivian, lifelong animosity and distrust among sibs. And sometimes more. In the biblical story, Joseph's brothers retaliate for their father's favoritism by selling Joseph into slavery. Skipping back a few generations before Joseph, Cain murders Abel, avenging himself against the brother whom God had favored.

The fact that one parent is partial to one child and the other parent to another, as in the case of Christina and Vivian, does not usually even the score or temper the resentment. Each child feels cheated by the nonfavoring parent. This is especially true when the parent the children regard as most dominant or closest to them, such as their mother for Christina and Vivian, favors another.

But there is a slight twist to the resentment reaction. A small percentage (13 percent in relation to father and 18 percent in relation to mother) who viewed themselves as *favored* also checked "resentful" as one of their responses. For them, resentment stems from the burdens that accompany the favored position.

A teacher explained it well. When he was about twelve years old, he said, a neighbor told him that everyone knew his mother favored him over his older sister and two younger brothers. He had not thought of himself as favored. What he knew was that his parents fought a lot and his mother confided her feelings to him more than to anybody in the family. By being his mother's confidant, he said, "I had found my own way of making my mother love me."

Over the years, and continuing to this day (he is now thirty-two years old), his mother found occasions to tell him openly of his favored position. But she attached some strings: Because she loves him best, he has the greatest capacity to hurt and disappoint her, and therefore the greatest responsibility *not* to hurt her. "Not hurting" means confiding in her more than he wishes to, phoning more frequently than he normally would, and generally trying to please her.

Such emotional blackmail, of course, is not restricted to parental choices for favoring. With or without favoritism, parents have been known to make their children feel that their love is conditional, to be withdrawn if the children do not meet the parents' demands or expectations. But the favoritism slant pulls the strings especially tight. "It's an untenable position," the teacher says. "I resent the responsibility she places on me and the fact that I can never get out from under. I like being favored—who doesn't? So I try to make her happy. But I'm constantly guilt-ridden for not living up to her expectations."

He also feels guilty, he explains, because his sister and brothers have always envied his special status, unaware of the burdens it carries. The guilt adds to his resentment.

"Guilty" is a reaction checked far more frequently on the questionnaire by people who regarded themselves as favored than by those who didn't (28 percent of those who considered themselves their mother's favorite feel guilty, for example, compared to only 6 percent of those who regard a sibling as the favorite).

Aside from the guilt of never pleasing parents enough, there is for the favored, says Dr. Neubauer, a kind of "survivor guilt" for having won out at the expense of others in the family. In the recesses of their hearts some chosen children believe the accusations leveled against them—that they have abetted the favoritism by their own activities. They suspect that they have betrayed their siblings by joining forces with their parents, even if unintentionally (and sometimes their behavior is intentional). Others, unsure of just why they have been chosen, feel a generalized guilt for whatever it is they may have done to beat out their sibs. The favored also feel guilty for enjoying their victory, a victory and an enjoyment they hold on to as tightly as they can despite their guilt.

Along with these reactions, there is a tendency—although the numbers are not great—for the favored to feel less independent, more dependent on parental approval, than the unfavored. Even without a manipulative parent like the teacher's mother, the favored children's desire to keep their chosen position can tie them more tightly into the family and make them less willing to take risks or fly on their own.

"You have to keep producing," is how one man described being favored. "There's an element in it of quid pro quo. They'll love you most but you have to perform. And since you've enjoyed the benefit of their approval, you live in fear that you may lose it." To which he later added, "I have spent my whole life needing approval, of my parents, my peers, everybody."

The favored may be less independent also in the sense that the guilt they feel toward their brothers and sisters gives those sibs a certain power over them. Christina described a time some years back when her sister and mother were not getting along at all. She was in a terrible position, she said, caught in the middle, unable to align with her sister for fear of losing her mother's love, and unable to defend her mother for fear of infuriating her sister. Feeling herself hurt by both mother and sister, Vivian was less trapped by the dilemma of trying to please both. And by having to cope with her mother's perceived rejection, she had developed a kind of inner strength and independence.

The unfavored child's edge on independence, of course, does not necessarily negate that child's need for parental approval. Shut out of the magic circle of chosenness, she or he may go through life hungrily seeking a parent's love and recognition, and the more unrequited, the more desperately sought after. Christina may not be off the mark when she says that Vivian is still waiting for their mother to give her the love she seeks and the love she can never get now that their mother is gone.

In the end, for both favored and unfavored, the losses favoritism imposes greatly outweigh the gains, and they can extend far beyond the family. Her experience with Vivian, Christina said, has made her more cautious with women friends than she would like to be. "I often get this feeling," she explained, "that, like Vivian, women who didn't get enough from their mothers are trying to turn me into their mother, so I break off before I become close to any of them. I don't want to be somebody's idealized mother. I don't want to have to make up, again and again, for the closeness I had to my mother that my sister didn't have."

Vivian also described difficulties with women friends. These she saw as resulting from the thick bond between Christina and their mother. Only after she became involved in the women's movement, she recalled, was she able to trust women without feeling they would ignore or turn against her.

Vivian speaks with particular unhappiness about the fact that she postponed marriage and family life because of her strained relationships with Christina and their mother. "I didn't make a conscious decision not to have children," she says. "But I used to think vaguely, 'If I had two daughters, I would kill myself.' I didn't want to repeat the difficulties that my mother had with her sister and that Christina and I have had." She now regrets the years gone by, and at the age of forty-three wants very much to become pregnant.

Most distressing for both Christina and Vivian are the continuous tensions that divide them. Their mother left her daughters a monetary inheritance from the family business that they have been able to invest cooperatively. But the legacy of pain, anger, resentment, and distrust family favoritism left has destroyed any real harmony between them.

In spite of the depth of hurt she has experienced, Vivian does not believe her mother intended to hurt her. Her own resemblance to her aunt and her mother's reliance on Christina acted together, she feels, to create an atmosphere of favoritism toward Christina. "If I had kidney failure and needed a kidney," she said, "I know my mother would not have hesitated for a moment to give me her kidney. All the things she did, the difference in the way she treated me and Christina—it was all on a very unconscious level."

On that unconscious level, parents slip from appropriately treating their children differently to treating one preferentially. On that unconscious level, some parents go much further, singling out one child to blame for all the problems and all the pain in the family.

CHAPTER EIGHT

The Scapegoat

SINGLED OUT FOR DISFAVOR

*I*n ancient times, the Bible relates, two goats were used as part of a ritual in which people atoned for their sins. One, chosen by lot from the two and known as the scapegoat, was symbolically laden with all the bad deeds and wrongdoings of the people and sent off into the wilderness. The other, the pure goat, was set aside as a special offering to the Lord.

In modern times, there exist families in which one child, like the scapegoat of old, is seen as the bearer of all bad deeds and wrongdoings. As a result, that child is picked on, blamed, and criticized by parents more often than their other children, and—while not sent off into the wilderness—treated as an outsider, more difficult and less easy to like than the others. Often that "bad" child is contrasted to a "good" one, who, like the pure goat, is regarded as special to parents and other family members. Like other roles children assume in the family, the roles of bad child and good one become implanted in their self-views and personalities.

The issue in such families is not favoritism but its opposite. Instead of being chosen for best treatment, the child (and often, later, the adult he or she becomes) is singled out for worst. Instead of arousing the envy of brothers and sisters, the way Vivian envies Christina's closeness to their mother, the disfavored child arouses the pity of siblings at some times, their protectiveness at others, but just as often

178

an animosity that equals the animosity of parents. And while a degree of favoritism seems to be part of normal family life for many siblings, disfavoring or scapegoating one child usually occurs in families in which overall relationships nudge past the borders of normalcy toward more troubled or disturbed ones.

When I began this project, I had intended to keep my focus directed only toward "normal" family relationships, but as my interviews grew, I realized how hazy the borders between normal and disturbed often are. It became clear that I needed to extend my investigation of sibling relations to include areas within those hazy borders that cropped up again and again.

Scapegoating is one of those areas. More often than I would have guessed, people spoke about the long-range effects of disfavoring and scapegoating in their families, either describing themselves as the victim or recognizing that a brother or sister had been assigned that role. And the effects they described could be far more malevolent than the consequences of favoritism. Roy Deveau, for example, the Dallas restaurant owner and gay activist, suffered terribly from the insults his father hurled at him during childhood. He did not simply feel less favored than his older brother Eddy; he felt unloved and unwanted. Still bitter about his treatment, he continues to long for recognition both from Eddy and the world at large.

More extreme was a description given by a journalist in Minneapolis about her father's behavior toward her older brother.

"He never criticized the deed," she said of the father, "he always criticized the boy. Sometimes, when I'm alone, I still hear the echoes of his voice shouting at my brother, 'You're a good-for-nothing.' "

Though she feels sorry for her brother, she sees little of him now because he keeps to himself, shut off from family and without friends. He has never had the confidence to marry or to hold a good job. When he speaks, which is rarely, he stutters and his voice is so low it can barely be heard, almost as if he wants to hide his very existence. The journalist attributes her own ability to succeed to the fact that as her father's "little girl" she was spared his barbs. Her success also comes, she is sure, from her decision as a teenager to leave home and turn to friends and other relatives for support lest her father's wrath fall on her one day.

Even when not that virulent, scapegoating can leave lifelong scars. A child can feel scapegoated by one parent or both, by siblings along with parents, or, occasionally, by siblings alone. When one parent badgers a child or constantly finds fault, the second may try to step in to offer protection. But even that protection cannot undo the anguish of a child who suffers the dislike of a mother or father. And in many cases, the second parent feels helpless to change the situation or remains passive and withdrawn, keeping marital peace by leaving spouse and child to fight their own battles. It helped Roy Deveau to know that his mother cared about him, but her caring could not make up for his father's nastiness.

Siblings may also feel powerless to help a sister or brother who is picked on by a parent. In fact, they may regard the "bad" sibling as an example to be avoided and keep their distance, afraid themselves of losing status in the eyes of the parent, or worse—like the journalist—becoming the next victim. Younger siblings, especially, feel helpless and fearful for their own safety when an older sib is oppressed. Older siblings are more likely to help younger ones, but they often do so by secretly providing comfort and sympathy rather than confronting a parent openly. Eddy Deveau did save Roy by serving as a buffer between him and their father, and Roy is forever grateful. But even Eddy, Roy said, got some satisfaction from not being the butt of his father's anger, and he did not seriously take on his protective role until later in life.

The first question that arises about families in which a child is made to feel disliked or rejected is, why? What makes parents, who for the most part truly care about their children and want to do what is best, behave in ways that can only hurt them? What leads a mother or father to set one child apart, not in such commonplace roles as the "brain" or the "beauty," the "scholar" or the "athlete," but in the role of difficult child or bad one, troublemaker or good-for-nothing?

On the most immediate level, the causes for scapegoating may seem simple, not that different from the various reasons parents favor one child over another. Gender bias is one such cause. Unknowingly, the journalist's father may have seen his son as a competitor or threat to himself, whereas his daughter, his "little girl," posed no challenge to him. Disappointment in a child's abilities or achievements is another, major cause. Parents who put great stock in school achievement, athletics, or even appearances may rebuff the child who does not meet their expectations, while adoring the one who does. Roy Deveau's father hated it that his younger son was a "sissy," uninterested in athletics, and devoted to the arts and music, for which neither father nor older brother had any regard.

Most important, on this level, is a basic incompatibility between parent and child, a "mismatch" of temperaments and personality. Norman Maclean describes such a mismatch in the novella "A River Runs Through It," a memoir about his younger brother Paul. Their Presbyterian minister father, explains Maclean, had strict ideas about how children were to be reared, and was enraged because his stubborn youngest son refused to eat oatmeal for breakfast.

"My mother and I watched horrified morning after morning," he writes, "while the Scottish minister tried to make his small child eat oatmeal. My father was also horrified—at first because a child of his own bowels would not eat God's oats, and, as the days went on, because his wee child proved tougher than he was. As the minister raged, the child bowed his head over the food and folded his hands as if his father were saying grace. . . . The hotter my father got, the colder the porridge. . . ."

For a parent like this who expects authority and control, his child's stubbornness and rebelliousness may be so irritating that he finally sees and treats the child as a problem. Although in his story Maclean describes his father as loving and sympathetic to both his sons, the younger son later became an alcoholic and part of the criminal world. It would be simplistic to link the adult behavior directly to the breakfast table scene. But in many cases, when that type of incompatibility exists between parent and child, the child eventually turns away from the family toward a destiny of his own.

It is worth mentioning, although it is far from universal practice, that among some ethnic groups parents may tend to view their children moralistically from birth, splitting them into the good and the bad or the strong and the weak, and then treating them according to their appointed roles. Writing about Irish-American families, therapist Monica McGoldrick describes a mother who always referred to her children as "my Denny, poor Betty, and that Kathleen," slotting them into places she had set for them. And sure enough, "that Kathleen" managed well to fit the bill of the troublesome child.

But most often, when parents persistently target one child for complaints or even excessively worry about that child, the immediate causes mask deeper underlying ones that are closely tied to family or personal issues.

Family therapists describe families as systems, organisms, in which each member, or part, works in tandem with every other one. In this way of thinking, family relationships follow patterns of behavior of which the individual participants are unaware. Within those patterns, whatever affects one member of a family affects all others, and a member who is regarded as a problem may actually *reflect* a problem in the larger family system. Often that problem is a marital one that the partners are not willing or able to acknowledge. By designating one child as troubled or difficult, they may, without awareness, be using that child to deflect the difficulties between them.

Here is how the system might work: Betty and Bob have a school-age son and a younger daughter. For several years Betty has been disappointed in Bob, who, she feels, has not advanced fast or far enough within the hierarchy of his electronics company. She accuses him of being lazy and berates him whenever a coworker moves ahead. He responds by withdrawing and becoming emotionally unavailable. Recently Betty has begun to be concerned that their son Bill, now in third grade, is also "lazy" as well as "sloppy" about his schoolwork. She talks to Bob about the boy, and both parents begin to pressure Bill to be more diligent. The greater the pressure they exert, though, the more defiant Bill becomes. Soon husband and wife join forces in viewing Bill as a problem child, disobedient and difficult to manage, especially compared to his sweet, compliant little sister. Over time, Bill gains a reputation as the black sheep in the family, sullen and stubborn at home and disruptive at school.

As Bill's difficulties escalate, Bob and Betty become a team, devoted parents deeply concerned about their son. Betty stops criticizing Bob, and he communicates freely with her about his disappointment in Bill. Together they have established a myth—were it not for the distress Bill causes them, they would have a perfect, conflict-free marriage.

In family systems terms, without realizing it, Bob and Betty have used Bill as a scapegoat in order to deny or bury their marital problems. For his part, and without being aware of doing so, Bill has colluded with them in becoming the family problem. Through his negative behavior, he has kept their marriage intact.

There are a variety of issues around which parents might single out one child for scapegoating within the family system. A problem child may be a cover for a parent's alcohol or drug abuse, for example. Or, the emotions aroused by that child can provide a degree of excitement to a dull, lifeless marriage. In every situation, as the family dance gets under way, all parties—parents, siblings, and scapegoated child—find their places and follow the steps that will push the real family difficulties underground.

Family systems theory offers one way of examining the dark, underlying causes of scapegoating. Another way is to look at the parents as individuals who may unconsciously displace their own internal conflicts onto one child. (Displacement is a psychological mechanism whereby people transfer unpleasant emotions away from the source of the emotions toward others. The man who kicks his dog after his boss yells at him is displacing his anger at the boss onto a safer target.)

To take Roy Deveau as an example again: While his differences from his brother made him an easy scapegoat for his father, the scapegoating can be seen also as growing from the elder Deveau's personal struggles. Angry at himself for failing to keep the family ranch going, he eased some of his self-blame by directing his rage toward the son who did not resemble him and taking pleasure in the son who did. Furthermore, at the worst time in his career, when he could barely provide for his family, his wife supplied needed income by working as a cook. Because her earnings were essential for survival, he could not express his shame and his resentment of her, so he channeled those feelings toward his younger son. Roy became the victim of his father's bitterness and sense of failure.

Among the most destructive feelings parents displace onto a child are hatred, fear, or envy of a relative from the past. Most destructive because these feelings can be searingly intense, yet their roots are so deep that parents rarely have any awareness of these associations. In the same vein, parents often project images of their own parents, grandparents, or other relatives onto a child, viewing that child as if she or he *were* that person. For example, a parent may name a child after a despised relative in the unconscious, magical hope that somehow the child will make up for all the unpleasantness associated with that relative. But cast in the shadow of the disliked relative, the child is treated badly, and hence starts out with little chance of succeeding.

Of the many images parents project onto their children, they are most likely to identify a son or daughter with their own brothers or sisters of the same sex or birth positions. And just as they may reenact their sibling experience by favoring a son or daughter who parallels them in birth order, they may reenact that experience by showing disapproval of one particular child. Vivian, in the last chapter, who felt her mother loved her less than her older sister, insisted that much of the unequal treatment came from the fact that she resembled an aunt whom her mother disliked. Without ever realizing it, said Vivian, her mother was treating her as though she were that aunt.

It's not unusual either, when parents connect a child to one of their own siblings, for them to hurl at that child the hidden fury or resentment that they had never dared reveal, thus using the child as an unconscious means of settling old scores.

A woman who sought counseling after the birth of her second son explained to the therapist that she had been "divinely happy" after her first son was born. The second, however, left her so cold that she came dangerously close to neglecting him completely. What emerged from her therapy was a recognition that as a middle child of ten, she had always longed to be an only child with easy access to her parents and no siblings in the way. In symbolic terms she saw herself in her first son and saw her second son as crowding him (herself) out, just as her siblings had crowded her. By neglecting him she was wishing away his existence.

Children who are treated as though they were their parents' disliked siblings, as well as children who are scapegoated for other reasons, often *become* the very beings they have been designated to be—mischief makers and black sheep in childhood and angry, wounded, or disturbed adolescents and adults. (That is, if they are not entirely crushed by the treatment, like the brother of the journalist mentioned above, who is passive and dead inside, unable to form any connections to others. Or unless they fall into that small group known as resilient children. These are children who seem to overcome even the most horrendous family upbringings and come out strong and whole, either because they are temperamentally tougher than others or because, like the journalist herself, they are able to find other people to shelter them.)

Strange as it may seem, children comply with those images because they recognize the need their parents have to see them in a certain light. By conforming to that need, they can please parents—albeit in a twisted way—and shore up their own sense of security. Stated in reverse: *Not* complying can be for a child too risky, too dangerous, too confusing as a way of life, even if complying means distorting oneself to fit parental molds. In the family systems framework, for example, a scapegoated child unconsciously collaborates with parents in burying the tensions within their marriage because the anxiety of a marital breakup may be even more unbearable to the child than following the script parents have devised.

Similarly, children have a need to believe that their parents are good and will always take care of them. As painful as it may be for them to take the blame for problems on themselves, that route is safer and less threatening than one that allows them to think that the parents on whom they utterly depend are really the bad or difficult ones, uncaring or disturbed.

Children also conform to the roles parents assign them, as negative as those roles may be, because the views parents hold of them shape their views of themselves. In her large-scale studies of young siblings in Cambridge, England, for example, Judy Dunn has found that the differences school-age children perceive in the ways their parents treat them make a marked difference in the children's sense of self-worth. Those children who perceive themselves as being treated worse than others in the family have the lowest self-esteem. So when a parent acts toward a child as if she were worthless, it's easy for the child (and later the adult) to think of herself as worthless.

From a different vantage point, children live up to their assigned role as the black sheep because the role carries benefits of its own. It can be exciting to be the nonconforming child, set apart from siblings and the center of everyone's concern. Labeled bad or troublesome, children who feel deprived of love and care discover that the more trouble they get into, the more notice they get; so the more notice they get, the more trouble they create.

And then, paradoxically, along with the "rewards" a scapegoated child receives, the child also suffers intense rage and frustration brought on by the constant criticisms of parents and siblings. Maintaining the role of bad child, especially during adolescence, can be a way of expressing that rage and frustration, of flinging back at family members the very accusations they make, of showing them that you can go them one better.

Natalie, a twenty-seven-year-old stenographer, described herself as always having been seen as the bad one in her family because she was outspoken and independent compared with her more conforming older sister and babied younger brother. During her teen years, as fights with her parents escalated, her mother accused her of being, among other things, "cold-hearted" and "devious." She responded by living out her mother's accusations. She grew distant from the family and "went underground" in her activities. She drank more than she should, chose friends—especially boyfriends—whom she knew her parents would dislike, and took off on car trips without giving anyone a clue as to where she was and when she would return.

The constant comparisons her parents made between her and her sister added to her determination to be "bad," Natalie says—one final and significant reason why children live up to their negative images. As with the Platt brothers in Chapter One, and many other siblings, the characteristics of one tend to prod the other toward the opposite pole. When one child is constantly touted as good, "bad" may seem the only place left for the other. Her sister, says Natalie, appeared to her for years as a "pillar of all the shoulds in my life, of all the right ways to do things." The more obedient she perceived that sister to be, the more rebellious did Natalie become; the closer the sister to their parents, the more withdrawn Natalie.

Like the scapegoats, who incorporate their negative labels into their sense of self, their opposites also incorporate labels, in their case positive ones. And one way the good ones keep their positive identity is by staying close to parents, as Natalie's sister did. Schachter and Stone, who studied siblings as opposites, point out that excessively favored children—the "angels" of the family—tend to cling to parents as a way of protecting themselves and establishing their difference from those seen as excessively bad—the "devils." Observing children in a clinical setting, they found that the angry and frustrated devil siblings would pester their angel sibs. Instead of standing up for themselves or fighting back, the angels would appeal for help to their parents, who would rush in to protect them. These behaviors not only reinforced the children's views of themselves and each other as bad and good, they prevented the children from ever learning how to settle their own differences, as do sibs in typical families.

But the good siblings themselves do not get off scot-free. Like the pure goat in ancient rituals, they too become sacrifices to the family system and their parents' internal needs. By being responsible and well behaved, they validate the parents' own goodness and skills. Clearly, their behavior seems to say, there is nothing wrong with parents who can produce a child as virtuous as this. Invested with their parents' idealized image of them, the good children must constantly live up to the role assigned them. In that way they can both retain their status and reinforce their parents' self-concept.

A woman in her fifties whose sister was written off by her parents years earlier as "wild" and "uncontrollable" wondered out loud whether her parents ever realized the costs she had borne. To remain the good one in the family, she'd had to spend her life catering to their needs. "Did it ever occur to them that I should have a real childhood? That someone should take care of *my* needs?" she asked angrily. Similarly, Natalie described her sister as miserable in an unhappy marriage but afraid to leave because it would upset her parents. "I think my sister is far more trapped than I," she said. "She's always *had* to be good, and she's just beginning to understand that."

Natalie expressed a "terrible sadness" over the fact that even now, as an adult, she "does not share a life" with her sister because of their polarization. Recently, as her sister has begun to recognize that in having to be good, she too was a scapegoat of sorts, they have become somewhat closer. They are more fortunate than many other siblings in similar situations, for whom the effects of scapegoating are never undone. The hurt and bitterness of the disfavored child and the demands made on the good one remain enduring burdens.

Of the several families I met burdened in this way, the Dorman family of New Jersey stands out for its extremes in scapegoating one child and idealizing another. These extremes have stretched across two generations of adults. Though their story is one of excess, it highlights elements found in more moderate families in which children have also been split into the roles of good and bad.

I speak of the family, yet the mother, the person responsible for much of the family drama, is dead now. The story came to me from the father and two of his daughters. The third daughter—the eldest, the one who suffered most—has cut herself off from her sisters and refuses to discuss her life.

It was Patty, the middle daughter, who first sketched the family history for me. She had contacted me after a talk I gave at a local community center because she wondered if I had ever encountered a family like hers. At that moment, she and her older sister, Meredith, had stopped speaking to each other, after years of an on-again, off-again relationship—"mostly off," she said with a half laugh. She understood that her sister's life had been difficult, but enough was enough, and she was not going to spend *her* life being blamed for everything that had happened in the past. The break was something of a tragedy, she allowed, especially since her mother had not spoken to her own three sisters for twenty-three years, finally reconciling with two of them shortly before her death. One of those sisters, Patty's youngest aunt, had pleaded with Patty not to fall into the same situation.

"She said, 'Don't do this, you don't know how terrible it is,' " Patty related. "I told her I understand. I do and I hate it, but too much has gone on for us ever to get together again."

Patty gave me the phone number of her youngest sister, Vicki, who lives in Mexico, suggesting that although Vicki had removed herself from much of the commotion in the family by moving away years earlier, she might have something to contribute. But the person from whom I could learn most, she advised, was her father. Following that advice, I called him first and set a date to meet.

In her early forties, trim, with long dark hair and green eyes, Patty is strikingly attractive, so I wasn't surprised when I met Lew Dorman, a man in his late sixties, to find him ruggedly handsome. He brimmed with excitement. He had never met a writer before, let alone been interviewed by one, and he could hardly wait to get started. A retired electrician, he had time on his hands and a penchant for talking. The first time he came to my office, I was in the process of moving. Cartons lined the hallway, and boxes of books were stacked to the ceiling. None of that did he notice. He sat down on the only available chair, pulled it up close to my desk, and proceeded to talk. Four hours later, as he prepared to leave, he took out his pocket calendar and suggested that we meet again in two days.

He was in particularly good spirits at that initial meeting. For the first time since his wife had died a year earlier, he had become emotionally involved with a woman. In fact, he had spent the night with her, and was as pleased with himself as a teenage boy after his first sexual conquest. Prouder, because he could make comparisons, and was not above doing so.

"I have to be honest," he said, "my wife was never affectionate with me the way this lady is. My wife—her name was Honey—was the first woman I ever touched in my life. We were married forty-five years, and I didn't know anything else. Now I meet this lady and she's so lovable. I think I've had more love from her in these two weeks than I ever had in my life."

"It sounds as though your wife was not a very warm woman," I commented in my best noncommittal interviewer's tone. Not that I wasn't tempted to pursue the story of his marriage, but I had already written a book about long marriages, and I was eager to get to the subject at hand. "How was she with your daughters?"

"This will tell you how." He leaned back, folded his hands behind his neck and shook his head. "When our first daughter, Meredith, got married, my wife refused to be in the ceremony. I walked Meredith down the aisle, and my other two girls were bridesmaids. The groom's father was his best man and his mother walked with an usher. But Honey, she just walked in with the guests and sat in the back as if she hardly knew the bride. To hate, to hate your own child! It was a terrible thing."

"Did she really hate Meredith?"

"She certainly acted as if she did. She used to beat her, scream at her. The scenes were terrible." He stared at me, itching to tell the family story, yet telling it as if it had nothing to do with him personally.

"How did she treat your other two daughters?"

"You've met Patty, so you know what a doll she is." He beamed as I nodded in agreement. "Honey loved her. She's easy to love."

"And Vicki?" I asked.

"She was tough, a very, very tough little cookie," he began, and elaborated, "and extremely clever. Great little girl. She knew her own mind and she kept out of her sister's fights. At eighteen, she got married and left us. Moved to Mexico with that husband of hers. I never liked him much, and they're divorced now. But she's stayed down there with her daughters." When I spoke to her by phone later, Vicki told me that she couldn't wait to get out of the house, away from "the yelling and screaming that went on between Mom and Meredith."

"What was it about Meredith that made your wife treat her the way she did?" I probed Mr. Dorman.

"It was her oldest sister who turned my wife against her own daughter," he replied. "Four years older than Honey, but she got married five years later than we did and she was always jealous of us. Her husband's a fireman who never paid any attention to her. I was real good to Honey, and I made more money than any of her sisters' husbands. Did I tell you, Honey also had two younger sisters? Anything the older one told them to do, they did. All of them. Anyway, the older one, she had three daughters, just like we did. But they were wild, always in trouble, so she was also jealous of our kids, and especially of my first, Meredith, 'cause she's such a beauty."

The jealousy angle was confirmed by both Patty and Vicki. "My aunts were all jealous because Mom was the first to marry and she wasn't the oldest," Patty explained. "Then she had Meredith, who was a gorgeous baby, and that bugged them even more." At one of our meetings, Patty showed me some photos of Meredith as a baby, a teenager, and an adult. She was and is indeed "gorgeous," displaying an almost ethereal beauty reminiscent of portraits of Renaissance women, with their high foreheads and translucent complexions.

"She's the prettiest one in the family," Patty said generously, "and my aunts couldn't stand it. There was always fighting between her and them, especially my oldest aunt. My parents should have told them to mind their own business, but they didn't."

Why the father didn't protect his daughter is a matter I saved for later. Why the mother, Honey, not only did not protect her daughter but joined her sisters in attacking her was the issue I pursued first. What I learned from Meredith's father and her two sisters was a strange tale of domination, hatred, and rage displaced.

The domination came from Honey's oldest sister, Ray, who, as Lew Dorman had said, controlled all three of her younger sibs. Their father, a gambler and drinker, had deserted the family when the sisters were children. Their mother, "a real old-fashioned fat little Polish lady" (in the words of her son-in-law), was always ill or complaining about being ill, leaving family affairs to Ray. She ruled the home with an iron hand, keeping her sisters in line with verbal and sometimes physical abuse. The younger daughters feared and obeyed her without question.

Her older sister continued to dominate Honey's life even after she married. "Any time we had a decision to make, she'd start telling me what her sister Ray thought," recalled Mr. Dorman. "I'd say, 'I'm your husband. Why do you always take her word over mine?' And she'd say, 'Because blood is thicker than water.'" Ray's interference accelerated with Meredith's birth. Still unmarried herself, she could find no good qualities in Honey's daughter. Under her influence the younger sisters joined in criticizing the baby and continued throughout her childhood.

Instead of defending her daughter or, as Patty said, telling her sisters to mind their own business, Honey not only allowed them to behave as they did but went beyond them herself.

"Oh, Honey was hard on Meredith," Mr. Dorman said several times, adding once or twice, "I never laid a hand on my children. She tried to get me to hit Meredith when I'd get home from work, but I wouldn't do it because I knew she was getting enough of it. And I imagine if I did, it would have been child abuse all around, because my wife was really rough on her."

"It was a very bad scene," Patty said. "Sometimes my mother would scream at my sister so loudly my father would shout, 'Stop screaming, the windows are open.' But nothing stopped her."

When I questioned Vicki about those scenes during one of our phone conversations, she said she could not really explain them. "My father writes the whole business off as my aunt's doing," she said, "but I think there must have been more to it. My mother was always harping on how stubborn and willful Meredith was. I don't know if this makes sense, but I used to feel there was some kind of competition there, as if Mom thought Meredith was trying to take her place in the family."

Not close to her mother herself, Vicki said, still she had never been attacked the way Meredith was. And Patty, of course, was "Miss Wonderful" to her mother, a standing both Vicki and Meredith resented.

Patty was everything her older sister was not in her mother's eyes, Lew Dorman confirmed: gentle, malleable, loving, devoted. She also knew how to handle her mother—"yessing her to death to get on her good side." But there was more to it than that. He, too, saw her as the best of his three daughters. You could talk to her, he said, and "always get something good out of it."

Still, in one of our later meetings, Mr. Dorman expressed some doubts about his favorite daughter.

"I've been thinking about Patty and Meredith," he said. "Vicki was too young to get involved, but what about Patty? Why didn't she ever do anything to help her sister? When Meredith got married, Patty said she was glad to get rid of her. Here her mother was beating her older sister all the time and Patty didn't even feel sorry for her."

(If he felt sorry for his daughter himself, he did little to show it. "He was around but not present," Vicki said of him, "stepping in once in a while, but stepping out again just as quickly." Each time I asked him why that was so, he evaded a direct answer. "There wasn't much I could do because my wife was home all day with the girls," he would say. "I worked night and day until I was fifty years old and they were grown up. What could I do? Divorce her? Throw her out of the house? Pull her by the hair? I wasn't like that. I felt things always weathered. Somehow they would work out.")

"As far as I'm concerned," Patty replied when I asked about her role in the fights between her mother and her sister, "I don't think there's anything I could have done, but to be honest, I didn't try. I didn't say to myself, 'God, I'm glad it's not me.' But it also wasn't a situation where I could say, 'Mom, why are you doing this?' The years just went by and there was always this bad blood between my mother, her older sister, and her firstborn daughter. As my sister got older and stronger and smarter, it became two women at each other all the time."

Things might have remained that way forever had Meredith not married. She was twenty at the time. She had dropped out of high school three years earlier and was earning a good living as a model in a large department store. "She could have supported herself," said Patty, "but in spite of everything that went on, she never ran away from home. She lived there until the day she got married."

That day became a turning point in Honey's life. She had refused to be included in the wedding ceremony, using as her reason Meredith's coldness to her aunts, Honey's sisters, especially their exclusion from prewedding parties. During the wedding festivities, Meredith ignored them, enraging them more than ever. "It was a mess," Patty recalled, "a huge, monstrous, ugly wedding, with my sister cutting my aunts, my mother furious at my sister as usual, and my oldest aunt, Ray, telling my other aunts not to speak to my mother because of Meredith's attitude toward them."

For several weeks after the wedding, the aunts, led by Ray, did speak to Honey—but only to berate her for her daughter's bad behavior. Perhaps it was the irony of being attacked by her sisters after she had deprived herself of participation in her daughter's wedding ceremony because of them, or perhaps she had just had enough. Whatever the reason, for the first time in her life Honey took a stand against her older sister. And what a stand it was:

"Ray," she said one day, "stay out of my house and out of my life. I want nothing more to do with you."

According to Lew Dorman, the migraines and backaches his wife had suffered for more than twenty years vanished the day she stood up to her older sister. For the next twenty-three years, Honey did not speak to any of her three sisters, for once she broke with the older one, the two youngers followed suit.

When Honey became ill with leukemia, a niece—daughter of one of the sisters—insisted that her mother establish contact again. Over the course of the next year, after almost a quarter century of mutual silence, Honey settled her quarrels with her two younger sisters. Although Ray, the oldest, tried also to reconnect, Honey would not budge. The day before she died, Ray pleaded to be able to see her, but Honey refused. And Lew Dorman would not allow her to attend her sister's funeral.

After Meredith married, she and her mother made peace of sorts, though they did not see a great deal of each other. Continuing the pattern they had adopted toward Meredith, the Dormans intensely disliked her husband, Charles, a clothing buyer she had met when she worked as a model. "A little Napoleon," Lew Dorman calls him. "He's short, and he struts around, putting on airs like he's a big shot." (By contrast, Patty's husband, Victor, a chiropractor, is "the greatest, a wonderful human being. I could live in the same home with him and be very happy.")

Nevertheless, when her mother became ill, Meredith devoted herself to the older woman, giving up days and many nights to be at the hospital with her. Since Honey's death, Meredith, according to her father, "runs up to the cemetery all the time looking for her mother. She spends hours at the graveside."

Now, however, the conflict has shifted, as Patty reported when we first met, and centers on Meredith and her. The two had drawn closer during their mother's illness. With Vicki away, they shared the burden of caring for her. But as Honey's strength ebbed, Meredith began insisting that the family take her home to die instead of keeping her in the hospital. When her father refused, she accused him of not caring enough about his wife and urged Patty to join her in pressuring him. "She began calling my father all sorts of names," Patty recalled. "I said to her, 'What good is this doing? It won't make Mom better.' "

Once Honey died, Meredith turned her anger away from her father to her sister. She blamed Patty for inciting their parents against her husband. She implied that the years of disagreement she had had with her mother had really been instigated by Patty, who had not once come to her defense. Patty responded by accusing Meredith's husband Charles of turning his wife against her family. Charles, in turn, joined the fray by forbidding Meredith from having any further association with her sister or brother-in-law, a ruling Meredith gladly accepted.

"They will probably have nothing to do with each other again until I become sick or die," said their father sadly. "Then they may come together for a little while, but it won't last. Too much has happened."

Patty agrees. "Meredith will probably move to California or someplace else far away from us, and that will be that. I'm sorry we could not have had a more natural relationship, but I can't be held accountable for all the problems in her life."

That, then, is the family story Lew Dorman and his daughters Patty and Vicki told me. Now I would like to retell it with the aim of interpreting the scapegoating of one daughter and idealization of another that it embodies.

Honey Dorman, dead now of leukemia, came from a home ruled by her oldest sister Ray, who had taken firm hold after their father abandoned their mother. Greatly dependent on Ray and in need of her approval, Honey also burned with fury at her domination, suffering internally with migraines and backaches. Caught in that double bind of dependency and rage, she was unable to stand up for herself against her sister. She even accepted, without protesting, Ray's mistreatment of her own daughter, Meredith.

At the same time, Honey may have unconsciously identified Meredith, who was her eldest daughter, with her eldest sister. (In Vicki's version of the family history, Honey thought Meredith was trying to replace her and take control of the family, much as Ray had controlled their original family.) That identification would have reinforced her treatment of Meredith as her scapegoat onto whom she displaced all the unspoken wrath she felt toward Ray.

Patty, a middle daughter like Honey, became the angel child. Easy-tempered and happy to placate Honey, Patty served as a symbol of her mothering capability. The troubles in the family, Patty's presence proclaimed, came from Meredith and her aunts and not from her mother. Patty's good nature and winning ways also reflected well on her father, and he, too, favored her, although he had some reservations about her behavior toward Meredith.

Lew Dorman did little himself to protect his eldest daughter from his wife's abuse. It's possible—using family systems theory—that the constant fighting between his wife and daughter served his own need to mask the emotional impoverishment of his marriage. As long as the family problem centered around Meredith and Honey, neither parent had to focus on their marital relationship. Mr. Dorman may also have felt helpless and overwhelmed by the turmoil in his home. It was easier to stand aside and convince himself that things would "weather" than to enter the fray by trying to help Meredith.

The drama took a different turn after Meredith married and left home. Without the availability of a convenient outlet, the rage within Honey could no longer be contained. It burst through in a major explosion some weeks after Meredith's wedding, freeing Honey to break, finally, with her sister.

Honey's story is filled with noise and tumult; Meredith's with sadness. She was so hurt and beaten down, so much in need of love and security that, like many abused children, she did not have the strength or self-esteem to disentangle herself from her mother. As much as she suffered from the yelling and fighting, at least she had some contact with Honey, at least she was noticed, even if only through denigration. Because of that contact and notice, Meredith chose to live at home until she married, though she could have supported herself away from her parents.

Meredith found some respite from her family life after her marriage. But when her mother became ill, she rushed to the older woman's bedside, and since her death, she—more than either of her sisters or her father—has tended the grave. That behavior, too, is a common response to a parent's death when a child has felt rejected. It reflects a yearning for the affection of the rejecting parent that can never be satisfied. That yearning may continue for years after a parent dies, living on as a futile fantasy that if the parent could see the child's dedication and loyalty, the longed-for acceptance and approval would be forthcoming.

Meredith's accusations against Patty fit the pattern of a scapegoated child as well. Just as Vivian blames Christina for being favored, children like Meredith who feel unloved accuse the most loved child of instigating their parents against them. Even as adults, these people find the notion that a parent truly did not love them too painful, impossible to accept. It is far more tolerable to place the blame for their mistreatment on a sibling.

The recriminations of a disfavored sibling bring a great deal of suffering and guilt to the "good" children like Patty. But they also arouse their anger and exasperation at being falsely accused and laden with the baggage of family discord.

I heard that mixture of feelings expressed most clearly by two other sisters, each one convinced of her absolute rightness. These women, in their thirties, are the daughters of a Russian immigrant father who, during the years of rigid communist rule in the Soviet Union, suffered terribly in a Siberian prison. The older daughter described his ruthlessness toward her. He found fault with everything she did and slapped her around with little provocation. For no reason that she could see, he treated her younger sister with love and kindness, as though she were a precious possession. The woman says that now, as an adult, she can find it in her heart to forgive her father because of his personal history of torture and suffering. She can never forgive her younger sister for not intervening to stop their father's cruelty.

"What could I have done?" the younger cries. "I was a child myself, and terrified of my father. How could I have protected her?"

"She should have found a way," the other insists. "There are children who would have found a way. There are children who have a moral center. She did not. She is immoral. She relished her role as the goody-goody and played up to him all the time."

"I have anguished over this," says the younger. "Did I get some pleasure out of seeing my father beat my sister, knowing that he loved me? Could I have done more to help her? By the time I might have been old enough to do anything for her, my sister had left home. It's getting harder and harder for me to be friendly toward her when I feel that she hates me and I can do nothing right."

"I don't hate her. I think she's immoral. She abandoned me when I needed her," the older persists.

Over the course of years, feelings may harden on both sides: the rage and resentment of disfavored children toward their more fortunate siblings, and the irritation and anger of the "good" ones, erasing all sympathy for the victimized. Long after parents are gone, the misery and strife caused by scapegoating can continue to divide a family, in some cases—as in the Dorman clan—for generations.

We usually think of scapegoating as something only a parent does to a child, the parent being all-powerful and the child weak and dependent. But there is another type of scapegoating that sometimes occurs in families, again pitting the strong against the weak. That is scapegoating by siblings of one another. It can happen between two siblings when jealousy and competition stretch beyond normal rivalry and one relentlessly bullies the other. In large families, scapegoating occurs when two or more siblings gang up on another.

In any family's life, of course, siblings do join forces to exclude one or another of them, negotiating alliances and shifting allegiances as events and situations change. But to speak of scapegoating is to speak of a persistent combining against one sibling, persistent badgering and hectoring and jeering until the victim feels excluded from what family therapists like to call the "sibling subsystem." In adult life, the impact on the scapegoat's self-esteem and attitudes can be as severe as any caused by rejecting parents.

Envy of a favored sibling is probably the most blatant reason why siblings will line up against one of their own, determined to "get back" at the favored for privileges enjoyed. Parental disfavoring of one child, as we've seen, can also cause sibs to turn away from that brother or sister. In some instances the sibs not only do not protect a scapegoated child from the wrath of parents, they join in the attacks. Like Cinderella's stepsisters, who gloried as much as her stepmother in overworking and underfeeding the beautiful child, they bolster their own sense of security by allying themselves with their parents. A child who becomes scapegoated by brothers or sisters in this way may, in turn, reject everybody else in the family. The child may insult and provoke siblings, pushing them further and further away (while desperately wanting their love and support) until they withdraw completely, leaving the scapegoat isolated, an outcast.

Such outcasts may break completely with their brothers and sisters as they get older. Or they may become troubled adolescents and adults, true "black sheep" who continue to nag their siblings for money and support, or to bully them, because this is the only means they know to get what they want. (Or if by some rare stroke of luck they have been able to find love and security away from home, like Cinderella they may float into a future a great deal happier than their past.)

Other motives of brothers and sisters who turn against one sib usually have to do with that sib's differentness. The difference may be one of gender—the only boy in a family of girls, for instance—or appearance, ability, temperament, age: whatever it is that sets the child apart. The scapegoating usually takes the form of bossiness, derision, name-calling, or labeling. (Little Dumbkin, in another fairy tale, was the third son of a king, and got his nickname from his clever brothers because he was simple and didn't talk much. But ah, in the wonderful world of fairy tales, Dumbkin outsmarts the others and wins the crown. This is not the usual fate for the scapegoated other.) The more insecure the other siblings, and the more jealous or threatened they feel by the sib who is different, the worse their behavior.

Twenty-one-year-old Heather, a professional ice skater, suffered the scapegoating of her two older brothers, Gavin, twenty-six, and Brian, twenty-four, because of her differences from them.

Gavin works for a large entertainment agency, in which he represents beginners in theater and movies, and Brian works as a sales representative for a computer software company. Shortly before I met her, Heather had been discharged from a hospital where she had been treated for a severe case of anorexia nervosa, the eating disorder in which a patient (usually a girl or young woman) who sees herself as fat refuses to eat, losing weight until she endangers her own life.

About five feet six, Heather had weighed seventy-five pounds when she was admitted to the hospital, cajoled into going by the combined efforts of parents, brothers, and skating coach. Still quite thin at ninety-five pounds when we met, she continued to gain some weight and appeared to feel better over the course of our month-long meetings. The turning point in her illness had come, she said, when her older brother Gavin had apologized for the cruelty with which he had always treated her.

From Heather, her brothers, and her parents, the story that emerged about the years leading up to her illness was of a close-knit family with caring parents who had been unaware of the profound effect their sons had on their daughter. As the only girl in the family, Heather had been both babied and teased mercilessly by her brothers, especially during her teen years, when she began to devote almost every free hour to practicing her ice skating. Aside from her skating prowess, there was something about Heather that set her apart from the others and lent itself to their harassment—a sensitivity, a curiosity that looked beyond superficialities, an interest in exploring feelings that other family members preferred to push aside.

Gavin started criticizing and bossing Heather at a young age, escalating his tactics over time. Her hair, her clothes, her friends, her eating habits all became grist for his mill. The criticism had intensified in recent years, as he began struggling to establish a career in the competitive entertainment field and she began earning public recognition for her skating. "He would shout at me about my practicing," Heather recalled, "as if I were committing some crime. The best thing he called me was 'stupid.' "

Brian, always less sure of himself, bolstered his own confidence by joining in Gavin's attacks or making a point of ignoring Heather's achievements.

Because skating required Heather to watch her weight, and because the activity itself kept her trim, no one in the family paid serious attention to her increasingly obsessive dieting. But in the year before her hospitalization, the weight loss became extreme, and she was diagnosed as being anorectic.

As an illness, anorexia expresses many underlying needs of a patient. One of them, and this was the case with Heather, is a need to gain some kind of control over one's life. Unable to stand up for herself with her brothers, and too emotionally beaten down by them to complain to her parents, Heather depended on her illness as her only form of self-assertion. She, and nobody else, could be in charge of her own body, even if it meant almost destroying that body.

Along with a regimen of learning to eat again, hospital treatment for Heather included family therapy sessions, some with siblings alone and some with parents and siblings. It took her brothers months to recognize their role in her illness and, having recognized it, to try to make amends. "The day Gavin looked at me in front of the whole family and said, 'I'm sorry for what I've done to you,'" Heather recounted, "was the day I knew everything would be all right for me and for them."

Scapegoating is one of the darker sides of family life for siblings, and one that usually requires professional help to undo. Unfortunately there are other dark times in the lives of sisters and brothers that go unattended and with which adult siblings must struggle to come to terms. Among them is a family history that included—and may still include—alcoholism, drugs, or other hidden and painful family secrets.

CHAPTER NINE

Family Secrets

ALCOHOL, DRUGS, AND SIBLING INCEST

"*I* know you've got a secret," a character says in the chilling play *Buried Child* by Sam Shepard, "You've all got a secret. It's so secret in fact, you're all convinced it never happened."

This family's gruesome secret is that buried in a field behind their house lie the remains of a baby boy born after three other sons in the family were already grown. As the play develops, the full horror of the secret is revealed: The father, Dodge, had murdered the baby whom he believed his wife had conceived by another man. "We had enough boys already," he mutters, drunk from alcohol and the power of the act he had committed.

But even as the secret is being made known, one brother shouts, "No! Don't listen to him. . . ." And the mother cries, "I'm not listening to this! I don't have to listen to this!"

So it is in many homes with long-held secrets. The secrets lie buried beneath the surface, known on some level by family members, yet rarely acknowledged openly, and if acknowledged, quickly pushed away, so secret that everybody acts as if the events never happened. There are, of course, harmless and humorous family secrets, bits of history that become incorporated into family lore—an elopement, a family feud generations earlier, the shady career of some distant ancestor. But many other secrets eat away at family life, insidiously spreading their malignancies until no member is left untouched.

A woman described being her mother's confidante as a child. What

199

that meant was that while her two older brothers were sheltered from hearing of their parents' marital troubles, by the age of thirteen this woman knew that the marriage was terrible. The other secret she knew that her brothers and father did not was that her mother had been involved in an affair that stretched on for years. Her mother died some ten years ago, and her father is old and ill. Her brothers carry around with them the myth of their parents' perfect, idyllic marriage. Yet they themselves have had great difficulties in forming close relationships. One brother, struggling now through divorce, is wrenched with guilt, feeling he has betrayed his parents by failing at marriage. And the woman is wrenched between wanting to tell the truth so that there is finally honesty in the family, and fearing to tell the truth lest her brothers turn against her for destroying their mythic view of their parents.

A man recalled the "weirdness" in his home during his childhood because his father had a disability that nobody was allowed to mention. "One of his hands was shriveled and he limped," the man said, "but if any of us kids asked about it, my parents treated us as if we had committed a grave sin. We all learned not to talk about it, even to each other, and to act as if there were nothing wrong. One of the things that has happened to me because of my father is that I don't trust my own perceptions. I'm never sure what's real and what isn't. Besides that, the cloud of mystery that still hangs over our heads has made us wonder what else our parents hid from us."

Another man spoke of more devastating secrets—a mother's mental illness and later her suicide, neither ever acknowledged until a daughter followed the same path in adult life. Still another is tormented because he didn't know, but suspects that somehow he did know, that his sister had been raped by an uncle when she was about ten years old and from then on had been treated as something of an outcast in his Arab-American family.

It would be nice to be able to report that when sibs have lived together under a veil of secrecy or when they have suffered together from hidden, dreadful conflicts in their family, they grow up close and supportive of one another. In fact, some do. Feeling themselves "alone together in the storm," as a woman with an abusive father wrote on the questionnaire about her sister and herself, they sustain and encourage each other. In adult life such siblings usually remain close, drawn together by a shared history of troubles.

More often, however, the troubles are not truly shared. In a home shrouded in secrecy and distrust, siblings often live in distrustful isolation from one another. The woman who has borne within her the secret of her mother's long-term extramarital affair says that the secret continues to divide her from her brothers. As long as she is not able to be honest with them, she relates to them only on the most superficial of levels. Ironically, the habit of hiding realities, donned long ago to protect her mother and hold the family together, has now become the source of family separateness.

The more disturbed a family, the more likely are the children within it to insulate themselves emotionally, each finding a separate corner in which to curl up, heads down, hands over ears, cut off from one another and the outside. Like survivors of a catastrophe, these siblings become survivors, too, looking out for themselves, getting by as best they can, using their energies to manage day-to-day living, with little left over for one another. Even when they do offer each other support, that support is usually incomplete, based on too much domination by one sibling or too much dependency by another. And all the while, on that level just below the surface, lies the relentless, twisted knot of secrets.

Of the many kinds of secrets that worm away at the guts of a family, probably the most widespread is the secret of alcoholism. In my survey, people listed the alcohol and drug abuse of parents or siblings as among the leading problems that confronted them. There has been, in fact, a great deal of attention paid over the last decade or so to the special problems of adult children of alcoholics (ACOA), making their concerns the focus of a network of support groups that provide help and understanding. As usual, with all that has been written and said, there have been few studies and little published about sibling interactions among this group of adult children.

What have been described—too patly, I believe—are some of the roles children of alcoholics take on in their homes while they are growing up. Too patly because the roles have been given names, and the names crop up again and again in writings by support organizations and family therapists, as though all alcoholic families were the same and every child in every one of these families could be neatly pegged into a specific slot. It's more correct to see these roles not as universal truths but as examples of the way children in alcoholic families may react to the turmoil surrounding them.

It's also more accurate—and this is the piece that is most frequently forgotten—to recognize that siblings in disturbed families, like those in healthy families, assume roles not only in reaction to parents, but also very much in reaction to *each other*. The roles give children an identity in the family distinct from any one else, and in the midst of chaos and conflict, a place that is their own, even if it's a negative place.

What *is* different about the roles children in alcoholic families carve out (and those in other troubled families as well) is their greater rigidity and unchangeableness. Whereas other siblings have the capacity to reverse roles with each other, to crawl into each other's skins and discover their alikenesses, these children may remain boxed into the positions they began with throughout life. For them, the security and control they gain from their roles are too important to give up. Scarred as adults by what they suffered as children, they continue to cling to the self-definitions that served them well when all around them was confusion. The roles also serve a purpose for the family as a whole, making it doubly difficult for any individual to shed them.

In many disturbed families, as we've seen, one child may be designated the scapegoat, victim of parental and sibling unhappiness. When alcoholism is the family problem, the child's difficulties or bad behavior serve to hide the devastation of a father or mother's drinking. Often the scapegoated child identifies with the alcoholic parent and also abuses alcohol or drugs. Then all the anger in the family gets directed to that child, and the myth is established that he or she, and not the parent, is the source of everyone's misery.

Standing in contrast to the scapegoat, as we've also seen, is the good child, the one parents love most. In alcoholic families, this child (whom alcoholism literature labels the "hero") is usually the one who achieves most—in school, athletics, music, or whatever the child's abilities and the family values call for. By achieving, the child makes the family look good to itself and the outside world. And with that achievement, the child secretly hopes that he or she can also bring an end to the shame of drinking and the conflicts that go with it.

As adults, these achieving children may feel driven to succeed, needing to hold tight to the image of themselves as different from their parents and siblings, as winners instead of losers. Because of the intensity of that need, they may become overbearing with others, brooking no criticism, determined to control and direct not only their own lives but those of everyone around them, making up—as it were—for the control over their lives they lacked as children.

When these family achievers are the eldest or one of the eldest, they usually also assume responsibility for younger brothers and sisters, a burden that can be overwhelming.

"Our mother was an alcoholic while we were growing up," wrote a thirty-seven-year-old office administrator on the questionnaire. "I took on major responsibility for raising my younger sister and younger brother and running the household. Once I was out of the house, I wanted nothing to do with the role of mother again. I cannot imagine that I will ever want to have children of my own." On another section of the questionnaire, which asked about problems with sibs, the administrator complained that to this day in any quarrel in the family, her mother places all her expectations for making things work on this older daughter, instead of "expecting three adult children to work on their own difficulties."

The expectations and responsibilities may cause deep resentment in the responsible brother or sister toward younger or more dependent sibs. The resentment, in turn, may lead to rigid disciplining of the others, so that while younger sibs get help and support from an older one, they also feel frustrated in their need for love.

The responsible brother or sister suffers different kinds of frustrations from siblings. A child who truly wishes to protect other siblings —to be their "guardian angel" in a terrible family situation—may sacrifice personal goals for the goals of the others. And because the others see that child as a parentlike figure, they take the nurturing and care for granted even when overdisciplined. Rarely do other siblings realize how much a caretaking child has sacrificed, or how desperately that child, too, needs succor and support. Well into adult life, the responsible sibling may continue to protect brothers or sisters but get little protection in return.

The frustrations of family life in alcoholic homes take their toll on other children in still different ways. Instead of assuming the extremes of bad or good child, some children simply give up, coping with their lives by *not* coping, by keeping out of everyone's way and remaining as inconspicuous as possible.

In families of more than two siblings, such a child (labeled the "lost child") is often in the middle, caught between an achieving older—or a maligned, scapegoated one—and a babied younger. Like other middle children, they need to function as both an older and a younger sibling within their family. But unlike other middles, they cannot rely on parents to help them. Left to their own devices, they often withdraw, building a thick wall around themselves to block out family pain. Such children may grow up to be shy and passive adults, lonely shadows crouching in the background of life.

The youngest children in alcoholic families tend to be less passive and more demanding of protection and support. Similar to youngests in healthy families in that they have been more sheltered than others,

these children may find themselves cut off from knowledge of the
dark undercurrents of family life even while they suffer their reper-
cussions.

"The three older kids were forbidden by my mom from telling me
about family secrets—the extent of alcoholism, violence, and mental
illness," wrote a thirty-one-year-old systems analyst. "My brother
committed suicide, but nobody had let me know how ill he was. His
death torments me still."

Aware of family misery but unable to understand it, the youngest or
most dependent children may be tense and anxious, wanting to love
and be loved. They may also become family clowns, the "cute" ones
who defuse conflict by making others laugh. Such children will continue to feel dependent as adults, sometimes marrying people who,
like their older sibs, can provide the strength they lack.

As I said, the inclination of therapists and support groups to cate-
gorize children of alcoholics and label them in terms of roles does not
mean, of course, that in every alcoholic or disturbed family, siblings
play out roles in exactly the same way. Siblings may find other niches
for themselves—as Mom's pal or Dad's caregiver, as rebel or "kook"
or conscience of the family. Or the roles may be less defined, with
more overlapping between one and the other. Furthermore, the gender of the children and the gender of the alcoholic parent have a great
deal to do with the parts the children play and their relations to each
other.

Daughters of alcoholic fathers, for example, like many daughters,
may cherish within themselves the belief that they are their dad's
favorite. But for them, that belief usually brings with it the vain hope
of rescuing their fathers from addiction. In that hope they feel superior to their mothers, whom they see as ineffectual for not having
stopped their husbands' drinking. To make up for their mothers'
weaknesses, these daughters serve as mothers to their fathers, both
nurturing them and attempting to control their alcoholism.

Eldest daughters in particular assume responsibility for their fathers' well-being along with responsibility for their younger siblings.
But that very closeness makes them susceptible to extra pain—the
pain of being forever manipulated by an alcoholic father and the much
greater pain of possible abuse by him, both physical and sexual.

Obviously, a father need not be an alcoholic to sexually abuse a
daughter. Men who are violent with their wives can be violent with
their daughters. Men who feel sexually inadequate and have a need to
prove themselves or assert their power also may become incestuous
with their daughters. Nor are all alcoholic fathers sexually abusive

toward their daughters. But such abuse occurs often enough among men who are heavy drinkers to say that their daughters are particularly vulnerable to it.

When a father does have incest with his daughter, she finds herself in a dreadful trap. Profoundly shamed, yet fearful of revealing her secret lest her father hurt her, she rarely tells even a sibling what is happening. Sometimes an older sister hopes that by continuing an incestuous relationship with her father, she can protect her younger sister from the same fate. More often, she is too ashamed and too locked into the mutual secret to reveal it to anyone within or outside the family.

Although eldest daughters are most at risk in regard to a father's sexual advances because they mature first, younger daughters can be in danger too. A girl with an older sister may feel a special seductiveness in being chosen by her father and sharing secrets with him that her sister does not know. Or, perceiving herself unprotected by her mother or older sister, she may feel she has no way out of the situation.

The sense of being unprotected when a father is alcoholic—not only against sexual abuse, but in all the ways parents should protect their children—makes some daughters feel more angry at their fathers than nurturing of them, more bitter than solicitous. These daughters often turn their backs on their fathers and leave home as soon as possible. They may keep in touch with their siblings, and even provide financial aid to the family if they can. But to the extent that they are able to, they try to put the horrors of their family history behind them.

When a mother is the alcoholic, a daughter is more likely to remain trapped in the family morass, especially if she is the eldest. With her mother inaccessible, such a daughter truly takes over family life, becoming "wife" to her father and mother to her siblings. In Freudian terms we might say that she has won the Oedipal struggle by winning her father away from her mother. Indeed, women who substitute for their alcoholic mothers describe getting some secret satisfaction out of being able to show their father and siblings how much more capable they are than their mothers. Three times in the course of an interview, a businesswoman whose mother drank heavily pointed to a photo of her and her sister taken when she was twelve and her sister eight. "Look how my sister is leaning her head on my breast," she said each time, "like mother and daughter. I was her mother for years, and I still am."

But a daughter's victory over an alcoholic mother is a hollow one.

Nurturing as she is, she may become embroiled in competition with her siblings for their father's attentions or for control over the household. More significant, like the others, she suffers the anguish of not having a mother to love and guide her.

Sons of alcoholic parents suffer their own anguish. A boy who has an alcoholic father may become a scapegoat for his elder's inadequacies. The father sees the son as a competitor and denigrates him for being the "good boy" the father is not. Yet the father also expects the son to achieve and present a healthy front to the outside, so he becomes furious at any sign of weakness or failure the son might show. Eldest sons, like eldest daughters, usually become family caretakers, providing support for both their mothers and their younger siblings even as they struggle within themselves with the burden of disdain and disgust they feel for their fathers.

Sons feel disgust also for an alcoholic mother. Such mothers often abuse their sons emotionally (there is less threat of sexual abuse, although that possibility always exists). Angry at their husbands, they turn their wrath against their sons, the easier and more available targets. A mother heavy with drink may belittle her son, making him feel inadequate as a son and a man. If there are no sisters in a family to provide some mothering, boys deprived of their mother's love may become deeply depressed and enraged at their rejecting mother. If there is more than one son, the brothers may band together to protect themselves from their mother. But just as often, they become increasingly rivalrous and angry with each other as each tries to eke out some semblance of mothering.

Whether a mother drinks or a father, or both, the anger brothers and sisters in disturbed homes often have toward each other is one more factor impairing closeness and mutual aid.

The anger stems from more than rivalry. It is a child's reaction to a parent's betrayal. A sibling who has been cared for by a brother or sister instead of a parent may be grateful, but he or she will always feel deprived and incomplete, never having received the full measure of adult affection and support that are a child's due. As is so often the case, it is easier for the child to displace onto a sibling the anger and resentment felt toward the parent. The businesswoman above who showed me the picture of her sister leaning on her breast spoke with irritation about the constant quarrels she and her sister have. "She never dealt with her rage at our mother," she said. "Instead she takes out that rage on me because I filled in for my mother."

The parenting sibling, like this woman, has anger and resentments in turn. As an adult, that child may feel guilty for not having given the other sufficient care and attention, yet enraged for being made to feel guilty about circumstances others have created. And this child, too, feels cheated, as do all children in alcoholic families, by parents who behave like children themselves while their children take on the role of parents.

I would not really use the word "resentful" to describe the feelings of Carolyn Pamela Mason Jennings, whom everyone calls Pam, toward her younger sister. Nor would I use the word "rage" to characterize that sister, Abigail Claire Mason Young, whom everybody calls Gail. But I would say that both feel hurt and cheated from having grown up in the home of a hard-drinking, hard-fighting father and stepmother. I would also say that both carry within them a profound sadness, and with it an unfulfilled longing for closeness that is overlaid with unrelieved guilt toward each other.

To watch these women together, however, is to see none of that. Six years apart in age—Pam is fifty-eight and Gail fifty-two—they could be mistaken for twins. Both are tall and thin, with sandy-colored hair—Pam's mixed with thick streaks of gray—and strong, straightforward features, the kind one associates with early American colonists and upright Puritans. Indeed, the sisters are descendants of Mayflower settlers on their mother's side and grew up in the New England home that belonged to their great-grandfather. Both speak slowly and thoughtfully, although Gail's words are spiced with a dry, acerbic wit, whereas Pam appears to be more open and easy in her manner. Most striking, each sister treats the other with a grace and cordiality that belie the complexity of their underlying emotions.

I first met the sisters together at the home of a mutual friend in Newport, Rhode Island, where Gail lives, and where I was visiting during a brief summer vacation. Pam and her husband Stephen, a naval officer, were vacationing also, the first trip north they had made in years from their condominium in Florida. I was struck by similarities, not only in the sisters but in their husbands as well. Stephen and Gail's husband, Richard, looked and sounded as much alike as did Gail and Pam. Physically, the sisters agreed, both men resembled their father somewhat, but unlike him, neither drank. The sisters had managed to avoid the trap so many adult children of alcoholics fall into of marrying alcoholics themselves—but not completely. Both men come from families of heavy drinkers ("more alcoholics than you can shake a stick at" is how Gail put it) and had themselves joined Al-Anon, the support group for relatives of alcoholics.

Each sister, I learned at that first meeting, has a son and a daughter. Pam carries a special burden—her son is retarded. Refusing to institutionalize him, she and her husband have cared for him at home since birth. It's care that Gail characterizes as "heroic," and about which Pam says simply she "feels good." Pam's daughter, just a year younger than her brother, is studying to be a nurse, with a special interest in mental retardation. Gail describes her children—her daughter who works for a town planning agency and her son who teaches in a local college—as "straight arrows," but she worries that the bad "family blood" will one day cause havoc in their lives.

The "bad blood" in their family, the sisters told me, was all on their father's side. Their mother, the "blueblood," had shocked her family by marrying a man of Scottish-Irish ancestry. So carried away had she been by his good nature and boisterous enthusiasm that within three weeks of meeting him, she had wed him. Her parents had reluctantly accepted him into the family, and shortly thereafter the couple had moved in with them in their home in Cape Cod, Massachusetts. The father owned and managed a real estate firm, and—not without misgivings—took his son-in-law into his business.

Although the couple had planned to make a home of their own as soon as they could, the years went by and they never moved out of the Cape Cod family house. When Pam was ten and Gail four, their mother died. Their grandfather died soon thereafter, and the girls and their father remained in the same home with their grandmother. By then their father had become a heavy drinker. He neglected the family business, and he and his daughters lived mainly off his mother-in-law's inheritance. Then, two years after his wife's death, he remarried —a woman half his age but easily his equal in drinking—and the new wife, Trudy, joined the family in the grandmother's house.

As long as their grandmother was alive, Pam and Gail had a protector. When she died a few years after her husband, an aunt took some interest in the girls, but for the most part they were left in the care of their father and stepmother.

That much of their story I heard from the sisters on the night we met. They were equally forthcoming in describing their background and equally agreeable to being interviewed separately. I worried secretly about whether I would learn anything more from those interviews; they had been so controlled in presenting their family history, like a team of reporters concerned only with facts.

I was dead wrong. Alone, each woman's objectivity vanished, like veiling that has been thrust aside, revealing beneath a layer of raw, pock-marked, unpolished emotion.

In Gail the emotion was kept taut, in tight check, yet all the more powerful for her guardedness. As we spoke on her screened-in porch —she stretched out on a wicker sofa, I seated on a nearby chair—she frequently put her hand in front of her mouth, rubbing her lips as she thought and at the same time smothering some of her words. It was a gesture that seemed to symbolize ambivalence, both about reaching into the pain of the past and exposing that pain to others. The facts had surely been easier to present.

Hers was the pain of a lost child—not the stereotypical lost child of alcoholism literature but a child for whom love was lost before it was fully experienced. Although Pam told me she has memories of her mother holding her and singing to her, Gail, so young at the time of the death, remembers almost nothing. "Just a hazy image of lace and softness, and even that is pretty shaky," she explained, shrugging as though it didn't matter to her whether her memories were real or not. I wondered to myself how many hours and hours she had spent trying to recapture even those wisps of motherly images.

About her father Gail was more definitive: She had loved him, drinking and all. And she had felt loved by him, drinking and all. "He was a gentle, kind New England gentleman except for the alcohol," she said. It was a description from which she would never waver even as her narrative painted a very different portrait.

The alcohol took over his life, like a devil determined to rule, especially on weekends. Their mother, Pam had told Gail, had been able to keep him "on the straight and narrow" to some extent. But with their stepmother, come Friday evenings he would go at the bottle with a vengeance, and the house would reverberate with loud laughter, fighting, and—eventually—screaming invectives.

"My friends wouldn't come near our house on weekends," Gail said. "I was too embarrassed." (Pam elaborated on this when we spoke: "You do all the things that children of alcoholics do. You don't go home. You don't want your friends to meet your father. You think nobody knows, and of course everybody in town knew.")

Summertimes the scene would shift to a small cottage the couple owned overlooking the bay. After her grandmother died, Gail was often alone with them there, her sister managing to visit friends or find odd jobs at resort hotels on the Cape.

The drinking was somewhat more contained during the week because Trudy ran a small mail-order business and needed to have her wits about her at work. She was a smart, tough businesswoman who cared a great deal about money and not at all about her stepdaughters. "Oh, she was cold," Gail said, "she never gave Pam or me any kind of love or attention. I guess she couldn't neglect us completely because people would have noticed. But she just had no interest in us."

As she spoke about her stepmother, Gail wrapped her arms around herself as though she still physically felt the coldness of Trudy's presence. Later she told me that after the sisters had left home, they had lost touch with Trudy for years. Some seven years ago, they heard that she died. Drank herself to death, folks said. "My reaction," said Gail, "was just relief. It still astounds me that I could be forty-five years old, with a successful marriage and two children, and still feel scared of this woman. I don't even know what I was scared of, but as long as she was alive, I felt unsafe."

In the chaos of Gail's life, it was Pam who provided some modicum of normalcy. As older sisters in disturbed families often do, she became a substitute mother to Gail to the extent that she was able to. "She offered me companionship," Gail recalled, "her own and that of others. She watered the social roots my mother had established. Because she was friendly with the children of my mother's friends, she saw to it that I had a social entrée. That kind of thing is terribly important in a small town. It determines how your life is shaped as long as you live there."

Even more important in shaping Gail's life, Pam introduced her to reading and through that to the world of the imagination, far from the sordidness of her existence. "In the absence of family life," Gail said, "books become your companions. Pam provided that for me, and gave me a lifelong love of literature. I'll always be grateful for that." Pam later confirmed her role with pride. "I remember reading to Gail in bed before she was a very big girl. We read *Heidi* and other classics," she recounted. "I've always hoped those are pleasant memories for her."

As pleasant as those memories might be, for both sisters they are overshadowed, always, by the harsher side of their existence.

"Pam suffered more than I did," Gail said softly after we'd spoken for some time.

"Why do you say that?"

"Because she was older and much more aware than I of whatever was happening. She was twelve when Daddy married Trudy. I was only six and never sure of what was going on. During those early, stormy years of that marriage she was much more exposed to everything. And even before that . . ."

She broke off, hand on mouth, then continued almost in a whisper. I cupped my own hand behind my ear surreptitiously so I might hear better.

"I have no concrete evidence for this," she said, "but there's so much in the news these days about fathers who sexually abuse their daughters and that kind of thing. It's the farthest thing I would ever have in my mind about my father, sober. But when he was drunk, is it possible he could have done something like that to Pam before he remarried?"

"What makes you think so?"

"She's been damaged so much more than I. Somehow I've managed to keep my demons at bay and she hasn't." She lowered her hand from her mouth and spoke more clearly, as if having made a decision. "I'm sure she'll tell you this, so I guess I can," she went on. "Years ago she had a nervous breakdown. After that she had psychoanalysis and some group therapy, I think. It's hard for me to picture myself in therapy, but it's helped her."

"So you think she may have experienced some terrible stress at home that you didn't?" I asked. I wondered whether there was something more Gail wanted to tell me but couldn't bring herself to say. "Did you ever feel endangered yourself in that way?"

"Never. I always knew my father loved me very much."

For all the misery of her life, Gail clung to that love, refusing to question how it was that a man who loved his daughter "very much" could so neglect her and her sister or subject them to the care of so unfeeling a woman. For her, alcohol explained everything in her father's behavior, even the possibility that he might have molested her sister. More than anything she had said, that reiteration of her father's love made my heart ache for her. For the child of an alcoholic even a glimmer of love can make the intolerable acceptable.

Gail elaborated on her sister's difficulties and her own.

"Maybe it's just that she's more sensitive than I," she said, picking up the thread of Pam's greater damage. "But I know she's had a harder time in coping. She still feels guilty about leaving me and moving out of that house when she was twenty, although I have never consciously begrudged her having gotten away."

I noted the word "consciously," questioning in my mind whether she suspected that somewhere within herself she did begrudge her sister's action.

Gail was fourteen and in her last year of junior high school when Pam decided to leave home for a job in New York. She was to go to New York by train from Boston on a Friday evening and had gone to the city in the morning to spend the day there before leaving. The train was departing at 6:25 P.M. Gail had to be in school during the day, but "desperate" to see her sister off, she talked her aunt into driving her straight from school to Boston. The station was jammed with people traveling for the weekend, and Gail had to push her way in. She knew Pam would be on the train, but she wanted at least to wave good-bye.

"I wanted more than anything for Pam to see me," she recalled, shaking her head as if to shake off the unhappiness of the memory. "I finally reached the gate and someone said, 'Don't bother, the train is gone.' I sat down on a bench, sick to my heart, and just sat there, numbed. About ten minutes later I heard an announcement that the train was *just* leaving. I had been given the wrong information. I could have seen her! I can't tell you what that did to me. I just broke down, totally collapsed."

Gail was crying openly. "I hate train stations," she said. "They're such sad places."

"It must have been so hard for you," I offered, thinking not only of the train incident but of her having been left alone with her father and stepmother.

"She hated leaving me," she answered almost defiantly, as if responding to my unspoken thought. "But she had to go. I did the same thing." She hesitated a moment. "Of course, there were no younger siblings, but I did the same thing when my time came."

But that difference is enormous. It seemed to me that as understanding as Gail is of her sister's departure, as not "consciously" begrudging as she is, she was indelibly wounded by it. I suspected—and suspect—that her sense of being abandoned by her sister and her sister's "hating" to abandon her are the central motifs in their relationship. The moment at the train station when one left and the other "totally collapsed" is frozen in time for both of them.

Thirty-eight years after the event, Pam still cannot shake off the guilt it caused her. She brought that guilt up within moments after we began speaking in the same screened-in porch where Gail and I had met, and she referred to it again and again when we continued our conversations by phone after she had returned home.

"I have a huge guilt about Gail," she said at our initial interview. "I left home when she was only fourteen, so I wasn't there for her teen years. It was a very, very difficult thing for me to do, that leaving, yet I knew that if I didn't get out, I would be very sick. That didn't mean, of course, that she wasn't going to be very sick by my leaving, and that's why I feel so guilty.

"I mean it was terrible, a catch-22. I remember, over and over, the week or two before I left. We slept in the same bed, and I would rub her back or try to hug her and make some sign of love, and all the while in my head I was packing my bags, ready to run. It was a terrible feeling for me, and I've never forgiven myself. Yet I know I had to do it. I really had to do it to survive . . ."

Pam's voice drifted off, and she looked away from me. Probably for the millionth time, she was convincing herself that she had not committed a crime by saving her own soul.

"Later," she picked up her argument, "after our father committed suicide—did Gail tell you our father killed himself?"

"Yes, she did." Gail had described the death almost in passing when we spoke, dryly and unemotionally, just as unemotionally as Pam was now referring to it. At the age of sixty, after months of being sober, and with Trudy at his side in their summer cabin, their father had shot himself through the head. Shocked as they had been, on some level they had expected the death—a meaningless culmination to a meaningless and wasted life.

"After he died," Pam went on, "Gail continued to live at home with our stepmother. She was about twenty by then. And when I came home one weekend, I noticed that they were barely speaking to each other. When Trudy would be in the room, Gail would step around her, as far away as she physically could. The indications of real hatred were obvious to me. So that weekend I said to her, 'You have to get out just the way I got out.' I was married by then and Stephen was stationed in New London, and I said, 'If you don't get out, I'm going to come get you and make you live with us.' "

Gail did get out. She moved to New York, where she met Richard. After they married, Richard entered the insurance business and they moved to Hartford, Connecticut, a major insurance center. His company later transferred him to Newport, their present home.

"You must feel good, then," I said, "about having turned Gail's life around in that way."

"I did feel later," Pam answered slowly, "that at least I had done that. Because I knew the situation I had been in and I could see and feel and smell and touch the experience that she was going through."

But still she is torn with guilt. And still she wishes she could undo the past.

Not that she underestimates her own suffering. "When my grandmother was alive, I was put into a hideous adult position," she told me once on the phone. "My grandmother would say, 'Your father's drinking again. Watch over him.' And I would try to talk to him. 'Can't you stop?' I'd cry, and like all alcoholics he would deny. 'But I'm only drinking wine,' or 'I'm only drinking beer,' he'd say."

And still what eats away at Pam is the belief that she did not give

her younger sister enough "nurturing." That she let Gail spend weekends alone in the summer cabin with her father and stepmother. That
she did not "comfort and reassure" and share experiences with Gail.
And, ultimately, that she left Gail.

"In my own heart," she said at one point, "I would hope that she
has some good feelings about something I did for her. I know I started
her reading, but I'm not sure that was such a big deal considering
everything else in our lives. I would like to have felt that I really made
a difference."

Adding to Pam's guilt is the fact that Gail, she feels, is "closed off,"
"zippered up tight." So tight, says Pam, that she "won't talk to me
about any of the things that hurt. I've left openings and I've referred to
things I'd want to talk to her about, yet if I try to bring up a subject
about our childhood, she simply won't pursue it. She will *not* pursue
it. I've had a nervous breakdown. I've had therapy, and I've learned to
speak about things. I guess she has not been able to deal with all the
pain, and that has been a source of great consternation to me."

Several times as I spoke with Pam, my mind flashed back to Gail's
concern about whether her older sister had been sexually abused by
their father. Did that idea come to her from one of the "openings"
Pam had left that she had not cared to pursue? What would happen if
she allowed Pam to talk to her about the "things that hurt"? Would
she, in fact, uncover a dread secret that she may not really want to
know about the father she loved?

Gail's closed-offness is especially poignant for Pam because she
knows things could be different. She described how, at Christmastime
a year ago, when Pam became ill with pneumonia, Gail gave up her
own vacation, left her family, and flew to Florida to nurse her sister.
"She literally saved our lives," Pam said. "She took care of Tommy,
our retarded son, and in her calm way just ran the household and
made everything work." It was a gesture of love, and a wonderful
week that in its very wonderfulness highlighted the things that Pam
feels are missing in the rest of their relationship.

"I would hate to die and not ever have gotten into a real, honest-to-
goodness conversation with her," Pam said. "But I never have. We've
not been able to assume and embrace the real love I think we have for
each other, and I find that such a shame."

Gail has similar misgivings. In one of our conversations she spoke
of her own guilt about not writing or phoning Pam as often as she
would like to, about not maintaining the close contact sisters "should
have." She admitted that it wasn't as easy for her to "open up" as it
was for Pam. And she looked into the future with foreboding.

"I am very much aware," she said, "that she is the only sibling I've got. Since her pneumonia she's not been in great health, and she becomes more burdened every day with the care of her son. I see our mortality, and I know the load of guilt I'll carry if anything happens to her and I've not been better about keeping up. Guilt, and great sorrow."

After I spoke with the sisters for the last time, I had a mental image of them standing on opposite sides across a great divide. Each wants to reach over and touch the other, to hug and cry openly and exchange good, honest talk. Yet the reach seems too far, the talk too difficult. Long ago each learned to cope by herself with the secret misery of her life and—perhaps—even to hide the darkest secrets from the other.

Like many children in families riddled by secrets, they are survivors. Pam survived by leaving home and—as torturous as it was to her—leaving Gail behind. Gail survived being left in the horror that was her home by continuing to shut off a part of herself, numbing her mind to the hurt that might otherwise have overwhelmed her. As gracious as they are to one another on the surface, and as devoted as they truly feel, neither sister has yet been able to bridge the emptiness that lies between them.

There is another kind of emptiness between siblings that secrets can create, and that is the sense of futility one sibling feels in trying to help another who denies needing help about drinking, drugs, or other secret problems.

A sibling's drug or alcohol abuse was ranked high as a concern on the survey. But whereas responses to growing up in an alcoholic home ranged from pity for the addicted parent to rage to understanding to self-pity for consequences suffered, one emotion stood out above all others in reaction to addicted or substance-abusing sibs: anger. There was anger at what these siblings had done or were doing to themselves and anger at what they had done or were doing to their families. And there was frustrated, helpless anger at being caught up in troubles that were not of one's own making.

"My brother is an alcoholic, and I was always running when he called because I felt intimidated by him," wrote a thirty-four-year-old secretary of her brother, four years older. "But his friends got sick of him and so did I. I talk to him, but I don't run for him anymore."

"My sister is obsessed with exercise, dieting, and food," a twenty-three-year-old receptionist reported. "I've offered to pay for a consultation for her with an agency specializing in eating disorders because she said she can't afford it herself (even though I know she can), but I've gotten no place."

"I was very close to my sister before her drug problem," wrote another woman, this one twenty-seven and a department manager, expressing the feelings and disappointments of many others, "but it has destroyed our relationship. It has also hurt our family, which in turn hurts me more. I feel sorry for her in a way, but I also believe we are all in control of our own lives, and she is weak and dumb for letting herself get so low." Then she added, almost as an afterthought, "I hope she gets her life back, and no matter what she has done, I would help her because she is still my sister and I love her."

That note of love, of wanting to help, of feeling responsible in spite of oneself is what makes the anger so frustrating, the rage more a plea to be set free than a statement of freedom and independence from a problem sibling. ("I just fucking don't want to have to deal with his problems anymore," said a man of his druggie brother. Then, "So why do I let him get to me?")

Norman Maclean, in "A River Runs Through It," captures these mixed feelings among siblings of the troubled. The little brother who refused to eat his oatmeal has become an adult alcoholic, picked up for the dozenth time by the local police. Irritated at being phoned by a police officer, Maclean says, "I had already heard more than I wanted. Maybe one of our ultimate troubles was that I never wanted to hear too much about my brother." But on reflection, he writes, "I knew there were others like me who had brothers they did not understand but wanted to help. We are probably those referred to as 'our brothers' keepers,' possessed of one of the oldest and possibly one of the most futile and certainly one of the most haunting of instincts. It will not let us go."

The "haunting instinct" of caring for a troubled sib is especially powerful and difficult during the teen years, a time when boys and girls begin to experiment with drugs and alcohol. Children whose brothers or sisters become part of the drug culture are torn in many directions. They may become their sib's confidant, sworn to secrecy, and thus split between loyalty to the sibling and worry about him or her, between wanting to guard the secret and wanting to hand responsibility for the sib and the secret over to parents.

When siblings have been close in adolescence or young adulthood, the involvement of one in drugs or alcohol can also leave the other feeling alone and different. It is as if there is now a barrier between them that one has crossed and the other hasn't, and they will no longer be as they once were. Younger siblings, especially, may be hurt and confused by an older's move into frightening and dangerous areas. I noticed—although I found no statistical significance for this—that many of the people who wrote about the problem of their sib's substance abuse were youngers complaining about older brothers or sisters. Because they have always looked up to their older siblings, younger ones feel betrayed when they find themselves having to look down on them.

In many cases, of course, especially during adolescence but later, too, younger siblings follow their elders' lead into drugs or alcohol, just as adult children of alcoholics often become alcoholics themselves. The model is there, and the pull toward imitation is difficult to resist.

What makes a sibling resist that pull, and what leads one child in a family and not others to alcohol and drugs, is a subject as complex as any other question of sibling differences. The answers are as varied as those for other differences: dissimilarities in personality, in friends, in the way parents treated each child, in the home environment each created for the other, in—as in so many other situations—a wish to *be* different.

A study of adult heroin addicts and their nonaddicted brothers conducted over the course of twenty years at the University of Texas at San Antonio turned up some interesting statements about that wish. All the subjects in the study had difficult family backgrounds. Their childhoods included the divorce of parents, the death of one or both parents, or substance abuse in the family. When asked why they thought they had become heroin addicts and their brothers had not, the addicts most frequently cited different peer groups—"hanging around with the wrong crowd."

When asked the same question, the nonaddicted brothers agreed that belonging to different groups of friends was an important factor. But they also emphasized their own deliberate decision to avoid drugs or alcohol. One spoke of having seen "what a mess my brother was always in," another of not wanting to cause his parents the "heartache" his brother had caused. The nonaddicts also described leaving home at an early age to escape their brother's influence, or becoming involved in after-school activities to stay away from the brother's crowd. They were determined to avoid the trap their brothers had fallen into.

Unfortunately, for these nonaddicts as for other siblings of substance abusers, avoiding the trap of addiction does not mean avoiding the burden of a sib's addictions. In a moving article, a reporter for the *Wall Street Journal*, Jonathan Dahl, described his search for his drug-addicted older brother Jeff. Nine years earlier, their father had evicted Jeff from their home after years of trying to get him off drugs. But shortly before he died, the remorseful father had pleaded with Jonathan to find his brother, who had quickly vanished.

Jonathan spent more than a year scouring bars, subway stations, drug rehabs, and shelters, seeking leads to his lost brother. With each dead end he became more determined. He remembered the big brother who had tied his shoelaces for him at the bus stop and had once "bloodied the noses of sixth-grade bullies" who tried to hurt him. But the Jeff he did finally find in a roach-infested apartment in Denver was a bloated, middle-aged man who had never been able to escape drugs. After spending a week with him, Jonathan returned home, confused and dejected by what he had seen.

"Part of me wants to help him," he writes, "but part of me realizes I can't be my brother's keeper. Until I figure out what to do, I think about Jeff all the time."

Haunted, as Maclean says, by one of the oldest of instincts, Jonathan, like most siblings of the addicted, will probably never stop thinking of Jeff or longing to help him.

Of all the disruptive secrets in a family, the best-kept may well be that of sibling incest. It is a secret rarely revealed to parents, siblings, or friends and rarely discussed in adult life even by the partners themselves. When Gail spoke of the possibility that her sister Pam had been sexually abused by their father, she attributed her concern to the ever-increasing public discussion about parent-child incest. There has been much less discussion and much less research about sibling sexual activities.

Even the term "sibling incest" is not clearly defined. All siblings show sexual curiosity, and all learn by looking, touching, and exploring their own and each other's bodies. Incest is something different. Strictly speaking, it refers to sexual intercourse between siblings. But children too young for intercourse can also be said to be incestuous when they go beyond normal sex play and engage in sexually explicit activities such as attempts at intercourse and frequent petting and genital touching.

Nor does anybody know how common sibling incest is. Some researchers estimate that it is five times more prevalent than incest between a parent and child. But because it is rarely reported to the police or to clinics, nobody has reliable figures. One clue to its occurrence is a 1978 survey by psychologist David Finkelhor of sibling sexual experiences among college students in New England. Of the nearly eight hundred students surveyed, 13 percent (15 percent of the women and 10 percent of the men) reported some type of sexual encounter with a sibling during childhood. But Finkelhor lumped together many types of sexual activities—from "exhibiting genitals" to intercourse—so it is hard to know what these figures signify, beyond recognizing that sibling sexuality in childhood is far from uncommon.

Unlike parent-child incest, which most people regard as repugnant and abusive to the child, incest between siblings is often brushed off —even by clinicians—as harmless. The incest may be condemned if one sibling is much older and in that sense exploitative of the other. But when sibs are close in age, the argument goes, and neither coerces the other, the experience is simply an extension of normal sex play and may actually be a positive one, promoting the sexual development of the young partners.

It is a point of view with which I strongly disagree.

I disagree because, as psychologists Stephen Bank and Michael Kahn point out, rarely is incest totally mutual even if both partners seem willing. One sibling—generally the older—initiates and promotes it, and the other becomes seduced or manipulated into it. In those cases in which a younger child is the initiator, the child usually does not understand the meaning or implications of the experience and may later feel both guilty and humiliated by it.

And I disagree because even without coercion there is often an element of sexual exploitation in sibling incest, with the sister the more likely victim. It is true that incestuous activities occur between older sisters and younger brothers and—far less frequently—between sibs of the same sex. But the most common form of incest is between older brother and younger sister. In such relationships the older brother is usually the dominant partner and the sister often finds herself feeling used by him. Indeed, in Finkelhor's study, women to a far greater extent than men were the junior partners in the incest and far more often reported the experience as unpleasant.

More than anything, I disagree with the upbeat view of sibling incest because—with any age difference, and regardless of who dominates—incest violates one of the most basic taboos of society. Such violation is bound to bring with it some psychic damage, especially for the person who feels victimized.

Arguments have raged over centuries about whether the taboo against incest—either between parent and child or between siblings— is "natural," or whether society has imposed it. Is there an innate abhorrence and avoidance of incest built into our genetic makeup? Those who say there is point out that even nonhuman primates—monkeys and apes, for example—rarely mate with parents or siblings unless no other mates are available. They point also to a study conducted some years ago of nonrelated children growing up on kibbutzim, Israel's collective settlements. Because these children spend a great deal of time together in peer groups and come to see one another as brothers and sisters, few of them marry each other in adult life, although adults do not discourage such marriages. There appears to be a natural avoidance on their part of sexual activity with each other.

Those who disagree, Freud among them, argue that if there is a natural aversion to incest, why do we have such a strong taboo against it? Why don't all people simply shun it? Rather, say Freud and others, family members have powerful sexual attractions to each other. The taboo has been imposed to maintain the social order, to protect children from being taken advantage of, and to insure that people marry and procreate with others beyond the family.

Those who hold this position remind us that there have been societies in which the taboo against sibling incest did not exist. It was not unusual, for example, for the pharaohs of ancient Egypt during the eighteenth and nineteenth dynasties (some three thousand years ago) to marry their sisters. Somewhat later, history records, the beautiful Queen Cleopatra married, consecutively, two of her brothers.

There is no definitive answer as to how innate the aversion to sibling incest actually is. But it is unquestionably a cultural taboo that has existed for thousands and thousands of years in almost every society, and the few cases—like that of ancient Egypt—in which it was not upheld are rare and probably politically motivated. (Cleopatra married and then murdered at least one of those brothers for political reasons.) Breaking that taboo is not a light matter.

That is not to say that family members are not drawn to each other with sexual desires and fascinations. Freud described the Oedipal wishes of children for parents of the opposite sex. Artists and poets have portrayed sibling longings.

The romantic poets of the nineteenth century in particular were fascinated by the mysteries of sibling attractions. Edgar Allan Poe's haunting short story "The Fall of the House of Usher" depicts the decadence permeating the home of an incestuous brother and sister. William Wordsworth's effusive poems about his sister Dorothy often equate her with the lost natural and imaginative self of his childhood. Some critics maintain that the two actually had an incestuous relationship, but nobody has proven that. Critics also suggest that the secret of incest between Nathaniel Hawthorne and his sister underlies many of his brooding stories.

Not only was the incest of one poet, Lord Byron, known, but it scandalized English society and destroyed his career. Byron had a long-standing affair with his half sister, Augusta. In a letter to her that has become famous, he wrote: "I have never ceased nor can cease to feel for a moment that perfect and boundless attachment which bound and binds me to you, which renders me utterly incapable of *real* love for any other human being. . . ."

The questions raised by the behavior of Byron and other incestuous siblings are: What leads to so "boundless" an attachment between brother and sister that it can defy ingrained taboos, and what effect does that attachment have on the partners?

Byron grew up in a home deserted by his father and controlled by a violent-tempered mother. He and Augusta, children of the same father, had been separated for years. When they came together again, they thought of themselves as orphans in an unfriendly world, their need for each other fueled by their lack of love early in life.

Feelings of neglect and abandonment by parents—if not physical, then emotional—are basic elements in most cases of sibling incest. Left on their own, a brother and sister may turn to one another— literally falling into each other's arms—for the warmth and comfort they miss from parents. Or, lacking parental supervision, an aggressive older sib may force or seduce a younger into forbidden sexual acts, knowing that the younger will be too shamed or fearful of being blamed to reveal the secret to parents.

Parental neglect has a range of meanings, from the physical abuse of children, to alcoholism, to parents who are cold and distant with their children or absent from home much of the time. Dr. Levay, the sex and marital therapist, described a family in which the parents ran a business together, leaving their children, who shared a bedroom, alone much of the time. In this case, it was the daughter, the eldest, who initiated her brother into sex. Frightened at what they had done, she spoke to her parents, pleading with them to find a way for each child to have a separate space. The shocked parents scolded the children for their behavior—and continued immersing themselves in their business. The children continued their sexual activities.

Parents can be neglectful, as these parents were, by ignoring all evidence of sexual activity among their children, even when informed of it directly. Women I interviewed spoke of complaining to their mothers about a brother's sexual aggressions, only to be told that they were exaggerating, or imagining things, or behaving badly themselves. Parents may be so overwhelmed by the idea that their child could actually defy such a deep-rooted taboo that they simply refuse to deal with it. They may also feel intimidated by the disruption that will occur in the family if they bring the subject into the open. They will have to take the word of one child over that of another if the initiator denies any wrongdoing. They will also have to find a way to control the aggressive child, who may have become aggressive in the first place for lack of discipline. Frightened by the thought of confronting a child about such a shameful matter, these parents deny its existence, and they frequently blame the victim for raising the issue.

Feeling themselves neglected, siblings may engage in incest, and sensing that parents will do little to interfere, one may force another into sexual acts. Yet, certainly, not every brother and sister who feel neglected by parents become incestuous. What other factors influence sibling sexual behavior? Holly Smith, of the Department of Social Services in Boulder, Colorado, tried to answer that question by studying twenty-five families in which sibling incest had occurred. (Since these were families that had come to the attention of the department, they may have been more troubled than others whose cases never reach authorities. Still, they do shed light on a shadowy subject.)

Smith found that along with parents' coldness or disinterest in their children, many of the families had secrets revolving around sexuality. A key secret—which was usually no secret to one or more of the children—was that the mother or father was having an extramarital affair. The parents' activities seemed to give the children license to break rules themselves.

Another feature of these incestuous families was a kind of climate of sexuality in the home. In a number of cases, daughters had been abused by their fathers before becoming their brothers' victims. In several, children had watched their parents make love, or had listened to their parents recount their own sexual adventures, becoming stimulated and excited themselves.

But the most interesting of Smith's findings was one that appears to contradict these others. The mothers in about a third of the families not only did not stimulate sexuality but were actually sexually repressive. Devoutly religious, rigid, and puritanical, they squelched any discussion of sexual matters. The end result of their repressive attitude, however, was to intensify their children's sexual curiosity and rebelliousness.

.   .   .

It was just such a repressive mother and rebellious son that led to incestuous behavior in the Nettles family, one of the few I met in which siblings were willing to discuss the subject of incest. To be more accurate, two of the siblings—John and Theresa—were willing to discuss their older brother Paul's incestuous behavior. The youngest sibling, Helen, a nun in an Ursuline convent, was unavailable for interviewing. Paul himself spoke only of their mother's "spooky" attachment to Catholicism, her absorption in the mystical writings of fourteenth-century saints, her rigid control of the family and constant warnings when the children were young not to "touch yourself," not to curse, not to know "there was such a thing as sex."

Also from Paul, forty-four and thrice divorced, I heard that because of their mother, "sexually the family was a disaster," with all of the children ill-prepared to face the "real" world or the opposite sex. As a result, Helen had become pregnant at the age of sixteen, given up her child for adoption, and—despondent—had entered one of the strictest of Roman Catholic orders. Theresa, in Paul's version of family history, was so sexually ignorant that the night before her wedding, he and John had to sit her down and explain sexual behavior in great detail. Not that John had much to offer. He had married just a year earlier, at the age of forty, having been involved for three years before that in a torrid love affair with one of Paul's ex-wives.

"She taught him everything," said Paul. "But it was weird, almost incestuous, his being with my wife in that way."

That was as close as Paul came to the concept of sibling incest, although I had tried to draw him out after speaking with John and hearing about his brother's sexual pursuits.

"My parents told me," John said early in our first interview, "that Paul was a difficult child. He's a brilliant character actor, and that brilliance showed at a young age. He always had a powerful personality, always wanting his own way."

Part of Paul's personality was his "strong sexual drive," intensified in John's opinion by their mother's rigidity and their father's passive acceptance of her religious fanaticism.

"He was a rebel," John said, "he went against everything my mother stood for, including raping her children."

"Raping?"

"I don't really know how far it went, whether he stopped at petting or whether he had intercourse with them, but he came on to both my sisters. I never knew anything about it for years, but finally when we were older my sisters began to tell me. I was really shocked. Still, to this day, I have never brought it up with Paul."

"What would happen if you did?" I asked.

"I would not want to hurt him by exposing him to that open wound. It's something he seems to want to repress."

"And your sisters, were they wounded?"

"Whether it affected Helen's pregnancy and decision to be a nun, I don't know. But Theresa told me just last summer that she had really suffered because of it, and in light of his behavior she had been repulsed by the lecture about sex that he gave her before her marriage."

Paul had gotten "buzzed," John explained, filling in the background of the prewedding sexual education Paul had mentioned. He had insisted on "graphically" describing to Theresa what to do on her wedding night, and she had found the experience "very traumatic."

Theresa confirmed this when we met. A pleasant-looking woman, she shows little emotion when she speaks, always smiling slightly as if determined to put the best face on anything life has to offer. We spoke at some length before touching on the subject of incest. Unlike her brothers, she said, she considers the "sheltered" life her parents gave their children "just right," and she is raising her children the same way.

"When I was younger and I did something I knew my parents would not approve of," she recalled, "I would feel guilty the minute I walked through the door of our house, and that would put me back on track. You have to have values and a moral commitment. My brothers don't have that. My husband does, and that is a great help to me."

Still, she admitted, it had been hard for her after she married to feel closer to her husband, an editor at a Catholic publishing house, than to her brothers. Adding to that difficulty was the fact that her husband did not want her to have anything to do with Paul. It was in answer to my question of "Why not?" that she ventured into the territory of incest. But first she described from her viewpoint the dinner at which Paul "persistently" portrayed to her every aspect of sexuality he could think of. She had become so upset that she had run out of the restaurant, leaving her brothers behind.

"For Paul to speak to me about those things, after all he had done . . ." she said. She stopped, the smile stiffened. "I might as well tell you," she continued, "that Paul used to force himself on me sexually when we were younger, and it went on for some years. I found out when I was older that he did the same thing to my sister, Helen. We never talked about it earlier. I hated it, and I was too ashamed."

"Did you ever tell your mother?"

"I did, and she just warned me to be more careful. I'm not sure she could have stopped him. He was so determined to get his way."

In her reluctance to intervene, Theresa's mother was no different from many other parents who avoid dealing with their children's incest. Her strong religiosity may also have stood in her way. Paul's behavior implied a defiance of all that she believed in. How much easier to ignore it than to have to confront such fundamentally "sinful" actions in her own home. For her part, Theresa found it more comforting to defend her mother than to acknowledge that she had not been properly protected.

Theresa did not say what exactly Paul had done to her, nor did I press. Whether he had actually "raped" her, as John implied, or only "petted," his determined sexuality had left a lasting mark.

"It took me a long time to adjust to the sexual side of marriage, maybe ten years or more," she said. "I was so frightened of even being touched. My husband was very patient with me. He's a kind, good, gentle man, and I'm very grateful to him."

Throughout our talks, Theresa kept her tight smile, her voice carefully modulated, flat really. Here was a woman who strained to hold herself in check, to be a perfect Catholic like her mother, to love her husband as a good wife should, all the while trying to come to terms with a secret, the depths of which only she and the brother who had hurt her knew.

"Have you ever spoken to Paul about your sexual activity together?" I asked her.

"Nothing can be gained from talking about it," she answered. "It's his problem as much as mine. We've both had to deal with it in our own way."

That there are vast differences in the ways Theresa and Paul have dealt with their incestuous behavior is obvious. She speaks honestly of the difficulties she's had in adjusting to marriage. Less openly, her insistence on maintaining her mother's rigid religious standards may be the only tolerable means she has of putting her lapse from those standards behind her. Paul acknowledges nothing. He blames all family problems on the destructiveness of his mother's religious extremism, in that way rationalizing his own behavior. (And John does nothing to make him confront that behavior. He may disapprove of his brother, but he treats Paul's "wound" as equal to Theresa's, although he knows the damage she has endured.)

With all that, Paul does not appear to be totally unscathed. Forcing himself on his sisters when they were young was a way of gaining sexual power over them. His sexual preoccupation with Theresa continued in adult life, as evidenced by his obsessive presentation to her of prenuptial instructions. It was a kind of verbal "incest" aimed at maintaining control even as she was about to leave him and the family for another man. She left, and has remained in a good marriage. His three failed marriages would seem to indicate that he has not been able to leave in the same way, or at least that he has not been successful at establishing intimate relationships with women outside the family. Unlike Theresa, Paul still suffers from not having dealt with the motives or consequences of his incestuous activities.

The different approaches of Theresa and Paul characterize other siblings in similar situations. In research projects or in therapy sessions, women report incidents of sibling incest far more frequently than do men. Like Theresa, they are more likely to see themselves as the victims. But even men who have been victimized by their sisters do not like to acknowledge that circumstance because it undermines the more desirable male view they have of themselves as stronger than their sisters. When they are the aggressors, men feel less disturbed by the incest because that role fits into the socially accepted image of themselves as more dominant. Those men who do feel guilty or embarrassed often make excuses for their behavior or put it out of their mind, not wishing to confront the issue. It may, however, affect them in the long run, as it does Paul.

There have been few studies of those long-range effects of sibling incest on women or men. David Finkelhor's survey of college students who had engaged in some kind of sexual experience with a sibling was limited to young adults who had not yet married. Generally, both male and female students whose sexual experience had been with a sibling several years older than they saw it in negative terms—in fact, the greater the age difference, the more negative the reaction. Students who regarded the experience as positive tended to see themselves as equally involved and equally responsible as their partners.

But even those experiences remembered as positive can have negative effects over time. Dr. Levay, seeing patients beyond college age, described both men and women who remembered enjoying their incestuous activities with their sibs but were unable to transfer that enjoyment to other sexual relationships or to marriage. "There's a bonding, a special intimacy that develops so that the spouse is more like a third party than a husband or wife," he explained.

Other consequences were depicted by psychologist Karin Meiselman from her studies of both father-daughter and brother-sister incest among her patients. Some of the women who had been victimized by older brothers, she found, continued to become involved with, and marry, older men who abused and mistreated them, as though they saw that treatment as their due. Others had sexual difficulties in their marriages. And several women, including some who had enjoyed sexual relations with their brothers, had problems relating to their own sons. One beat and punished her son relentlessly, displacing onto him the anger she felt toward her brother. Another allowed her son to bully her the way her brother had. Still another acted seductive toward her teenage son, as she had toward her brother, frightening the boy so that he withdrew from her as much as possible.

There may be brothers and sisters who had incestuous childhood relationships that have not affected their adult lives. There may be sisters and brothers who happily continue sexual behavior well into adult life. But more often, like Theresa and Paul, incestuous siblings suffer consequences, some more obvious than others. And overall, this secret of secrets within a family often remains the most hidden and has the potential for becoming the most harmful of all for adult siblings.

CHAPTER TEN

A Piercing Pain

SIBLING ILLNESS/
SIBLING DEATH

*F*or the first hour of our interview Hugh Shea paced the floor of my
office, back and forth, up and down, smoking one cigarette after another and marking his path with a trail of light gray ash. He had come
to speak to me about a mentally ill sister—dead some ten years—but
he was musing now on why he had agreed to do so.

"All the unhappiness in my life," he said in one of his pacing
rounds, "all the neurotic things I've thought and done, can be traced
back to the situation at home with Rosie. But I've never spoken about
this to anyone, not even my analyst—and I've been in analysis twice."
He stopped, smiling for a moment. "I guess that's why neither of them
worked," he said, and resumed pacing.

He was a chunky man of middling height, mid-fifties, with clumps
of dark brown hair surrounding a balding scalp and deep-set, intense
blue eyes. As he walked, his entire body seemed to be in motion, one
hand dragging on his cigarette, the other fiddling with objects around
the room. When he finally sat down, he still seemed to be in motion,
responding to some inner beat. His fingers tapped the surface of the
desk as he crossed and uncrossed his legs, and every few minutes he
turned away from me with a jerking movement to stare out the window, as if he expected to see someone there. This was not a man
comfortable with others—or himself.

As settled as he could be, he began talking about himself and his
family background. He would not go out of his way, he warned, to

228

discuss Rosie, but maybe some of that would emerge, and if it did, he would not censor himself. He had a feeling he would be freer with a total stranger than he had been with his analyst, whom—he said, smiling for a second time—he had never really trusted anyway.

The Rosie story did emerge, of course, almost instantly, for she was at the center of the family history. Without her the history would not have been much different from that of other immigrant families racked with poverty and struggling for survival in the promised land of America. This family happened to be Irish, the parents having married before leaving the old country, and their children born Americans. There were five children in all—three who died in infancy or childhood and two who survived: Rosie, the oldest, and Hugh, the youngest.

It was a piece of divine mischief that had brought about this order of survival, Hugh was convinced, for the three who died might have grown into good and useful human beings, while Rosie, the survivor, became in her teenage years severely schizophrenic. At least that is what we would label her condition today. The Sheas labeled her "bad," and reacted accordingly.

Both before and after the onset of Rosie's illness, the family lived not far from Hugh's grandparents in one of the poorest and roughest sections of New York, known then as Hell's Kitchen. Hugh's father worked as a trainman on the Third Avenue El, and his mother took in boarders to supplement the family income. To accommodate the boarders, the children slept in odd corners of the family's railroad apartment, Rosie usually in the kitchen, Hugh on a couch in the living room. Still, they managed, until Rosie turned ill.

Hugh, five years younger than Rosie, had only vague memories of her before her illness. The later memories are far more vivid. As he delved into the family story, he lost his reluctance to describe those memories, and his sister. She was, as a teenager, he recalled without trying to soften his words, "a wild person, fat as a blob, with matted hair and tragic eyes." She cursed uncontrollably, lashed out in rage, cried as though in dreadful agony, and frequently walked about mumbling to herself. Because his parents didn't understand that his sister was ill, they responded to her wildness with shouting and beatings. At the same time, his mother tied herself into a knot with her daughter from which she never escaped. She scolded and hit, then repented and comforted, then scolded and hit again in a cycle that repeated itself time and again.

As Rosie moved from early to late adolescence, the cycle intensified. To escape her parents, she took to the streets, becoming a prostitute, to the horror of the family. To escape the violence of the streets, she took on a pimp named Danny, on whom she became totally dependent, speaking in her calmer moments of marrying him. Nothing came of that, of course, and many a time Rosie would stumble home in the small hours of the morning, black and blue and swollen-faced from the beatings she took from Danny or some client. Other times her parents would search the streets to find her and drag her home, dirty and disheveled. Then the beatings would be meted out by her father, whose rage and shame knew no bounds.

Hugh witnessed it all, his sister's behavior, his father's beatings, his mother's shouting and reconciliations and attempts to control her husband's violence against Rosie.

"They protected me from nothing," he said bitterly, "any of them. My parents were too caught up in their own misfortunes to think about me, and Rosie was too sick to control herself. I learned more than I should at too tender an age. I couldn't absorb it, couldn't assimilate it."

Hardest to absorb was the onslaught of sexuality connected with his sister's life, surrounding him at a time when he was just becoming sexually aware himself. Sometimes his sister would drop her purse, and Hugh would see prophylactics fall to the floor, titillated by what they represented, repelled by the associations between them and his sister. Twice he observed—because nobody noticed that he was present—abortions performed on his sister in their dimly lit kitchen by some "slimy man" in a dirty white doctor's jacket. And once, walking through the street in the late evening with a friend, he saw his sister out "whoring." He turned away, pretending not to have seen, but he knew that the friend knew who she was, and he was humiliated. Even in his rough neighborhood, none of his friends had a sister like his.

As his narrative progressed, Hugh became very still. No more tapping or turning or leg crossing. He stared at me, puffing on his cigarette, his mind some place far from my office.

"More than once, then and in later years," he said slowly, "I wished her dead. Why couldn't I have a life like everybody else's? Why couldn't I have parents who paid more attention to me instead of focusing all their energies on my sister? And if I had a sister, why couldn't she be a real big sister, the kind who looks out for you and takes care of you the way sisters do in Irish families?

"I hated her," he went on, swallowing hard, "and I loved her. I had so much compassion for her. Sometimes, after my father would beat her, I'd go to her and stroke her head, trying to comfort her. I used to fantasize about her. I used to picture myself her protector, instead of that pimp Danny. I used to picture myself holding her in my arms, loving her the way a man should love her, the way she was not being loved by the men who had her night after night.

"Were they sexual fantasies?" he asked himself, and answered, "In a way, yes. They were fantasies of the love that was missing from both our lives, missing because of who she was. I had such pity for her, and for myself. In some strange manner I felt there was a bond between us that was separate from our connections to our parents. In whatever way she was able to understand, I think she felt that too. We identified with each other as sister and brother, in spite of everything that went on."

So strong was that identification, Hugh later explained, that some years ago, as he approached his fifty-first birthday—the age at which Rosie had died—he began brooding about the possibility that her last birthday would be his as well. It was then that he entered analysis for a second time, but dropped it soon after passing that landmark date. "I've got to deal with things in my own way," he said simply, and I suspected that speaking to me now about Rosie's life and death was one aspect of that dealing.

The death came several years after she had been institutionalized—finally. For years the Sheas had refused to hospitalize Rosie, even after they recognized that her behavior did not come from badness but from sickness. They were more willing to suffer the shame of her prostitution than the shame of having a daughter in an "insane asylum," as mental hospitals were called at that time. There was a brief period when they did place her in an institution—secretly, so that no neighbors or family members knew. Hugh remembers, at about age eighteen, going with them for visits, taking a long train ride and then walking four miles from the train station to the hospital, to save taxi money. When at last they saw her, Rosie would greet them with "heartrending" pleas to be taken home, or would wander around staring blankly at them, overmedicated and not recognizing them.

Later, when she was in her late twenties, Rosie had a lobotomy, an operation (now in disrepute) in which the frontal lobes of the brain are removed to calm a disturbed patient. The surgery did calm her, but left her emotionally dead, flattened into a kind of walking vegetable. By now Hugh's mother had decided to care for her daughter at home herself, and she continued that care long after her husband had died and she herself reached her seventies. When her strength ran out, she finally agreed with Hugh to place Rosie permanently in a state psychiatric hospital, and it was there that she died, about five years after their mother's death. Hugh visited Rosie regularly until the end, but they were empty visits in which, for the most part, brother and sister sat and stared at each other, saying little.

I had asked Hugh few questions during the hours of our interview. His intensity was such that once he began delving into Rosie's history and his, I did not want to interrupt. As his narrative was drawing to a close he turned to me, as if noticing my presence for the first time.

"It's a sad story, isn't it?" he asked.

"Yes, it is, so sad for all of you. But I'd like to ask you something." I felt he would not mind my intruding on his privacy now after he had revealed so much. "You said when we began that all your unhappiness and neuroses stemmed from your relationship with Rosie. What did you mean by that?"

"Look at me," he answered, standing up and looking down at himself. "I'm the loneliest man in the world. All alone, except for my students, and they can't help me."

Hugh teaches seventh-grade English in a Queens junior high school. Occasionally he publishes poems and essays in elite literary journals, although he admits readily that his talent is a small one—"I may be Irish, but I'm no Joyce or Yeats." Unmarried, he lives alone in a modest ground-floor apartment that has bars on the windows to protect against the frequent thefts in his neighborhood. Summers he travels a bit—sometimes with a friend—and gathers material to use in his classes.

"Because of Rosie," he continued, "I never wanted to marry or have a family. I no longer worry that I will get sick like her, but with so much emphasis these days on genetics, I certainly would never take the chance of having a child who might become like her."

"That doesn't sound neurotic," I interjected.

"Neurotic? What's neurotic . . ." He was up pacing and chain-smoking again. "What's neurotic is that I never married and that I have no interest in sex." He seemed to spit the words out, daring me to laugh, daring himself to go on. "I was too young. I saw too much, and it was hideous. I grew up with a revulsion toward sex. The whole thing disgusts me, so I keep my distance from it. And I live alone.",

He turned toward me as if disgusted with himself. "Through much of my life I felt overwhelmed by my sister's misery and by the constant noise and commotion in our house. I found refuge in school and in reading. I used to hide in corners at home or at my grandparents' house when I could get away to read stories about happy families. Because of my reading, I may be the only fellow from my old neighborhood who made it through high school, let alone college."

He paused, asked for a glass of water, walked around my office.

"For years and years I felt burdened by my sister and by my parents' treatment of her," he continued. "All I wanted was quiet, and peace. And now I've got it, all the peace and quiet in the world. And I'm so terribly lonely."

Throughout childhood and adolescence, brothers and sisters experience each other's illnesses, from ordinary colds to broken arms or legs to more serious or life-threatening diseases. Depending on the age of a child and the nature of the illness, the reaction to a sick sib may be sympathy and commiseration, jealousy over the attention the other receives, or fear for the other's life and for one's own. My brother still remembers vividly the day we waited for an ambulance that would take me to the hospital for emergency surgery after an acute attack of appendicitis. I was about seven, and he has a mental image of me lying in bed crying, the window blinds shut tight as if to close out all joy and sunshine, and my mother hovering by, pale with worry.

"It was such a shock," he says. "I was totally unprepared. It was the first time I realized that something bad could happen to someone in my family, or to me, and I was so scared."

In adulthood the fears that accompany the serious illness of a sibling stem not from lack of preparation or understanding but from understanding too well the possible consequences. Along with fears about one's own health, such illness arouses powerful feelings of love, wishful dreams of holding on to that sibling forever, and a deep sorrow that pushes aside old competitions and angers.

When illness strikes, adult siblings often become bulwarks of support and consolation for each other. They sweat out with a sick sib agonizing waits for results of biopsies and CAT scans. They make themselves available to the other's family, and they serve as conduits to parents. In many families, it is a healthy sibling who breaks the news of another's illness to parents—or helps hide it from them—in order to spare the other the extra burden of a mother's or father's anxieties.

When a crisis ends and a sib recovers, old patterns of relating usually take hold again. But the illness, with its foreshadowing of future loss, can also leave a residue of sadness and longings for greater closeness. After Pam—in the last chapter—contracted pneumonia, Gail put aside work and family responsibilities to care for her. Now, more aware than ever of their "mortality," she feels guilty about not phoning or writing her sister more frequently.

The story is different, the feelings more twisted and complex for both children and adults, when the illness of a sibling—like the illness of Hugh's sister Rosie—is chronic, when a sickness or disability stretches from childhood or adolescence into adult life, when it defines that sibling as different and becomes a major focus of family life. Then the sadness the other feels may be tinged with self-pity for the unfairness of it all; the love with hate for an illness—or the bearer of that illness—that has disrupted the normal course of living, and the dreams with fantasies of having a "real" brother or sister with whom to share one's life.

There are millions of people, like Hugh, who grow up with a sibling who is chronically ill or disabled, either mentally or physically. (Sibling support and advocacy groups place the number of disabled at thirty-seven million. The number of siblings of the disabled is obviously much greater.) Not all speak of suffering as Hugh does. Many describe in far more positive terms the satisfactions of helping a sick or disturbed sibling, the joy of observing a sib's progress—the small increments as well as large strides—and the rewards that come from understanding, because of the sibling, others who have difficulties.

The impact on family members can also vary with different kinds of disabilities. As upsetting as it may be to have a brother or sister who is blind or deaf, for example, that person's behavior will generally be more predictable and easier to relate to both in childhood and later years than the behavior of a severely retarded sibling, whose mental world is impossible to penetrate.

Even so, there are certain childhood experiences and attitudes that hold true for all families of the handicapped, whether the impairment is physical or mental. As normal a life as the blind child may lead in comparison with the severely retarded one, for instance, sibs can never play the same rough-and-tumble games with that child as they do with other children. They can never look into that child's eyes and know what she is thinking as they can with other people. Nor can they ever really understand what it is like to *be* that child.

"Actually, it hardly matters how we label these people," says Helen Featherstone, in *A Difference in the Family*, one of the best books written on disabilities in children. "Their limitations will touch the lives of their sisters and brothers, their mothers and fathers."

For siblings, the limitations a child's disability imposes will affect the relationship between them probably all their lives. The normal ups and downs of the sibling seesaw, the angers and jealousies, the affections and loyalties, the ambivalences—all are intensified and distorted when one sib is handicapped. Hugh loved Rosie, but he also wanted her dead. He longed for a big sister, but instead, he, the youngest, had to become a big brother. He could barely communicate with Rosie, yet he knew they had a bond between them independent of their parents.

A large part of that bond for Hugh was his identification with Rosie. In spite of her extreme illness, he could put himself in her place and comfort her. But he also worried that he might die at the same age she had. Identification, which occurs among all siblings, can be the source of some of the greatest warmth and greatest frustrations for those with a disabled or chronically ill brother or sister. Because of their identification, nonhandicapped sibs like Hugh are able to empathize with handicapped ones. Because of their identification, they may also be frightened or overwhelmed by the other's disability.

The more alike a child is to a sick or disabled sibling, the greater the identification will be and, often, the greater the frustration and pain. A child who has diabetes or a chronic form of leukemia does not look or sound different from other children. A sister or brother can identify with that child's suffering. But precisely because of that identification, the sibling might feel distraught by the other's illness and fearful of becoming ill in a similar way. To shut out those fears and the other's pain, the healthy sibling might avoid hospital visits or act cold and distant at home.

In a study of college students with retarded siblings, psychologist Frances K. Grossman found that students had the greatest difficulty coping when their sib was only mildly retarded and therefore most like them. The identification was too threatening to the well sib, especially if both were of the same sex. "Whenever I see something in him that reminds me of myself," said one student, referring to his mildly retarded older brother, "it really bothers me. That's why . . . I guess I avoided him at times."

There can be special frustration if a sibling had identified closely with a disabled child before the disability began. Hugh cannot remember Rosie before she became schizophrenic, but others speak emotionally of the "befores." Connie, a college senior, had been inseparable from her older brother Ron. Only ten months apart in age, they had shared the same interests and the same circle of friends. Six years ago he became "a different person," Connie explains, when a car crash left him physically and mentally impaired. In spite of plastic surgery, his face still "looks funny and distorted" and his thinking is slow and disorganized.

"I look at photos of us taken just a few weeks before the accident," Connie says, "and I still bleed inside. Until I was fifteen, I had a loving brother who was almost like a twin to me. Now we're worlds apart."

For many people the frustrations of having lost—or never having had—a sibling with whom one could identify in a normal way include a deep, smoldering, pervasive anger at the disabled other. It's an anger that siblings of the handicapped may not express in the matter-of-fact way other siblings are allowed to show anger. Yet the anger exists, and even when not put into words, it may reveal itself.

"I used to have a recurring dream that I killed someone, buried someone, and I'd wake up in the morning terrified that I was going to be discovered," said a forty-three-year-old man, youngest of three brothers—an older whom he adores and a middle who is retarded. "Then I'd say, 'Oh, I was dreaming.' When I got older, I realized what it was about. In my mind I had buried my retarded brother Henry because in my mind I hated him. I didn't even know I felt that way. But I knew that whenever my older brother Larry and I would want to go someplace, he'd try to come along, and I'd have this tremendous anger. I'd think, 'Does he have to come along? Does he have to be here?' "

Anger at a handicapped sibling exists because that sib often interferes with family life and relationships. It also exists because having a disabled sib saddles the children in a family with extra responsibilities, sometimes even the actual care of the disabled one.

The college students in Grossman's study emphasized the burden of responsibilities that fell on their shoulders because of a retarded sibling. Community-college students from working-class homes suffered especially compared with private-college students whose parents were more likely to have obtained help from outside the family. And—as they do in so many other caregiving situations—sisters more often than brothers bore the weight of a sib's handicap, in many cases curtailing their social lives and career goals to help out at home.

Mostly, children feel angry at a disabled sibling because of the inordinate amount of time, attention, energy, and resources their parents give the child with special needs. From their point of view, it is as if that child is the only child in the family, with little room for others. Connie described how, after her brother's automobile accident, he was hospitalized for three months and during that time her parents spent every free moment they had with him. She could understand that, she said. But her bitterness and resentment grew as he recuperated during the next three years and her parents continued to devote almost all their time and energy to him. "I went off on my own," she said. "I had not only lost the brother I knew and loved, I also lost my parents because of him. It was hard not to resent him."

For many siblings a special kind of resentment may surround another subject, one so sensitive they rarely dare raise it with parents. That is the question of whether a severely disabled sibling should be placed in an institution. A baby born with Down's syndrome, for example, is destined to be mentally retarded and, often, to suffer physical disabilities as well. Whereas years ago physicians usually advised parents to institutionalize such children, medical opinion today emphasizes the progress they can make at home.

Parents who elect to raise children with Down's syndrome or other forms of retardation at home feel they are giving them the best opportunities possible to reach their potential. The children's siblings would probably agree. Yet deep within themselves they may wonder what it might have been like if the disabled child were *not* at home. Like Hugh, they may think, "Why couldn't I have parents who paid more attention to me?" instead of organizing family life for the sake of the child with special needs.

Such thinking, of course, brings guilt—the handmaiden of anger and resentment. And siblings of the disabled do feel guilt—about their anger, about their own good health, about wishing the other one away. Paradoxically, if the sibling *is* away, siblings may also feel guilty about that. In Grossman's study, a number of college students whose retarded siblings had been institutionalized at an early age felt guilty and uncomfortable with that situation, as if they bore some responsibility for it. Unless the family had maintained close and meaningful contact with the institutionalized child, they also felt embarrassed that a sibling had been so completely rejected. (The decision about whether to institutionalize a severely disabled child is complex and multifaceted, and one that parents need to base on their own wishes and needs and those of all their children.)

"Embarrassment" is a word that comes up again and again in recollections about handicapped siblings. Almost more than any other emotion, adults looking back remember their sense of being embarrassed by their handicapped sib's appearance and behavior, by noises and mannerisms. They also remember feeling protective, wishing they could shield their sib from the stares of adults or the taunts of other children—but not so protective that they were willing to risk their friendships because of the other's differentness.

Connie spoke of a "terrible" time after Ron recovered from his accident. The friends they had in common rejected him because of his slowness and strange appearance. Deeply loyal to him, Connie tried to include him in parties and outings but was afraid she'd lose all her friends if she pressed too hard. At one point she heard some of them exchanging crude jokes about Ron, and she felt herself torn between wanting to lash out at them and wanting to hold on to their friendship. Her mother finally said to her, "Your friends are shits! Is that who you want to hang out with?" With that, she broke away and moved toward a new circle of friends.

Anger, resentment, guilt, embarrassment—these are some of the most painful feelings siblings of the disabled carry within them. And what of the disabled sibling? What feelings do the mentally disturbed, the physically handicapped, the chronically ill children and adults have toward their well brothers and sisters?

Anger and resentment also, of course. They are angry at their bodies that have failed them, at their parents who created them imperfectly, at their siblings who enjoy the good health they lack. They are also frustrated at the dissimilarities between their siblings and themselves. From her studies Grossman concluded that retarded siblings who are older than their well ones and are aware of their situation are particularly frustrated. These children are able to recognize that their roles as leaders have been usurped. The younger handicapped may be less unhappy, for like all youngers, they are willing to accept their elders' care and protection. What is true in this regard of retarded siblings is also true of those who are physically disabled.

But disabled children also have warm, loving, and appreciative feelings for their siblings. What a handicapped child wants more than anything is to be accepted, included, and treated as if normal by others. Siblings provide that treatment in a way that nobody else does. Parents worry, shelter, and guard over their disabled children; other children hold the disabled at arm's length or—cruelly—mock them. Siblings, accustomed to living with a brother or sister's disability, can be accepting and even casual about it, and that acceptance adds normalcy to the handicapped child's life.

A librarian whose younger brother, Stanley, had severe mental illness could nevertheless recall playing games together as children that gave Stanley great pleasure. In one game, in which they pretended to be spiders, the older brother would create "spider webs" by crisscrossing strings throughout the household. "My mother would yell at us about the strings all over," he said, "but Stanley loved it because for once he and I were in league against our parents instead of his always feeling like the outsider."

Over time, the nature of a handicap will influence the disabled's connections to siblings. As they reach adolescence and adulthood, numbers of the blind, deaf, palsied, or otherwise physically disabled gain control over their disability and live satisfying lives that draw them closer to siblings. The mentally disabled usually are not able to achieve these goals, and, in fact, they often fall further behind as the years go on. Tragically, the very tactics they use in their desperate need for closeness and normalcy often push their siblings further away.

A woman portrayed a Thanksgiving dinner at her parents' home that she and her older brother attended with their families, from which her schizophrenic—often violent—younger brother was excluded. "Every half hour," she related, "Michael would call and say, 'Is Allison having a good time? Is Carl having a good time? Are you having a good time?' " After that, her parents never again had a family Thanksgiving or Christmas dinner. "Mother knew she could not have Michael with us, but if she couldn't have all her children together, she decided she would have none of them. We've all missed out because of Michael, and that's made us push him away more than ever," the woman said.

In a thousand ways, well children in a family, like this woman, like Hugh, learn that the disability of a brother or sister can disrupt not only normal relations between siblings but also normal relations with parents.

With every birth, say psychiatrists, parents harbor within them the fantasy of having a perfect child, and each of us, at birth, is the recipient of this fantasy. Because no one can truly be that magical child, parents must try, as their children grow, to come to terms with realities. For children, part of the task of growing up is to kill off their parents' visions of who they are supposed to be and to become who they *are*, individuals in their own right.

When a child is disabled or deformed, these fantasies of perfection are quickly and cruelly destroyed, and more than ever parents must struggle to give up what some psychiatrists have called "the ghost of the perfect child." In that struggle they often turn with greater intensity to their other children, to fill in for the losses and the smothered dreams.

For nondisabled children, that intensity can make relations with their parents seem like a double-edged sword. On the one hand, they feel shortchanged by their parents' utter devotion to the handicapped sib. On the other, they perceive themselves to be the *real* center of their parents' lives because they bear the weight of the parents' deepest wishes and expectations. For these sibs the task of killing off the magical fantasies and finding their real selves is fraught with special difficulty.

Sue Miller portrays this difficulty in her book *Family Pictures*. Nina, the narrator, speaks of herself and her younger sisters as having been born to "make up for" their autistic older brother Randall. In one conversation, she accuses her mother of having loved her only conditionally, in contrast to her unconditional love for Randall. The condition? "It's be quiet, be good, be happy, be well. Be well. And I'll love you. I'll love you, *my perfect baby.*"

To be well and perfect, happy and successful, to achieve, and bestow on parents that portion of life's joys they have been deprived of —these are the pressures normal children carry within them for life when they have a sibling who is handicapped.

Along with the pressures well siblings feel to be perfect, they also suffer from the stresses weighing on their parents. The enormous burden of caring for a handicapped child can create marital difficulties that in turn lead to tensions within the family as a whole. Often, too, absorbed in the care of their special child, parents neglect to explain the nature of the child's disability to the others in the family. Or they avoid doing so because they find the subject too painful to discuss. But without that knowledge, children become fearful and anxious about their siblings and themselves. As they get older the well siblings often worry about transmitting the disorder to their own children, or—like Hugh—they brood about dying at the same age as the other.

Grossman's study of college students with retarded siblings found that even among these educated young adults, many had little information about the nature of their sibs' handicap, and many were confused and somewhat overwhelmed by it. Those who handled the situation best came from homes in which the illness had been discussed openly, siblings' questions had been answered honestly, and feelings and fears were not shrouded in secrecy or shame.

In adult life siblings of the disabled struggle with new feelings and fears. When parents age, grow frail, and die, siblings often inherit responsibility, and sometimes custody, for another who is handicapped, and brothers and sisters who may earlier have separated themselves from family problems—either physically or emotionally—are now drawn into the orbit of the other one's life. Margaret Moorman, writing in the *New York Times* after her mother's death about a sister with manic-depressive illness, admitted that "I once thought that when my mother died I would rather kill myself than have to take care of Sally as she did." She saw her choices as devastating: either give up her own life and move to Virginia, where her sister lived, or "fail my sister utterly and be unable to live with myself."

As it turned out, Moorman did neither. Instead she kept in close touch with Sally and monitored her care from afar. For herself, she found support through a self-help and advocacy organization called Siblings and Adult Children Network, a committee of the National Alliance for the Mentally Ill. (Other organizations that offer support and information to siblings of the chronically ill include the Sibling Information Network, with headquarters in Connecticut, and Siblings for Significant Change, based in New York.) With the support she received and the support she gave, she and her sister have been able to draw closer together yet maintain their separate lives.

One of the major lessons Moorman learned was to respect Sally's wish for—and ability to handle—a certain amount of independence. It is a lesson others in her circumstances also have to learn, for in their zeal to replace parents and do the right thing, well sibs sometimes overprotect and overcontrol their handicapped ones. The man who had recurring dreams of burying his retarded brother Henry described his older brother's rush to take Henry into his own home after their mother's death. "It was a disaster," he said. "Henry had nobody to talk to all day—my other brother and sister-in-law both worked—and he sat and stared into space for hours. Now they've put him into a group home for the mentally retarded, and he has companions and goes to work from there. Everybody's much happier."

But solutions like this are not always possible, and then the lesson may be painful: The only way to preserve oneself is to hold the other at a distance, even while assuming the required duties. The librarian mentioned earlier learned, he says, to deal with bureaucracy in keeping his brother—who became violent as he grew older—hospitalized, despite federal and state cuts in hospitalization for the mentally ill. He also learned to deal with his own anguish in turning down his brother's pleas not to live out his days in an institution. " 'I love you very much,' I would tell Stanley,' " he said, " 'but I can't let you live with me and trample over my life.' "

The end results of his brother's illness for this man, as for others, are bitterness, anger, and guilt—always guilt—because of the fate that burdened him with a disabled brother and because of the brother himself. "I don't remember resenting the time my parents gave Stanley," he said. "What I resented then and until he died a few years ago was the time he took out of *my* life." Although married, he—like Hugh

—has chosen not to have children, not only for genetic reasons but because "having a child seems like one more heavy weight."

Nevertheless, the librarian says, the outcome of having grown up with a disabled brother is not all negative. Because of his parents' preoccupation with Stanley, he became as a child more self-sufficient and self-directed than other children and maintained through adulthood an ability to be decisive in his work and his personal life. And because of his loneliness as a child, he has come to value and therefore to sustain strong and good friendships as an adult.

For Hugh, the horrors of his childhood experience with his mentally ill sister Rosie have had the opposite effect; he has been left lonely and unsatisfied. But he, too, speaks of another side of himself, an ability, because of the enormous compassion he felt for Rosie, to empathize with others in difficulty.

That attribute of compassion marks many other siblings of the chronically disabled. Grossman found that college students with retarded sibs were often more tolerant of differences among their classmates and more willing to take a stand against prejudice than other students. As adults many siblings of the disabled enter such helping professions as medicine, social work, nursing, or psychiatry. The ability to help others may never outweigh the pain of growing up with a severely disabled sib or the ongoing responsibility of caring for one, but for many it has made those difficulties far easier to bear.

The death of Hugh Shea's sister Rosie left him sad and fearful that he might also die at a young age. The death of the librarian's brother Stanley left him, too, feeling sad for the tragedy of his brother's life. Yet he also felt relieved that decades of torment were over for both of them. The death of a deaf brother in childhood, a Detroit physician related, has left him with snatches of memory and waves of love that wash over him at unexpected moments.

"Deaf people make strange sounds," he said. "There's a loudness that's totally unmodulated and everything is inappropriate. When I was a child, I was embarrassed by the noises my deaf brother Ernest made, but I'd forgotten about them over time. Then one day recently I got on the elevator at work and there was a deaf child making sounds I had not heard in forty years. I was overwhelmed with emotion, with longing for Ernest, and with a love for my little brother I did not even know I felt so deeply."

What he did know he felt, the physician went on, was guilt that his secret wishes to be rid of his brother had come true. A child in London during World War II, he remembers the first air raid by German planes, soon after Ernest's death: "Bombs came crashing down. I was in the basement, and I kept saying, 'I'll never be bad again.' It was this association I had made—I was nine and he was six when he died—that somehow my badness toward him had caused his death."

That association remained in adult life, and it shows itself, the physician is convinced, on the anniversary of his brother's birthday. Then, invariably, without being conscious of the date, he does something "outrageously self-inconveniencing" to punish himself for his "badness" as a child and for his own survival. Most recently, he left his car unlocked with his medical kit inside when he went to teach a class, only to find—as might be expected—both gone when he returned. " 'Oh, my God,' I said," the physician recalled, " 'this must be Ernest's birthday.' And it was."

Although the reactions of this physician, of Hugh, of the librarian, are to sibling deaths complicated by lives of disability, they hold true for many other sibling deaths. When a brother or sister dies, whatever the circumstances, siblings experience feelings of profound loss, of love and identification, sometimes of relief, and frequently of self-blame.

If the loss is abrupt, as in an accidental death or sudden illness, it can crush sibling survivors. Robbed of the chance to say good-bye or make peace with a sibling, they become tormented with fantasies of undoing the death. "If only I could see him one more time," they think. "If only I could tell her how much I love her." "If only I could say I'm sorry." Long after the death, all the fights they had ever had with that sibling, all the angry words exchanged or hateful wishes imagined, continue to reverberate through their minds while they try to come to terms with the reality of their loss.

If a death has resulted from a long illness, siblings, like other family members, often feel relief that the other's suffering has ended. But relief also brings guilt for having wished for the end or for impatience during the course of the illness. And the death brings sorrow and loneliness, regardless of how much the sibling or the family had suffered.

Unfortunately, these sibling reactions often go unrecognized and unacknowledged. For when a daughter or son dies, the monumental grief of parents overshadows all other feelings in the family, and siblings find themselves in the position of being their parents' comforters, their pillars of strength. When a husband or wife dies, the grief of the surviving spouse and of children "takes precedence," as a friend wrote me after the death of her brother, over that of the person's sibs, who are relegated to the role of "loyal supporters" of the bereaved family.

Yet grief for a sibling who has died can be as intense as the grief for any family member, whether that death occurs in childhood, like that of the physician's brother, or adulthood, like Hugh's sister Rosie. Or even before the sibling's own birth.

Before my brother and I were born, my parents had another baby, a boy, who died at about eighteen months of age. Though we never knew that baby, we heard about him throughout our lives, always indirectly, through a sigh from my mother, a sentence or two from my father. I knew from early childhood that the lost baby had been bright and beautiful, everything a parent might wish for. I knew that he died of pneumonia and that when my brother and I had pneumonia ourselves as children, my parents were beside themselves with fear. I knew that my mother always blamed herself irrationally for that death and that my father has never stopped thinking of his firstborn son, not even for a single day of his long life.

More recently I knew, because my father told me, that when my mother became pregnant for a second time, they prayed for a son to replace the one lost to them. They were joyously grateful when their prayers were answered and my brother was born.

I have not devoted years or even days in morbid dwelling on that child I never knew; it was not until recently, in fact, that I became aware that he occupied a greater part of my life than I had ever realized. The awareness came with a rush of emotion when I received a letter from my father sent to my brother and me and all our cousins detailing the location and rules about a family cemetery plot he and his four younger brothers had purchased years ago. None of us have had the slightest interest in that plot except to visit it more often than we would have liked in recent years as we buried each of those four brothers.

My father's letter had a small addendum. It described the location of one tiny grave where "our first child Sidney is buried," in case anybody was interested. Sidney. They had never said his name aloud, but somehow I had heard it before. Suddenly he was real, and fragments of thoughts that had flitted through my mind over the years came together as a whole.

"Sidney." I spoke the name. What would it have been like if you had lived? What would it have been like to have two older brothers? I remembered thinking as a child during various of our country's wars that had he been alive, he might have been of an age to fight, might have died in those wars, causing my parents even greater pain than had his actual baby death. But if he had lived, what would he be now? What would he look like? I ached to know. And Robert. How different would he be if he were a middle child instead of the elder of us two? What if he were a second son? Would he have been jealous of Sidney? Would I have been left out of a league the two boys formed?

And more: Would I have been left out altogether? Literally never have been born? None of my aunts and uncles on either side of the family had more than two children. It was the fashion in my parents' Depression generation to have small families. Would my parents have stopped at two—two sons, no daughter—if Sidney had lived? Did we swap lives, he and I, he losing his so that I could be born?

The questions flooded my mind as I read my father's addendum about little Sidney's grave. I wondered what Robert thought when he saw that note. We have never discussed the older brother we might have had, or any of the other "might-have-beens." Robert would probably find my ruminations foolish. The baby died, after all, more than a half century ago. He's a phantom brother. He barely existed. He has no relevance to our lives.

Yet Robert was what the experts call a replacement child. Upon him were placed the hopes and strivings of grief-stricken parents bereaved of their son. Surely their thwarted dreams for the first had to have influenced their behavior toward the second. Does Robert's conviction that he was their center, their pride and joy, come of the place he filled for them? Are his many successes products of some unconscious knowledge that he *had* to fill the place of that idealized first child? Are his insecurities?

Most times, the death of the brother I never had is a tiny shadow hovering in an obscure corner of my memory, to emerge when a letter or word, a name, prods it into consciousness. For others, such deaths loom larger, affecting their thoughts and behavior more directly.

Anna O., one of the most famous case studies in the annals of psychoanalysis, was haunted by sibling death. In reality a well-known German social worker of the early 1900s named Bertha Pappenheim, "Anna" had an extreme, pathological reaction to the death of her father, and her illness was described by her analyst, Josef Breuer. In a study of the case, psychoanalyst George Pollock contends that Bertha regarded herself as a replacement for a sister who died before she was born and possibly for a second sister who died later. The deaths of those sisters and her position as a replacement child may have contributed significantly to her excessive reaction to her father's death. Pappenheim's life's work of rescuing young women trapped into prostitution and delinquency may also have been an unconscious attempt to atone for her own survival and her inability to rescue the sisters whose places she had taken.

To replace a dead sibling can often mean finding oneself swaddled for life under the fervent protection of parents terrified of ever losing another child. It can also mean competing with a ghost, an image fixed in time and forever perfect in the eyes of parents. ("He was so smart, he walked and talked before he was a year old," my father told me when I asked about the baby who had died.) That impossible position has led a college student I know—bright, achieving, ranking high in his Ivy League class—to contemplate dropping out of school. "All my life I've had the feeling my parents wanted me to be two people," he says, "me and the baby boy who died before I was born. I can't keep up anymore with the wonderful person he was going to be. I have to find out who *I* am."

If the death of a child who existed before you did can have such a powerful impact, the death of a sibling one has known, loved, played with, and fought against can be devastating.

When such a death occurs in childhood, siblings are likely to be confused and frightened as well as deeply saddened. Because young children do not completely comprehend the meaning of death, they may feel abandoned yet unable to understand what has happened to a brother or sister. They may also be overwhelmed and disturbed by their parents' anguish, and wonder whether they have done something to cause it.

Despite their sorrow, children do not mourn the way adults do. A child may cry briefly over the death of a brother or sister, then go off to play, only to spend hours alone later daydreaming about the lost sib. Or the child may bury her grief and become a perfect "angel," trying in every way possible to make up to her parents for their loss. Consumed by their own pain, parents do not usually recognize how hurt their children are, and they neglect to help them deal with the loss. Doubly bereft, then—of their sibling and of their parents as a source of comfort—surviving children often close themselves off, rarely revealing their innermost sorrows and fears.

In adult life that pattern of burying painful feelings may reappear in responses to other losses: an inwardness and seeming lack of emotion on the outside; inside profound pain and a terror of death. People who have not been helped to come to terms with the loss of a sibling as children often become anxious and fearful adults, overreacting to illness, needing to be in control and therefore afraid to take risks, frightened of any unknown situation lest they feel as they had once felt in childhood, helpless, confused, and afraid.

Twisted into the raw pain and sorrow children feel are strands of self-blame. Like the physician who still punishes himself for his deaf brother's death, children interpret their secret wishes to be rid of their rival as having supernatural powers to come true, to destroy the other. Freud commented that the death of his baby brother Julius "left the germ of self-reproaches in me," because of the angry thoughts and childish jealousy he had harbored.

For some children and adults as well (although probably not so for Freud, who was adored by his mother) the self-reproaches come also of feeling inadequate in comparison to a dead sib, of tortured self-questioning about why you lived while the other died. Again and again people recalled that when a brother or sister had died, they had suffered feelings that it was *they* who should have been taken instead. Typical of such thinking was a thirty-two-year-old woman whose older sister had been killed during childhood in a car crash. "Even when she was alive, I used to wonder of what use I was to my parents," she said. "My sister was everything they wanted. When she died, their lives fell apart, and I still believe that if they had to choose to lose one of us, I'm the one they would have given up."

To some extent those feelings express the haunting "survivor guilt" common to people who feel they have escaped death or the tragic fate of others through no special virtue of their own. More explicitly, however, siblings' feelings that they are the ones who should have died instead of another are often planted unwittingly by parents. Their grief and concentration on the loss of one child can make the others feel unwanted and unneeded.

In a collection of vignettes about his patients, psychotherapist Irvin Yalom describes a mother so inconsolable even four years after the death of her daughter that she finally blurted out, "The wrong one died." Her confession articulated the message she had been giving her two surviving sons. And that message, she discovered, had helped turn one son to drugs and the other to petty crime as they grew up in the shadow of their sister's death.

Feelings of inadequacy and identification with a sibling who dies become especially intense for teenagers, who understand the meaning of death and are able to think about it in terms of themselves. Aside from a grinding, sometimes intolerable, grief over their loss, they may suffer unrelenting remorse about not having spent more time with a sick sibling or not having visited more frequently when that sib was in the hospital. They may also become preoccupied with fears and thoughts of dying. Or, with the bravado of youth, and with rage at the fate that took their sibling, they may defy death by taking life-threatening risks that show *they* will beat the system even if their sib could not.

The French aviator and writer Antoine de Saint-Exupéry, author of *The Little Prince*, identified so closely with a younger brother who died when the author was seventeen that even as an adult he took careless chances while flying, almost as if he didn't care whether he lived or died. He finally disappeared—nobody knows exactly what happened—on a flying mission in the midst of World War II. In *The Little Prince*, before the boy-prince dies, he promises to remain present, always, in the stars in the sky—the author's fantasy, perhaps, of not truly losing his brother.

Like younger children, adolescents may not mourn a sibling openly, or at least not in the way their parents expect them to. Teenagers have a powerful need to conform to their friends' behavior, and open expressions of grief can be embarrassing because they set the young person apart from others. "I hate the devastating words of kindness and the looks of pity my friends give me," said an eighteen-year-old boy who had recently lost a sister to cancer. To avoid special attention and looks of pity, to avoid being different, teenagers often lean over backward to act "normal" after a sibling's death.

That facade of normalcy may hurt parents, who wonder how their son or daughter can be so unfeeling. Yet the more demanding a parent may be of "proper" mourning behavior, the more a teenager may move in the other direction, sometimes openly rebelling, sometimes simply avoiding parents. Beyond the need for normalcy, such behavior by teenagers also stems from their need to get on with the job of growing up. As they struggle to find their own footing, they resist being pulled back into family life by parents who may try to hold on more tightly than ever now that one child is gone.

Instead of expressing their grief, teenagers may become withdrawn, may drink more than usual, or may become immersed in a frenzy of activity that helps muffle the dreadful reality of the sibling's death. In adult years, such repression may make people especially frightened by illness and death, especially distraught after a loss, and unable to cope, just as they had been unable to cope in their youth.

The most haunting of all sibling deaths a teenager can experience, and most long-lasting in its effects on later life, may be a sibling's suicide. It is a sudden death that weighs survivors down with feelings of fear, failure, guilt, and rage.

The fear that grips siblings is the fear that they, too, might allow despair and unhappiness to overpower them one day. They, too, might lose control and act on their most dangerous impulses. The sense of failure comes from feeling that they should have been able to prevent the suicide, from having failed the sibling at the most important moment of life—the moment he or she chose death. The guilt is all-pervasive: the guilt of old conflicts that might have contributed to the sib's despondency, of not having shown enough love, and of being alive when the other is dead.

And the rage, which may appear later, results from feeling betrayed by the dead sibling, rejected along with life itself, and left behind to help parents make some sense out of a universe that has been shattered.

A Harvard student described a wake in which a young man named Stan mourned and raged at his brother Peter, who had committed suicide.

"Be kind to your parents, Stan," a friend of his mother said early in the evening.

"But who will be a comfort to me?" Stan asked.

"I think you can take care of yourself," the woman replied, leaving Stan, as his parents had left him, alone with his feelings.

Later, making love to a girlfriend, Stan thought about his brother: "I hoped that somewhere above us in the smoke circled the shade of my brother Peter, who had taken his life. I hoped that he watched us embrace, that he watched me begin to tear myself from him. I wanted him to gnash his teeth and drift out of all reckoning, I wanted to ruin him as he had ruined us. . . ."

Occasionally, from the "ruin" of a sibling's suicide can come some benefits. Surviving siblings often say that as adults they have been driven to achievement and success, as though through their accomplishments they will be able to wipe out the stigma of failure that clings to their family. But for others the suicide becomes a precursor to their own self-destruction. For once one has broken the barrier into death, it becomes less hard for another.

I saw that barrier being broken for a second time in a family in which an older brother, at age seventeen, had gone out into the woods and shot himself through the heart. Ten years later his younger sister, now aged twenty-five, mother of two children, depressed and facing divorce, went to the same spot in the woods and shot herself in the same way. It was the ultimate statement of the impact of a sibling's death in adolescence.

And what of the death of a sibling in adult life? What effect does it have?

Sometimes, oddly, like a suicide, it can lead to a unique kind of creativity and achievement. John F. Kennedy was slated by his powerfully controlling father to be a teacher or writer, his older brother, Joe, to be a politician and eventually run for President. With Joe's death in a bombing mission during World War II, the torch was passed to John, who became the thirty-fifth President of the United States. John's assassination inspired Robert Kennedy, the next younger brother, to try to step into his place by seeking the Democratic nomination for President, a campaign that ended in the tragedy of his own assassination. The youngest of the brothers, Edward Kennedy, later unsuccessfully sought the presidential nomination and has remained a senator. He often invokes the names of his brothers as his ideals and guides.

But such spurs to achievement are rare after the death of a sibling in adulthood. Mostly the aftermath is an overpowering sense of loss. When a brother or sister dies, siblings feel they have lost something of themselves. A piece of their history no longer exists, for that sibling connected them with the past as nobody else in the world can. A sibling's death in adult life, even more than a parent's, leaves survivors alone with their deepest memories. There will never again be anybody who knows them in the same way.

These feelings of loss are made all the more poignant by the knowledge that there remains with that sibling "unfinished business" that will now never get resolved. In the natural order of things, we expect our siblings to live as long as we do, and most of us put off thoughts of death until old age—and may avoid them even then. We assume there will always be plenty of time to catch up, plenty of time to talk. When that time is cut short and the things we would have liked to say are left unspoken, the loss reaches into the heart of our being. There will not be another chance. Whatever has been left unsettled will stay that way forever. A woman whose younger brother had recently died of AIDS put it simply. "All the possibilities we expected to have are gone," she said.

The epidemic of AIDS, tragically, has wiped out those possibilities at a young age for many siblings. Deaths from AIDS (along with drug abuse, automobile accidents, murder, and other unexpected and shocking causes, whose rates among young adults seem continually to rise) have also brought the realities of their own mortality to the forefront of siblings' consciousness long before most expected to have to face those realities.

Barbara Lazear Ascher, writing of the funeral procession for her younger brother, dead of AIDS at thirty-one, describes sitting with her parents and sister "still as stones" as they rode through the streets of New Orleans. She speaks of the shock of learning of his illness, of the terrible grief that followed his death. And of the fears: "When a sibling dies, the absolute certainty of death replaces the cherished illusion that maybe we'll be the exceptions. When a sibling dies, death tugs at our own shirttails. There's no unclasping its persistent grip. 'You too,' it says. 'Yes, even you.' "

When death occurs, adults recognize in ways children cannot the finality of a sibling's life and the fragility of their own. But like younger survivors of a sibling death, adult survivors often bury their own feelings, not so much because they do not know how to mourn, but because so many others—their parents, their children, their in-laws and nieces and nephews—lean on them for help. Siblings who have been thought of as the most responsible in the family may find themselves becoming the mainstay of other sisters and brothers but also the target of their anguish and disappointments. "My sisters are angry at me," said a woman whose brother had died of heart disease. "They think as oldest I should have been able to keep him from dying."

The demands of others combined with enduring pain after a sibling's death were brought home to me by a nursery school teacher, Melissa Fields. Having heard of my research on siblings, she called to say she would like to speak to me about her older sister Cara, who had died eighteen months earlier of breast cancer.

"I'm glad to see you have the Kleenex out," she said as she spotted the tissue box I always kept handy during interviews. "I'll need them."

In fact she turned to the box less frequently than others who had not come to discuss loss. Their tears had resulted from difficult relationships, from ambivalence toward a sibling, or from longings for closeness that could never be realized. Melissa described none of that with Cara. She knew sorrow and loneliness and grief, but she knew also that there had been an unequivocal friendship between them and a mutual admiration that allowed her to see Cara as her mentor.

" 'Much of her leadership role flowed naturally from her ascribed status as first child,' " Melissa read to me from a eulogy she had given at her sister's funeral. " 'Thus it was Cara who was first with braces, glasses, piano lessons; it was Cara who paved the way for her sister and brother with the first date, the first driver's license, and the first college applications.' "

Cara had been four years older than Melissa and ten years older than their younger brother Walter, to whom she had been "without doubt" a second mother. Melissa had never been close to Walter, seeing herself much more a younger sister to Cara than a middle child with a younger brother. In fact her relationship to Walter was one of the issues concerning her.

"It's been awkward," she said. "He's thirty-two and single, and kind of dependent. He always counted on Cara for advice. Now he's turning to me. I've been suddenly catapulted into this role of older sister, and it's very hard to figure out just what it means. Am I supposed to take over with him for my sister even if we've never had that kind of relationship? Am I supposed to be his support system?

"And what about my mother? My father died a long time ago, and I vaguely imagined that at some advanced state my mother would just not wake up one day—you know, something casual like that—and Cara would call me and we would go out to Mom's and I would stand by while my sister made all the necessary arrangements. When Cara died, it occurred to me, of course, that it's not going to be this way. Whatever happens, I will be the one responsible."

Melissa half smiled, as if to mock her naive vision of the future. A plump woman, she nevertheless projected an image of energy and activity, not unlike her portrayal of her sister. Cara, she related, had undergone a mastectomy four years earlier, but within a year the cancer had spread throughout her body. She suffered for another three years, and during that time did not give in to the illness for a single day. Refusing to be hospitalized ever again, she followed every course of treatment available that might make it possible for her to be alert and functioning. She had taught early education courses at a teachers college (Melissa had turned to her often for advice in handling her nursery school charges), and when she could no longer teach, she wrote articles and essays on education.

Melissa doubted, she said, that she could have acted as courageously. But it was clear to me that she had shown her own determination from the day she learned of the spread of her sister's disease.

"My first reaction to the phone call in which she gave me the grim results of her CAT scan was an overwhelming feeling that I had to have another baby," she said emphatically. "I told my husband that we had to get pregnant." Already the mother of two, she did become pregnant "with extreme promptness," and her baby girl was born well before her sister's death. It was her form of "creativity," and not an unusual response to death, psychiatrists point out.

"This was not a matter of replacement," she explained. "It was something deeper, more primal. You hear about the force of life and it's just a marvel to me that I felt it. In the thrust of death, there has to be some life."

Throughout the course of the illness, Melissa kept in close touch with Cara, although they lived geographically apart, consulting her sister about her work as she had always done, because she knew Cara wanted that.

"I wanted it also," Melissa said. "I couldn't imagine her not being there for me. But I began to deal with the reality. I cried a great deal— I did so much of my mourning for her before she died, in a sense, it was a little easier for me afterward."

But not much. For afterward, along with her grief, came other matters Melissa had to confront: her brother, her mother, and—most difficult—her connections to Cara's husband and children.

She had always felt close to Barr, Cara's husband, regarding him almost as a brother. She admired him especially for the unflagging support he gave Cara until the very end. But now she is torn, for within a month after her sister's death Barr began dating another woman, whom he married just a few weeks before I met Melissa.

"Amazing, isn't it?" Melissa asked rhetorically. "A woman can go years and years without finding an available man, but a man—he can meet someone almost immediately."

Melissa has nothing against Barr's new wife, Wanda ("She's a paler version of my sister—not so feisty, but warm and comforting"). Nor was she shocked that Barr would become involved with someone else. Her sister's illness had gone on, after all, for three years, so he had begun the process of separating as well as grieving. What has bothered her most is a dreadful feeling of loss, a second loss, this time of her brother-in-law.

"We were so much a part of each other's lives," she said. "Of course, what we shared was a person in between, and without her, how could it ever be the same? I kept telling myself when he got engaged to Wanda that I was worried on behalf of my niece and nephew—how they would adjust to a new person—but I knew I was much more worried on my own behalf."

In the year after her sister's death Melissa helped Barr clear out Cara's belongings, all the time mourning her "two losses." Because she had felt close, she spoke to Barr about her feelings. He "made all the right noises about still being part of the family," but she could tell that he was moving on to the next phase of his life.

Melissa had planned to be at Barr's wedding; he had wanted her there. At the last minute, however, she became ill and couldn't make it.

"It was very important to me that I be included," she said, "and I had really meant to be there, but I was so glad I wasn't. I don't know how I could have gotten through it all."

Now Melissa feels that she and Barr will remain friends, sharing a mutual concern for her niece and nephew, but she knows that he will not really be part of her life nor she of his. Now, too, she sees herself as the chief repository for Cara's children of knowledge about her sister. "When the time comes, and they are interested in picking up pieces of their mother's life," she said, "I hope I will be there for them."

As for herself, Melissa said with resignation, "Life *does* go on. Still, what I lost when I lost my sister is something I can never make up. Cara was the only human being who came anywhere close to sharing my memories. There's nobody left now who knew our world the way we did. Not my mother, who is too old, and not my brother, who was too young. When I lost my sister, so much of my past was lost. When my sister died, a part of me died with her."

The death of a sibling in adult life can mean the loss of more than one person. It can mean the loss of in-laws who had become almost like siblings themselves. It can mean the loss of nieces and nephews who had been kept close because of the sibling. It can mean the loss of a part of ourselves that we can never recapture.

In some families, siblings lose each other not through illness or death but through anger and endless fighting. When the fighting is vitriolic, the loss may be permanent. With more moderate quarrels, sore feelings may heal, but words spoken in anger and accusations made may still leave behind a sense of irrevocable loss.

CHAPTER ELEVEN

Intimate Enemies

THE THINGS SIBLINGS FIGHT ABOUT
(Parents and Possessions and In-Laws and Money and Parents and Possessions)

A popular television talk show shortly before Christmas: Three sisters sit together facing the audience. Two of them have not spoken to each other for twenty years, nor in that span of time have the three celebrated even one Christmas holiday together. The oldest one weeps as she describes how the youngest did not help out in any way when their father was dying. They talk about their angers, avoiding gazes, finding it easier in these few minutes to speak their minds before millions of television viewers than for decades it has been to speak to each other. A commercial break. The sisters are cut off from TV viewers. When they reappear, they're smiling.

"My sister's right. I should have been there," says the youngest, "I didn't take any responsibility."

They have patched up twenty years of fighting during the few minutes of commercial pitches. This year, they announce, they will celebrate Christmas together. The audience applauds wildly. Millions of viewers have been privy to their reconciliation.

And maybe it will last and maybe it won't. But even if it doesn't, we will never know, nor would we want to. For on television everything is possible, and on television even deep-rooted sibling enmities can disappear as quickly as grime wiped away by some magical new detergent. And the magic is reassuring.

In real life, alas, the magic is not so handy, and enmities that have run for decades sometimes continue for decades more. In real life, some siblings begin fighting as children and carry their fights unendingly into adulthood, so that no matter what they seem to be fighting about, they are still fighting about the same things. Others go along peacefully for years, riding the seesaw of competition and love, bickering sometimes, drawing close at others, until some incident (which may be as trivial as a birthday party) or some life event (which may be as monumental as the death of a parent) reawakens old angers or triggers new ones. Then warfare can break out, like a sudden rash that erupts, red and burning, becoming more inflamed, more purulent, the more intensely it is rubbed or scratched. In a few cases the rash becomes permanent, the warfare a way of life in which brothers and sisters break off all contact, connected only by silence until the end of their days.

The roots of sibling angers and fighting in adult life, like the roots of love and loyalty, go deep into the beginnings of time, into the earliest days of childhood. Those childhood fights have their origins in the fundamental rivalries—among older and younger sibs, same-sex or opposite-sex ones—for the love and attention of parents and for power and dominance over one another. Children in a family fight to be noticed, by parents and each other. They fight to get privileges and gain possessions, to hold on to their property or to take away another's, to secure their own turf or to undermine the other's. They fight sometimes to gain control and sometimes just to irritate one another. They fight, for all these reasons, far more among themselves than they do with other children.

As we have seen, the fights and power struggles of childhood have an impact on adult life. The lower self-esteem of some younger siblings, the need to remain on top of some older ones, continue, reflecting in large measure the rivalries and battles of earlier years. So, for some adults, do feelings of guilt for having hurt a brother or sister or feelings of anger for having been hurt during the relentless quarrels of youth.

But along with the hurts or guilts, the shaky self-esteem or strife they leave behind, the fights of childhood also serve positive and useful purposes. Through tugs-of-war within the safety of the family, children gain experience for the less safe larger world. By fighting over possessions, they come to distinguish between what is rightfully theirs and what is somebody else's. By competing over skills and abilities, they sharpen their ability to gauge their own strengths and limitations. By jockeying for position in relation to parents, they find out about fairness and equality. And by making up as well as fighting, they begin to solve problems, to negotiate differences, and—ultimately—to understand other points of view.

Conflicts with siblings are so important in learning to get along with others, insist psychologists, that only children may be at a disadvantage in maneuvering out in the wide world beyond their family. Because they do not argue and compete within their family, they often are not prepared to argue and compete outside it. Instead they become too trusting, too expectant that the world and its people will be as helpful and caring of them as their parents. Discovering that others can trick them, undermine them, or deal with them dishonestly can be a shock to adult only children. Even having suffered the cruelties and chicaneries of schoolmates and friends does not quite prepare them for the real world of competition the way most adults with siblings are prepared.

The fighting lessons siblings learn in early childhood are reinforced and extended during early and later adolescence. Acutely sensitive to their appearance, their sprouting sexuality, their vacillating emotions, teenagers are also especially vulnerable to the insults and taunts of siblings. And because they have become skilled practitioners by now, teenage brothers and sisters know better than anyone outside the family exactly how to twist the knife into the weakest spots, how to torture with the precision of an inquisitor, and how to cover over their own actions: "Maybe you ought to get professional help to deal with your temper tantrums," said one brother sweetly to a sister he had provoked into paroxysms of incoherent rage.

But again, from the conflict and the rage can come learning, forward steps in development toward adulthood. To explore the nature of that learning, a researcher at the University of Chicago compared fights between siblings to fights between friends among a group of students from fifth to eighth grade. He found a number of differences. The fights girls had with their friends, for example, differed from the fights boys had with their friends, the girls fighting over aspects of their relationship ("She's supposed to be my best friend and she didn't pick me for her team"), the boys over specific incidents ("We were playing football. I thought they had a fourth down, he thought they had a first"). Gender, on the other hand, was *not* a significant factor in the fights among siblings, with both girls and boys fighting equally over typical sibling issues of power and personal property. It may be, suggests the researcher, Marcela Raffaelli, that while the friends' fights strengthen the differences between the sexes, the sibling fights help both boys and girls learn universal lessons in how far they can go before provoking retaliation.

In sibling fights, also, Raffaelli found, the young adolescents felt free to say whatever was on their minds, expressing their anger and hostility openly. Friends were more cautious about showing their negative feelings to each other for fear of losing the friendship. While learning to repress feelings in order to hold on to friends is a basic skill for adult life, being able to speak their minds, speculates Raffaelli, provides siblings with other vital lessons. In the shelter of their homes and with the knowledge that siblings will remain siblings even after fights, youngsters get to know themselves and to recognize their own emotions and desires as distinct from those of their brothers or sisters. That recognition and separation can provide vital boosts toward maturity.

Because sibling fights are so important and so usual during childhood and adolescence, child development experts often advise parents not to interfere in them unless one child is physically abusing another or a battle has become vicious and out of control. Some studies have shown that parental intervention may actually escalate fighting among young children. When younger siblings know that parents will intervene and come to their aid, these studies indicate, they are more likely to provoke fights with older ones (whom parents then tend to blame for the fights). The fact, also, that children often fight to gain parental attention means that providing that attention can reinforce the fighting.

But this advice needs some qualifications. Without intervening in every sibling fight, parents do need to establish rules and boundaries that help children and adolescents contain their rage and settle their differences. They need to set a tone within the family so that siblings recognize that this level of shouting or cursing is not acceptable, or that degree of name-calling will not be tolerated. If necessary, they need to separate the combatants until tempers cool and a calmer atmosphere prevails so that siblings can get back to the business of negotiating their disagreements without trying to destroy each other.

For many people, by adulthood the lessons of early fights have been well learned and the fights themselves put to rest. As brothers and sisters move out of their common home and go off on their own, they no longer have to argue about space or property or the myriad other issues that filled their days when they were together with parents under one roof. While rivalries and resentments or comparisons with one another may continue well into adult life, the ceaseless squabbling of childhood usually subsides or disappears altogether.

Except for some siblings, like Christina and Vivian in Chapter Seven, who—when I last spoke to them—had just had a huge blowout over the question of whether their father spoke English with a Greek accent. Christina insisted his English was imperfect and accented; Vivian that it was just fine, and that Christina wanted only to criticize him because she knew he had favored Vivian.

Or Patty and Meredith in Chapter Eight, who cannot say two words to each other without fighting, and as a result communicate, if at all, through their father Lew Dorman.

Or two brothers—both in their late twenties—who described, separately, a brawl they had had when attending a wedding together a few weeks earlier. "We were in the bathroom and Marty pushed me," said one, "so I pushed him back. Then he slugged me, so I slugged him back, and we were off." Said Marty, "I can't say exactly why, but he has always brought out so much anger in me that I want to pummel him physically. I don't think there's another person in the world who can do that to me."

For these people and numbers of others, the quarrels of childhood continue unabated, and never mind the fact that they no longer live together. It is as if whatever happened between them years ago had happened just yesterday, and every meeting is a continuation of yesterday's fight.

What motivates such adult siblings to keep stoking the flames of anger again and again, never permitting them to die down?

The answers group, as do so many others in regard to siblings, around the two areas that influence adult relationships—the way parents have treated sibs and the way sibs have treated each other.

To start with parents this time: Parental favoritism in childhood and later—as might be expected—stands out as a major source of ongoing troubles among adult siblings. When it has been keenly felt, as it was with Christina and Vivian, it can remain not only a cause for underlying tensions, but an open sore, picked at again and again.

Parental disfavoring of one child remains an equally sore point among siblings. We've seen that a scapegoating parent is often forgiven and idealized—the way Meredith idealizes her mother Honey—while the parental "good child" becomes the bad one in the eyes of the maligned sibling. When fighting is constant, it is usually because the disfavored child-turned-adult wants some repayment from others for injuries suffered. Yet that person may be so demanding of siblings, or so angry, that no amount of goodwill on the part of the others can make up for past pain.

In one family a woman who always felt devalued in the eyes of her father has so consistently attacked her younger sister, the "good one" in the family, that the younger has kept herself "invisible," she says, as a way of appeasing her sister. "My being noticed causes my sister so much suffering and anger," she explains, "that I've stayed in the shadows." For her that has meant not writing a novel she wants to write and not accepting a political appointment she has been offered. In recent years it has also meant becoming as resentful of her sister as the sister is of her, and responding to her sister's anger with angry outbursts of her own, leading to ever-spiraling arguments.

For many siblings it is not parental favoring or disfavoring that turns one against another but parental roadblocks mounted to keep them apart. Unknowingly, usually, a mother or father will play off one child against another by openly comparing them and inciting competition. "If I buy a new carpet," says a woman, "my mother will say, 'Oh, but you should see your sister Becky's new carpet. It's so beautiful and it cost a lot less.'" Another woman characterizes family gatherings with her four sisters as "The Pillsbury Mother-off." Always goaded into rivalry by a mother whose "love and approval were conditional," the sisters are now fighting about who has given their mother the best grandchildren.

A parent's conscious motive in this type of competition may be to urge the children to greater achievement, to inspire one with the deeds of another. The unconscious one—whether the sibs are children or adults—is to maintain control by drawing them closer to the parent than to one another. If sibs never join forces, the parent remains all-powerful, the center of family life.

Although the Ginetti sisters, in Chapter Four, get along well, they have experienced some of that parental pitting of one against the other. Intent on keeping her hold on her daughters, Mrs. Ginetti, matriarch of the family, has gossiped with each of the women about the others, stirring up angers among them. The gossiping stopped, said Lisa, when she and her sisters united in forbidding their mother from ever speaking to any one against another.

In more disturbed families, where young siblings have not felt loved and protected by parents, this type of undermining may be more destructive because the children feel bereft of support from either parents or siblings. The lifelong distrust siblings develop for each other in these situations may carry over to others outside the family as well. For, after all, if you discover early that you can't trust your brothers and sisters, how can you ever learn to trust anybody?

Equally destructive in the pantheon of parental causes for sibling conflicts is the influence of *parental* conflicts. As children, siblings identify with their mothers and fathers and model themselves on them. If parents bicker all the time, the children learn to bicker in the same way. If a father constantly denigrates a mother, or a mother belittles a father, children quickly pick up the techniques of denigrating and belittling each other. Those attitudes and techniques, learned at an early age, follow the siblings into adult life as their way of relating to each other.

Moreover, battling parents often use their children as pawns, each cultivating a different child to serve as an ally against the other. Trapped in their parents' skirmishes, the children become enemies themselves, and long after the parents are no longer on the scene, they may continue their own hostilities.

Turning away from parents, the second—and even more fundamental—source for never-ending sibling squabbles may be found in the nature of the siblings themselves. It may well be that some brothers and sisters have a basic incompatibility that causes lifelong unhappiness with each other. Like some parents and children, these siblings are temperamentally mismatched. Or, to use the term psychiatrists Stella Chess and Alexander Thomas coined, they lack a "goodness of fit."

Like parents and children, siblings do not need to be temperamentally similar to fit well together, but they need to be able to understand and empathize with each other. When they are poorly matched, they lack that understanding and empathy. One child may be easily excitable, demanding, and crushingly cruel to another who is slower and more docile; or both may be high-strung, given to screaming and tearing away at each other. Just as parents need to accommodate to their childrens' temperaments, poorly fit children need to learn how to accommodate to each other—to keep out of one another's way when that is necessary, and to cooperate when that is possible.

But the task is not simple, and siblings do not always achieve goodness of fit. Chess and Thomas describe some children who, from birth, are highly intense, difficult to calm, and have a tendency to withdraw when faced with any new situation. For them, a new baby's arrival can be especially stressful, and without a great deal of help from parents they may never accept a younger child. Dunn and Kendrick, in their observations of very young children, saw several families in which one child—usually the elder—consistently rejected another who consistently tried to please and be friendly.

It is a great leap to go from earliest childhood to adult life in placing some of the blame for sibling hostilities onto temperamental mismatches. Siblings change over time and do accommodate to each other, and many who fought like cats and dogs as children become best friends as adults. Nevertheless, for some, core incompatibilities and poornesses of fit that begin in childhood never disappear. They are the people who, when asked about siblings, say such things as "My brother hated me from the moment I was born," or "We never got along for one second." Such siblings may eventually break off completely, or they may go on wrestling forever, like the brothers who brawled in the bathroom because one "brought out so much anger" in another.

Contradictorily, unending bickering among sibs may come from *too much* compatibility, or more accurately, too much alikeness, or too much dependence of one sib on another. Some brothers and sisters wrangle over everything because what they are really wrangling over is their inability to separate and form independent selves.

The process siblings go through of forming those selves extends from childhood through adolescence and often into adult life. Sibs of the same sex and those close in age, as we've seen, may find that process especially difficult because they identify easily with each other and can easily become overattached. The Platt brothers affirm their separateness—and control competition between them—by de-identifying, viewing themselves as opposites. Rita, in Chapter Four, has been able to maintain her distinctness from her sister only by keeping distance between them. The sisters do not see each other often lest they get dragged back into the kind of suffocating closeness they had as children.

Other siblings, who have not found a way to separate from each other, may fight as their means of asserting independence. But the fights are fought over and over because of the very fact that these siblings are *not* independent. They are locked into each other, frustrated and angry at their intense connectedness, yet unable to pull apart. A younger sibling may constantly rail against an older's domination. He might also invite that domination by always seeking the other's advice and opinion, still wanting—despite noisy protests—to be told what to do. An older sibling may constantly fight off a younger's dependencies, loudly criticizing the younger for not being more self-sufficient. She might also enjoy those dependencies and encourage them by using the fights and criticisms to belittle the younger.

An extreme in fighting as a form of separating for siblings who are unable to separate is the case of two sisters, both in their late seventies. For them, the disputes are exacerbated by the fact that, never married, they have lived together for years.

The sisters are literally inseparable, says a cousin who spoke to me about them. "We all call them 'the girls,' " he said in describing them. When asked their names, he tore off a sheet from the pad I held and wrote, *CarolandSelma*, explaining that they are so bound together that everyone thinks of them as one person.

"Nobody would dream of inviting one to dinner without the other," he explained. "But when you do spend time with them, you find they argue a lot; they snap at each other. One will say something, and the other will get all huffy. The kinds of things others will discuss, they get explosive about with each other."

Elaborating on his theme, he told me that Carol, the elder, was the dominant sister. "Selma might express an opinion about something and Carol will jump in and say, 'Oh, shut up, you don't know what you're talking about.' Selma will look miserable after that, or she might shoot back with something of her own. They're always at it, and who knows how much fighting takes place when they're alone."

Caught in a sibling bind, one might say.

Finally, trapped in another kind of bind are those sibs who quarrel endlessly because quarreling is better than nothing at all. Like husbands and wives who continually jab at each other to fill in the dead spaces in their marriage, for these siblings, quarrels are a form of energizing, of adding life to what otherwise might be lifeless, stagnant. Or, as someone once said, hate also is a relationship.

The many causes of ongoing sibling fights—the parent causes and the sibling causes—are not necessarily isolated from one another. Temperamental mismatches, for instance, may also lead parents to favor one sib over another—most often the easygoing, sunny one over the temperamentally more difficult one—and the favoring may serve to increase the mismatching conflicts. Or, the siblings' overinvolvement and inability to separate may make them particularly sensitive to any hint of parental favoring or disfavoring, aggravating their rows. If Vivian and Christina, for example, were freer of each other, they might lead their separate lives peacefully without always becoming embroiled in fights about which parent favored which daughter.

·   ·   ·

Ever-battling sibs make up one group of adult brothers and sisters. A much larger and more widespread group consists of those who don't fight most of the time, whose relationships are generally calm and compatible until some special event or life crisis sparks storms of rage that leave all parties shocked and shaken by the depths of acrimony revealed.

A crisis, in psychological terms, refers not to some dire circumstance, but to a period of transition, a turning point in which earlier attitudes and relationships may change.

For siblings, separating and moving away from home is one such life crisis, and in terms of fighting, a time, as noted, when earlier differences may recede into the background.

Marriage—one's own or a sibling's—is another crisis point in sibling relations, one in which old animosities may crop up in different form and include, often, new family members—the spouses of siblings.

Some disputes begin at the wedding, a time of joy that can also be a time of stress. More than one bride has flown into a fury when a sister appeared at her wedding wearing white, and more than one sister has done just that—to compete with the bride, to provoke her, to share the spotlight, to use this precise moment to get even for an accumulation of past hurts. The mother of Christina and Vivian had always been jealous of her younger and more beautiful sister. When the sister, dressed in white, outshone her at her own wedding, the jealousy solidified into hatred.

At the opposite pole is a hairdresser who has not spoken to her sister for a year, since her wedding, she says, because the sister dressed for the occasion in her oldest, drabbest clothes, with no makeup and hair "a mess," indications of her "disrespect" for the bride. "If I were a mature adult," said the hairdresser, "I might have said, 'Well, she's jealous. I'm getting married, and she doesn't even have a boyfriend.' But I didn't want to deal with her problems. It was my day and she was taking it away from me, and that got me very angry."

Then there are the older siblings whose younger ones have married first. Jealous and angry at being upstaged, they sulk their way through the wedding festivities or find fault with every detail, including the new marriage partner. In the Bible, Jacob fell in love with Rachel and not her older sister Leah. With the conniving of their father Laban, Leah stealthily replaced Rachel in the bridal chamber. "It is not the practice in our place to marry off the younger before the older," Laban declared to Jacob in defending his deception. Rachel and Leah spent much of the rest of their lives competing over who could produce the most children.

Beneath many of the clashes during the wedding and later lie complex emotions. Younger siblings can be overwhelmed with feelings of hurt and abandonment when an older one weds, especially if they depended greatly on that elder. Roy Deveau, in his brother Eddy's words, became "sullen and depressed" when Eddy married, afraid of losing "direct and immediate access" to the older brother on whom he relied for so much.

Even less dependent younger siblings may suffer an acute sense of loss when an older one marries. On a deep level, old feelings of inferiority and deprivation reemerge. In earlier years such feelings came from perceiving oneself to be smaller, less powerful, and less important than an older sib. Now the feeling that one is less important recurs—this time in relation to the sibling's new spouse. So does the feeling of being deprived—this time pushed aside by somebody who is the new and enduring focus of that sibling's life.

Older siblings also experience loss when a younger brother or sister marries, but the feeling may be less intense. Because they generally see themselves as less affected by a younger sib than the other way around, they tend not to feel rejected or abandoned when the younger marries, especially if the older has married first. What is reawakened when a sib-in-law appears on the scene is the very old perception of being dethroned, as they had once been when a newborn sibling entered their lives back in childhood. And what they lose, as they lost then, is the exuberance of being in charge, in control, at the center.

At a sib's wedding these buried emotions can translate into tensions and anger. With a marriage under way, they may reveal themselves in jealousies or open hostilities between the new spouse and siblings. "I was VERY upset," wrote a secretary, making sure she got her message across, "when my older brother got married. We used to be so close, and I felt I had lost him to someone who didn't hold a candle to me. I still feel that way. My sister-in-law is no peach!"

Tradition has it that the second most difficult marital family relationship is between sisters-in-law, particularly a woman and her brother's wife (mothers-in-law are supposedly the number one difficulty). The tradition did not hold up in my survey. Many more people wrote of the positive effects of husbands and wives on their relations with siblings than of negative effects, with sisters-in-law faring best of all. Like sisters, sisters-in-law tend to pay more attention to family matters than do their husbands, and can be instrumental in keeping families close.

But envies do exist, and scraps often do occur among sibs-in-law. Like the upset secretary, a woman who has been close to her brother may resent the wife he has taken, and find dozens of ways to criticize her or pick a fight. The wife, in turn, threatened by her husband's closeness to his sister, may make a determined effort to keep them apart, alienating her sister-in-law even further. The wife of a man who has several sisters may be hurt and angry because she feels left out of the sisters' intimacies. The sisters may be annoyed at her pushiness, as in, "But after all, a sister-in-law is *not* the same as a sister," said by a woman with three sisters and a brother whose wife the others dislike. Or siblings may complain that their sister's spouse "cares only about his own family and never has time for us," as another woman wrote of her brother-in-law.

In some families a husband or wife will take up a spouse's old antagonisms toward siblings, expressing feelings the spouse dare not act on openly. Then the husband or wife becomes the "bad cop," the one siblings blame for a sister or brother's distance from the family. Meredith, who had been mistreated by her mother and unprotected by her sisters or father, married an assertive man—Charles—whom her father labeled "the little Napoleon." Knowing his wife's history, but unburdened himself by it, Charles stood up to her family in a way she was never able to. The official family story is that he has forbidden Meredith from associating with her sister; the reality is that he has acted out her own underlying wish to dissociate.

In other cases a brother- or sister-in-law transfers a lifetime habit of fighting with his or her own sibling to relations with a sib-in-law. It's a hard habit to unlearn, and if a spouse accepts it, or ignores it, relations between the in-laws can remain rocky for years.

Intensifying fights among sisters- and brothers-in-law is the fact that the parties involved do not have the history of fighting and making up that sisters and brothers have with each other. Most of us know how to fight with our siblings—having perfected our techniques through years of experience—without allowing each fight to turn into an all-out disaster. Without that backdrop of history and experience, in-law fights can escalate quickly from an insignificant tiff to a major family battle.

For the sister or brother caught in the middle of these fights, the frustration and pain can be unnerving. With whom do you side, your spouse or your sibling? Yes, your first loyalties should be to your spouse. But if you love your sib, if you understand that person's pain, how do you show it without betraying the other? And what of your feelings of being betrayed by the sib who has attacked your spouse? And how do you behave toward your sib's spouse, who may be torn as well between loyalty to husband or wife and loyalty to an in-law who has become a friend?

Sometimes that person caught in the middle is able to act as go-between, pulling all sides together by emphasizing family loyalties. In other situations the person in the middle can get stuck there forever, playing a long-term balancing act between spouse and sib. Often such fights simply get papered over, the in-laws maintaining cordial relations on the surface while angers simmer beneath, unresolved.

This has been the circumstance in the Ginetti clan, allowing the family's closeness to remain intact, but with an unhealed injury that continues to cause pain. The quarrel centered around business, and was between Nancy, second of the sisters, and Vince, husband of her older sister Mary Ann, over some mutually held property.

Angry at Nancy and her husband, Tony, Vince did not speak to either for two years. When they were thrown together at family events, Vince sat, according to Nancy, "without opening his mouth—a terrible, terrible thing." As terrible for Nancy was Mary Ann's refusal to discuss the situation with her. Although the sisters kept up outward appearances of friendship, the atmosphere between them was thick with tension. If Nancy ever brought up the subject, Mary Ann withdrew ("I had nothing to say to her about it," she explains, "I just thought she was wrong"). The dispute finally simmered down, and peace was restored. But to this day, says Nancy, "we have never been allowed to clear the air by speaking openly about it. For me, the hurt is always there."

People often assume that all sibling fights in adult life are actually a continuation of earlier ones that have been frozen in time, the same fights repeated in different settings and with different language. Actually, this view of sibling quarrels is not quite correct. In-law fights and business fights frequently *are* current fights, not necessarily extensions of the past. Nancy and Vince had a real disagreement about Vince's management of their property, and Mary Ann sided with her husband partly out of loyalty, but largely because she thought he was right.

What intruded from the past for these sisters were echoes of how they had dealt with each other from their earliest childhood: Nancy's wish to assert herself with her elder sister, yet great need for that sister's love and approval; Mary Ann's stance, as eldest in the family, of being above the fray, not required to discuss her feelings with her younger sibling (just as she had never felt called upon to explain why she thought she could wear Nancy's black ball gown before Nancy did). The echoes reverberated in the background during the two years of this family's business fight, while the real quarrel occupied the foreground.

It is during those times of life that come closest to resembling other times siblings shared that the echoes of the past become strongest, so strong that voices and angers of long ago come crashing through, drowning out the sounds of the present. Then it is hard to know where old fights have left off and new ones begun, hard to separate the words of adult siblings from those of the children within them.

In the normal course of days and years, holidays and family gatherings can become the occasions for replaying the fights of yore— around the Thanksgiving or Christmas, Easter or Passover table. For on these occasions adult children are together as they once were with parents, slipping easily into their old roles. If a mother pays attention to one daughter's child, another may become enraged that her child is being neglected, just as she had felt neglected or displaced in comparison with her sister years earlier. If a brother talks about a new job or promotion, another may become irritated that once again he is unnoticed while his brother hogs center stage.

Adding to holiday tensions are the discrepancies, again carried over from childhood, between what siblings think the event ought to be and what it is. Most of us hold idealized versions of family gatherings, in which beaming parents and perfect children frolic happily with nary a cross word between them. When in actuality a brother drinks too much and argues with everybody, or a sister, bitter after a horrendous divorce, is sullenly silent, the reality seems even more painful because it falls so far short of the ideal. Strains between brother and sister—and voices—rise as each blames the other for destroying the mythical holiday spirit.

Despite their unpleasantness, fights centered around holidays and family events usually blow over, at least until the next time (although some do become entrenched, as in the sister who wrote on my questionnaire that her brother has cut off contact with her because accidentally he was omitted from the list of invitees to her surprise birthday party). Fights that arise during more serious times of crisis can be more disruptive and longer-lasting.

Most serious of those times, and most reminiscent of childhood, are the years in which aging parents become increasingly dependent until eventually they die, leaving their adult children orphaned and alone together. For many siblings those years bring a renewed strength and support that draws brothers and sisters toward one another as never before. For others they stir up the worst in sibling relations. And when this happens, the pain is increased, as it is with holiday letdowns, because the actualities are so far removed from idealized expectations of cooperation and closeness.

When parents are ill and their children rally around, the siblings' lives begin to focus on their parents and brothers and sisters, as in childhood. If one sib is perceived to be doing less than his share, the others grow incensed, just as when they were young and one of them dodged doing chores. But even when each shoulders responsibilities, the situation corresponds closely enough to the family structure of their childhood to arouse jealousies, angers, and cunning power plays as they compete for parental attentions.

Does one daughter insist on bearing the major burden or making the major decisions? Others might accuse her, covertly if not directly, of fawning over Mom or Dad for her own purposes as she had always done, or of wanting to be boss as always. (And secretly they might use their rage at her as their excuse for not doing more.) She might accuse them, covertly if not directly, of dumping the problem on her as usual and forcing her into doing everything because she is oldest or youngest or the one who invariably bears the brunt of family difficulties. (And secretly she might relish the role of best daughter and the parental gratitude that goes with it.)

Layered beneath the accusations will be adult children's aching sadness at the impending loss of their parent. And there will be, unspoken and often unacknowledged even to themselves, haunting questions: Who will emerge, with so little time left, as a parent's favorite? Who will be seen as the truly good one, the one who loves and is loved best? And more personal ruminations: "Can I get now the recognition from parents or from siblings that I have not received in the past?" "Can I balance the scales of power and status by demonstrating to a more successful sib that at least I have won within the family?" "Can I even the score, finally, for all the hurts and slights I have suffered from parents?"

("I'll never forgive the bastard!" says one brother of another in discussing the care of their sick, elderly father. True, the "bastard" had experienced difficult times with this father, who had made many demands of him. Still, says the other, "he refuses to help out in any way at a time when Dad most needs our support. At what point do you stop blaming parents and become accountable for your own life?")

Mixed into the emotional cauldron are long-standing parental assumptions rooted in gender differences. Just about every study made on the care of aging parents has found that the burden falls most often on daughters (and sometimes daughters-in-law). To be specific: Daughters outnumber sons by three to one among children who care for their parents. Furthermore, because life expectancy has increased greatly, a woman today might spend seventeen years of her life caring for a dependent child, but *eighteen* assisting elderly parents. In fact, so many women are caught between the care demands of their children and their elderly parents that they have been labeled the "sandwich" generation.

Regardless of the many changes feminism has brought, parents still *expect* their daughters to be available to them on an everyday basis, and many women give up much-needed jobs and careers to care for their aging or ill parents. Most parents hesitate to make similar demands of sons, whose jobs—no matter what—they still see as somehow more important.

("Will you be here tomorrow?" my father asks after my mother is taken to the hospital for emergency surgery on a broken hip and before we are able to arrange outside help for him.

"Yes, don't worry, I'll be here," I assure him.

"And the next day?"

"Yes, the next day also."

"And the day after that?"

"Yes, the day after that as well."

"Good. By then we'll be able to hire somebody."

"Maybe Robert can come one day so I can get back to work on my book," I venture.

"Robert? I know he wants to help, but how would he know what to do? *Daughters* know about taking care of a home.")

Trapped into their roles as parental caregivers, daughters become enraged if brothers do little to help out, and even more so when brothers who have taken no responsibility offer advice from the sidelines. That rage feeds the tensions and traumas surrounding parents' fragilities and illnesses.

The many grievances and annoyances connected with the care of old or ill parents do not necessarily turn into outright fights. In their study of adult siblings, Ross and Milgram found that those who had always had rivalrous and conflict-laden relationships were most likely as adults to have negative reactions to a parent's sickness, but those who had been close since childhood remained close at this time.

I discovered this to be true in my research as well, but I did find that when the stresses of parental illnesses are very great, they can create difficulties even among siblings who generally had good relations. "Because I was much younger than my brother or sister," wrote a secretary, "I never felt much childhood sibling rivalry with them. I do see it surfacing in myself now, around issues of dealing with our father, who has had a stroke."

In fact, conflicts stemming from concerns about aging parents are so commonplace that respondents to my survey listed the care of parents most often as the cause of a problem with siblings. Disputes ranged from "his not visiting Mother in the nursing home because he said he couldn't 'handle' seeing her that way," to "our inability to pitch in together to get Dad settled after Mom died," to "her ambivalence about contributing to Mother's support even though my mother has great need of money."

Money, of course, is an underlying, often insidious element in many of the sibling problems related to elderly parents. Actually, money can be an underlying and insidious problem long before it begins to revolve around parents.

What is it about money that brings out the most primitive, hateful, and vengeful impulses in adult siblings?

Its real value, certainly, is crucial. When one sibling has a great deal and others have little, the differences in possessions, positions, and possibilities for the future can be galling to those with less. Although all once shared equally in family resources, now one might be able to enjoy vacations the others can only dream of; one's children may live in luxuries the others' children can see only from the outside, noses pressed hard against the window. And if the wealthier sibling is condescending toward the others or brags or—worse—refuses to aid a brother or sister who needs financial help, the hatred and fury of the others can be boundless.

But for siblings money is also something more than money. It has symbolic meaning beyond its literal one. For one sibling, acquiring wealth may symbolize winning out over others in the old competitions; for another, wealth may be a means of achieving authority in the family, becoming the person others respect and admire. And the converse—having less money than others may be regarded as a sign of inferiority or defeat in the sibling derby. Several respondents to the survey wrote with great irritation about brothers or sisters who borrowed money they neglected to repay or who continued to ask parents for money because they "couldn't make it on their own," as one man said of his two younger brothers.

Both aspects of money, its literal value and its symbolic one, come into play more forcefully than ever as parents age, and especially after they die. The discord among siblings engaged in a struggle over parental money has to do in part with cash and the real value of assets. When a family has a great deal of money, that discord can reach volcanic proportions—witness huge business dynasties such as the Koch family of Kansas, whose public bloodlettings have revealed an astounding mass of hatred among four brothers wrestling viciously for control of the family fortunes. Bitterness and outright warfare can be equally poisonous, although less public, when money is scarce and sibs try to fill their coffers with the family inheritance.

Stemming from even deeper sources within sibling psyches, fights about money when connected with parents are fights about parental love and recognition. The dollars are concrete symbols to adult children of what, finally, really counts from parents: affection, gratitude, praise, reward for devotedness.

Philip Roth, who has written about brotherly relationships in several works, writes in *Patrimony*, a book about his father's death, of his feelings in connection with his father's modest estate. Some years earlier, knowing himself to be financially more secure than his older brother Sandy, Roth had generously instructed his father to leave his entire inheritance to Sandy. Now dying, Roth's father tells him that his wishes have been followed, and Roth finds himself distraught. Why had he made such an offer? Wasn't this inheritance his due?

"Didn't I think I deserved it?" he asks himself. "Did I consider my brother and his children more deserving inheritors than I, perhaps because my brother, by having given him grandchildren, was more legitimately a father's heir than was the son who had been childless? Was I a younger brother who suddenly had become unable to assert his claim against the seniority of someone who had been there first? Or, to the contrary, was I a younger brother who felt he had encroached too much upon an older brother's prerogatives already?"

For Roth, as for many other siblings, money as such is not really the issue. The money is emblematic of each sibling's worth in the eyes of parents. It validates each one's history in the family.

Sometimes parents themselves promote bitter rivalries about money by using their wills or promises of their estates as weapons with which to threaten adult children into demonstrating ever greater devotion.

More usually, parents who instigate money conflicts among their adult children do so unintentionally, sometimes with the most admirable of goals. Like Roth's father, a parent may leave the greater portion of an inheritance to the son or daughter who has the fewest resources, because this seems a logical way to protect the offspring whose needs are greatest. Unfortunately, the parent does not realize that adult siblings, still carrying within them the emotional baggage of childhood, remain always on the alert for signs of favoritism. Choosing one child over another, even for the best of reasons, can make the unchosen jealous and unforgiving of the chosen.

Max, a fifty-four-year-old stockbroker, accuses his younger brother James, a sometime opera singer and most times waiter, of turning their mother against him, and thus winning the promise of her entire estate. James accuses Max of doing little to care for their mother. From the mother's point of view, one son has plenty of money and one has none, so it seems obvious she should provide for the needy one after she is gone. But all that Max sees in his mother's announcement that James will inherit everything is betrayal and rejection. Max's anger has deep roots.

"My brother always resented my closeness to my father," Max says. "Now, it's as if he's saying 'Gotcha' to both of us. Everything my mother inherited from my father will go to James, and I will have nothing." All he can feel, he says, is disgust and hatred for his brother, and for his mother a "cold deadness."

With the death of parents can come frenzied wrangles for possessions left in the parental home—a silver teapot, a piece of jewelry, a television set, or something far more trivial: one brother and sister have not spoken to each other for twenty years because of a fight, when clearing out their mother's home, over a set of plastic napkin rings used on holidays.

Aside from any real worth they may have, for surviving children, parents' possessions symbolize both a part of the parent and a part of the life siblings shared with their parents at home.

Many of those possessions carry within them the mysteries of parents' lives—the bed they shared that we were not allowed into, the places they went without us, the secrets they had that we longed to know. Their possessions tell us about them—what they thought beautiful or useful, and what they considered important enough to keep when they threw out other things. When parents are gone, we want to know them through their possessions, and we want to keep them with us always, by wearing the watch a father wore, or baking in a pan a mother used, or pulling napkins through the plastic rings that signaled a holiday dinner.

Through those possessions, also, we want to hold on to our own past. The teapot, the napkin rings, the worn-out flatware, evoke memories of childhood, be they happy or unhappy, sad or eccentric. They serve as links to a world that we once inhabited and that now is long since gone. We can never recover that world, but we want to own the tangible reminders of it.

Then, too, the echoes of rivalries past push their way through any current discussion of dividing up parental property. Siblings may fight greedily over items that have intrinsic worth. They may fight over worthless pieces of furniture or clothing simply to win or beat out the others, as they once fought for toys or privileges. Says a reporter of a battle over possessions with her sister: "On the one hand, I say to myself, 'What difference does it make? Isn't it better to have peace in the family?' But another voice says, 'It's mine! I want it!' and I'll do anything to win."

The fights that erupt among siblings over marriage partners or money, parental illness or parental possessions, can shake the very foundation of their relationship. Resentments that had been repressed for years can burst through and flood out all feelings of affection for the duration of the fight. A brother who has fought with another because of money can feel "betrayed," as one man said, "sick with the knowledge that he wasn't here for me, and I don't know if I can ever count on him again." A sister embroiled in a struggle with another over their mother's jewelry can utterly convince herself that "I really don't care if I never see or speak to her again," as one woman in that situation reported.

Yet, for most siblings, the rage subsides with time, and dire predictions and threats of a permanent rupture never materialize. It may take longer for them to revert to feeling the same "unguarded trust" they had previously shared, as a writer friend put it after a bout with her sister; indeed, they may never again achieve that type of innocent belief in each other. But most will manage somehow to reach into the depths of their hearts and rediscover the loyalty and love they had pushed aside in the heat of their battle.

Only a quarter of respondents to my survey indicated that there had been periods of time when they had not spoken to a sibling out of anger; the great majority kept their connections, no matter what. And generally, of those brothers and sisters who continue not speaking to each other out of anger for some time, only a small number remain that way permanently.

But there are some siblings who do separate so completely that even in the next generation nieces and nephews do not associate with each other.

Family therapist Murray Bowen uses the term "emotional cutoff" to describe people who break off all contact with their parents, and makes the point that such cutoff harms more than it helps because it is a form of running away from family problems instead of finding a way to deal with them. Emotional cutoff from siblings can be just as harmful (although on occasion it may serve a good purpose—as in the case of Honey and her domineering older sister Ray in Chapter Eight). People who have shut out their siblings from their lives often express profound feelings of loss and sadness, and in many cases confusion about just what had happened.

When asked, many sibs who no longer speak to each other give vague answers as to why. "She's crazy; I don't want anything to do with her," one will say. "He was always a problem; I've just decided to give up," says another. Or there will be a specific, apparently trivial reason, as in, "I hated the eulogy he gave at Mom's funeral."

Actually, the real motives behind such radical surgery usually lie not in the specific issues that led to the break but in broader sibling histories. For a variety of reasons, the rejecting sibs have come to epitomize to each other all that has been hurtful or bad in their life together, whether it was bad childhood experiences, or bad relations between parents, or bad family life in general. The "crazy" sister, in a brother's mind, may be identified with a "crazy" mother who fought with the father the brother adored. The "problem" brother may have been a family scapegoat, and is now an unremitting reminder of devastating family troubles. The unacceptable eulogy may have triggered unacceptable feelings toward the deceased mother that are displaced on to the sibling eulogizer.

When siblings sever the connections between them, the cause is almost always the culmination of stored-up angers or misfortunes.

For Chuck Franklin and his sister Sandy Hastings, there is not even a particular fight either can point to as the springboard for their mutual avoidance. Nor can either articulate specific reasons for it. Chuck says simply that he feels "no connectedness," and Sandy that what there is between them "happened over a lifetime" and can no longer be "erased."

I met Chuck on a plane to Washington, D.C., where he lives and where I was scheduled to speak at a convention. Within moments of our striking up a casual airplane conversation, he had launched into his sibling story—"to add to your research." He was still talking as the plane landed, and suggested that we continue the next day in his office at the National Institutes of Health, where he works as a public health administrator. He also gave me his sister's phone number at her home in Bethesda, Maryland, clearly eager for me to get in touch with her, although he refused to serve as go-between.

Protesting, when I called, that it would be too painful for her to "unearth" the past, Sandy nevertheless agreed to an interview and then proved to be as forthcoming as her brother. She, like him (and many other people), found it less difficult to talk to a stranger than to the sibling whose life she had once shared.

The last contact they'd had, both told me, had been about a year earlier when their father died, and another several years before that when he had become ill. Prior to that they had not spoken for fifteen years, except for an encounter at a family party.

"I've had a great deal of anger toward Sandy," Chuck said on the plane. "She has a habit of using people."

"I have no animosity at all toward Chuck," Sandy told me over the phone. "Things just happened. We're strangers to each other."

The contrasting evaluations were just a hint, I would find, of contrasting views and recollections.

About some basic things the two agreed: They had grown up in a run-down house in Baltimore's inner city, surrounded by other poor African-American families like their own. When Sandy was eight (she had just turned forty-seven when we met) and Chuck six, their mother died of cancer. The children continued to live with their father, whose job as an able-bodied seaman on a cargo ship took him away from home much of the time. He brought in a stream of girlfriends to care for the house, and it was the children's job to get rid of them when he grew bored. For a few summers after their mother's death, Chuck lived with her sister and Sandy with their father's sister. Other than that, the children were so much on their own that a social service agency threatened several times to take them from their father and place them in foster homes.

Chuck, both related, had been a "bad boy," hanging out with a "bunch of hoodlums" and running away almost a dozen times from the Roman Catholic boarding school in which his father placed him after the public schools were fed up with him. The brothers assured him and his father that he would amount to no good, and they might have been right, except that at eighteen Chuck joined the Army. Being away from home led to an interest for the first time in reading, and then in studying. Out of the service, he finished high school, attended college at night, and went on to graduate school, where he received a master's degree in public health.

"I decided I would show all the bastards who had no use for black boys like me," Chuck said. "No one I knew valued education. But I worked my ass off, just for spite. I know my father was proud of me."

So was his sister, who wishes to this day that some of those brothers who ran the boarding school could see *her* brother now. As for her, she finished high school and got married for the first time when she was eighteen. She has been divorced and remarried twice since then, now happily to her third husband, a car salesman. She herself runs a tiny gourmet food take-out shop.

Those were the basics. The different viewpoints, and the essence of the quarrels, come in interpreting these facts. Chuck regards his chaotic childhood as a time in which he and his sister led "parallel lives," he "running around" with his gang, and she becoming involved with boyfriends. "I don't remember my sister doing a thing for me," he said. "She never even cooked me a meal."

"Chuck was like my child," recalled Sandy in contrast. "I cleaned and cooked for him and listened to my father yelling all the time because he hated being stuck with two kids. Sometimes we'd be alone on weekends with no food and no money, and I'd have to make do. I think after a while Chuck resented my mothering him, which maybe he still does. I'd say, 'Clean up your room,' and he'd shout, 'Leave me alone,' and lock his door."

While Chuck remembers neither Sandy's mothering nor his anger at it, he does remember the anger he felt later when Sandy, in the midst of her first divorce, tried to move back into their father's home. At that point, Chuck, now out of the service, was married to his first wife. Too poor to support a place of their own, they were living with their father. "That's when the cutoff began," he recalled. "My sister wanted to come back home and take over my space, and I got furious about it. I felt, that's who she is, always wanting something. She didn't belong in that house with us. She and my wife didn't get along."

Sandy's version: "Chuck never even told me he was getting married; one day he and his wife were just living there with my father. Right away there was something that didn't work between his wife and me. She didn't like having to keep house for my father, and he made things worse because he was always telling her what a great cook *I* was. She and Chuck were having their troubles, and she took that out on me, too."

Sandy was having her own troubles. Her husband had turned out to be an alcoholic, and she, too, had begun drinking and popping tranquilizers. When she would call on her father for help, Chuck would get angry and accuse her of "making Pop cry." When she stayed over at the family house once or twice, Chuck's wife made it clear she was not welcome. One day she walked out the door of her own home and down the driveway to a neighbor who took away all her pills and invited Sandy to live with her for a while. The next day she tried to call her brother at her father's home to tell him where she was. He had disconnected the telephone line.

"I was told," she related, " 'Sorry, this is not a working number.' "

Brother and sister stopped seeing and speaking to each other after that. During the years that followed, Sandy remarried and moved to Bethesda with her second husband. She stayed in touch with her father but rarely saw him. Chuck, who had divorced his wife, remarried and became the father of twin girls. His education completed, he took a job in Washington, D.C. His father eventually gave up the family house and lived with him. Then he moved to Florida, living alone in a small apartment Chuck set up for him.

The one brief contact Sandy and Chuck had during those years was at a large family gathering to which both had been invited.

"We didn't have much to say to each other," Chuck remembered. "But there was an emotional kind of twinge, seeing her again. I know I welled up slightly. It was strange."

"There we were at the same table," Sandy recounted. "I would look at him, and he was looking at me. He was very quiet, and I kept staring at him."

The next meetings, the last ones, took place because of their father, now old and becoming sick. During the years of estrangement between his children, the elder Franklin tried on occasion to have them phone each other, but for the most part he kept out of their affairs. As he grew older, Chuck, the more established of the siblings, took over his care, flying down to Florida to check up on him and, when he became seriously ill, arranging to have him placed in a nursing home.

"I kept my sister informed," he said, "but she did nothing, and never offered to help. Once my father was in the home, we almost came to blows because she didn't visit him."

Sandy fills in what Chuck omits: "My father stayed with me for about four days after Chuck brought him up from Florida and while he was arranging the nursing home for him. I thought I'd be able to take him in permanently so he would not have to go to the home, but I couldn't. He was like a baby, and I had to miss work in order to watch him every minute. I said to myself, 'I spent my childhood taking care of my brother, and now I'm going to take care of my father?' I couldn't do it."

The one thing Sandy felt good about was that she was able to cook for her father. She made him hominy grits, "real old-fashioned food that he could chew easily," she said. "It made him happy, and it made me happy to give him pleasure." But when she told her brother, she recalled, "he said sarcastically, 'That's what you did for him? You made him hominy grits?' "

Sandy is a heavyset woman who projects intense emotion when she speaks. "My brother's life," she said, "is so established, so different. It's as if he doesn't want any part of the past. That's why the hominy grits bothered him."

Sandy admits that she did not visit her father in the nursing home—"I just couldn't stand seeing him that way, and now I'm ashamed"—and that Chuck took "excellent" care of him. She's also grateful that Chuck acceded to her request not to hold their father's funeral in the same home from which their mother had been buried.

"When my mother died, they told me to put on my best dress because I was going to a party," she said. "So I did. I was all dressed up, and then I saw her laid out. It was horrible. I could never go back there."

Sandy's fuss about the funeral parlor made Chuck realize for the first time that she had been at their mother's funeral and he had not. He is pleased that he obliged her, but has not changed his feelings. "I've had tremendous resentment of her," he said in describing his sister's response to their father's illness and death.

After the old man's funeral, the family gathered in the home of a relative. "I made a point of not sitting with my sister and not talking to her," Chuck recalled. "I didn't want to be around her." He has not seen or spoken to her since.

"At the cemetery," he said, "I remember thinking I might never see her again, and, in fact, it would be hard to think under what conditions I would see her."

From Sandy's perspective, it's all "very sad." She would like to "sit down with Chuck over a cup of coffee and ask some hard questions." Yet she is afraid to open the door to painful memories. "I just can't push twenty-five years away," she says.

So the cutoff continues for both these siblings, and may continue until the end of their days. Exactly why, neither can say. Chuck sees his sister as selfish, trying to grab his space, demanding of him and unwilling to care for their father. Sandy regards her brother as unfeeling, shutting her out when she most needed his help, a man trying to cut loose from his past, although admittedly dedicated to his father, the one tender link to it he kept.

Yet, as the outsider each was ready to speak to, I would speculate that neither is quite right about the other, and that neither has truly taken into consideration the effect of the past on the other.

For both siblings their mother's death when they were very young was a trauma that could never be healed, certainly not by a father who yelled, screamed, and had little time for his children. For Chuck, the younger, his sister filled in for the lost mother, but only as much as a child could. She could represent authority, "mothering" him by making him behave, but she could not supply the nurturing and love of an adult. As siblings so often do, Chuck directed against his sister the rage and pain he felt, while showering his father with affection. Sandy's bossiness as a child, her pill popping as an adult, and her inability to care for her father as Chuck did gave him concrete reasons for rejecting her.

Sandy is more aware than Chuck of the pain of their early years. If she didn't care for their father in his old age as much as she might have, perhaps it was because she had too much anger toward him or because she simply wasn't able to, having received so little love or support herself. And if she is angry with Chuck (although she claims she bears no animosity toward him), it may be because she wants, but has never been given, some expression of gratitude from him for her early role of mothering.

Both children were saved from greater hardships by the aunts who looked after them during the summers. But, according to Sandy, each aunt added to the ill feeling between sister and brother by favoring the child in her care and criticizing the other.

Sandy and Chuck led parallel lives, as Chuck said, and continue to do so. "If you were to sit down and talk to Chuck," I asked Sandy, "what would you ask him?"

"I'd ask him what happened. What happened in those twenty-five years? Why did you let me cross that driveway to my neighbor's and not respond to my calls? Why didn't you let me know when you were getting married? How did you feel growing up when they told you you'd wind up no good? And why don't you ever contact me?"

In different forms, but with the same need to know, these are the questions all sibs who have broken with one another or who are deeply angry might like to ask. If they do, they might discover that, as with Chuck and Sandy, the issues they are fighting about only skim the surface of the real pressure points between them.

PART III
Endings and Beginnings

"But if it is a question of pardon between us human beings, then it is I myself must beg for it. . . ."
Thus he spoke to them and they laughed and wept together and stretched out their hands. . . .

—Thomas Mann, *Joseph and His Brothers*

CHAPTER TWELVE

How Near? How Far?—Part 1

WHAT MAKES
SOME SIBS CLOSE
AND OTHERS NOT

"*W*hy do you suppose we feel so close to each other?" I asked my brother. For in spite of childhood battles and occasional adult spats, we have no doubt, either of us, of the depth of the love we share and the commitment we have to each other.

"I think the folks set a standard of support among their brothers and sisters that we were always aware of," he answered instantly. "They had such powerful family relationships."

Indeed they had. My mother, her sister, and three brothers were never out of touch with one another, although they often lived far apart. But my father, especially, maintained an uninterrupted attachment to his four brothers that had not, as my brother would put it, "a shred of cynicism about it." It was straightforward, honest, and full hearted.

We grew up under the canopy of that attachment. Through all of our childhood and teen years, we lived within blocks of our uncles and their families. We attended synagogue together, shared holiday celebrations, and took for granted the presence of one or another family member dropping by to say hello.

The relationships were not all equal. The two youngest brothers were closest to each other, sharing a business for almost forty years, and the two oldest—my father and his brother Morris—had their own tight-knit bond. ("He was so funny," my father said of that brother not long ago. "No one could make me laugh the way Morris could.") But there were numerous crossovers. My parents continued well into old age to live as neighbors and good friends with the youngest brother and his wife, in houses separated by a few feet of driveway. And while the middle brother, the most affluent, may sometimes have felt himself apart from the others, he was with them all the way in their devotion to their parents and loyalties to one another.

That, as my brother said, is the standard "the folks" set for us, and one that has played so large a part in our own assumption that the way one is with a sibling is close and supportive.

What has contributed to the closeness, or the distance, other siblings feel toward one another?

That is a question that comes up again and again in any discussion about siblings. In a sense, it is the ultimate sibling relationship question. When all is said and done, what is it that leads some sisters and brothers to see themselves as close and caring and others to shrug one another off with indifference?

And, to take a step backward, what does closeness actually mean? How close is close?

Many siblings I interviewed had wrestled with these questions, and many still do. Although devoted to each other, Gail and Pam, in Chapter Nine, find the closeness they seek elusive, having been stifled before it could fully develop by the destructive atmosphere of family secrets in which the sisters grew up. Eddy and Roy Deveau, one straight and the other gay, insist that their closeness has remained intact in spite of fundamental life differences and a number of serious blowups between them. The stepbrothers Jared and Bill seem to be constantly reevaluating the degree of closeness they wish to have with each other, whereas Meredith and Patty, blood sisters, insist that they want no closeness at all, their feelings poisoned during all those years in which Meredith was seen as the bad child and Patty the good one.

Deborah Gold, a researcher who studies aging and developmental changes in later life, has suggested that sibling relationships among older people can be classified into five types: intimate, congenial, loyal, apathetic, and hostile. Gold based her classification on interviews with men and women over the age of sixty-five. In a general way, those types might be applied as well to younger siblings, at all stages of adult life.

Intimate, Gold's first category, refers to those brothers and sisters

who see themselves as "best friends." These siblings are deeply devoted to one another, share their innermost thoughts, and may even
feel more psychologically connected to each other than they do to
their own spouses and children. Occasionally, they may become angry
at or envious of one another, but the feelings do not last.

Congenial siblings, in Gold's typology, may view themselves as
"good" rather than "best" friends, but are still warmly caring and
supportive. Although they may become annoyed or competitive with
one another or argue at times, they usually enjoy strong, positive
feelings.

For *loyal* siblings, closeness is based more on a sense of family
responsibility than on personal involvement, a "blood is thicker than
water" approach. Such sibs help out when needed, as a "good" sister
or brother should, but are less emotionally connected, and may be
less accepting and more critical of one another than are intimate or
congenial siblings.

As might be expected, *apathetic* siblings have little interest in or
contact with one another and no feelings of loyalty or connectedness.
"We were never close, even as children," is their usual explanation for
the distance they maintain, and they maintain that distance with
seemingly little feeling.

Hostile siblings, on the other hand, keep their distance out of deep
feelings of rage and resentment that accumulated over years. Some
fight whenever they see each other; others may have been pushed to
the breaking point by a particular fight, such as that of Max and James
over their mother's inheritance; and still others, like Chuck and Sandy
in Chapter Eleven, cannot trace their hostility to one specific cause,
but refuse to see or speak to each other.

Of course many sibling connections do not fall neatly into one of
these five types. These are human relationships, and they cannot be
packaged into the tidy and useful categories the social scientists devise. Thus siblings who might be labeled "loyal" in some respects
might in others fit into the slot of "congenial." Moreover, Gold's
scheme was not designed to take into consideration variations within
each group. The category of "intimate," for example, can cover a
range of intimacy, including such overclose and overinvolved relationships as that of "CarolandSelma."

Nevertheless, these categories do offer a broad overview of the
continuum from closeness to distance on which sibling relationships
exist. Family therapist Salvador Minuchin uses the more technical
terms "enmeshment" versus "disengagement." My survey tapped into
that continuum in another way by asking subjects to choose from

several responses the degree of closeness they felt toward their siblings.

To the question "How close are you?" most respondents checked "close" (31 percent) and "somewhat close" (31 percent), fewer "very close" (21 percent), and the smallest number "not close at all" (17 percent). Despite all the complaints siblings make about each other, despite the ups and downs in their relationships, in the end, relatively few place themselves in the most distant categories of apathy or hostility. Nor do the majority see themselves as "very close," intimate and unqualified best friends. Most people view themselves in the middle range of "close" or "somewhat close," that place for mixed feelings, where warmth can sometimes slide into hostility, and resentment can be contained, when desired, by love and loyalty.

Closeness, in other words, does not negate all problems and difficulties, and difficulties and problems do not necessarily rule out feelings of closeness. It is only when differences or conflicts dominate a relationship that sibs rate themselves "not close at all," or, in Gold's formula, apathetic or hostile.

(Even the extremes of closeness and distance are not free of ambivalences. Gold describes hostile siblings—the most alienated of all —as being as emotionally involved with one another as the most intimate ones. They expend a great deal of psychological energy criticizing their sibs, remembering past slights and anticipating future hurts. Their anger and denigrations may be the only means they know for remaining involved. The most intimate sibs, like CarolandSelma, on the other hand, may find themselves fighting and competing all the time *because* they are so intimate.)

How close is close?

Siblings need to set their own thermostats, find their own comfort zones for involvement in one another's lives. The siblings I met who longed for greater closeness were not seeking some ideal state of perfect intimacy and love. They were more realistic than that, and most had other friends whom they trusted and in whom they could confide. What they wanted from each other was something else. Pam and Gail did not speak of needing one another as best friends, but only of needing to help and be helped by each other in overcoming the horrors of their past. Neither Christina nor Vivian, in Chapter Seven, has expectations of freeing herself completely of the pains and resentments that have piled up from the early favoritism in their family. What each desires from the other is recognition of her own pain and the freedom to speak of her personal suffering without this escalating into greater rage and acrimony.

The yearning for closeness among siblings is usually a wish to draw a little nearer, to give and get a little extra support, to tilt the seesaw a little more toward intimacy than distance, toward warmth than coolness. It is certainly a wish for a satisfying friendship if that is possible, but it will accept the congeniality, or at least the loyalty, that should be part of the singular tie connecting one sib to another.

How siblings might go about fulfilling their wishes is the subject of the last chapter of this book. How they got to where they are—what makes some brothers and sisters close and others not—is the focus here. To begin with, what are the factors in family background and childhood that influence the way siblings relate to each other later as adults?

Family relationships like those my brother and I grew up with are one such factor. The visits from my uncles, the shared joking, the pitching in when one or another needed help—these are the kinds of models that influence many siblings. Respondents who felt close or very close to their siblings tended to report that their mothers or fathers, or both, had felt close or very close to their own brothers or sisters. Conversely, those people who felt distant from their brothers or sisters were more likely to have parents who were distant from *their* siblings.

That is not to say that there is always a straight-line cause-and-effect relationship at work here. Siblings from families filled with conflict and disturbance may make a conscious effort *not* to behave as their parents had, and may succeed in breaking the family pattern. An antiques dealer explained:

"My sister and I vaguely knew that my father had a sister, but we never met her until my sister's wedding. Apparently they'd had a tumultuous relationship, always at odds with each other. At the wedding, we saw these strange people who my father introduced to us as our aunt and uncle. My sister and I looked at each other, and there was this unspoken agreement between us that nothing like that would ever happen to us. I'm sure it won't. We became more precious to each other after seeing that mysterious aunt with my father."

Still, the magnetism of family patterns is very powerful. We do not necessarily copy our parents' behavior with their own families, but that behavior becomes subliminally encoded in our minds, serving as a guidepost that we follow, usually unawares.

Family systems therapists speak of the likelihood that people who cut themselves off from their parents will have children who themselves break away, having learned by example to deal with problems by *not* dealing, escaping instead. The same holds true for siblings. There are enough tensions in family life for the idea of simply walking away from them, of turning your back on a sibling who is irritating or provocative, to be a tempting one. And if as you grew up you witnessed just that kind of behavior among your parents and their siblings, the temptation may become irresistible.

Certainly Patty and Meredith have not resisted it. They have handled their differences by splitting from each other as their mother Honey had from her three sisters. Although one of their aunts pleaded with Patty not to reenact the family agony with Meredith, the two sisters have done just that. The powerful patterns that governed the behavior of their mother and aunts have been transmitted to them not genetically but environmentally, through the atmosphere that pervaded their home and the angers that hovered like black clouds around the older women.

There are other patterns of family life that play on the consciousness of brothers and sisters as they grow up, influencing their attitudes toward each other. The warm devotion of my father's brothers to one another and to their parents typified the close ties of many other Jewish immigrant families as they pulled together to make their way in a strange and frightening new land. That those attitudes were also part of a broader, ethnic approach to family relationships added to their strength and their enduring impact on my brother and me and on our cousins as well.

Ethnicity is difficult to discuss because it lends itself so easily to simplistic generalizations and stereotypes. For every ethnic characteristic you can describe, I can name half a dozen exceptions. Are Italian families warm and intimate? I have met Italian brothers who are closed off and cold to each other. Do Asian men take charge of family life, becoming their sisters' protectors? I have spoken with an Asian man who abandoned his sister during the Vietnam War and has made no attempt to contact her since.

Yet there proved to be no way to ignore the ethnic differences that came through clearly in my interviews and questionnaire. These differences also fit into patterns documented by sociologists and psychologists who study families. Exceptions notwithstanding, what they find is that our ethnicity is part of our identity, and we cannot truly understand ourselves without recognizing it.

Ethnic identities are strongest in new immigrant groups—like my father and his brothers—who protect themselves in their unfamiliar surroundings by clustering near each other in tight-knit communities. The children and grandchildren of these immigrants lose many of their distinctive ethnic characteristics as they move out into the larger world and become part of the dominant culture. But they do not lose everything. Patterns of ethnicity are passed along from parents to children and continue to influence group behavior for generations. In family life these ethnic patterns affect the degree of heat siblings want and can tolerate from each other.

When Mary Ann, eldest of the Ginetti sisters, moved to Seattle, far from the rest of the clan in Connecticut, nobody thought it unusual for the second sister, Nancy, to cry "every night for a year," as she said. Though Nancy's special attachment to Mary Ann made the separation particularly difficult, the move itself cut into the closeness typical of many Italian-American families like the Ginettis. It is a closeness that also characterizes other ethnic groups whose origins stem from various Mediterranean cultures—Greek-Americans, for example. In these families siblings not only keep strong ties, they openly express their feelings—both positive and negative—to and about each other.

I saw some of that openness, and great devotion among siblings, in Latino families as well. In California I met three Mexican-American brothers, all businessmen, each of whom told me independently that while wife and children come first in commanding his loyalty, "my brothers are very close behind."

The youngest of these brothers had just completed a one-year jail sentence for a white-collar crime that had scandalized the community and shattered his parents. The other two brothers, who jointly owned an import company, had suffered business losses by association and were enraged at the third for his "stupidity" as well as dishonesty. Nevertheless, when their brother came out of jail, they managed to arrange a good job for him even as they continued to reestablish their own firm's reputation. And as critical of him as they are themselves, they will not tolerate criticisms from others.

"A person I'd been very close to said bad things about Rudolfo," said the eldest, "and I told him, 'That's it. I don't want anything more to do with you.' My brother is my brother no matter what."

That intensity of sibling loyalty can exist in an Irish-American family, but there it is not likely be expressed as freely. In interviews I often found brothers and sisters of ethnic Irish families to have strong feelings for each other, yet they tended more to joke about those feelings than to admit to them. Hugh Shea, whose sister Rosie had been schizophrenic, was surprised to find himself revealing things to me that he had not even told his analyst, preferring through most of his life to keep his deepest emotions to himself.

Hugh's longing for a "real big sister" who might have watched over him "the way sisters do in Irish families" fit into another pattern of this culture. Mothers and sons may have a special closeness, but sisters may actually be seen as the "strong ones" who care for their brothers and hold the family together. Traditionally, girls have been as well educated as boys in these families and are expected to be as independent. In keeping with that, I did have a sense that of the many women I interviewed, Irish-American women complained less that their brothers had dominant roles. The woman who said that the girls in her family casually accepted the fact that "Mom liked her boys a whole lot" reflected the confidence of others.

Independence is less the issue in African-American families than connectedness with a large network of relatives beyond the immediate family. The importance blacks give to their extended families of grandparents, aunts, uncles, cousins, in-laws, and even close friends, along with parents and siblings, may have its roots in the complex kinship systems that existed in Africa. But broad and strong family ties have also helped black families cope with the struggles they have faced and the oppression they have experienced.

These close family ties promote sibling loyalties. Journalist Brent Staples broke out of the poverty and violence that marked his childhood in an industrial city in Pennsylvania. His younger brother Blake did not. Although Brent lived a comfortable middle-class life, he desperately tried to reach out to Blake and save him from the crime and hopelessness that trap many young black men. He failed; Blake was murdered at the age of twenty-two. More than two years later, Brent wrote of the death, "I felt as though part of my soul had been cut away. I questioned myself then, and I still do. Did I not reach back soon or earnestly enough for him?"

Sibling ties become weakened in African-American families when poverty or other dire circumstances force sibs to be separated and cared for by different members of their extended family. Away from immediate family members, children may become confused about their loyalties and lose their connections to each other. After Chuck and Sandy's mother died, for example, aunts from different sides of the family cared for each child. Each aunt favored the child in her care and criticized the other, augmenting the bad feelings the children developed for each other.

"Ethnic" is hardly the term one usually applies to members of the dominant American culture, Protestant Anglo-Saxons, whose roots go back to the earliest days of America's history. But this culture, too, acts on siblings' feelings for each other. Among its great strengths is its emphasis on independence and individualism—what we often think of as our basic American values—along with attitudes of self-sufficiency and stoicism. The New England sisters Pam and Gail, for example, did not indulge in an iota of self-pity about their horrendous early lives with their alcoholic father and stepmother.

Yet that self-sufficiency can also stand in the way of intimacy. Pam, the more expressive of the two sisters, complained that Gail was "zippered up" and couldn't be reached. Gail wanted very much to draw closer to Pam but felt unable to, inhibited by her own inner torments but also by the pattern of emotional restraint and control that was part of the sisters' heritage.

Taught to hold back their feelings and keep a "stiff upper lip," Anglo-Americans like Pam and Gail are more likely to present a cheerful front and suffer internally than to share problems with each other. As a result, family members may feel emotionally isolated, lonely and cut off in a profound way from one another even when they keep up regular contact. The author John Cheever often wrote about such families. In his short story "Goodbye, My Brother," a family that traces its beginnings to early American Puritans gathers for a reunion at its summer home on a Massachusetts island. The narrator grows increasingly irritated with his youngest brother Lawrence, who finds fault with everything. Wanting only to have a good time, and unwilling to confront family failings himself, he finally strikes his brother from behind, knocking him over and bloodying his head.

"Oh, what can you do with a man like that?" the narrator says after Lawrence and his family leave the summer house. He immediately turns to enjoy the sunshine and the sea without dwelling on the significance of the violent act he has committed against his brother.

Expressiveness or reserve, intimacy or independence—these are some of the ethnic traits siblings absorb along with other family characteristics as they grow up. It is against this backdrop of family and ethnic patterns that they will establish their own unique relationships with each other.

How those relationships build and develop throughout childhood will help determine the level of warmth or distance siblings will carry with them to adult life. One way to examine early sibling relationships is to use as a model the relationships of parents to their children, the attachments they form to each other from an infant's first moments.

Attachment theory, a mainstay of modern psychology, emphasizes the need children have for a warm, close bond with a parent. A central tenet of this theory is that the response of a parent—usually the mother—to her child strongly influences the nature of the attachment the child forms to the mother, and ultimately, through that attachment, the nature of the child's view of itself and the larger world. Mothers who respond comfortably to their babies, easily picking up their feeding signals and quickly returning their smiles, are more likely to give their children a sense of security than those who are uncomfortable, tense, inconsistent, or—of course—openly rejecting.

It is not that the mothers of securely attached children are perfect; but they are "good enough," in the words of psychoanalyst Donald Winnicott. They do the best they can, and because they approach their children with tenderness and care, they give the children a feeling of being both loved and worthy of love.

What is true of attachments between children and parents is true in its own way of attachments among children themselves. Siblings form strong bonds by identifying with one another and by responding to each other. The attachments are far from perfect, but when there is a base of empathy and responsiveness, they can be "good enough" to offer each sib the sense of being loved and cared about by the other. A woman who has become extremely close to her older sister in adult life remembers always fighting with that sister in childhood. "But that doesn't mean we didn't also have fun together," she explained. "We really liked playing together, and it's the liking that we've picked up on."

The compatibility among sibs—their "goodness of fit," to use Chess and Thomas's term again—contributes to that liking and to sibling attachments from earliest days. Those children whose temperaments and personalities fit each other well usually get off to a good start, laying the foundation for continuing good relations. When psychologist Michael Lamb observed pairs of preschool children with their infant siblings, he found that the more sociable and responsive the infants were to their elders at that point, the friendlier the elders were six months later when the children were observed again. The infants and their big sisters and brothers reinforced each other's good feelings from the beginning.

Early good feelings can last for years, according to Dunn and Kendrick. In their investigations, they discovered that when firstborn children showed affection toward their baby siblings during the first few weeks after the baby's birth, both children were especially friendly fourteen months later. They remained consistently friendly when seen in follow-up studies three years later. The goodness of fit between the sibs from the outset had set them on the path toward a happy relationship.

Dunn and Kendrick also concluded that parents can encourage

goodness of fit by involving an older child in a new baby's life. They noticed in their studies that older children seemed happiest with their new sibs when parents spoke to them about why a baby was crying or what the baby might be feeling or whether the baby was hungry. In their follow-up studies fourteen months later they found that those children whose parents had talked to them about a new baby and made them feel involved were much friendlier toward younger sibs than were other children. The youngers, in turn, were particularly friendly toward these older brothers or sisters.

None of these findings suggest that infants who are shy or unresponsive to older sibs, or elders who have no interest in their baby sibs, are doomed to a lifetime of alienation. Nor do they imply that friendly sibs never fight or feel jealous of each other. But they do signify that a comfortable compatibility and strong early attachments among siblings lead to closeness later in childhood. The compatibility and the closeness often stretch into adulthood.

The age gap between siblings is another important component in the kinds of attachments they form among themselves, but nobody has yet been able to prove exactly *how* it influences those attachments.

Ask child development experts and, for the most part, they will tell you that the best age spacing between siblings is about three years. Why? Because children under that age are still trying to find their own bearings, to create themselves as beings separate and apart from their parents. The appearance of a new baby before an older child has planted a firm foot on his own soil can cause rage and resentment against the baby and send the child running right back into the arms of his parents, fearful of letting go lest he lose everything.

Many advocates of this at-least-three-years-between-siblings philosophy cite the research of psychoanalyst Margaret Mahler, who pictured the months between the ages of two and three as stormy ones for a toddler—what is often referred to as "the terrible twos." This is the time when children suffer a series of losses: they begin to give up the bottle, they begin toilet training, and some of them begin to attend play groups or even nursery school. All these beginnings move them away from the global protection of their parents. That move, an inevitable part of growth, can be frightening until children have matured enough to realize that even when they are separated from their parents, the parents will continue to love and protect them. The maturity that accompanies that realization makes it easier for a child to accept a new baby, and with acceptance to be caring and friendly.

Less psychoanalytically, and with a slight switch on the above thinking, some psychologists argue that the best age gap between siblings is either less than two years or more than four. Less than two because when a second baby is born within a year or so of the first, the children share their parents almost from the start. Firstborns in that situation feel less resentful of a newcomer than do those who have had their parents to themselves for a longer time. Siblings more than four years apart, the argument goes, also feel less threatened by a new baby because they are more independent and have lives of their own apart from their parents.

Ask parents about the best spacing of children, and they will tell you the pluses and minuses of what *they* did. Some will argue that a narrow range has brought their children close together; others that this narrowness squeezed each child into feeling cheated of parental care. Some will insist that a four- or five-year gap gave each son or daughter a chance to develop as an individual; others that if they had it to do over, they would shorten that gap so that the children could have more in common. And if you probe a little further, you will discover that the way parents planned their families had much to do with their own sibling experience—consciously or unconsciously they were trying to re-create the good or rectify the bad.

Ask schoolchildren how they feel about siblings of different ages, as did psychologists Wyndol Furman and Duane Buhrmester, and you will get some contradictory answers. The fifth- and sixth-grade children whom these psychologists interviewed indicated that they felt closest to siblings nearest them in age, especially those of the same sex. But they also fought most with siblings nearest in age. Younger children felt they had the least amount of status and power when siblings were four or more years older than they, and, in their weaker position, could offer little support or nurturing to those older sibs. Older children, however, felt most nurturing and supportive toward siblings four or more years younger than they.

Now ask adults how close they feel to their own siblings of different ages, and you will get another mixed bag of responses. In general, adult respondents to my questionnaire, like the young ones interviewed by Furman and Buhrmester, considered themselves closest to siblings nearest to them in age—closest of all to those only one or two years apart and more distant from those whose age difference was five or more years.

But there were some puzzles here: When the results were analyzed according to birth positions, they showed that younger siblings felt significantly closer to brothers or sisters only one to four years older than to sibs five or more years older. Older siblings did not make such clear-cut distinctions in regard to younger ones. The differences in their feelings toward younger siblings near to them in age and those further apart were not striking or statistically significant.

These different attitudes among younger and older adult siblings may relate to the attitudes of the school-age children studied by Furman and Buhrmester. Perhaps younger brothers and sisters continue throughout life to feel most powerless with siblings quite a bit older than they, regarding them more as parentlike figures than as contemporaries. Perhaps older siblings continue even in adult life to feel nurturing and protective toward their younger sibs and therefore close to them regardless of the age gap between them. Or, as a secretary wrote: "I have always enjoyed my relationship with my brother and feel it has added a great deal to my life. He (five years younger) followed me everywhere until I left for college. He was known in our town as Brother, and I still think of him that way."

Despite these differences between older and younger siblings, in terms of the broad numbers I have to conclude that the warmest feelings among sibs come not—as some child experts imply—from wide spacings but from narrow ones. Both as children and adults, siblings closer in age see themselves as closer in feelings. People in the survey who described themselves as uninvolved with one or another sibling often blamed that distance on a large age difference, which culminated in one's being out of the house and off to college or career while another was growing up.

But the experts are right in one concern about narrow age spacing. For many sibs, nearness in age generates conflict and competition that coexist with feelings of closeness. The eldest Ginetti sisters, Mary Ann and Nancy, a year apart in age, are a case in point. Nancy speaks of adoring her older sister and feeling deeply connected to her, and Mary Ann, although less effusive, admits that she feels closest to Nancy and would confide in her before anyone else in the family. Yet most of the family tensions have occurred between them, from squabbles over clothes in their earlier years to their business fight more recently.

As with the Ginetti sisters, I should point out, in families of more than two children, siblings tend to pair off, marching to life's rhythms two by two. It was always a surprise to me in interviews to hear people speak with great emotion about "my brother" or "my sister" as if there were only one, and then to discover as our meeting progressed that there were three or four siblings—or eight or nine—in the family. But for that person, I came to recognize, there was only one brother or sister who really mattered, the one who was "*my* sister" or *"my* brother." (Said a nurse, eldest of seven, "Oh sure, I know the addresses of the others and would be invited to their weddings and things, but my sister and I are really *sisters."*)

Sometimes in these families, alternate sibs—the first and third or second and fourth, for instance—establish the closest ties with each other. In that way they avoid the conflict or intense rivalry that close age spacing may bring. But more often, like Mary Ann and Nancy, brothers and sisters nearest each other in birth order become most connected emotionally. In fact, in their classic study of large families, Bossard and Boll ranked closeness of age as a main cause for the "cliques" typical of such families.

Whether in large families or small, one more basic element affects the nature of the attachments siblings form with each other: gender. I found little difference in the degree of closeness reported by brothers from that reported by brothers and sisters. But, as noted earlier, the one finding that stood out clearly and strongly is that sisters form the closest and tightest bonds with their sisters. On almost every scale of closeness—from how often they see each other to how much they confide in one another—sisters topped the charts for intimacy and warmth toward one another.

Educator Carol Gilligan contends that women have been raised to speak in a "different voice" than men. That voice is softer and often drowned out by the more dominant sounds of men in our society. Yet it is a voice of connectedness, of a morality that concerns itself with the interpersonal, of deeper involvement with children and parents and siblings. It is a voice that more freely expresses feelings and sentiment. And those qualities of connectedness and expressiveness can bring sisters close together.

These sisterly qualities are so important that researchers have found that the elderly, both men and women, fare better when they have a sister they feel they can count on for emotional—and sometimes material—support than if there is no sister in the family. Just as elderly parents depend more often on their daughters than their sons for help, elderly siblings with a sister to whom they feel close gain a sense of well-being that closeness to a brother does not seem to provide. Conversely, fighting or other disruptions of the bond with a sister cut into an elderly person's well-being, making that person more prone to depression. It would seem, then, that even if it takes a lifetime to realize it, brothers as well as sisters eventually recognize that having a sister is something special.

.   .   .

The final, and crucial, area to be investigated in seeking clues to the origins of sibling closeness or detachment is, of course, the profound influence of parents. Not the overall atmosphere of family solidarity or ethnic behaviors that children breathe in as they grow up, but what it is that parents literally do or don't do in regard to their children that influences the children's attitudes toward each other.

Most fundamentally, in their behavior toward each other and their children, parents serve as models with whom the children identify. Through the nurturing and care they give, they set an example for the children to be nurturing and caring toward one another. Through the intimacy and warmth they project, they spread an aura of intimacy and warmth throughout the family. Adults who regard themselves as having tight, intimate connections with their siblings often credit those connections to lessons learned at their parents' feet.

"My sisters and I have always had good feelings about each other because our parents treated each one of us with respect and taught us to respect one another," said a woman, youngest of three sisters.

"The values and role models our parents gave us had a great influence on all of us," wrote a fifty-two-year-old man, the middle of five, on the questionnaire. "They simply assumed we'd be close because family was all-important to them. Even though my father has been dead twenty years and my mother almost twelve, we follow in their footsteps."

"I believe my brother and I are close," summed up a secretary, "because of my parents' attitude: 'Life is so short, be friends. Don't ever regret saying you're sorry because if something happens to one of you and you neglected to clear things up, you'll regret *that.*' With this direction we have remained close, and to this day—no regrets!"

Obviously, words of advice—or platitudes—from parents do not in themselves create congenial children. Nor is it necessary for parents to push their children to be best friends in order to foster closeness between them. It is more important for the children to learn to be supportive friends, "there" for each other when needed. Most important, parental advice can bring about good relations among siblings only if it is backed up by good (or good enough) parenting that provides models of empathy and trust for the children to emulate in their conduct with each other.

The survey bears out the interrelationships of family behavior. There was a strong and significant statistical correlation between the degree of closeness people felt toward their siblings and toward their parents. Those who felt close or very close to their mother or father or both also tended to feel that way toward their siblings. And those who felt close or very close to their siblings had similar feelings toward their parents. Deep family feelings breed deep family feelings.

Paradoxically, some of the most intense sibling ties can result from an *absence* of parental care. On the continuum of sibling closeness, the most intertwined of the intimate siblings are often those who preserved their selves, in coping with hardship in their early lives, by clinging to each other. Left on their own, their parents either physically or psychologically unavailable, these brothers and sisters became unwavering in their loyalty and supplied one another with the solace and sustenance they lacked from parents.

Psychologists Bank and Kahn label such extremely loyal and close siblings with the fairy-tale name of "Hansels and Gretels." In childhood they become each other's caregivers. Like Hansel, the elder often takes the lead in protecting and sheltering younger siblings. But like Gretel, who outwitted the wicked witch when Hansel was locked in a cage, youngers can also come to their elders' rescue through their allegiance and devotion. More than best friends, these siblings are both parents and children to each other, depending on one another for emotional and physical survival.

The death of a parent in childhood can create such strong, mutual sibling dependencies. When a surviving parent is consumed by grief, siblings often must rely only on each other for comfort and relief from their own pain. The even more tragic death of both parents can push sibs into still closer bonds as they struggle together to master the feelings of terror and abandonment that accompany orphanhood.

Eileen Simpson, in her autobiography *Orphans*, describes the ardent devotion she and her sister Marie, ten months older, felt for each other after their parents died—their mother when Eileen was eleven months old and their father shortly before her seventh birthday. In the various convents and homes in which they lived, she writes, adults held so little importance to them that, unlike other children, they never competed for "favors and attention" and were never rivalrous or possessive. The bedrock of their lives was their loyalty to each other.

Parental divorce, which causes its own wrenching loss for children, can also draw siblings into powerful emotional connectedness. Feeling themselves physically abandoned by the parent who has moved out, they may also feel emotionally abandoned by both parents, bereft of the family life they had shared. In that rapidly disintegrating world, siblings hang on to each other for support. Jared, in Chapter Six, watched over his younger brother Chip when their parents divorced. Although Chip died in young adulthood, Jared still regards himself as closer to him than to Bill, the stepbrother with whom he lived for years.

Psychological abandonment can occur in many other ways, and emotional orphanhood can be as devastating as literal orphanhood. Children feel orphaned when parents are too busy to pay attention to them, or—in large families—too exhausted from family responsibilities to devote time to any individual child. They feel orphaned when parents drink to excess, or abuse each other and the children, or are chillingly distant and unloving. They feel orphaned when they sense themselves to be alone with each other and lacking in the protective powers only parents can provide.

"A hole in the world" is how Richard Rhodes, in his book of the same name, characterizes the emptiness that engulfs the life of a child abandoned or mistreated by parents. Starved, beaten, and humiliated by a cruel stepmother and uncared for by his father, Rhodes relied throughout childhood on his brother Stanley, a year and a half older than he, for humanity and salvation. The brothers became so close that years later, as an adult, Richard dreamt once that he was being beaten in the eye at the very moment that Stanley—miles away from him—was, in fact, being beaten that way in a brutal fight.

"My brother's fear and pain called out to me," he writes. "I felt that close to him. Though we reside a continent apart and have lived these past thirty years in notably different circumstances, I still do."

Closeness can serve as a shield for all Hansels and Gretels who have been literally or emotionally orphaned. In that closeness they find security, and by depending on each other, they discover that they can make their way through frightening forests. Unfortunately, they can also become entrapped by that very closeness, security, and dependency. Because they so utterly needed each other as children, they may find it extremely difficult later to break free and establish independence. For them the task of separating and individuating from siblings may be especially challenging because the pull toward oneness can be not only powerful but particularly seductive.

Eileen Simpson describes the pleasure and security she felt as a child in being treated exactly like her older sister. Although she knew Marie sometimes became annoyed at their "twinness," Eileen felt content to be dressed like her sister, receive identical gifts, and always to order the same flavor ice cream. Only after an aunt forced her to make her own decisions did she begin to realize that "I also had a self that was unique."

Helped by her aunt and others, Simpson was able to free herself from a dependent and crippling closeness to her sister. For some profoundly connected siblings, that freedom comes only with great struggle and at great cost. When John Cheever portrayed one brother bloodying the head of another in "Goodbye, My Brother," he was also portraying his own attempts to strike loose from the older brother with whom he, like Simpson, had been "twinned" through the early part of his life. In their case the brothers' extreme closeness was a reaction to their father's drinking, their parents' constant quarrels, and the lack of any warmth or affection toward them in this Yankee household. John and Fred relied on each other for comfort well into young adulthood.

"It was the strongest love of my life," Cheever once told his daughter Susan. So strong that it became "ungainly" and "psychologically incestuous," and he knew he had to separate. After sharing an apartment in Boston with Fred for several years, John moved alone to New York. But he continued to wrestle with his attachment to Fred through his stories, which time and again pick up the theme of brotherly violence mixed with brotherly closeness.

Some deeply attached siblings never separate. They remain so scarred by parental loss or rejection that they become incapable of establishing mature, satisfying relationships outside their own bond. On the continuum of closeness and distance, they belong at the most extreme end of closeness, their ties stretching beyond the edges of normalcy.

The sisters "CarolandSelma," as their cousin describes them, have lived most of their lives almost as one person. "If you speak to one on the phone," says the cousin, "the other calls you back thirty seconds later to get in on the conversation."

Long ago, in a modest house in the town in North Carolina where the sisters grew up, there were parents who disliked each other and had little interest in their daughters. The father, who managed the farms of wealthy landowners, was consumed with bitterness at being a worker and not an owner of the property he supervised. He took out his frustrations on his wife, whom he insulted regularly and humiliated publicly by flaunting his liaisons with some of the best-known prostitutes in town. The mother, a librarian, morose by nature, dealt with her husband's behavior by withdrawing into herself. What she required most from her daughters was invisibility; she kept her home as silent as her library's reading room.

Repressed by their mother and ignored by their father, the sisters huddled together for companionship. The one refuge from their oppressive home was an aunt, their mother's sister, who taught them to laugh and play with her children. But it was not enough. Never given a chance to develop separate selves, the sisters seemed to blend into each other over time, each giving up some of herself for the larger protection of being part of the other. Like the alga and fungus that are joined to form a lichen, these sisters now seem joined forever, neither able to live separate from the other.

It is only through their quarrels that CarolandSelma ever appear to try to separate from each other, just as John Cheever used violence in his stories about brothers as a way to extract his own brother from his soul. But the quarrels or violence of these and other closely bound siblings may also reflect their deep-seated angers at each other and at their parents. As dedicated and loyal as they may be, children themselves cannot fill the hole in the world created when parents desert them, and in their need and frustration they may lash out at each other.

As with CarolandSelma, some of the fiercest angers exist among children who have experienced the most dreadful parental deprivations. Older siblings, as noted earlier, may seethe with anger if they have been saddled with the care of younger ones, and they may treat the youngers harshly even while caring for them. Ironically, in the very worst situations, family secrets such as incest, parental abuse, or severe alcoholism may so damage children that they have little feeling at all for each other, not even anger. Hurt and beaten down, they strive mainly to survive, and without a model of love and compassion with whom to identify, they find it difficult to provide even grudging care for each other.

For—and we return now to the role parents play in fostering closeness—even when parents are absent or emotionally unavailable or have died, in order for siblings to be caring about each other, they need to have received some care themselves, to have known in some way the protection and security only an adult can offer a child. They need to have had some exposure to a kindly adult who served as an example with whom they could identify and from whom they could learn what it means to reach out to another.

Eileen Simpson and her sister Marie saw such examples among the nuns who ran the convent where they lived for a while and among the various aunts who took them in at different times. CarolandSelma, warped as they may be, also had a loving and concerned aunt. And three sisters—Jill, Blythe, and Sherry—orphaned when they were eleven, ten, and eight, respectively, had hazy memories of a mother's love to sustain their closeness even as they grew up in separate homes.

The mother died two years before the father. When he died, the girls lived with their elderly grandfather, and when he died a year or two later, they were sent to different foster homes, where each lived until she married. Jill, as the eldest, has the clearest recollections of their original family as being very close, and has been determined to follow that tradition with her sisters.

"I was the oldest," she explains, "so I always felt it was my responsibility to keep the three of us in touch. But it wasn't just responsibility," she adds. "I wanted them near me because they were all I had. You don't cry on foster parents' shoulders. My sisters were the only ones who could relate to what I was going through because they were going through the same thing."

She recognizes that she may be "bossy" in still urging her sisters to get together as often as possible, but "it's all the family we have," she says, although each sister has children of her own.

Sherry, as youngest, gets most annoyed at Jill's bossiness and control, "as if she always has to run the family." Yet she says, "I'm only twenty-nine, but I worry about our mortality all the time. God forbid anything should ever happen to one of my sisters. I couldn't bear it."

And Blythe, regretful that the sisters live about an hour away from each other, tells of a daydream "that we would live in the same community so that we could just go back and forth. If you wanted to have a cup of coffee and be comfortable together, you could, any time you felt like it."

Each carries within snippets of mother memories. Sherry's, the saddest, is of a "wake, confusion, a party atmosphere, and me crying." Blythe's is of "the three of us and our mother going into a store and looking at Ginny doll clothes and laughing together." And Jill, keeper of family lore, of "sitting with her, and she'd be hugging us or holding us on her lap, and I just never felt cheated that Blythe or Sherry was getting more of her than I was." Three sisters—three Gretels—holding on to one another because they had been left alone, and because in their aloneness they were able to follow a faded blueprint bequeathed by their mother.

The blueprints for closeness or distance that siblings and their parents draw up in early childhood become the basis for the more solid structures of adolescence. By the time young people reach their teen years, each has taken the measure of the other. Each has an understanding of the other's temperament and knows how to placate as well as irritate. Each, also, has absorbed family values and ethnic attitudes and become a careful observer of parental behaviors. Everyday rivalries and fighting aside, a general bent toward closeness or coolness may be, by now, an integral part of the relationship.

But now other influences may begin to act on that relationship. By adolescence, for instance, the roles siblings have carved out for themselves are fairly well established. The scholar in the family pursues his studies and the athlete her tennis, and the sense of differentness both have allows them to draw close without stepping on each other's toes. But those very qualities also separate their lives more than ever at this time. No longer thrust as fully as they once were into family activities, teenage siblings may tunnel into their own worlds, spending far less time together than they had before.

Then, too, if there is an age gap of four years or more, one sib may be out of the house, off to college or working at a job, while another is in high school. One may be caught up in dating or sexual adventures while another has barely begun the rites of puberty. One may test out new waters and take on new values or mannerisms shocking or frightening to another. (How well I remember my brother's return after his first few months at an Ivy League law school while I was still attending a city college and living at home. He wore crew neck sweaters and khaki pants, spoke casually of friends whose family names I had seen in social columns, and appeared to have lost all interest in anything I was doing. I locked myself in my bedroom and cried my heart out, convinced I had lost forever the companion of my youth.) Or one may go further, becoming involved with drugs or alcohol, leaving another feeling helpless, cut off—or, sometimes, eager to follow suit.

Yet at the same time, different forces are pulling sibs together during adolescence. As they become more independent, teenage sisters and brothers often forge strong alliances. They exchange secrets and confidences, especially about sexual matters, that they wouldn't dream of telling parents. They also share criticisms of their parents they had never dared to acknowledge to themselves or each other when they were younger. Mark Platt attributed some of the closeness he and Jerry found in their late teen years to their ability to talk about their parents "as though they were vulnerable people who had problems just the way we all had problems."

As teenagers and young adults, siblings also offer one another encouragement in striking out on their own, and they begin to turn up areas of common interest they may not have noticed earlier. (My brother and I began to enjoy discussing books we were both reading after I regained my composure and discovered he hadn't changed *that* much—and he regained his interest in me.)

For those siblings to whom mutual interests and alliances are important, a new, more mature closeness gets built—especially during later adolescence—on the older foundations of the early years. That closeness and maturity includes a stronger sense of themselves as individuals, secure enough to put aside open warfare and the most burning rivalry and separate enough to appreciate one another's uniqueness. Many siblings say that during their college years they really came to know each other and to regard themselves as good friends, even when they were at different schools. A surprising finding about that closeness of the college years points up its importance in ways that had never been thought of before.

For more than forty years a group of men who attended Harvard during the early 1940s have been the subject of a long-range study known as the Grant Study. Its purpose has been to discover the factors in the men's lives that led to physical and emotional health as they grew older. George Vaillant, a psychiatrist, became head of the study in 1967, and has reported periodically on the men at different ages. By 1990, of the original 204 men selected for the study 173 remained in it (some had died; others dropped out). By then Vaillant had come to some conclusions about what it was in earlier life that most affected the health of these men at age sixty-five.

High on the list of elements important for the men's adjustment—meaning general good health and satisfaction with life—was being close to one's siblings at college age. Those men who had had a warm and close relationship with their siblings during their college years fared much better in their overall well-being later in life than did those who had been distant from or hostile to their siblings.

Vaillant's finding suggests that the closeness siblings develop in their youth stands them in good stead later in life. The closeness builds step by step from early childhood, shaped by siblings and their parents and the culture they share. Then, as sibs move on through the life cycle, the degree of heat and coolness between them varies, influenced by each new rite of passage. But when feelings of warmth and congeniality have been established at a young age, they rarely disappear completely. In older age they become once more a source of comfort and companionship among sisters and brothers.

CHAPTER THIRTEEN

How Near? How Far?—Part 2

CLOSENESS AND DISTANCE ACROSS SPACE AND TIME

*W*hen siblings leave adolescence and move away from their family home, they put behind them a way of life that, in most cases, will never recur: the condition of living together under one roof. The experience of being children together, the shared bedrooms and hand-me-down clothes, the struggles for power and for parents, the friendships and fights now become part of the storehouse of memories that brothers and sisters carry with them into their separate lives. These memories, intertwined with layers of feelings that have grown over the years, form the underpinnings for sibling attitudes and actions in decades to come.

Memories are an essential part of continuing attachments in adult life, say attachment theorists, and the ways in which people remember are clues to the nature of the attachments they have made and will sustain. Again, we can glean some understanding of sibling attachments by examining the attachments of parents to their children, in this case the connection between their memories and the quality of their attachments.

Trying to understand why some children appear secure in their

attachments to their parents and others tense and anxious, researchers began looking into the parents' own history. They soon discovered
that *how* the parents remembered that history was more important in
understanding their behavior toward their children than *what* the history actually was.

Specifically, psychologist Mary Main noted that parents she interviewed fell into three general groups according to their ways of remembering. One group had clear memories about events and feelings
of their childhood and their links to their parents and were able to
discuss those memories coherently. If their early experiences had
been painful or difficult, they managed to face those experiences and
integrate them into their memories. Because of the ease with which
these people spoke of their memories, Main speculated, they must
have had secure attachments themselves in childhood, or had coped
with their insecurities in a way that allowed them to relate comfortably to others. For the most part, such parents conveyed their ability
to be insightful and secure to their children, and, like them, the children were securely attached and self-reliant.

A second group of parents remembered very little about their childhood and apparently repressed incidents and emotions that were
painful to deal with. They might portray their relationships to their
parents in idealized terms as "fine" or "excellent," but when probed,
they would recall incidents of parental neglect and rejection. Their
inability or reluctance to remember events as they had occurred was
an indication of their detachment from the past. That detachment
carried over in their relationships to their own children, who also
seemed detached, or, in Main's terms, "avoidant."

The third group of parents had somewhat confused memories of
their childhoods and their relationships to their own parents, swinging between positive and negative descriptions. Their descriptions
suggested that these people were somewhat overwhelmed by their
early experiences and the memories of them, unable to sort out how
they really felt. In their confusion, they still remained dependent on
their parents for approval and recognition. Their children, like them,
were highly ambivalent and unsure of their feelings, seeming to want
independence yet clinging to their parents for security.

Parallels can be made between the way people remember their
attachments to parents and the way they remember their attachments
to siblings. For siblings those patterns of remembering are an important yardstick for the kinds of relationships they had with one another
and the kinds they will continue to have.

In most of my interviews with brothers and sisters, the past constantly jutted forward to interrupt the present. As hard as I might try to center a discussion on what was going on with a sibling *now*, the interviewee always slipped back to *then*. Back then an older sister took care of a younger, and that is why the younger one now feels grateful or resentful or needing to separate from the older. Back then a younger brother tried hard to push an older one aside and get ahead, and that is why the older is proud or guilty or modest about his accomplishments today. Although the siblings in a family might differ in their personal memories, they usually managed to convey a larger picture of family history that all shared.

But there were a small number of people who did not have memories of back then. They could remember little, if anything, about playing or fighting with their sister or brother, little about their feelings toward one another or their interactions with parents. Their interviews were usually fairly brief and bland, lacking the richness and texture of most of the others. Turner, in Chapter Five, was typical of such people. His younger sister Claire spoke many times of a "yearning" to be "loved and admired" by her brother. She described sharing a bedroom with him until he was thirteen and she nine, and his insistence on wrestling and pinning her down to helplessness. Turner remembered nothing at all of this period, not even the feelings he'd had sharing a room with his sister until puberty. Their four-year age gap made her "so much younger," he said, that they had always had little in common.

Like Main's detached parents, and in many ways like the apathetic siblings in Deborah Gold's typology, Turner has maintained only minimal connections to Claire. The memories that might have been a link either do not exist or have been repressed, and the forgetting and repression symbolize the coldness he felt and continues to feel toward his sister.

Claire herself, through her memories, represents the third type of attachment between siblings that can be compared to the third kind of attachment parents showed to their original families in Main's study. Claire swings back and forth emotionally as she remembers her anger at Turner's rejections and her longing for his affection and approval. Diffuse and embellished with a stream of words, the memories hint at her inability, still, to sort out her emotions. Deeply resentful of Turner, she remains trapped by her feelings for him, wearing her heart on her sleeve while she longs to be noticed.

The memories of early experiences and feelings that siblings take with them as they move off in different directions serve as the base upon which new experiences and new feelings will act. For those siblings whose memories are cold and flat, unbroken by emotion or understanding, the new experiences and feelings will simply come and go, washing over their lives like so many waves, making little impression. Connections among these siblings will remain not much different from what they have always been—distant, uninvolved. ("We have maintained a cool civility in our relationship, no matter how hard I try to break through," wrote a thirty-four-year-old switchboard operator about her thirty-six-year-old brother. "Our conversation consists of, 'Hi, how are you?' 'Fine. You?' 'Fine. The kids?' 'Fine.' 'Work?' 'Fine.' 'Good.' ")

For those, like Claire, whose memories and the feelings they evoke are convoluted, unsifted, and unclear, the waves of new events may bring about some changes in connectedness, building upon some areas of feeling, eroding others. Claire described, for example, a brief "respite" from the old, cold relationship with Turner when their mother's death brought them closer together for a short time. But too few memories on Turner's part and too many negative ones on Claire's made the change a fleeting one.

But for the majority of siblings, whose memories are like a rich underground landscape studded with ridges and crevices of every shape and size, the waves of change will flow over and around and inside those memories, building new configurations on top of old ones, shaping additional high points and low ones, yet always leaving that solid base, that seabed, of memory and feeling that will stretch through life.

The first changes siblings face as they enter the early years of adult life may be the most fundamental of all: geographic moves that take them miles away from each other. The moves usually grow from ordinary life events—jobs, schools, marriages, or other circumstances that cause sibs to live in different cities, states, or even continents.

Distance almost always limits physical contact, but it does not necessarily limit emotional contact. That contrast between physical and emotional distance showed up clearly on the survey.

There was a significant difference in the contact siblings had, depending on how far apart they lived. Eighty-two percent of respondents who lived within a hundred miles of a sibling saw or spoke to that sibling once a month or more, but only 39 percent of those who lived more than a hundred miles from a sib saw or spoke to that sib monthly or more often. In contrast, there was only a slight difference in *feelings* of closeness to siblings who lived nearby and those who lived farther away. Of respondents who lived within a hundred miles of a sibling, 84 percent rated themselves "very close," "close," or "somewhat close" to that sibling, and almost as many—81 percent—described themselves similarly in relation to siblings who lived at a greater distance. The invisible threads of closeness, of memories and feelings, it appears, are able to span vast spaces.

Describing that span, a bookkeeper in New York wrote of her sister in California, "We both wish we lived closer to each other so we could be together more. But every time we visit, we manage to pick up right where we left off, with much spontaneous affection and enjoyment of each other's company."

It does sometimes happen, if much time has elapsed, that the "pick-up" is less spontaneous, no matter how close the remembered feelings. My father recalls going to meet his brother Morris when Morris arrived on the shores of America from the family's native Russia. They had not seen each other for three years because my father, like many immigrant elder sons, had come to the States earlier with his father to earn enough money to pay the way for the rest of the family. An adolescent fifteen when he left Russia, he was now a young man of eighteen. Morris, a strapping youth two years younger, stared at him uncomfortably.

"Was machts ihr?"—"How are you?"—he asked shyly in Yiddish, using the formal word "ihr" for you, instead of the more appropriate and intimate word "du." Intimidated by the grown-up before him, he lost the brotherly familiarity they had always known. It took a while for awkwardness to fade and old feelings to take hold again.

(A contemporary version of this story concerns two brothers in their late twenties who greeted each other at the airport after a separation of two years. Russell, who lives in Cleveland, leaned forward to embrace his brother Alex, who lives in London. Noticing Alex's perfectly tailored British suit, he suddenly felt embarrassed, wondering whether British men hugged each other. He pulled back and, instead, stretched out his arm for a handshake just as Alex was leaning forward to hug *him*. The men clumsily touched fingers and shoulders, then stared at each other in silence, each unsure of whether the other was the same brother he had always known.

"I got scared that Russell had become different," said Alex in relating the incident, "until I realized that he was scared of the same thing in me. We had to find our footing with each other again.")

For some siblings distance can actually be an asset to closeness. "I love having two sisters, but I love even more having them live far away. I don't have to think about how I feel about them," said a real estate agent who usually knows clearly how she feels about everything. Or, "I'm so glad that they're there and I'm here. I can really love them from a distance, and if we were closer we probably wouldn't be talking," the words of a piano teacher with four older brothers and three younger sisters. For these people, being apart makes it possible to cling to good memories and feelings without having to cope with the stresses of everyday reality.

During the early years of adulthood, distance may also advance the ongoing struggle sibs have to become individuals separate from one another. Because they are apart, they must make independent decisions, going about their work and lives without seeking one another's advice or approval. Nancy Ginetti was heartbroken when her sister Mary Ann moved to Seattle. Nevertheless, the move freed Nancy—both physically and psychologically—to return to school and carve out a career as an interior designer.

The obvious danger of distance is that even when sibs have strong memories and ties, it can lead to permanent estrangement unless they make a conscious effort to keep in regular contact. (Compounding this danger is the "telegraph messenger" parent who carries news from sib to sib to keep their connections for them. When such a parent becomes ill or passes away, the whole sib system can break down.)

There are, of course, those siblings who welcome this danger. They are the ones who do not want closeness and contact and who deliberately move miles away to avoid them. Sometimes adult children move away to cut themselves off from parents and in the process shut out the siblings who have remained associated with the parents. The siblings left behind, relegated to the "enemy camp" because of their connection to parents, often suffer greatly at losing a brother or sister in this way. A soft-spoken physical therapist said almost apologetically that she lives a "conventional American life" and had therefore found herself despised by her artist brother, who "moved to Europe, became anti-American, and rejected family values." Brother and sister remain, she related with sadness, "separated by life philosophy as well as physical distance."

Yet with all our mobility, and the many reasons that might lead brothers and sisters to live at long distances from each other, more than might be expected stay close by. A Gallup poll conducted in 1989 found that more than half of adults—57 percent—live within an hour's drive of a brother or sister, a number only about 10 percent smaller than the number of adults who live about an hour's drive from a parent.

For these siblings and others who are within easy reach of each other, the choices of how near or how far are more pressing than for those who live far apart, and the changing stages of life may bring differing responses.

As they go about pursuing careers or occupations, young men and women continue in their task of shaping their individuality and asserting their independence from parents. In doing so, some find themselves drawing closer to their siblings: As peers, sisters and brothers are able to aid one another in adjusting to their new lives away from a common home. The strong attachment Mark and Jerry Platt developed during their college years has grown, Mark said, because as adults the brothers are "more willing to share feelings and experiences." On their own and away from parents, they have also had an opportunity "to have a relationship based on nothing more than the fact that we like being with each other."

But even with loving feelings and newfound friendship, the thrust toward self-sufficiency is so powerful in early adulthood that many siblings feel compelled to assert their differences from each other more vehemently than ever.

Here is Philip Roth talking about his older brother Sandy, a commercial artist, who once had been an inspiration to Philip. In early adulthood, as he is launching his career in writing, Roth explains in his autobiography, *The Facts*, "I did my best to suppress my disdain . . . for the advertising man's point of view; but he was hardly less aware of it than I was of his uneasiness around university types and highbrow intellectuals or of the provocation that he sensed in what he took to be their pretensions. . . . A suspicious undercurrent between us, fostered by strong professional polarities, made for self-consciousness and even shyness when we met or telephoned."

Those siblings who had been deeply involved with each other—the loyal Hansels and Gretels or the overly dependent brothers and sisters —may now find themselves stifled by the closeness that had once saved their lives. Determined to become their own persons, they move forward with the unfinished business of defining limits that will differentiate one from another.

It was as a young man of twenty-two that John Cheever set out alone for New York, leaving his brother Fred, his alter ego, behind in Boston. He knew that if they remained together much longer, they would "wear out their lives like old clothes, in a devotion that would defeat its own purpose," as a character in one of his short stories says of his brother and himself.

Ben, a twenty-seven-year-old mathematician, has made a determined effort to separate himself from a brilliant older brother who had both "overwhelmed" Ben with his abilities and "dominated" him because of them. Having espoused radical political causes and an anti-establishment life, Ben mocks his brother's staid conservative style. That hasn't stopped him, however, from entering the identical field of research as his brother, which may mean that he has not broken away as much as he thinks he has, or may mean that the only way he *can* make the break is by competing on the brother's own turf and showing that he can kill him there.

Stephanie, a politician, who is most articulate about the struggle for separateness, described having become her younger sister's "mother" ever since their mother died when she was fifteen and her sister ten. "The lines between us were never clear," she said. "I was mother, but if I gave her advice or criticized something she did, she would become furious at my 'domineering.' I was sister, but if I didn't treat her like a daughter and help her with her problems, she would feel hurt and neglected."

Some time ago, after a long discussion, the sisters decided to keep their distance from each other for an entire year. "But each of us knew," said Stephanie, "that if we really needed each other, we could pick up the phone and call." When they did pick up the phone and get together again, she said, "it was as adults. We had grown up. She was less dependent and I less bossy, and that's how it's been ever since."

The most obvious affirmation of sibling separation in young adulthood is marriage, a stepping away from one's original family to assume responsibility for a new family. For siblings who have been closely attached, the marriage of one or another leads to what Judith Viorst calls a "necessary loss," a giving up of one thing (a special intimacy and exclusivity with the sibling) in order to gain another (a new friendship with the sib's spouse; a mature friendship with the sib).

I was surprised to find in the survey the general feeling that husbands and wives improved relations between siblings rather than hindered them, and that sisters-in-law—so often maligned—were the most helpful. But when you think about it, these findings make good sense. Busy at this stage of their lives with settling into their unique identities, siblings may loosen the bonds between them, sometimes to the point of dropping them altogether. Their spouses do not carry the emotional baggage they do, nor need they fear losing their identities by drawing close to their sibs-in-law. So they can tighten family commitment even while they aid their own spouses in becoming autonomous individuals. Along with sisters, sisters-in-law can be the glue for family togetherness.

A sibling's spouse may also fill an emotional hole that existed in the sib's original family, becoming a substitute brother, sister, or even parent to his or her new in-laws. Lisa, youngest of the Ginetti sisters, turned Chris, husband of her older sister Kate, into the big brother she never had. Later she almost married a man much like him. For his part, Chris, an only child, loved having a "little sister." For both, the in-law connection enhanced rather than diminished family feelings.

With all that, marriages do—and should—create boundaries between siblings, and sibs need to maintain those boundaries in order to preserve their marriages and their friendships with each other. A sister's open envy of her sister-in-law, a brother's bitter rivalry with his brother-in-law, can create havoc in family relationships. People who keep those relationships compatible recognize that even if they do not like a brother's or sister's spouse, to stay connected to that brother or sister they need to maintain ties to the spouse as well.

Matt Elliot, mentioned in Chapter Five, admired his older sister, Debra, for many things, not least among them her niceness to his wife. She had opposed the marriage beforehand, but once it became a reality, she proffered warm support to both Matt and his wife.

Boundary lines also need to be clearly defined from within a marriage. Some years ago while researching a book about people in long marriages, I came to the conclusion that one of the factors that keeps marriages strong as well as long is the ability of husbands and wives to put their loyalties to each other above loyalties to parents, siblings, or friends. That means that they do not confide details of their marriage outside the marriage, nor do they allow the outside to slip in, to dilute the intimacy between them with criticisms of one or gossip about another. And that means that even in the most intimate sibling relationships, there are barriers that a married brother or sister cannot or should not cross.

Gail, searching for ways to increase closeness to her sister Pam, with whom she had shared a dreadful childhood, still ruled out marital talebearing. "Maybe if we'd had severe marital problems, we would have been closer out of need," she said. "But neither of us has ever criticized the other's husband or exchanged secrets about our own, and that rule has helped keep both our marriages strong."

Unfortunately, this golden rule of marital and sibling behavior is not always obeyed.

In her book *Blue Collar Marriage*, sociologist Mirra Komarovsky points out that among working-class families, husbands are often so inexpressive, so shut off from feelings, that their wives feel they must turn to their own families, particularly sisters, for the warmth and emotional intimacy lacking in their marriages.

In my own research, first on long marriages and now on sibling relations, I met siblings who remained as intertwined after marriage as they had been before, leaving little room in their sealed-off system for spouses. For these people marriage did not bring the separation or sense of loss it did for others. Overinvolved as they were with each other, they did not flinch at sharing conjugal confidences along with other secrets, or placing the intimacy of their bond above intimacy with marital partners.

At its worst, such tightness between siblings can drive a thick wedge between husband and wife. Here, for instance, is a tale told by a grown-up daughter, Lynn, about the heat between her mother and her uncle and about her aunt, who was left out in the cold.

The mother and the uncle, the mother's younger brother, had been reared in an upper-crust British family with socialite parents too busy to spend time with their children. The two children became deeply attached to each other, the brother teaching his sister about sports, the sister teaching the brother—who knows what? After both married, they lived with their families in the same building. Every evening when the brother returned from work, he stopped first at his sister's flat to have a drink, relax, and talk over the day's events before going home to his own family. Because he worked in the family's banking business, he always knew he had a sympathetic ear in his sister. His wife, Lynn's aunt, had little of the same interest in the business. What she had instead was an unmitigated rage against the sister-in-law who preempted her time with her husband. She displayed her feelings through coolness toward her sister-in-law as well as her nieces, Lynn and her sister.

Matters became much worse when Lynn's aunt discovered that her husband was having an affair and was meeting his lover at his sister's flat with her full blessings. Although the marriage managed to survive the affair, not surprisingly, no shred of good will survived between the sisters-in-law. If ever they met by chance, the aunt would turn her back on Lynn's mother and her children.

"Oh, she's just crazy," Lynn's mother would say in explanation of her sister-in-law's behavior.

"It doesn't seem crazy to me," Lynn said in telling me the story. "I used to see my uncle in our home all the time, and I loved him because he brought us candy. Later, when I understood what had gone on, I sympathized tremendously with my aunt."

Although overcloseness among any combination of siblings may affect one or another's marriage, excessive brother-sister intimacy like that in Lynn's family has the greatest potential for causing marital problems. Older brothers, who tend to see themselves as protectors of their younger sisters in any event, may have an especially difficult time relinquishing that role after the marriage of a beloved sister, and the sister may find it just as difficult to put her full trust in a man other than her adored, protective older brother. Older sisters, so often mother figures to their younger brothers, may find it hard after a cherished brother marries to hand over to another woman their special seat as advisor and confidante, and the brother may find it just as hard to give up his dependency on his sister.

Underlying these often unconscious attitudes are even more deeply unconscious sexual feelings, the old erotic attractions between opposite-sex sibs that such sisters and brothers may never be able to transfer fully to husbands, wives, or lovers.

When, in George Eliot's novel *The Mill on the Floss*, adult brother and sister, the novel's protagonists, die wrapped in each other's arms during a flood, the death symbolizes their profound wish to be united, although on the surface each has found or sought love elsewhere. And the words on their tombstone, "In their death they were not divided," are words that can be applied to other sisters and brothers who live out their lives in conventional marriages yet remain even unto death locked in an emotional embrace with each another.

Countering these siblings who stay inordinately close to each other in spite of their marriages are others who turn far away from each other because of those marriages. A sibling's extreme devotion to a spouse's family, for example, may lead to much less concern about the sib's own family of origin. Such is the case with Stephanie and her younger sister, mentioned earlier, who had little to do with each other for a year while the sister freed herself of her dependency on Stephanie. Now, it seems, she is so free and so taken with her husband's large, comfortable family that she barely has time for Stephanie. "I hate being left out all the time," Stephanie says. "She had Christmas dinner with her husband's family and never thought to invite me. They invited twenty-seven people. Would it have hurt to have twenty-eight?"

Probably yes, at least in the sister's mind. Sharing the enjoyment of her new family life would have hurt her determination to remain disengaged from Stephanie. For when people drop their own families to pick up a spouse's, they usually do so for a reason. They may want to shed all traces of dependency on siblings or parents or want to get out from under a burden of responsibility for parents or siblings. Or they may feel they are acquiring something from the new family that the old one lacked—status, perhaps, or warmth and camaraderie and the satisfaction of being appreciated. "I feel good that I have married into a family that allows me to experience 'a family' that loves and accepts me," wrote a thirty-one-year-old man. "My own family never knew the real me."

Other life situations can create chasms between siblings after they marry: different values, which may lead one to disapprove of the way another lives or spends money or raises children; different levels of income, which may make it impossible for siblings to share vacations or evenings out or to reciprocate one another's invitations; different religious practices, in which one may be churchgoing and religiously committed and another totally disinterested; and different relationships with parents, which may pit one sib's family against another.

This last can be among the most pernicious forms of divisiveness unless sibs and their spouses unite to fight it. When parents disapprove of a son- or daughter-in-law, they unbalance the equation between siblings in the same way that favoritism does. Their criticisms of a son's or daughter's spouse to other adult children is likely to stir up or reinforce these others' negative feelings. Lew Dorman added fuel to his daughters' disagreements by contrasting Meredith's "little Napoleon" husband to Patty's husband, "the greatest, a wonderful human being." Equally important, a mother or father's disapproval of one in-law and approval of another awakens old jealousies among siblings, that ancient jostling for position that never totally disappears from the sibling landscape.

Divorce undoes much of the sibling separateness that marriage creates. As painful as a divorce is for the person going through it, one positive result it often has is that of rallying other family members to that sib's side. The negative aspect of that is that siblings who are not secure in themselves may revert to an earlier dependency on a brother or sister at this time. And brothers and sisters may too willingly welcome a sib's divorce, secretly pleased, as one woman said of her brother, that the sibling isn't "taken" anymore.

But for a person struggling with a marital breakup, a sibling's support can be a life preserver in an overwhelming sea of despair and confusion. People describe reversing roles at this time, with younger siblings taking on the role of big sister or big brother, when necessary, to comfort and sustain an older one. Women speak of their gratitude to brothers who become substitute fathers for their children after a divorce, offering "a man's perspective," in the words of an office manager trying to care alone for her teenage sons. Siblings also report gaining new understanding of one another as each helps the other grapple with crises of separation and divorce.

The exceptions to such family solidarity when a sib divorces come when family members disapprove of the divorce, either for religious reasons or because they think, as one man said of his brother, that "the divorce is a piece of selfishness that's hurting innocent children. My sisters and I are no longer speaking to him because of it."

Fondness for a sister's or brother's divorced husband or wife can also complicate reactions. When a sibling's marriage has lasted for some time and the spouse has been accepted as a friend and family member by brothers and sisters, divorce leaves the status of the spouse in limbo. How far does loyalty to a sibling extend? Must a brother or sister "divorce" a sib's spouse who has become a friend because of the sibling's divorce? If you keep that person as your friend, are you betraying your sibling, or at least making that sib feel betrayed?

The answers depend to a great extent on the causes for the divorce and the degree of animosity that exists between the parties. In general, though, I have found that siblings who have been divorced expect loyalty above everything from brothers and sisters. They are more willing to tolerate continuing contact between friends and ex-spouses than between their siblings and ex-spouses—one more example of the fact that the sibling relationship is more than friendship, even when siblings are less than best friends.

The matter of how one behaves with a former in-law, I should add, applies to a sibling's death as well as to divorce, and can be even more trying. When a marriage has lasted over time, in-law relationships often become close enough that even after a spouse's death sisters- or brothers-in-law continue to consider themselves part of that spouse's family. But if siblings are younger, and a deceased sibling's spouse remarries, surviving sisters and brothers are often not sure how to respond. Melissa Fields, in Chapter Ten, still mourns the loss of her beloved older sister, Cara, and added to her mourning is the second loss—through remarriage—of Cara's husband, Barr. The second loss has left her confused as well as sad. What should her relationship to Barr be now? Once, when he was her sister's husband, she had embraced him as her brother. Now he is someone else's husband and she no longer feels related to him.

In some ancient communities a practice known as the *levirate* was mandated by law. According to this practice, when a man died, under certain prescribed conditions his brother was required to marry the man's wife. Other early societies practiced the *sororate*—marriage between a woman and her sister's husband if the sister had died. These forced marriages could cause great hardship for the parties involved, and certainly nobody misses them today. Yet the one thing these laws did was designate clear-cut places and positions for sibs-in-law after the death of a sibling.

Today in our open societies we have no forms with which to adapt to the changed status of a sister- or brother-in-law when a sibling dies or is divorced, and brothers and sisters often flounder in trying to find the proper degree of warmth or distance to take with an in-law. Perhaps if the powerful connections between sisters and brothers were more openly celebrated, and their extension to brothers- and sisters-in-law more clearly recognized, we might find suitable conventions for these difficult sibling situations.

Another complex situation concerns the children of one's siblings, a subject in itself, and not technically within the scope of this book. Two things need to be said, however: There is almost nothing that can pull siblings closer together during their married years than having children of similar ages. And there is almost nothing more likely to keep latent rivalries alive through the course of siblings' adult lives than having children of similar ages.

The first statement refers to the exchange of experiences, knowledge, joys, anxieties, and support siblings have when they are rearing children at about the same time. The childrearing years bring about a closeness—particularly for sisters—that may exceed anything that existed in childhood, and even siblings separated by large age gaps find a new commonality and a new level of intimacy when they are involved in similar childcare tasks. "More than anything," a woman wrote on the questionnaire, "becoming mothers has served to join my sister and me at the hip!"

The second statement refers to the exchange of bulletins about report cards, athletic awards, SAT scores, job advancements, and marital status that siblings pursue when they are rearing children at about the same time. It is not that siblings do not love each other's children and go out of their way to help them (most do). Nor is it that they overtly compete about their children's achievements (although some do). It is only that children, whom parents so often regard as extensions of themselves, also become extensions of deep-rooted rivalries between their sibling parents. Sometimes, in fact, the children become vehicles for rivalries their parents had never openly expressed.

I saw some of that in my own family. As devoted and close-knit as were my father and his four brothers, and as close as were my brother and I to our cousins in our growing-up years, we always knew that each family made comparisons about the children and continued to compare us into our adult lives. It was as if the brothers had displaced onto their children competitive feelings they had never risked acting upon themselves. So brothers and their wives carried stories to one another about this child's scholastic success or that one's creative talents, this one's financial acumen or that one's excellent marriage. And while they lauded one another's offspring and were happy for their successes, the muffled message beneath all the news was directed at their own offspring: You need to do as well as, or preferably better than, your cousins.

As adults, most of the cousins see less of each other than they did in childhood, when the entire family celebrated all holidays together. But there remain strong friendships among some and occasional flashes of jealousy and rivalry among all, muted by time but there to be aroused at such family gatherings as weddings and bar mitzvahs, even funerals.

Such competition seems to be fairly common among grown-up cousins. It is created by parental comparisons, and it endures in differing degrees depending on parents' attitudes and the amount of contact cousins have in childhood and later. (Grandparents who favor one grandchild over others can also incite lifelong jealousies and rivalries among their children's children.)

Cousin friendships are also fairly common, stemming back as do ours to the years when an older generation of brothers and sisters was rearing children together. In some cases, cousins use one another as substitutes for siblings with whom they don't get along. For only children, cousins often fill in for nonexistent brothers and sisters. And some cousins who may not have been close earlier enter a new phase of friendship in mid-adulthood when parents and aunts and uncles are no longer alive and they have become the frontline of larger family continuity.

Midlife is a time of change for siblings as well. Investigating that change, psychologist Victoria Bedford gave thirty men and thirty women, ranging in age from thirty to sixty-nine, a projective test designed to uncover underlying feelings about their sibling relationships. Subjects were asked to make up stories about pairs of siblings pictured on cards, on the assumption that through the stories they composed, they would project feelings they had about their own siblings. Bedford was particularly interested in knowing whether siblings' concerns about independence and separation from each other changed over the course of adult life.

She found that, indeed, such change did occur. Subjects who were in the earlier years of marriage and involved in raising their children showed significantly greater concern with themes of independence, separation, and differences than did those who were older and whose children had moved away from home.

Her findings speak to the varying attitudes and interests of siblings as they move from one life stage to the next. Still struggling in early adulthood with the task of disentwining from one another, they project their concerns about autonomy and separateness onto the stories they read into the test cards. As the years progress and they become less absorbed in establishing their individual selves, they feel freer to ease the boundaries between them, less fearful now that sibling intimacy will stifle them or cut into marital intimacy. The stories they devise reflect that greater freedom.

Certainly it is toward midlife that siblings begin to allow themselves to "turn into" each other as did the brothers in the Sam Shepard play *True West*, the screenwriter becoming a thief and the thief becoming a screenwriter. More specifically, now is the time when the barriers of de-identification may begin to crumble. Siblings who feel strong in their individual identities begin to give up the rigid roles that set them apart and to rediscover the traits they have in common and with which they can identify.

This is the time, in midlife, when Philip Roth, so polarized earlier from his older brother, is able to dedicate *The Facts*, the book that described that early polarization, "To my brother at sixty."

This is the time of life when a woman named Ariella has decided that her younger sister Gilda, the "ditsy" one, is not so ditsy after all. Gilda, a professional midwife, had been, according to Ariella, "obsessed" with diet, exercise, and health issues, a "walking encyclopedia" of largely "useless" gynecological information. Now Ariella, a clearheaded statistical analyst, has had a series of gynecological problems and a hard decision to make about whether to have a hysterectomy. Sister Gilda has become a main resource of knowledge, advice, and comfort. Ariella, the conservative and cautious, wants to push ahead with the surgery, "to get it over with." Gilda, the unreliable and impetuous, urges caution and conservatism, and a little more research to make the right decision. Both sisters are discovering for the first time that behind the roles they had held for years are real people not very different from one another.

The brothers Platt have not yet dropped their roles as "Mr. Serious" and "the Clown," but they are heading in that direction. Mark is considering dipping his toes into Jerry's world of performing but worries that doing so might set off ripples of trouble between them and churn up rivalries they had suppressed long ago by assuming their opposite roles. He worries also about how he will fare if he tests himself on his brother's turf.

Perhaps he need not worry. Perhaps if Jerry continues his professional accomplishments and feels comfortable with them, he will welcome Mark's forays into his territory. He might enjoy sharing his satisfactions and his worries as a performer with his brother. With time, he might also feel good that he, the younger, the clown, was able to help the elder, the brainy one, in his own arena, and he might feel proud of any success his help will have engendered.

For midlife, these brothers might find when they reach it, is a time when pride in a sibling's accomplishments is possible even without dividers that split up territories. Ross and Milgram, who have made several studies of adult siblings, interviewed siblings of the rich and famous to see how they felt about themselves in relation to their brothers and sisters. (Milgram had a personal stake in this research; his older brother, Stanley Milgram, is better known than he for his work in psychological experimentation.) Although their subjects admitted to "twinges of envy" of their celebrity siblings, they also spoke of their admiration and the inspiration the other's success had been to them. Many pointed with confidence to personal talents and strengths that allowed them to accept the other's fame.

And that is one more midlife secret that makes it possible for the older siblings on Bedford's projective test to be less concerned about separateness than younger ones; that makes it possible for siblings to allow their roles to overlap without rushing to opposite corners; that makes it possible for brothers and sisters to accept, even enjoy, the success of their more famous sibs: the secret of a self that is not only separate but also more secure and more accomplished than before, and therefore less directly in competition with another.

Midlife is a time of integration, a pulling together of ideas and ambitions, of dreams and emotions of earlier years, into a more complete whole, a more satisfying self. In short, this is a time of maturity for individuals and for siblings in relation to each other.

Does that mean that all competitive or envious feelings toward siblings are gone now forever?

Not a chance.

Victoria Bedford found that the basic, underlying ambivalences of sibling relationships remain constant throughout adult life. In her projective tests, people of the later, empty-nest years, no less than people of the earlier, childrearing ones, composed stories about conflict and competition as well as connection and spoke about "emotional turmoil" as well as deep affection in their feelings toward siblings.

Dark feelings, which begin in childhood, continue, then, into the middle years of life. But many siblings (except for those who go on squabbling endlessly) push those feelings more than ever into the background, preferring harmony among themselves. For them, angers or resentments will reemerge in full force only under great stress or when revitalized by a major life event—a reversal of power relationships that places an older sibling in an inferior position to a younger one, a change of fortune that brings sharp contrasts into the lives of brothers and sisters, or the like.

Of all the stressful situations in which midlife siblings find themselves, as we've seen, the care of elderly parents can provoke the fiercest competition of all, disrupting even long-established peace in families. In fact, siblings speak so frequently about the fights and bad feelings that surrounded a parent's illness or death that it is hard to remember that these same events can inspire completely different emotions and behaviors in other brothers and sisters.

There are siblings for whom the increasing frailty and eventual death of parents become turning points—rites of passage—into a new form of family unity that includes fuller and stronger bonds of loyalty and affection than ever before. These are the siblings who cooperate in caring for parents without constant complaints, who share financial burdens when necessary and divide up the even weightier burdens of visiting parents in hospitals and nursing homes. And when, finally, the time comes for last good-byes to parents, these siblings offer each other consolation and comfort in ways that nobody else can.

Adult only children often say that, from their perspective, far worse than fighting with siblings over the care of parents is not having siblings with whom to fight or—more to the point—with whom to share the duties of caring for a parent, as these siblings do. What they miss just as much, they say, is not having brothers or sisters with whom they can mourn after losing a parent.

Nor do all siblings necessarily become trapped into fights about property and possessions after parents die. Some of those who do not have idyllic relationships during their parents' lifetime still support each other later. In spite of their incessant arguments over favoritism, for instance, Christina and Vivian have cooperated in investing the money they inherited from their parents, money that they knew had been scrupulously divided between them. Proud of their ability to help each other at least in this regard, they speak of honoring their parents by respecting their inheritance.

Sometimes new alliances are formed. A lab technician who had always been closer to her younger sister than her older brother developed a new intimacy with that brother when their father became ill. The sister, busy with young children, pleaded that she had little time to give to the father's care. Irritated at her attitude yet understanding of it, the lab technician and her brother took over completely. They discovered in the process that they had a great deal more in common than they thought, and have remained good friends since.

And sometimes the loss of a parent as mediator forces siblings to come to their own terms with each other. It was not uncommon to hear from a brother or sister who had lost a parent, especially a second parent, that "we had nothing left to fight about after Mother [or Father] died, so we became friends."

Summing up the good feelings that can grow even in the midst of the confusion and sadness of a parent's death, an advertising director wrote of herself and her brother, "There were periods of time during my parents' illnesses (they died of cancer eight years apart) when we fought with each other. But we realized that with the loss of our parents we were all the family we had and that that kind of behavior was stupid. If our parents' deaths were necessary, it would be for the purpose of bringing us closer together. That they have accomplished."

In the years after parents die, and as siblings themselves age, many of the patterns of closeness and distance established earlier become fairly well entrenched. Those brothers and sisters who regarded themselves as close during the earlier stages of adult life, and those who became closer after the death of parents, will probably remain that way. Those who drifted apart decades earlier are not likely to strike up strong new bonds of warmth and affection during the later years of life. Still, there is a tendency among elderly siblings, and even those who have had little contact, to want to narrow the emotional distance between them if possible as they grow older. As the years ahead become fewer in number than the years behind, sisters and brothers value their ties more and more.

In her studies of elderly siblings Deborah Gold found that only 10 percent of her sample could be classified as "hostile," actively disliking and distrusting each other. Only another 10 percent could be labeled "apathetic," having no interest in or connections with one another. The rest fell into various categories of closeness, if not as intimate friends, then certainly as ones who are congenial or loyal to each other.

Several researchers have examined how older siblings show their congeniality or loyalty or intimacy. Gold found in her interviews with men and women over age sixty-five that many go out of their way to visit one another, and make a point of telephoning often. In fact, 53 percent said that their contact with sisters and brothers had increased in late adulthood. When asked why they keep up contact, or try to increase it, these sisters and brothers speak of feeling more keenly connected now that they are the lone survivors of their original families. Some describe a new importance siblings have taken on in their lives since their spouses died, offering comfort and understanding even their own children cannot provide. Others emphasize their shared history and refer fondly to the reminiscing they are able to do together.

Reminiscences come increasingly to the foreground in sibling relationships of later years. The memories elderly siblings have, says psychologist Victor Cicirelli, provide "symbolic representations" of early intimacies, of shared goals and values, of roles played, of places and positions held within the family. As such, they keep the siblings linked over time and across space, helping them to maintain affection and loyalty that may last even after a brother or sister has died.

"Morris and I used to go on dates together," my father recalls, laughing. "We were always together. I remember when I was courting Mama, and he would stand in the next room while I kissed her good night." And off he goes, roaming back almost seventy years, to a past with his brothers that is as real to him as anything in the present.

"Molly," my mother says at Thanksgiving dinner to her younger sister, an octogenarian like herself, "remember the cats we always used to have at home?"

"Sure," Molly responds. "We needed the cats to eat the mice. Everybody had mice where we lived. We were all so poor."

"We were so poor," my mother echoes, "but we never realized how poor we were because we didn't know there was another way to live." And off they launch into memories of their father hauling bags of coal to heat the stove and their mother struggling to feed and clothe five children, mentally holding hands, the two of them, as they amble back into a world neither their stories nor my imagination can help me to really know.

The memories siblings carry with them from childhood into old age and the ability to reminisce with each other add to their sense of well-being, decreasing loneliness and bolstering feelings of belonging.

The knowledge that there is a brother or sister out there on whom they can depend—no matter how far away—also gives elderly sibs a base of security. It is not surprising that, as noted earlier, the base is sturdiest for both men and women when the family includes a sister. Sisters traditionally have served as family connectors and caregivers. But regardless of gender, the very fact of having a sibling is important to many older women and men. In George Vaillant's study, only children did not fare as well in psychological adjustment at age sixty-five as did men who had siblings with whom they had been close during adolescence and on whom they could, presumably, still count.

Yet, surprisingly, brothers and sisters rarely ask each other for concrete help as they age. That is, they do not turn to each other for financial loans or for physical aid, such as running errands, unless faced with a severe crisis. Ordinarily, in the hierarchy of care during the advancing years of life, people look first to their spouses and then to their adult children for assistance if needed. But even when spouses are gone and children inaccessible, siblings hesitate to call on one another. They seem to feel safer knowing a sibling is available for help, yet reluctant to actually seek that help.

Why the reluctance? It may be that sibs, recognizing one another's fragility, do not want to add to each other's burdens. It may be that brothers and sisters like to keep one another in reserve, a kind of insurance that if all else fails, in times of emergency they will have this untapped resource left. It may also be that old competitions and power pulls prevent them from fully admitting their needs. Even in this late stage of life, and with their shared closeness and affection, elderly sibs are not ready to spill the beans completely to each other about their weaknesses or failures, not ready to give another the upper hand in this way.

Throughout life, from childhood to old age, siblings shift back and forth between closeness and distance, becoming increasingly closer as they move into the middle years and even more so in old age. But flickers of rivalry endure, swept forward in the vast seabed of memories and feelings from earliest days to latest ones, remaining, always, at the core of sibling attachments.

How that core shapes siblings as individuals, in relation to themselves and to the world outside the family, is what we turn to next.

CHAPTER FOURTEEN

Patterns that Repeat . . .
Repeat . . . Repeat . . .

IN LOVE AND
FAMILY LIFE,
AT WORK, AND
AMONG FRIENDS

*T*he eighty-year-old man has been rushed to the emergency room of a local hospital, doubled over in agonizing pain. The diagnosis is a gallbladder attack. The doctors on call hospitalize the man and medicate him so that the pain subsides. "You must have surgery," they tell him, "that gallbladder is badly diseased and will only get worse."

The man, a widower, declares that surgery is out of the question. He'll live with the pain, but he'll not allow himself to go under the knife. His son and daughter are called in and told that he will not survive long unless he has the gallbladder removed. The son and daughter speak to their father; he refuses. They plead with him; he is adamant. Surgery kills you, he insists. He'd rather take his chances with the disease.

His friends visit him in the hospital, adding their voices to those of the doctors and his children. The man won't budge. He will *not* have surgery.

His eighty-five-year-old brother arrives.

"You've gotta have surgery, so cut out all this nonsense," he says. "I'll tell the doctors to get you ready, and I don't want to hear another word about it."

The man signs a consent form to be operated on two days later.

"It's amazing," says the social worker who tells me the story. "This man had been married and widowed, had grown children and good friends, and was receiving the best medical advice. But the only one who could make an impression on him was his older brother. To the end, they're playing out their roles of big brother, little brother. Some things in life never change."

Actually, such things do change, as we've seen. Marriage, in-laws, economic issues, achievements, geographic distance, gender, or simply age may transform the ways siblings relate to each other at different times in their history. But as with these aging brothers, many patterns of behavior established in childhood are so implanted, so fixed, so natural, that even if the sibs have been married or divorced, had children and grandchildren, won Nobel prizes or climbed Mount Everest, they see each other as they have always seen each other—big kid, little kid, caregiver or care receiver, strong one or needy—and they act accordingly.

And sometimes that's fine. There can be profound satisfaction in knowing someone at his or her deepest gut level, and in falling into behaviors so habitual and intimate that they need no discussion, no explanation.

Two brothers in a business that sells electronic equipment independently described the exhilaration of sitting together at a meeting with a client and knowing by just exchanging a glance exactly what the other is thinking and exactly what each should say to win over the client and gain an order. The knowing glance is part of the overall pattern of behavior the brothers have had with each other all their lives. The older, like many elders, is responsible and staid, the decision maker. The younger is the "bad boy," who is also the creative one. In their personal lives, the elder clucks about the other's irresponsibility yet enjoys his brother's freewheeling spirit, an approach to life he doesn't allow himself. The younger pokes fun at the elder's stuffiness yet knows that *he* can be free as long as his older brother is around to cushion his falls. Their steadfast routines of relating to each other work well in their lives and their business.

But there are many instances in which repetitious behaviors among siblings do not serve them well and can become deeply destructive.

Turner, in his mid-forties, falls immediately into his old stance of being "dismissive and critical" of his younger sister Claire whenever they meet, she says. His attitude, in turn, renders her "exactly" as she has always been, longing for his approval, trying to impress him, and finding herself feeling, instead, "incompetent . . . somehow fucking up." The result is an inability on the part of either to touch the other, to gain a longed-for warmth.

Roy and Eddy also replay the scenarios of their early lives over and over, with Roy, according to Eddy, "posing all sorts of horseshit dilemmas" that force Eddy into taking care of him. While these brothers love and admire one another, they get trapped into a cycle of emotionally draining squabbles in which Roy, feeling he is not getting enough from Eddy, provokes him into an argument that ultimately leads Eddy to apologize and protect Roy but also to feel resentful toward him.

Most destructive of all the patterns sibs repeat with one another from childhood are their patterns of fighting, both the fights that go on incessantly and those that burst forth, like tornadoes, around crises involving money, married life, or parental illness and death. The fights echo those of an earlier era, but their consequences can be far more serious in adult life. As we've seen, the childhood threat "I'll never speak to you again" can become an adult credo that keeps branches of families mute for generations.

It's easy for siblings to slip into old practices with each other, especially during times of stress, when passions are high and defenses low. These habits of behavior, learned in earliest childhood, are so deeply ingrained in our consciousness that we're rarely aware of them; we fall into them naturally, with little recognition and less thought.

Then—an extension of the same idea—sibling relations do not lend themselves easily to change. With parents, our roles, of necessity, reverse over time. As they grow older they become more dependent, increasingly turning to us for the sustenance and care we once obtained from them. But as members of the same generation, siblings travel together across life's time lines, and nothing in the natural course of events forces them to uproot their deep-seated ways of behaving and assume new roles or new responsibilities.

That we do modify our behaviors toward each other at all is testament to the flexibility of human nature and the process of growth and maturation. But change is not built into sibling relationships, as it is with parents, and new situations often parallel earlier ones closely enough for the old patterns to simply take over: the eighty-year-old man was once an eight-year-old boy idolizing an older brother who accepted no nonsense and brooked no disobedience.

Most important, we often continue with siblings the patterns of behavior learned long ago because those familiar patterns are comfortable; we feel most secure in them. Particularly when we face difficulties (but even when we do not), we find safety in sameness and risk in change, no matter how painful or destructive the sameness may be.

"I thought I was liberated from her," a shopkeeper says, speaking of her younger sister. "But with this latest episode I fell right back in." The sisters live in different cities but keep up regular contact. More accurately, the shopkeeper calls regularly and the sister calls mostly when she has a problem. The "latest episode" involved a cancer scare the younger sister had after a physician discovered some enlarged lymph nodes under her arm. Tears and desperate phone calls to her older sister followed the physician's discovery. Frantic with worry, the shopkeeper prepared to fly out to her sister's home but decided to wait for a biopsy report before disrupting her family life and making the expensive trip.

She waited and waited, repeatedly calling the sister's home and receiving no answer. Finally, she reached her sister. Oh, said the younger woman, sorry she hadn't gotten around to calling, everything was fine, the biopsy was negative, and she had been busy preparing for a vacation.

"Why do I do it?" the shopkeeper asks, not expecting an answer. "Why do I get caught up in her life again and again when I get nothing in return?"

Most likely because she can't help herself. The pattern of looking out for her sister has been firmly instilled in her, and the more so, perhaps, because the sister takes her for granted. If she were to break that pattern and risk not being available when her sister called, she would live in fear that something might actually happen and she would not be there to help. She might also live in fear, although less consciously so, that her sister would no longer need her, a need that is crucial to her identity as the mothering elder. The security of the old responses outweighs their discomfort. (A woman, powerful president of her local city council, is still referred to by her older brother as "my itty-bitty sister." She hates the appellation, yet she never tells him so —for fear of offending him, she says, but also, I would wager, for fear of losing that long-held status as the adored and protected sister, even when she no longer needs protection. For the brother, the comfort of the phrase comes from the comfort of keeping his baby sister in her place, and forgetting the power she now wields.)

In many situations also—and this is true for the shopkeeper—part of the security of sameness comes from the belief, or the fantasy, that by not rocking the boat, by keeping to the same steady course, by repeating the same routines of behavior, this time you might make things come out right. This time the end will be different, and this time the little sister will finally be satisfied with the care and concern of the big one and stop making demands (and this time the big brother will see his "itty" sister's irritation at his condescension and find a more adult way to show affection and protectiveness).

For Claire, in every encounter with Turner, there springs the hope that at this meeting he will finally accept and appreciate her. As often as her brother rejects her, and as painful as that rejection is, she finds it safer to try once more and once more again to please him than to turn her back on him and his coldness and face unknown consequences. Even for Christina and Vivian there may be an underlying hope, as they repeat and repeat their agonizing fights over favoritism, that at last one will really understand how the other feels and give up her claim to parental chosenness.

Though we are not usually conscious of the ways in which we replicate childhood behaviors with our siblings, it's not very difficult to spot repetitions once we become aware of them. But there are other sibling reenactments in adult life that take place outside the bond itself, and these can be far more concealed and convoluted, more mysterious. Those mysterious reenactments have wound their way through many of the life stories in this book. Claire, determined to be free of her brother's criticisms, married someone she considered his opposite, someone warm and appreciative of her—who, it soon became evident, was really as cold and contemptuous as Turner. For a long time, Vivian, hungry as she was for friendships with women to make up for the closeness she perceived between her mother and sister, managed only to push other women away, competing with them as she did with Christina.

Freud used the term "memory-traces" in portraying lasting childhood imprints that shape our personalities and our dealings with other people.

"The nature and quality of the human child's relations to people of his own and the opposite sex have already been laid down in the first six years of his life," he wrote. "He may afterwards develop and transform them in certain directions, but he can no longer get rid of them. The people to whom he is in this way fixed are his parents and his brothers and sisters. All those whom he gets to know later become substitute figures for these first objects of his feelings. . . . All of his later choices of friendship and love follow upon the basis of the memory-traces left behind by these first prototypes."

Reviewing his own life, he described how memory-traces of his relationship with his nephew John, who was actually a year older than he, influenced all the friendships he made later. "Until the end of my third year," he recalled, "we had been inseparable: we had loved each other and fought each other, and this childhood relationship . . . had a determining influence on all my subsequent relations with contemporaries."

Indeed, throughout his life, Freud said, "an intimate friend and a hated enemy" had always been indispensable to him—often combined in the same person, as they had been in John. And in interpreting a dream he had after the death of one friend-turned-enemy he referred to all his friends as "revenants . . . a series of reincarnations of the friend of my childhood."

The process by which we use others as substitutes for the first important persons in our lives, our parents and siblings, is—to turn again to a psychoanalytic concept—the process of transference. Today the term transference is usually defined narrowly to describe an important aspect of psychoanalysis whereby a patient sees an analyst as a figure from the past through whom the patient can work out earlier conflicts. But transference has a broader meaning, and refers to the ways in which we transfer to later relationships the loves and longings, conflicts and fears, we had experienced with important people in our earlier lives; in other words, the ways in which we see others through the lens of childhood attachments.

The journalist Janet Malcolm, who wrote an in-depth study of psychoanalysis, put it nicely. Defining transference as "how we all invent each other according to early blueprints," she describes the human tragedy of never being able to really know one another. "We must grope around for each other through a dense thicket of absent others," she writes. "We cannot see each other plain."

The internal images of "absent others" that we carry within us are not necessarily exact reproductions; they are overlaid with our feelings and fantasies about those others. A man may recognize today that his elderly father is weak and dependent. But the internal image he bears of that father, imprinted in childhood, is of a powerful, domineering person whom one obeys unquestioningly. Projecting these overlaid images of long ago onto the people who fill our present lives, we relate to these people as if they were the original figures our minds knew in the past. The man may associate all other authority figures in his life—teachers, supervisors, the internal revenue officer—with the image he holds of his powerful father.

That social scientists have traditionally concentrated on parents as the most crucial absent others in our lives does not mean that "imagos" of brothers and sisters, as Freud and his followers called these images of the past, do not make up a large part of that dense thicket that surrounds our relationships. So much so that even in their consultation rooms, therapists who have begun paying attention to such things have noticed sibling imagos at work.

A female patient, for instance, who had a heavy, dark-haired sister dreamt that a heavy, dark-haired girl had left her therapist's office shortly before she arrived and that she had been so upset and jealous that she had refused to lie on the same couch, spending her session, instead, shouting at the therapist. Jerry, a forty-year-old group therapy patient, had been an only child for seven years and then found himself with two brothers, a year apart in age. A mild-mannered man, Jerry rarely spoke out—except to viciously attack new members who entered the group and the therapist who allowed them in. He had no tolerance for such "new siblings."

I would argue, in fact, that internal sibling images can sometimes have an even greater impact on our adult relationships than parental ones. Because so many of our interactions are with peers—with our spouses, friends, or coworkers—it is easier, in many cases, to identify them as sibling substitutes than as parent stand-ins, and to direct toward them many of the attitudes and feelings we had toward brothers and sisters.

Certainly some of the most positive aspects of the sibling experience get transferred to our peers. From siblings we learn habits of cooperation and companionship. We learn to compare ourselves to others and to assess our strengths and weaknesses as well as theirs, to negotiate conflicts and arrive at compromises.

We learn some good things even from sibling jealousy and rivalry, Freud taught, for these provide the foundation for group unity and collaboration with others. Once children recognize that they cannot win through rivalry and that they must share their parents' love with their siblings, he said, they begin to identify with other children like themselves. Through that identification come the seeds of a sense of justice—a decision that if one cannot be loved more than another, all must be treated equally and fairly. And that understanding of equality and justice in dealing with others gets transported into adult life.

Again, only children learn many of these lessons from their peers, in the sandbox and the playground, the classroom and the clubhouse.

And with the undivided love and attention they get from parents, they often feel confident and secure enough to make friends easily and cooperate with other children. They may have more difficulty, however, learning to negotiate to get what they want, not having the knowledge in this realm that people who grew up with sibs amass out of necessity.

For those with siblings, that necessary knowledge is carried into adult relationships, and what gets transferred, when the learning has been positive and productive, is an ability to compromise and collaborate, to form close ties and repeat with others the insights gained from brothers or sisters.

Unfortunately, internal images of the past also influence the present in negative, unhealthy ways, and here, too, sibling experiences reappear and reassert themselves in our many relationships with peers.

Freud spoke of the need to repeat as a compulsion, emphasizing especially the compelling need people have to repeat what has been painful and unpleasant in the past. Repeating, he said, is a form of remembering those things that have been pushed out of consciousness, submerged because they are too difficult to face. The patient, he wrote, "remembers nothing of what is forgotten and repressed, but he expresses it in *action*. He reproduces it not in his memory but in his behavior; he *repeats* it, without, of course, knowing that he is repeating it."

What is it that we—all of us, and not only psychiatric patients—repeat in this way? Old longings and wishes, conflicts, emotions, and angers. We repeat also our ways of protecting ourselves against the pain of these longings or conflicts or wishes or angers. In terms of siblings, we repeat rivalries and jealousies, self-images of inferiority and sometimes of grandiosity, guilt and fears, power plays and struggles for separateness. We turn others in our lives into the siblings we had or wish we had or wish we had handled differently, and see ourselves as we once were or wish we were or wish we had not been. In a dozen different ways with a dozen different people, we reenact strains or difficulties or unfulfilled desires of our sibling history.

And the question is, why?

It is easy to understand why we reenact our loving sibling selves with others in our lives, but why the unpleasant, the difficult?

Freud explained the need to repeat our most devastating histories as part of a larger death instinct, but that theory, never clearly developed, has been discounted by many. In more everyday terms, I believe we repeat unpleasant as well as pleasant sibling behaviors with those whom we unconsciously see as sibling stand-ins for much the same reasons that we replay our pasts over and over with sibs themselves: the old patterns are familiar, comfortable, and secure. They may be destructive, they may be hurtful, but they are the known, the natural, and in that sense the safe.

So safe and familiar are these patterns that we automatically slip into them without being aware of doing so. So safe and familiar that even when we think we are making an effort not to repeat with others what we had with our siblings, we may find ourselves treading the same old path, like Claire, whose warm, kind husband turns out to be the spitting image of her cold, critical brother.

In fact, we may find ourselves reshaping the present to make it conform to the past. Another woman, a successful talk-show host who all her life had hated being overshadowed by her even more successful and achieving younger brother, tried to gain the limelight by marrying a low-key, quiet, professorial type. Then she pushed and prodded him to publish and lecture, eventually to become a TV consultant, and he got himself so well known that once again she felt herself upstaged. Her stated wishes aside, safety for her was having a husband like her brother, whom she could look up to—and hate for having overshadowed her.

There may also be in some of our repetitions of sibling patterns with others, probably even more than in our repetitions with siblings themselves, the ever-present hope and dream of rewriting the past. Falling in love is an example of that hope and dream, says psychoanalyst Martin Bergmann. When we are in love, he explains, we find ourselves in a "strange paradox." In the person we love, "we seek to refind all or some of the people to whom we were attached as children. On the other hand, we want the beloved to correct all or some of the wrongs that these early parents or siblings inflicted on us." The result is that "love contains within it the contradiction of the attempt to return to the past and the attempt to undo the past."

What he says about love applies also to many other relationships. We want to relive what is known and familiar to us. But we want to undo what is painful in order to make it right this time, or at least to settle for once old scores—or, in the case of sibs, ongoing ones as well. Eddy Deveau is "Pop" to younger colleagues in his office, playing with them the fatherly role he has always had with his brother Roy. But whereas he makes few demands on Roy, he can be tough and ruthless with the colleagues, as if to make up for the blows he suffers from his brother. Honey Dorman identified her eldest daughter, Meredith, with her own older sister, Ray, but she treated Meredith to the rage and hatred she never dared express toward Ray.

We want to relive and we want to undo, and the tragedy is that we can do neither. We cannot make the past happen again, and we cannot arrange for it not to have happened. No matter how many times we repeat old forms of behavior and how many ways we devise to do so, we cannot change the past. Nor can repetitious behavior with others change our present relationships with siblings. Nor can it make up for the original slights, hurts, or injustices we may have suffered and continue to suffer at the hands of brothers or sisters. In fact, it is in large part because repetitions *cannot* serve any of these purposes that they go futilely on and on.

I doubt that any of us can break out of all the patterns of our lives, and we would surely not want to end the positive sibling transferences that help us adjust to the world of our peers. But most people can learn to recognize sibling reenactments in their current lives, especially those that may stand in the way, intruding on other relationships, whether in love and family life, at work, or among friends.

Because the revivals and the repetitions that grow from them are usually far outside any individual's awareness, probably the best way to become familiar with them is through the examples of others. Some of those that follow come from conversations with or writings by therapists or from people who have, through therapy, learned to understand many of their own behavior patterns. That does not mean, however, that therapy is the only route to recognizing these forces within ourselves. So the examples and vignettes in this chapter also are meant to alert readers to the imprints of their own sibling experiences in many areas of life.

"Mary Ann is very much like my husband Tony," Nancy, second of the Ginetti sisters, had said, adding that there have been times when she calls her husband by her sister's name. What she sees in both, she explained, are cover-ups for their own insecurities, and her understanding of those cover-ups makes her feel stronger than either one. Not given to great introspection, Nancy was nonchalant about the similarity between her sister and her husband, simply accepting the idea that her years of growing up with the one have made her feel comfortable with the other.

German psychologist Walter Toman would probably have approved of Nancy's attitude. Toman was the first person to attempt to show systematically how sibling relationships can have a lasting influence not only on personality but on marital happiness as well. In his book *Family Constellation*, published in 1961, he mapped out in almost compulsive detail the effects on marriage of the birth order position of each partner. His thesis was that the more "complementary" the birth order places of spouses, the better their chances of a good marriage. By complementary he meant replicating the original family positions of each spouse. Nancy and Tony, for example, have a complementary marriage in Toman's terms: Nancy as a secondborn is used to looking up to an older sibling, and Tony, a firstborn, is used to guiding others.

Toman worked out scores of combinations of sibling positions, analyzing, in addition to order, such variables as the number and gender of siblings in each spouse's family. One of the best "fits," in his thinking, even better than that of Nancy and Tony, is between an older brother of sisters and a younger sister of brothers. The husband in this combination has learned about the opposite sex from his siblings and has also learned to protect and lead women, and the wife has knowledge of the opposite sex from her brothers and is used to being protected and led by them. (Toman, don't forget, was writing before the women's movement made it clear that men are not the only leaders in society and women do not necessarily grow up wanting to be led and protected by them.)

An older sister of brothers and a younger brother of sisters is another winning marital combination in Toman's theory—the wife because she will be used to playing a supportive maternal role to her younger brothers, the husband because he will expect that kind of role from his wife, having enjoyed it with his sister.

Less cheerful prognoses for marital happiness exist, according to Toman, when each spouse has siblings only of the same sex and has therefore gained little firsthand knowledge of the opposite sex. Combinations in which each spouse has the same birth position are also less promising. Two firstborn partners, for example, might identify with and understand each other, but they would also be likely to reenact their original leadership roles and therefore vie for power and family supremacy.

The worst prediction of all, in this scheme of things, is for a marriage between two only children, because neither has learned what it is like to live with a peer, and each may wish the other to take on the role of a parent figure. Toman did modify this worst-case scenario by theorizing that only children often adopt the birth order characteristics of their same-sex parent. So, for example, if an only daughter who identifies herself with a mother who had an older brother marries an only son identified with a father who had a younger sister, the marriage has a chance at complementarity.

A number of family therapists—most notably Murray Bowen—latched on to Toman's ideas and incorporated them into larger family systems theories that highlight the influence on marriage of each spouse's family of origin. But psychologists who have tried to test Toman's theories among married couples have found them contradictory and inconclusive. Like other birth order schemes, his are seen as too rigid and too sweeping, not giving enough importance to the hundreds of variables that influence sibling relations other than order or gender.

My own feeling is that although quite a few of Toman's ideas about complementarity are badly outdated, his concepts still offer an interesting perspective on married life and are especially interesting because they call much-needed attention to the impact of sibling experiences on marriage. His mechanistic approach, however, as researchers have found, does not hold up across the board, simply because human relations cannot be measured and quantified like so many laws of physics. In reality, the effects of sibling transferences on love relationships of any sort are subtler, more amorphous, and usually more complicated. In a variety of ways, and not only in terms of ordinal position or gender, we may relate to lovers and spouses as we once did to siblings.

One means of sorting out these ways is to examine their occurrence on three levels, one more complex than the next.

On the most basic level, individuals directly repeat in their love relationships—as they do in other relationships—various aspects of their sibling histories. The repetitions may be beneficial, like those of the young woman who wrote me that of her friends, she and another who grew up surrounded by brothers know best how to "charm" men. (Along the same lines, Lou Andreas-Salomé, a disciple and correspondent of Freud's, wrote that as an adored younger sister of several brothers, she felt deeply that all men were her brothers. Indeed, she was known for both her many love affairs and her friendships with men.) The repetitions may be neutral, not especially helpful or harmful, like those of Nancy Ginetti, who simply recognizes aspects of her older sister in her husband but is not profoundly affected by the similarities. Or they may be hurtful, like those of the man who complained that he was attracted only to older women, like his older sister, and then found himself turning them off because he fell right into his pattern of playing "kid brother" with each one.

It is the hurtful type of repetition, of course, that usually comes to therapists' attention. Sex therapist Alexander Levay sometimes sees women who grew up angry and resentful because they felt their brothers had been favored over them. Their resentment did not stop them, however, from marrying men below them in ability, treating their husbands in the same privileged way their brothers had been treated, and then resenting their indulged husbands as they resented their indulged brothers.

Dr. Levay also described a kind of reverse repetition that often occurs, especially in instances of sexual abuse. "Whatever was done to them, they cannot do with others," he says. So, for example, a man whose older brother smothered him with physical affection, constantly kissing and hugging him just short of actual incest, now finds himself incapable of kissing or hugging his wife or showing any kind of physical affection, even in the course of having sex.

Other direct sibling reenactments have their own powerful effects on love relationships.

Ms. L. entered treatment after twelve years of marriage to a demanding, needy, dependent man. Although enraged at her husband's little-boy ways, she was unable to speak up or state her own wishes for a more balanced union. Through many hours of therapy she barely mentioned her sister, four years younger than she, until the day the sister, who lived out of town, arrived for an extended visit.

Now Ms. L. found herself in a rage, not unlike the rage she consistently felt toward her husband.

"Before she camed," she began saying to her therapist, then stopped herself and questioned how she, usually well-spoken, could say "camed" instead of "came." The therapist suggested that she may have slipped back, in her anger, to the four-year-old self she had been when her sister was born.

The interpretation loosened memories of the sister's constant demands when the women were children and Ms. L's persistent sense—continuing to today—that she had to give in to whatever the sister wanted. "You are the older sister," her mother drummed into her, implying that you must be grown-up, hold back your own feelings, and take whatever your younger sister dishes out.

Her husband, Ms. L. began to realize as she delved into her past with her sister, also dished out plenty that she felt she must accept. Her husband, in fact, was her little sister all over again, and she the big one, enraged yet keeping anger bridled, and going along with all demands and cries of need. It took some probing, but she finally made the sibling connection in her marriage.

Similar connections may exist in more limited areas of marital and other love relationships. An example is the building superintendent, middle of three brothers, who cannot bring himself to share anything with his wife, not even a morsel of dessert when dining out. He'd had enough "grabbers" in his life, he has said many times. Far more destructive in this realm of repetitions were the "brotherly and sisterly" feeling that replaced sexual passion in Claire's first marriage.

Claire's view of herself as "bumbling" and "incompetent," stamped on her from the earliest moments of her life with her brother and continued into her marriage, illustrates the second level of complexity in sibling replays in love and marriage. What is replayed on this level is an image of *oneself*, shaped to a great extent by siblings, that colors a person's responses to love situations. Lisa, youngest of the Ginetti sisters, feels herself, by virtue of her sibling position, most independent of all, and that confident independence has helped her manage a difficult marriage to a tough-minded man quite a bit older than she.

On the negative side, like Claire's—and the negatives tend most often to be emphasized—is the situation described by a mother, Jessica Prescott, whose son and daughter, Fred and Ashley, were as tied to each other as any two siblings could be.

Although there is another son, Blake, six years younger than Ashley, the drama was between Fred and Ashley, four years apart in age. And it *was* a drama, *My Fair Lady* with a sibling slant.

"He was Pygmalion," said Jessica of Fred. "He molded her like a piece of clay. He made her what she is." What Ashley turned out to be is his clone: a lover of theater and dance, a reader of fine literature, a music aficionada, a teacher of philosophy.

"Little Blake had his own life. He was too young for them, and he was different—an all-around kid. He read comic books and played baseball. But the older two," Jessica explained, "were always together. He would read to her and test her in her homework. And she followed him around like a lovesick puppy."

Whether there was anything physical in Ashley's lovesickness Jessica didn't know. She worried sometimes because the two would "lie around on the couch for hours, reading to each other." But her worries dissipated for a while when Fred began dating, looking away from his sister to other girls his age.

The worries soon came crashing back. Jessica and her husband may have been pleased with their son's social life, but his sister was devastated. She gained pounds and pounds of weight until she became almost obese. She withdrew from family and friends, started cutting classes, and became sloppy and neglectful of all that had previously interested her. In short, she behaved like a woman rejected, who sees herself now as worthless.

"She pulled a veil over herself," said her mother. "She couldn't compete with Fred's girlfriends, and she didn't want any other boy. She hid behind a veil of fat and sloppiness, and the more so because the girls he went out with were always thin and beautiful."

Now in her late twenties, Ashley is in therapy, has lost some of her excess weight, and has launched into a modest social life of her own. But she continues to struggle, she told me when we talked, with her own sorry self-image. She still sees herself only through her brother's eyes, and, in comparison to the women he dates, she finds herself wanting. At the same time, she uses Fred as her standard for judging all other men, and in so doing she finds the others wanting. She is yet to have an independent view of herself or others.

For his part, it would appear that Fred came out unscathed by the intense emotional closeness he had with his sister for so many years. In his early thirties, he is handsome and successful in his academic profession. Regarded as a good catch, he doesn't lack for dates with beautiful women. His only problem: He still sees himself as Pygmalion. In every relationship he undertakes, he tries to shape his lover into his own ideal, as he had once shaped his sister. But unlike his sister, these women rebel, and the relationship ends. Now he, too, is in therapy, seeking to find out who he is apart from his sister, learning that the image of all-powerful brother he built of himself then does not hold up now with women who are not his sisters.

Finally, on the third and most complex level of sibling transferences in settings of love and matrimony is the replay of angers and aggressions directed not at the sibling who has aroused the angers and aggressions but toward the partner who has become a sibling stand-in. One illustration can make the point:

A sixty-year-old executive of a large automobile company is highly regarded in his field, a frequent speaker at sales conventions, and a pillar of community life—and he treats his wife like dirt.

The wife physically resembles the executive's older sister, who died some years ago, but temperamentally they are as different as night and day. The wife is warmly devoted to her husband and four children, affectionate, and good-hearted. The sister, married but without children, was sharp-tongued and critical, especially of her brother.

Years ago the sister had helped support her brother through school, setting aside her own education to do so. Although he had gone to a large university and graduated in the top 10 percent of his class, he had not done well enough to suit her. She regarded him as lazy, an underachiever, not good enough to have stolen her chance at an education. No matter what he accomplished in life, he could never please her. She criticized his wife, his home, and his business associates and thought little of his public acclaim. Because he wasn't perfect, he was a failure in her eyes.

The executive absorbed all his sister's guff without ever responding. Then he took out his rage and neediness on his wife, criticizing her mercilessly and showing not a shred of gratitude for her devotion to him. His wife was a safe target, his sister a fearsome one; his wife was in his power, his sister controlled him. After his sister died and he recognized that all hope of winning her approval was gone, his frustration increased, and with it came ever-worse behavior toward his wife. Now he is ill and dependent on his wife, but his attacks continue. She has replaced his sister in his mind, and all the repressed anger at his sister has been dumped on her.

For this man, reenactment means displacing anger at a feared and hated sister onto a wife whose image is connected in his mind with that sister. The displacement is an unconscious attempt to right the wrongs done him by the sister, but the attempt at repair has become as destructive as the original damage.

If love and marriage reopen sibling scenes of the past, having children pushes those scenes to center stage. For it is in the birth order and gender of children and the interplay between these that people are most likely to glimpse themselves and their sisters and brothers.

Actually, it would seem odd at first blush that this should be so. After all, the parent-child relationship is not one of equals or peers as is marriage or friendship. It is hierarchical, the parents above and the children leaning on them, a far different configuration from the horizontal connections among siblings.

Yet the creation of a new family comes closer than anything else in life to reawakening feelings from one's original family. It is as if, even while we establish those new families, some part of us is standing on the sidelines watching our own early story being played again. Circumstances are different this time, personalities are different, yet so much of the new story resonates with sounds and emotions of the old one that we easily identify with the characters and events before us. We may recognize our childhood selves in this son or daughter, point out a brother or sister in that one, feel empathic with one child, put off by another. We react to the players in this story according to the parts they have in the present production, but we also react to them in accordance with memories they stir up of other players in other parts at other times.

A nurse fought repeatedly with her husband, a printer, about how permissive or strict to be with their youngest child, a boy. They'd had no difficulties in regard to their first two children, a boy and a girl, but they were at each other's throats about this one.

Martin, the son, might ask for the keys to the car. The nurse would hand them over to him, no matter what time of day or night or whether his using the car meant that she or anyone else in the family could not. Her husband, on the other hand, would automatically refuse the request, no matter how good a reason the boy had or whether or not someone else needed the car.

The incessant fighting about Martin so upset the entire family that the couple decided to enter therapy together. What they learned about themselves was that for each of them Martin served as a stand-in for a sibling situation in their original families.

"For me," said the nurse, "he was my youngest brother. With my first son it was different. He was the eldest, the special one. But my daughter, in a way, was me, and Martin was my little brother. I'd had a lot of angry, jealous feelings toward that brother, and I think I was permissive toward Martin because I wanted to undo those feelings. I felt guilty, and I wanted to make up for my bad attitude."

Her husband's story was just the opposite. "In his family," she said, "he was the youngest son, used to being babied and catered to by his parents. He resented my overindulgence of Martin almost as if Martin were *his* sibling and had usurped his place. So he reacted by being extra strict and trying to keep Martin down."

The revivals in family life, like other sibling reenactments, may take many forms, depending on the personalities involved and earlier family history. A man who is a second child between two sisters may react to having a son and two daughters of his own by indulging the son, as he had been indulged by his sisters and parents; by pushing his son to be a masculine "macho" man, as he would have liked to be but was not; or by encouraging the son's dependency on his sisters, reflecting the man's dependency on his own sisters.

In the example above, instead of replaying her guilt toward her younger brother in her dealings with her youngest son, the nurse might have displaced her jealousy of her brother onto her son and treated him accordingly. Instead of acting jealous of his youngest son, the nurse's husband, also a youngest son, might have identified himself with the boy and favored him over his other children.

Parents cannot map out every possible combination of ways in which they may be identifying their children with themselves or their siblings. But being aware that these possibilities exist can help them spot reenactments in their lives.

The reenactments can be most harmful in extreme cases in which persons who have been treated especially badly by a sib "identify with the aggressor," to use a technical phrase. That is, they see themselves as the other saw them—weak, or slow, or otherwise inadequate. They then project that poor image of themselves onto a child who resembles them in birth order, gender, temperament, or personality, and treat that child the way they were treated. Roy Deveau's father, browbeaten by his older brother, browbeat Roy, a second son like him. While he identified himself with Roy in that way, he also identified himself with his brother, the strong, aggressive one, and gave himself a sense of power by belittling his weaker son.

The identifications parents make between their children and their sibs usually begin with the birth of a second child. That does not mean people never make such connections in other circumstances. Vivian, wanting very much now at age forty-three to become pregnant, put off marriage and childbearing for years because of her terror of having two daughters wrestling with each other for mother love, as she and Christina do. Others have spoken of having only one child because they did not want the child to feel "jealous" and "deprived," as they did competing with a sibling. (Or, less known to them, they themselves did not want to relive through their children their old sibling tensions.)

Then, too, parents of only children will sometimes say that they relate to their child as if he or she were a brother or sister. A mother became irritated "out of proportion," she said, when her teenage daughter, a single child, began borrowing her clothes and jewelry. For her, the daughter was her younger sister incarnate, "stealing what didn't belong to her."

But the birth, or even the anticipation, of a second child—and others after that—may stir up old sibling emotions more powerfully than anything else. I say "anticipation" because some research has shown that just as parents may mentally slot their children into particular roles even before they are born, early in pregnancy with a second child women may begin to fantasize about their children as sibs and in the process relive their own sibling experiences.

Psychologist Janice Abarbanel followed four mothers of toddlers carefully through the course of their second pregnancies by visiting them frequently, spending many hours talking to them, and observing them at play with their children. She discovered that the pregnancy itself reawakened each mother's sibling history, and by doing so influenced not only her behavior toward her firstborn child but also her manner of preparing the firstborn for the new baby.

One mother, Ms. C., had always felt deeply competitive with her sister Marcie, older by fourteen months, and had also resented being treated as the family "baby" while Marcie took the role of big sister or "Mommy." It happened that Marcie herself became pregnant at about the same time as Ms. C., leading to a competition between the two women about who could have a more "perfect" pregnancy.

As Ms. C.'s pregnancy progressed, she increasingly identified her firstborn, Caren, with Marcie and herself with the growing fetus. She withdrew from Caren, complaining of fatigue. With little preparation she moved Caren from a small crib to a larger one that turned into a junior bed. And she rarely discussed her pregnancy or the upcoming birth with Caren. When the baby, a boy, was born, Ms. C. asserted that he resembled her, both in his appearance and in his calm temperament. Little Caren found herself labeled "cranky" by her mother as she sulked about, angry at her mother and new brother.

In contrast, Ms. B. had a warm and loving relationship with her older sister Janet. She recognized that Janet, who was divorced, may have been envious of her happy marriage, so she went out of her way to show her support and interest in Janet's life. Ms. B. timed her pregnancy so that there would be the same two-year age difference between her daughter Beth and the new baby as there was between her and Janet.

Throughout the pregnancy, Ms. B. visited with her mother and sister, taking Beth along. She often spoke to Beth about her pregnancy and the new baby on the way, and when she bought Beth a new bed, she helped her feel grown-up because of it.

Janet stayed with Ms. B. during her labor, which was difficult. After the baby, also a boy, was born, Ms. B. announced that he looked "just like Beth." As the big sister, Beth was excited with the new baby, and if she had moments of anger, she also loved being involved in his care. Ms. B.'s mother said that Janet had acted in much the same way when her baby sister, Ms. B., had been born.

In both cases, the pregnancy itself pressed into conscious and unconscious thought associations between the women, their sisters, and their children. For Ms. C., unpleasant emotions toward her sister translated throughout her pregnancy and afterward into distance from the daughter she was beginning to associate with that sister. For Ms. B., strong affection for her older sister led, from the beginning, to a positive, supportive attitude toward her daughter's new role as big sister.

Particularly noteworthy in both these stories is the fact that in each situation, as early as the mother's pregnancy, the seeds for future relationships between her children were being planted. Caren, absorbing, through the way she was treated, the overriding jealousy and competition between Ms. C. and Marcie, becomes resentful of her new brother. Beth, experiencing through her treatment the strong sibling ties between Ms. B. and Janet, greets her new brother with interest and approval.

Family systems theorists speak of a "multigenerational transmission process" in describing how parental models come to influence generations of children. In their framework, family traits, including mental illness, are passed on through the ages because each new generation repeats the previous one's behavior patterns. Parents might project their internal conflicts onto one child, say a son. He, in turn, might treat one or more of his children the way he was treated, and that child or children will transmit the same treatment and its conflicts to the next generation, and on and on through time.

"The multigenerational process," writes Murray Bowen, "provides a base from which to make predictions in the present generation and gives an overview of what to expect in coming generations."

I have never completely subscribed to the emphasis in this theory on the automatic transmission of family characteristics, as though every child's fate is fixed at birth and we are all trapped into reliving our parents' psychological problems and then passing them on to our children. Reality, it seems to me, is more flexible, and such factors as temperament, personality, or the simple happenstances of life may bring about change over the course of time.

Still, the theory is illuminating in that it forces people not only to look backward at patterns of the past to help understand their behavior in the present, but also to look forward to recognize how they may be handing down their own patterns into the future. Although this theory focuses mostly on relationships between parents and children, it can be applied also to the recurrent patterns of sibling relationships.

Through her behavior Ms. C. projected onto Caren her own negative attitude toward her older sister Marcie. If she continues treating Caren as if she were Marcie, Caren might continue behaving toward her younger brother as Marcie behaved toward Ms. C.—with jealousy and rivalry. And if the brother grows up feeling resentful of Caren, he might identify his first child with his older sister, as Ms. C. identified

Caren with Marcie, and treat the child accordingly, thus continuing the pattern. Through her behavior Ms. B. has transmitted to Beth a loving attitude toward her younger brother, so that she would not be consumed by envy, nor he by resentment. If he, in turn, like Ms. B., imparts that attitude to his children, close family relations might extend into the next generation and beyond.

Directions have been set in both families that may be crucial to sibling relationships in the future.

"Ghosts in the nursery" is the label psychoanalyst Selma Fraiberg gives to early family influences that intrude on the present. The ghosts, she says, are "visitors from the unremembered past" who steal in unnoticed and make their presence felt in the many reactions parents have to their children.

For many people, the ghosts of siblings past frequently step unabashedly out of the nursery and into the workplace.

That place—whether it is an office or university, a bank or beauty salon—tends, in and of itself, to re-create a family environment. That is, irrespective of any individual's sibling position or history, the arenas in which people work together are haunted by shades of family life. There may be a male boss, the kindly "Daddy" who encourages his "sons" and "daughters" by taking a personal interest in them, or the authoritarian "Father" who is distant and demanding. There may be a "Mommy" woman executive, who protects and defends staff members and sometimes infantilizes them, or a more severe "Mother," who has high expectations of her "children" but is short on approval.

Of course, every work situation, even with a small staff, includes "brothers" and "sisters," coworkers, who may support and enjoy one another but may also compete for power and recognition. Sometimes employers themselves foster "sibling" rivalry by pitting employees against each other to win the notice of those above. In other cases, one person may set colleagues on a competitive edge by undermining their work to others or carrying tales from one to another. Even in the best of circumstances, childlike sibling games get played out—who has a window, a corner office, a key to the executive washroom, and who can get ahead of the pack to gain position as a favored "son" or "daughter."

Now into this established mix, so reminiscent of family life, float each individual's special ghosts of early sibling roles and conflicts, heightening the existing familial feelings and reactions. All the insecurities, self-doubts, and fears of failure that may have existed in the family get carried to work in so many briefcases or backpacks and are transferred to relationships with sibling stand-ins. All the power plays between older and younger sibs, the wishes to dominate, the appeals to parents for help, get reactivated.

A sales manager with two younger sisters turns young male salesmen in his company into the younger brothers he always dreamed of having, becoming their mentor and adviser, introducing them to the company's "old boys' network," and totally ignoring women staff members in the process. A dress designer, youngest in a family of six, constantly changes jobs and is constantly dissatisfied. Wherever she works and whatever she does, she remains the baby sister who always wants to do what someone else is doing and always feels that someone else has got to where she wants to be first.

The stories abound:

A banking loan officer had a brother four years older than she who, she felt, never took her seriously. At work she had a male colleague, also four years older, who she believed treated her the same way. He, eldest son in his family, paid little attention to his colleague's complaints, and the two were often at loggerheads.

One day, when their office was out of pencils, she bought a new box which she kept all to herself, arranging them openly on her desk. She knew her colleague would be envious because he prided himself on always having a neatly arranged collection of new, sharpened pencils on his desk.

"I did it to irk him, to make him jealous," she said gleefully.

Discovering after lunch that half her pencils were missing, she asked her colleague if he had taken them. Unapologetically, he acknowledged that he had.

"Those were my pencils," she retorted with irritation.

"Oh," he answered, unbudging.

With great effort she resisted her impulse to pound on his desk and shout in her best five-year-old voice, "Those were *MY* pencils!"

Instead, she left the room, and with time came to recognize that she was responding to her colleague as if he were her brother and that she would have to separate her dealings with each.

For years Julian, a computer programmer, would be overwhelmed when placed in a work position with a certain type of man: "pugnacious, aggressively smart, and older." His reaction invariably was to feel inferior and pull back in fear, allowing the other to get ahead of him. It took years more, some of them in therapy, to make the connection between such men and an older brother, who, in reality, was not more able than Julian himself.

"Even as a child, my brother was socially awkward and unable to make friends," he recalled. "In retrospect, I think my mother compensated for his awkwardness—and for my ease with others—by creating an awesome image of him as brilliant and infallible. He intimidated me, and so did men like him, until I began to understand the association, and to explore my own abilities."

The real-life actor and director Leonard Nimoy, who played Mr. Spock in the *Star Trek* TV series and movies, was relieved, he told a reporter, when nominated for an Emmy award as best supporting actor even though his was the star role. As a second son, he said, he was educated to the idea that he was "not to upstage" his brother. Consequently he was most comfortable as a character actor, a supporting player.

Not all the stories are negative. A personnel director insists that women employees with several sisters have the best records for cooperation and an ability to negotiate on the job. "Sisters learn to help one another and rotate leadership positions at home," she says, "and they carry those skills to work. Brothers learn more about competition with each other."

And the helping professions include many people who chose their fields because of their experiences at home with a disabled sibling. Pam, herself the victim of an alcoholic family, takes special pride in her daughter's work as a nurse with the mentally retarded, a direct outgrowth, she knows, of having grown up with a mentally retarded brother. The Detroit physician who has guilt reactions on the anniversary of his deaf brother's death recognizes, he says, that his lasting emotions about that brother led him to choose cardiology as his specialty. He feels tremendous empathy for his patients, many of them male, and wants very much to help them because he identifies them with his impaired brother.

It is worth noting, although it means veering away for a moment from the subject of sibling transferences and back to their reenactments with each other, that of all the work spheres in which sibling lives are relived, the most intense is probably that of sibs in business together. Loyalties may be so powerful that sibs will place their devotion to each other above any other commitment, including that to the adult children who may be in the business with them. In one family business, the owner kept his two brothers on the payroll for years after they no longer contributed to the business, draining income from his two daughters, who actually ran the business. If either of the daughters dared complain about an uncle, the father would cast an icy glare at her and state sharply, "He's my brother."

Ironically, those very loyalties can be the cause of failure in a family-run business. Because of them, brothers and sisters find it difficult to evaluate one another's performance, tolerating, in the words of one business consultant, "all sorts of incompetencies and nuttiness that another business company would never put up with." Similarly, sibs in business expect to re-create what they had at home, regardless of their skills and responsibilities.

"The thinking," says the consultant Theodore Cohn, "goes like this: I slept in the same size room as you did and I got the same allowance and graduated from high school or college the same as you did, so if we are in business together we have to be paid the same. We both have to be vice presidents and have the same size offices and secretaries of the same quality." Those assumptions, he continues, can be very destructive to the business and the family.

Even more destructive is the repetition of ancient and ongoing rivalries, the cause for the downfall of many a family business. Another consultant and lawyer, John F. Goodson, labels such rivalry the "Dandelion Seed Syndrome." Each sibling in the business feels pushed and crowded by the others, much the way a dandelion seed spreads and crowds out the grass around it. So each pushes back in return, determined to seize the ground. The feelings are not much different from those of childhood, when siblings try to gain the upper hand over each other or to win the exclusive love of parents.

The best work situation in family businesses or any other kind of employment, say the experts, is a "participative" one in which employees share in making decisions and cooperate in shaping policy, feeling themselves, as a result, important and valued by colleagues. In other words, workplaces in which the best of the sibling condition is re-created and office siblings or real-life ones can act like grown-ups.

Like associations with coworkers, relations among friends come close to mimicking the sibling bond. Because friends, like sibs, are peers who deal with each other on an equal basis, the inclination toward sibling reenactments can be gripping.

For one woman the reenactment is of guilt for being the prettiest and therefore most favored of three sisters. So when she remarried not long after a divorce, she was torn with guilt because a friend, divorced for a longer time, had not met a man to marry. And when she was invited to a big party to which another friend was not, she could barely look the friend in the face, so filled was she with guilt. It's the sibling guilt that stalks her, she says, the sense of having won out and made her sisters (and now her friends) unhappy to boot.

For another woman the revival is of always feeling rejected by her older sister and angry because of it. So after the older one moved to Australia, a continent away, the woman pursued the sister's best friend, hoping to replace the sister and triumph over her in that way. But she pursued so hard and demanded so much that once again she set up the same pattern of rejection and anger.

For Roy Deveau there exists a continuous rerun of feeling like a kid brother, and it is replayed with all friends and colleagues no matter their age. Some other laterborns mention similar feelings and speak of finding themselves always on the receiving end of advice, always a bit cowed by friends who have an air of authority—or always angry at them. But some youngers take on airs of authority themselves, repeating with others—as did Roy's father—the treatment they themselves received.

Some family elders may try to dominate in friendships, to rush in with suggestions and directions; some may have difficulty choosing friends who are their intellectual or social equals, preferring those who are younger, weaker, or more dependent, as their siblings had been. (But then there is the sculptor, eldest of two sisters, who consistently becomes involved in friendships with women who have older sisters. They like her, she is sure, because *she* becomes the dependent one—an older sister to whom they can feel superior.)

Some middle children, used to negotiating the ends, manage to put themselves into peacekeeping roles among friends; others to play off one friend against another so that they always come out on top. And some only children who had longed for siblings while growing up can never have enough friends in adult life; others repeat their aloneness, making acquaintances but few close companions.

Another carryover: On my survey there was a statistically significant correlation between feeling close to siblings and having close friends. Persons who regarded themselves as close or very close to brothers or sisters tended to be people who also had four or more close friends. Those with fewer than two friends tended to be people who did not see themselves as close to their siblings. These findings suggest to me that closeness and good relations with sibs set the groundwork for intimate relations with other peers.

Siblinglike problems in those intimate relations can come when several friends jockey with each other for closeness to one in the group. One of the more bizarre examples of such jockeying came, a homemaker related, when she and two friends tried to help another whose husband had died. In the heightened emotional atmosphere after the death, each friend sought to outdo the next in displaying loyalty, and each jealously looked over her shoulder to see which of them was leaned on more, confided in most, appreciated best by the bereaved widow. The competition became so formidable that by the morning of the funeral none of the three friends was on speaking terms with the others.

"It was really funny, except that it's sad because we're no longer friends," the homemaker said, pointing out in passing that each friend was a secondborn with an older sister.

At its worst, sibling transference among peers becomes what the Germans call *Schadenfreude,* meaning a malicious gloating over someone else's misfortune. Put another way, in the words of the old aphorism, it is a belief that "success is not enough; friends must fail." Reflected in this way of thinking are the most primitive of sibling emotions. It's as if all the "I wants" and "Me toos" and "I hate yous" from childhood are rolled into one large ball and mentally hurled at a sib replacement, a contemporary who may be viewed the way a sibling once was—as an interference or a threat to one's position, self-esteem, or security.

At its best, sibling transference among peers exemplifies the very essence of strong sibling ties, centered around loyalty, love, and devotion. Sometimes, in fact, those best sibling qualities can be created more easily with friends than with siblings themselves. Free of the baggage of early pain and hard feelings, women and men may form friendships that rise to the fulfillment of the highest ideals of brotherhood and sisterhood.

The Bible, to which I have referred frequently because of its textbooklike portrayals of sibling jealousies and misdeeds, also portrays sibling-style friendships among people who are not siblings. One of the most moving is the friendship of Ruth and Naomi, who, although mother-in-law and daughter-in-law, treat each other in many ways like devoted sisters. For the sake of her friendship with Naomi, Ruth, the younger of the two, gives up her own land and family to live in Naomi's land, among her people. And Naomi watches over Ruth in that land, helping her to get her bearings and eventually to wed a loving husband.

Another, better-known friendship is that of Ruth's descendant David with Jonathan, son of King Saul of Israel. So faithful is Jonathan that he helps David escape Saul's wrath and ultimately become king in

Jonathan's own place. When Jonathan is slain in battle, David cries in anguish, "I grieve for you, / My brother Jonathan, / You were most dear to me."

Friends who are not siblings may achieve the pinnacles of brotherhood and sisterhood. The question now becomes how those ideals can be reached within the bond itself, among true brothers and sisters.

CHAPTER FIFTEEN

*"There's a Certain Kind of Laughing
You Can Do with a Sister or Brother
That You Can't Do with Anybody Else"*

BALANCING THE SEESAW

*T*here is an intriguing theory in the field of cognitive psychology that ostensibly has little to do with siblings, yet seems to me to have everything to do with them. Unlike those fields of psychology that emphasize unconscious drives and longings or the emotional attachments of children to parents, cognitive psychologists study the workings of the human mind, with its ability to learn, store, and recall information. The theory concerns the connection between the way we think and the way we relate to other people.

It contends that much of our ability to get along with others stems from the skills we have in "reading" people's thoughts. Because we know from our own experience what another person may be thinking, we are able to put ourselves in that person's place, to anticipate what he or she will do or say next, and to respond appropriately. This skill is called a "theory of mind," and it emerges in young children at about the time language begins to develop, a time when children are able to form mental pictures of objects and people. It is thought that autistic children, who often echo the words of others or respond in ways unrelated to what has been said to them, may lack a theory of mind. Although these children are able to learn concrete information, such as music notes or railroad schedules, they are not able to think about the thoughts of others and therefore to respond meaningfully to them.

One quality necessary for the existence of a theory of mind, say the psychologists, is the development among children of the ability to pretend-play. Children between the ages of one and two are able to pretend that a block is a train or a stick is a spoon. As they get older they are able to play pretend roles with each other, as in "I must be the mommy and you must be the baby." Children's ability to know who they are and at the same time to pretend to be something they are not is a precursor to being able to know what they think and feel and at the same time know what someone else thinks and feels; to understand "mental states," in the language of the cognitive psychologists.

Now—and here is where the sibling angle comes in—in a different field of psychology, developmental psychologists have been observing the pretend play of children in order to learn more about it. In their observations, some have discovered that pretend play is a vital part of sibling relations. They have found that young siblings who have the closest relations with each other also engage in the greatest amount of pretend play, although not necessarily greater amounts of real play than other siblings. They also engage in more pretend play with each other than they do with their mother. Whether these children get along particularly well because they pretend-play so much or whether they are able to pretend-play because they get along so well to begin with is not clear. Most likely both equations are true. Those siblings who pretend-play a great deal sharpen their abilities to think about one another's thoughts and feelings, and thus to understand one another and become good friends. And siblings who get along well and are able to anticipate one another's thoughts are more adept at playing pretend games with each other.

What is intriguing about the work of the cognitive psychologists on the value of pretend play and a theory of mind, and the work of the developmental psychologists on pretend play among siblings, is that together their findings offer one more piece of evidence for the importance of sibling relations as a training ground for broader relations outside the family. For just as sibs carry the negotiating skills they learn from fighting and competing to their relationships to the outside world, they carry over from playing and pretending together crucial skills of reading others' mental states and putting themselves in the place of others.

The findings of the psychologists also attest, once again, to the specialness of the sibling bond itself. Along with their many other interactions, through their play as children, siblings develop a singular capacity to understand each other, to think what the other is thinking and feel what the other is feeling, to know each other in ways that not even their parents know them. For many, that capacity endures throughout life, and sibs remain attuned to each other's thoughts and feelings no matter the vicissitudes and changes that sweep over them —like the two brothers in business together, in the last chapter, who with just a glance know exactly what each is thinking and precisely how to deal together with a client.

Throughout this investigation I have tried to tap into that specialness of the sibling tie. To that purpose, toward the end of every interview or series of interviews I asked the same question: "What does this relationship mean to you?"

The question was deliberately open-ended, meant not for one-line answers but for a thoughtful summary, an integration, of all that had been said in the course of our meetings. Sometimes the question was followed by another even more general query: "Do you think you can say how this relationship has influenced you as an individual?" For people who had several siblings, the questions were posed about each one and about all as a group.

Nobody responded immediately. Sometimes there were long silences; at other times there would be a groping for words, or hesitant phrases strung together in no particular order, as the person tried to synthesize thoughts and emotions that had been stirred up. Rarely was an answer direct. Usually it began with a qualification, or was surrounded with an anecdote, or was told to me in the context of a response to someone else about something else.

"I can't think clearly when I think about him," an older brother began in trying to capture his overall feelings about a younger one who had cut off connections.

"When Jane became sick, I could speak to my family," was the opening of another man, whose daughter had died two years earlier of cancer. He was a man who had, in our interview, persistently described himself as a "loner," not estranged from, but not particularly close to, his older sister and younger brother.

"My sister and brother were involved," he elaborated. "They knew what my wife and I were going through. It was good having a family that was supportive, that was there for us, whether that meant giving us a place to stay that was near the hospital, or visiting, or thinking about our needs. We had plenty of friends who were involved, but you know, my brother and sister understood in a way that none of our friends could. They were family."

"A friend of mine asked why I don't just stop talking to Vivian with all the grief she causes me," said Christina in answer to my question. "I thought about it, and I thought, 'She's right.' Then I thought, 'There are billions of human beings in this world, but there is only one human being out of all those billions who had the same mother and father as I did, who was there and shared my childhood. How can I never talk to her again?' "

In many instances the answer people finally came up with was a statement not about them at all, but about the state of being and having a brother or sister.

"It's a relationship based on trust," said a woman who had spoken warmly of her older sister's financial success and generosity toward her two younger siblings. "Even if you disagree, you have to have each other's best interests at heart and to trust one another's motivations."

"In the final analysis," said Nancy Ginetti, perhaps more down-to-earth and more to the point than anyone else, "there's a certain kind of laughing you can do with a sister or brother that you can't do with anybody else in the world."

In their own ways, everyone was saying—as the psychologists have been finding in their studies—that there is a certain kind of laughing, of crying, of *knowing*, that exists with a sibling that does not exist with anybody else in the world. In their own ways also, no matter how close or distant they felt toward their sibs at the time of an interview, no matter how angry or loving, all agreed that their ties to brothers and sisters had been profoundly significant in their lives.

Because of that significance, and because the sibling connection continues to be significant in the lives of individuals and families, this investigation ends now with some conclusions and suggestions for adult sibs based on the interviews, the survey, research into scholarly studies, and discussions with social scientists.

These conclusions and suggestions are not meant to be hard and fast rules—do's and don'ts for sibling well-being. This relationship is too complex and rich to be reduced to that. Rather, what follows is meant to trigger thoughts for adult siblings about themselves and each other. It is meant to help brothers and sisters find ways to strengthen their connections to each other when that is possible, to accept what cannot be strengthened when that is necessary, and, ultimately, to enjoy the laughter—that certain way of being siblings have with one another that they don't have with anybody else in the world.

COMPETITION, UNRESOLVED

A Harvard scientist has proposed a controversial theory about the development of the fetus in its mother's womb. The accepted theory is that the cells in each organ of the fetus are genetically programmed to grow in an orderly sequence as they form that organ. In contrast, says this scientist, James Michaelson, cells within each organ compete with one another, with the strongest or most "fit" cells eventually shaping each body organ.

Whether or not Dr. Michaelson is correct—and scientists will continue debating this for years—his theory points up a truth of existence: Competition in one form or another is intrinsic to life. It may begin at the very inception of life, as Michaelson says, before an organism is even formed, but if not, it surely begins for most species moments after birth—witness a litter of puppies vying for their mother's milk.

For human siblings competition begins with the birth of a second child, and it may last a lifetime. The first part of that statement is widely known and acknowledged, requiring no elaboration at this point. The second part, discussed throughout this study, is still a matter of denial and some shame for many sibs. The many people in the survey who asserted that they did not compare themselves to their siblings, and the large numbers in interviews who pointed to siblings —never themselves—as the source of competition, bear this out.

When books and articles, both popular and professional, speak of those competitions and power struggles that continue into adult life, they usually speak of them as stemming from "unresolved" rivalries of childhood. The implication is that if rivalries can be "resolved," in childhood or adolescence, they will no longer interfere in sibling relations. It's a point of view I don't share, mainly because I don't believe "resolved" is the correct word to use for rivalries.

To resolve, the dictionary says, means, among other things, "to deal with conclusively." I don't believe siblings can deal *conclusively* with rivalry, certainly not in childhood, and not later either. Rivalry exists among siblings, a fact of life and an entity in itself, overlaid by maturity and increased closeness or decreased contact in adulthood, but ready to be sparked into life again with the flash of a word or incident.

What siblings *can* do about rivalry, jealousies, and the power struggles that accompany them is acknowledge these feelings and struggles, not necessarily to the other person, but certainly to themselves.

Acknowledging feelings of competition in oneself and to oneself is the beginning of gaining control over those feelings so that they don't come through as put-downs or judgments that provoke retaliatory competition in another. Linguist Deborah Tannen writes in *You Just Don't Understand* of the criticisms implicit in the supposedly helpful suggestions or praise people often give one another. "Your new beau is fabulous—he's not boring like the last one" may sound like praise of a new boyfriend, but includes a slap at the old one. It is that kind of concealed criticism, which implies hidden hostility and competitiveness, that sibs complain about in one another.

The older sister who compliments a younger one on a new jacket by saying, "This fits you so much better than the one you wore last week," leaves the younger feeling that she looked terrible last week, and angry at her sister's know-it-all attitude. A younger brother who has been told of some work problem an older is having and constantly asks, with excessive concern, "Will it be all right? Do you think you can get through it?" is both undercutting the older and placing himself in the superior position of the comforter, the understanding "parent."

In recognizing their hidden jealousies or wishes for power and dominance, sibs can prevent themselves from using language or behavior that angers and provokes another. They can also prevent themselves from behavior that hurts *them*. The adult daughter who finds herself incensed at a sister's "fawning" over a sick father may also find herself in a foolish—and exhausting—contest to do more and still more unless she recognizes the competitive urge behind her rage.

To acknowledge to oneself ongoing twinges of rivalry or larger envies is to be able to take the first steps toward overcoming those feelings. Psychologists hold that underlying some of the strongest rivalries among young siblings is the belief that a parent's love is limited, so that if one child is loved, there may not be enough left over for others. As children mature they learn that love can be shared by all without loss to any one. It's a lesson adult sibs often have to relearn in regard to life's other bounties. That is, a brother or sister's accomplishments do not threaten one's own; the other's success does not mean we have failed. More than one person in a family can win at life's games.

Acknowledging, controlling, and overcoming envies and rivalries toward siblings also aids us in acknowledging, controlling, and overcoming those emotions toward others. *Schadenfreude* springs from the most primal of sibling impulses, the child's wish to see another punished so that he can come out on top. Understanding such feelings, and the envy behind them, can help eliminate them.

Women often find it more difficult than men to admit their competitive feelings, even to themselves. From earliest infancy, they are socialized to be cooperative and caring. They are expected to help Mommy, to be "cute" and "sweet" and "nice," and to leave physical aggressiveness to their brothers. The very qualities that pull them close to each other—their ability to nurture and support others—may lead them to feel shame or embarrassment about their competitive urges. In the survey men reported comparing themselves to their brothers in significantly greater numbers than did women to their sisters. Yet it is clear from two other findings that sisters have rivalrous feelings—they are more likely than any other combination not to have spoken to each other out of anger and they are more likely to be bothered by each other's habits.

Women who can accept the reality of their own jealousies or rivalries and then put those feelings aside may be able to avoid the angers that lead to not speaking to each other. (Similarly, men who can admit to themselves that they not only compare and compete openly but also, often, secretly covet what a sibling has, may also be able to contain conflicts before they occur.)

Finally, for both women and men, identifying competitive feelings in oneself may make it possible to speak openly about such feelings with sibs. Ross and Milgram found that siblings don't have such conversations not only because they may be ashamed of their feelings but because they fear that admitting their own competitiveness will give a brother or sister the upper hand. But if these feelings can be openly exchanged, brothers and sisters may find it easier "to reach a point together," as one woman said, "where when something positive happens to one of us it is shared as positive to the other. And something that happens that is negative is a shared hurt."

THE SEARCH FOR CLOSENESS

If siblings don't like to talk openly about competition, they do talk openly, again and again, about another feeling: the longing to be closer to each other than they currently are. They do this even as they emphasize their differentness from one another. "I'm introspective," said Mark Platt, "he's outgoing." "I'm sports-minded," said another man. "My brother sits home weekends and reads books." And so on.

Some people I met, while insisting on a wish for greater closeness, concluded simply that because of their differences they had too "little in common" with a brother or sister to allow for such closeness. Two sisters stand out particularly. Both spoke independently and at length of their envy of friends who said they had warm, intimate relationships with their siblings. Their father, they said, had two main interests in life—history and music, leading one sister to become an historian and the other a singer. As a result, their interests are so different that neither feels she knows much about her sister, although they have never lost contact.

"My relationship with my sister was initially formed by the fact that we lived in the same house together," said the singer. "But that is now forty-odd years ago, and my memories of the past are foggy. We move in different worlds. I don't know what led her to make her professional choices, for example. I can't tell you when or why she stopped teaching history in order to write and lecture. I don't know why, when she was teaching, she decided to teach one subject and not another. I never had those kinds of conversations with her."

Affirming differences, as has been said earlier, can serve some important functions for siblings in childhood. It helps them in forming separate identities, and it helps in controlling competition so that each can win on a different turf. But in adult life, identities are fairly well formed. The need for separate turfs becomes less pressing as siblings gain security and confidence in their own abilities. Now some sibs begin to give up their old roles, to put aside some of their differences and permit their similarities to emerge. Usually that change, when it happens, is unconscious, a part of aging and maturing.

What I want to argue now is that a *conscious* emphasis on similarities rather than differences, a *conscious* search for common ground, is an important route for those who yearn for greater sibling closeness.

The first step on that route is to break the habit of emphasizing differences. Most of us, as siblings, are so used to defining ourselves by dissimilarities that we don't think to look for the core of similarities that lies beneath the surface. The singer, for instance, described her decision to switch her field of study from composing—her father's passion—to singing classical music. She had been "petrified" to tell her father of the change, and when she finally did, his response was "Well, that's okay, you never really had any leaning toward composing anyway." She had been deeply hurt by his words and convinced that she had disappointed him terribly. Her sister, however, had insisted that her father's response had not been a sign of disappointment but had been intended only to make her feel better.

The sister, the historian, described a different, but related, incident. After she had decided to get a divorce, she had been "terrified" of telling her father, knowing that he held strict views about marriage. He had said little when she finally broke the news, but that Christmas, after the divorce had been arranged, she received a card from him addressed to "Mr. and Mrs.," with her husband's name. She believed it was her father's way of showing disapproval, and she saw herself as a dreadful disappointment to him. Her sister, however, had assured her that her father had meant only to show his support by not treating her as a divorced woman until the event was finalized.

The women told their stories as an example of their differences— in this case their different perceptions of their father—never noting the much more important alikeness of their reactions. They both lived in fear of disappointing a controlling, strong-minded father. Each made excuses for him, and both were so in need of his acceptance that they responded to his slightest sign of disapproval with shame and self-blame. Had they discussed the samenesses of their responses to their father, not only in these incidents but throughout their lives, they might have discovered a deep commonality that was merely glossed over with differences.

Shared history, such as these women's shared experiences with their father, is a major source of commonality, and focusing on that history is another step toward greater closeness among siblings. Mark and Jerry Platt have become increasingly closer since they have begun to speak about their parents as "vulnerable people," in Mark's words, and to discuss their home life together. Other people describe incessantly analyzing their parents with their brothers and sisters as a way of making sense out of themselves as individuals and as siblings. But shared recollections of childhood—of that seabed of memory and feelings that remains with us through life—extend beyond parents. They are powerful forces drawing many brothers and sisters together.

In fact, the fogginess of the singer's memories of the past goes hand in hand with her feelings of dissimilarity and distance from her sister. (It is also reminiscent of Mary Main's findings that parents who had detached themselves from their own past had children who were detached from them.) Jogging one's own memory—and each other's —out of the fog, and consciously recalling alone and together images of family events, ideas, values, expectations, humor, even sadnesses, can awaken feelings of sameness and attachment among sibs.

Similarities can be awakened, of course, when siblings spend time together. Even if they manage to stay in touch across vast distances, regular meetings to see each other face-to-face can make a difference. Together, sibs become accustomed to each other's aging. Together, they can notice gestures, ways of speaking, attitudes, and smiles that resemble one another's, the legacy of their shared genes as well as shared family life. (When I was younger, I used to hate being told how much alike my brother and I looked. I wanted to be my own person—as different from him in appearance as in interests. Now I watch him when we're together, and I see my parents in him, and I see myself, and there is intimacy in that seeing.)

Paying attention to similarities instead of differences encourages brothers and sisters to move away from the de-identification of earlier years and toward closer selves, shaped by a stronger identification with each other. It may be that if the identification gets to be too close, if the sibs step too far into each other's territories, they will become caught up in old rivalries and will have to move apart again.

But it may also be that sisters and brothers will discover with maturity that focusing on the ways in which they are alike rather than different becomes the lifeblood of a new cooperation and mutual enjoyment. The real-life social scientists Roger and David Johnson, third and fourth from a family of seven children, work together, write together, and consider themselves best friends. From their own closeness has grown their philosophy of education—that children learn better in an atmosphere of cooperation and interdependence than of competition and rugged individualism. Mutuality and cooperation, they say from experience, leads to great satisfaction and achievement.

There is one reservation to be added to the subject of closeness. The wish many siblings have for greater closeness is a basic and valid one and should be pursued when felt. That is not the same as a wish for "best friendship," for some ideal of sibling intimacy portrayed by novelists—or parents—which can be futile and frustrating. Although there are numbers of siblings, like the Johnson brothers, who see themselves as intimate, powerfully linked best friends, the majority of sibling ties, as this study and Gold's typology found, are not like that. Most include some jealousies, some conflicts, some ups and downs of closeness and distance. Few people are capable of giving ideal love or loyalty to a sister or brother, and a sibling who expects and demands that ideal may lose everything for want of an unattainable dream.

So a brother should not give up in anger at another who fails him at times. A sister should not write off a sib with whom she quarrels or competes. As the many life stories in this book attest, among siblings, as in other relationships, imperfect attachments can also offer enjoyments, satisfactions, and numerous rewards. Stephanie, in Chapter Thirteen, who had mothered a sister who later pulled away to assert her independence, summed up their current, mutually acceptable status. "We're not best friends," she said. "We're special friends."

"GROWING UP" FROM SIBLINGS

Stephanie and her sister arrived at their status of special friends only after a painful period of separation. Feeling themselves too intertwined, the women broke off contact for a year, agreeing that they could call on each other for help if necessary. In that time they "grew up," Stephanie said, coming together again as adults.

We usually think of growing up in relation to parents: affirming our independence yet maintaining closeness and connection to them and the values they instilled in us. But siblings, too, need to establish separate selves even while they remain connected and caring of each other. They need to find a balance between closeness and overcloseness, between a healthy interdependency and a harmful overdependency, between cooperation with each other and intrusion on one another's lives. In that sense, they, too, need to make a conscious effort to "grow up" from one another.

With their nearness in age and tendency to identify with each other, siblings may find their growing up even more difficult than growing up in respect to parents.

A woman came up to speak to me after a lecture because in the course of my talk she had started thinking about her entanglement in her younger sister's life. The younger one—aged thirty-five—confides *everything* to this sister, who is three years older, including the most minute details of marital problems or spats. "There are times," related the elder, "when I get caught in the middle trying to patch up a fight between her and her husband. Now I'm realizing for the first time how bad the role I've been playing is for all of us. I've got to do something about it."

The process of growing up for an adult sibling begins with a sense of dissatisfaction with the status quo. But to become a process it needs to involve dissatisfaction not only with a situation or with another person but also with oneself. It's when a woman, like this one, says, "I don't like the way I've been acting," not only, "I don't like the way she's been acting," or when a man asks himself angrily, "Why can't I ever make a decision without consulting my older brother?" not only, "Why is he always forcing his advice on me?" that the process can truly begin.

Growing up involves both a decision to change and a decision to cope with the anxieties that change engenders. The anxieties can be many. If the elder sister stops allowing the younger to pour out her marital woes, will the younger feel hurt and rejected and pull away altogether? If the man makes an important career decision without seeking the counsel of his older brother, will the brother become enraged and abandon him completely? There are no guarantees in this process, only chances taken and hopes held.

To be most effective, the chances taken must hinge on specific goals. What does the woman want in regard to her younger sister? To be kept out of her marital problems only, or not to be confided in at all? Does she really want to be freed of giving any advice, forcing the other to rely on herself in all matters, or does she want to make clear that she will always be available for the most serious problems? What does the man want to change in his relationship to his older brother? His own dependency, or the brother's expectations of dependency from him? How independent does he feel he can be without becoming frightened of failing or of facing big brother's admonitions?

A decision needs to be made, also, about what kind of action to take. Feeling themselves too merged with another, some people simply withdraw from a sibling, making a point of phoning less or, in conversation, confiding less. A twenty-eight-year-old marketing coordinator wrote on the questionnaire that the main problem she has with her twenty-six-year-old brother is that he doesn't approve of the man she has been dating for the past two years and whom she will probably marry. In the space left for explaining how the problem had been handled, she wrote, "I try to avoid discussing my boyfriend with my brother," and in the space left to say how the problem had been resolved, she indicated that it was "not yet resolved."

Such avoidance can serve the purpose of separating from a brother or sister, but the purpose can usually be better served if the sibling who wants the change can find a way to explain that desire to the other with words, not only behavior. And because a sister or brother is likely to misunderstand or feel rejected by a sib's desire for greater independence or for less responsibility for the other, the words need to be stated in the most sensitive way possible that demonstrates an appreciation of the other's point of view.

Stephanie and her sister, for example, made a joint decision to have little contact for a year, to allow the sister a chance to stand on her own feet and Stephanie a chance to recognize that her sister had her own feet to stand on. They arrived at that decision, Stephanie said, after the sister explained how important it was for her to take responsibility for herself, although she was deeply grateful for the nurturing and love Stephanie had given her.

Clear in her own mind about her goals yet respectful of Stephanie, the sister achieved the results she wanted. Those results may not always be achieved, and the response to a call for change may be laughter, a bitter retort, a look of withering disdain. Yet many people would consider the gamble worth taking. For when the results are good, adult siblings can find the greatest satisfactions in being *adult* siblings.

The process of growing up need not necessarily be a global one, changing the entire pattern of being in relation to a brother or sister. It may have narrower goals, or revolve around more specific character- istics. It may involve speaking to a sib about repetitive power plays that are galling to the recipient, or repetitive boastings and braggings that set another's teeth on edge.

Growing up may involve changing gender patterns that began with the different roles that boys or girls played within a family and that became fixed by adult life. Study after study has pointed out that sisters, far more than brothers, carry the major responsibilities for the care of parents and for family solidarity. Yet in an age when women spend almost as much time in the workplace as do men, many are questioning why the work of family life, including adult family life, should not be equalized, and many are seeking change.

Sometimes the process of growing up and changing in regard to sibs can be an internal one only. In such cases, the patterns of a person's own behavior may cause such pain that the person finally determines to break those patterns even if there can be no expecta- tion of change on the part of a sibling. Claire, for instance, suffers terribly each time she strives to win the approval and recognition of her brother Turner, who continually withholds both. She might save herself from suffering if she stopped trying to please him. She might feel herself in control if she admitted that she will probably never gain from him the appreciation she wants. She might have to live in sad- ness knowing that her brother cannot be the brother she dreamed of having. But she will live as a grown-up at last, free of a pattern that no amount of repetition can make right.

For some people, growing up means taking more extreme and even more painful action than what Claire might do to change. For these people, it means actually cutting off contact with a brother or sister because not cutting off is so hurtful and destructive. In a sense it means mourning the necessary loss of a sister or brother with whom one can find no understanding and no peace, and going on from there, as difficult as that might be.

George Vaillant writes in his book *Adaptation to Life* that the men in his study who have fared worst are not those who had lost a parent in childhood but those who had to live in the constant presence of a disturbed parent, or in a disturbed childhood environment. "No whim of fate, no Freudian trauma, no loss of a loved one," he explains, "will be as devastating to the human spirit as some prolonged ambivalent relationship that leaves us forever unable to say good-bye."

The sibling relationship by its nature is ambivalent. But when disturbances are constant and extreme, when the negative end of the seesaw so outweighs the positive that there can be no balance, one sibling may feel the need to say good-bye. Most brothers and sisters consider this kind of leave-taking a very last resort. Most find that change is possible, and that in growing up, the benefits of keeping sibling ties in place outweigh the costs.

PARENTS AND PARTINGS

A letter arrived in the mail a few days after my final interview with Philip, the pediatrician who has become a staunch feminist because of his experience of being favored, as the boy in the family, over his sister Regina.

"At the end of the taping," he wrote, "you asked for a summing up. I think it was too soon after, but now, thinking about it all, I'd say:

"I long to be near my sister, to be kind and helpful to her, loving to her—and for her to be loving and close to me—and for her to be happy with herself and her life. I don't know if I can be or she can be. The time is too long ago—we parted somewhere in the mists. I don't know where. I think it was close to the very beginning."

The partings for Philip and Regina that began in those mists of time and continue to this day are not about deep-seated competitions or polarized differences, and certainly not about an overabundance of intimacy that has forced them to separate from each other. They are about Regina's continued resentment of Philip's glorified position in their family and his subsequent achievements in adult life, and about Philip's guilt over the same things. It was he who grew up seeing himself as "handsome, smart, and sweet," and she who felt "short-changed." It was she who had to drop out of college and give her place to him when family funds could not support both.

As it is for Philip and Regina, for many siblings the hurtful things that happened "close to the very beginning" have little to do with anything that occurred between the sibs themselves and much to do with what occurred between parents and each child. Yet one of my most consistent findings has been that siblings blame each other for hurts done to them by parents, paying little attention to the origins.

This reluctance by siblings to blame parents, and their practice of shifting that blame to one another, remain sources of difficulties as powerful in adult life as they are in childhood.

This is not to propose that every problem between siblings be placed at their parents' doorsteps. The emphasis throughout this book has been on the unique relationships of brothers and sisters to one another, and that is where it remains. But when troubles arise among sibs, or when a brother or sister seeks greater closeness or an end to bitter enmities, parental contributors to the difficulties need to be considered. Were there things that happened long ago over which sibs had no control but which harmed them as individuals and in relation to each other? Did parents poison the atmosphere for friendship among them?

Such poisonous parental behaviors might include comparisons openly made, favoritism and scapegoating, fights between parents that drew the children into them, or, more devastatingly, family secrets such as alcoholism or incest. For an adult sibling who becomes aware of such ancient sources of problems and wants to bring about change, there are two tasks to consider.

The first is to approach parents, if that is possible and reasonable, meaning that a parent is not only alive and well enough but would also be receptive to a discussion that may touch on sensitive subjects. The purpose of such a discussion is not to point an accusing finger at a mother or hand a father a laundry list of his mistakes. The purpose is to allow the adult child to articulate views and air perceptions that have been bottled up for decades, and in the process to give parents a chance to state their views and perceptions.

The elder daughter whose taped conversation with her mother is presented in Chapter Seven discovered in that conversation that her mother had thought her capable of anything. What the woman regarded as favoritism was, in her mother's view, an attempt to protect her weaker younger daughter. That information did not change the elder's sense of having lost out on her mother's attentions, but it gave her an opportunity to speak her mind. It is conceivable that she will soften her attitude toward her sister because of that opportunity.

The eldest of four sons who has always resented his younger sibs because he had to bear the burden of responsibility for them may uncover in talking to his parents a deep well of respect for him that they had always felt but neglected to express. That respect may not ease the continuing burden the man feels, but it might give him a sense of pride in bearing it.

Unfortunately, no one can guarantee that the discoveries an adult child may make in talking to parents about the past will be as satisfactory as these; there exists always the possibility of finding out what you don't really want to know. But even then, going back to the sources may allow for new understandings of parents and siblings.

A mother may admit, for example, that she *was* harder on one daughter than another, perhaps because she expected more of that daughter or because that daughter was most like her and she felt insecure and unhappy in herself. The admission will be disturbing, but it will also give the daughter insight into herself and her sister that she didn't have before. Another mother may acknowledge that although she loved her children equally, she did think "boys are special." The acknowledgment may not please her daughter, but it will confirm what the daughter always felt—that she was no less loved than her brother, although he enjoyed male privileges in their family.

Talking history with parents—or, if they are not available or approachable, an aunt or uncle who is—will not undo that history, but it might make it more comprehensible, and in that way make the present more manageable for adult children.

The second task for a man or woman who seeks to unearth the germ of problems planted by parents is to approach the siblings who share those problems. And that, too, carries risks, and no guarantees of success.

Regina refuses to speak to Philip about the most painful parts of their past. "My sister's view of herself and of me is filtered through her anger and jealousy of my better lot in life, but she won't talk about it," he said at one of our meetings. "And I, filled with guilt, want nothing more than to talk." Other siblings may shrug off such discussions as "irrelevant," or too embarrassing. ("It makes me uncomfortable," my brother said when I prodded him into speaking about our different perceptions of family life.)

Yet siblings could learn so much about each other and themselves if they would investigate together the unfinished business of their past lives. By exchanging perceptions and perspectives, they might illuminate corners of the "mists" that none has been able to penetrate alone. They might also free themselves to speak about matters they had never risked touching on before.

A woman sits in my office, weeping as she tells of a brother nine months younger whom she "idolizes" and about whom she feels dreadful guilt. Her mother had become pregnant with the brother while nursing the woman, and had a difficult pregnancy and even more difficult labor. The baby's birth had been breech, and the child's foot had been crushed in the course of it, so that he has limped all his life.

This woman has always felt her mother unconsciously blamed her for her brother's difficult birth and injury and, more consciously, treated him as special because of those difficulties. She is tormented with her guilt for having "injured" her brother and also for resenting the specialness of his treatment.

But listen, I want to say and don't because of my promise of confidentiality to all interviewees, your brother told me that he knows you blame yourself. Your brother told me that for years he took advantage of your guilt by letting you get punished for things he did. Your brother thinks your mother was cruel to treat you as she did, and he feels ashamed of the way he treated you but doesn't know how to tell you that.

A man spends many hours of an interview pouring out wrath about the older brother whom his parents incessantly held up to him as ideal. His brother is unapproachable, the man says, because he has always seen himself as a star, never having had to struggle to keep up with anyone.

But listen, I want to say and don't, your brother spent much of his time talking about an older cousin to whom your parents constantly compared him and for whom he felt he was no match. Your brother spoke about always wanting your friendship but fearing your resentment and your rejection.

In our last interview, Christina said that she and Vivian have made a pact not to talk about the past because they fight too much when they do. But maybe they would be better served if the pact they made was to talk about the past but not to fight when they do. Maybe if they approached each other without confrontation, in search of understanding, they might find that they had a great deal they could talk about. They might find that what they had in common was not their rancor and not their jealousy, but their sense of being cheated by parents who used them as pawns for their own problems.

Many siblings do find ways of talking about some of the most painful parts of the past, and with talking they find healing and comfort. "My sister and I have become very close emotionally," wrote a thirty-four-year-old secretary. "We had problems for a long time because we both thought we were Mom's favorite child. We talked over our feelings about this four years ago and realized it didn't matter who was the favorite. Now we're just happy we have each other."

.   .   .

Sisters and brothers from seriously disturbed families may have a harder time than others in traveling back to the parental past, not because they necessarily avoid talking to each other, but because their pain may be so deep and so sharp that they cannot reach its origins. Pam and Gail, for instance, have spoken many times of events and incidents in their alcohol-ridden home. But what remains unspoken and perhaps unrecognized is what may be most important: the extent of Pam's anguish while she lived at home, including the possibility of sexual abuse by their father; the frightening sense of abandonment Gail felt after Pam left her alone with an uncaring stepmother and drunken father; the hole in the world each inhabited without the love of a mother or protection of a father, a space that neither could fill for the other.

The extent to which sibs can probe on their own into hurts imposed on them by parents depends on how deep and how obscure the sources of those hurts are. In some situations, one or another may need therapy or counseling to deal with the problems. (Cases of sibling incest fall into this category. Parental neglect, or sexuality, or repression of sexuality in the family are all contributing factors to such incest. But the act itself was between the siblings, and the emotional ramifications of trying to discuss it may be overwhelming.) In other instances, family therapy that includes all sibs (and possibly parents) may be useful.

As parents age, the role they played in the past in shaping sibling relations recedes into the background. But without an understanding of that role, siblings may go on forever blaming each other for deeds that were not their doing.

COPING WITH CONFLICT

At the deathbed of a friend of mine sat a younger sister with whom she had broken off contact some years earlier because of a fight. The sister had been called when my friend became ill, and from the moment of her arrival had not left the bedside. Even as the elder drew her last breaths, the younger sat with her, holding her hand and speaking words of love and comfort. It was a scene of sisterly devotion that moved all of us, the friends, to tears, until someone said, "Yes, but how tragic that it took her dying to bring peace between them."

As much as adult siblings try to avoid open conflict with each other, those conflicts do erupt in the lives of many. Based on survey responses, the most common center around the care of parents. Money and financial problems, drug and alcohol abuse by sibs or parents, and in-law squabbles are also fairly high up on the list. Personality differences and everyday irritations command their own share of complaints.

How do siblings resolve these conflicts so that they do not lead to years of coldness that persist to the end or conclude with tragic deathbed scenes like that of my friend?

Respondents to the survey were asked to choose from a list those techniques they might use in handling a problem with a brother or sister. The list, with some revisions, was based on the Ways of Coping Questionnaire developed by psychologists Susan Folkman and Richard S. Lazarus. It included two types of strategies. The first entailed taking direct action, as in "Talked to my brother or sister to find out more about the situation" or "Stood my ground and fought for what I wanted." The second involved passive responses, such as "Had fantasies or wishes about things I might have said or done" or "Kept my feelings to myself." At the end of the list respondents were asked how the problem had been resolved—"satisfactorily," "unsatisfactorily," or "not yet resolved."

The responses showed that active strategies are far more often associated with solving problems than are passive ones. For example, an overwhelming number (87 percent) of those who had talked to a sibling and more than half (51 percent) who had stood their ground indicated that the problem had been satisfactorily resolved. Those who fantasized about what they might have said, held in their feelings, or even made light of a situation were less likely to arrive at a satisfactory resolution.

What this tells us is that shoving a problem under the rug will not make it disappear, nor will amusement at something another considers serious. (Don't misunderstand: a sense of humor is crucial in sib relationships as in all others, but hiding angry feelings behind laughter does not usually bring the best results.)

How to go about talking to a sibling or standing your ground about a particular problem depends on the nature of the problem and the degree of anger surrounding it. Sibs who have a minor spat may be able to get past it quickly with a phone call, a lunch date, a friendly greeting card. Even weightier arguments—about whom to vote for or how to educate the kids—can often be handled by agreeing to disagree or to stay away from the subject.

It is when arguments have serious overtones, and subjects (which may indeed include politics or educating the kids) have deep meaning to one or another sib, that making peace becomes a more delicate matter.

Before even attempting to settle a dispute, a sib who wants to make the first move needs to sort out the immediate cause from underlying ones. Although adult sibling fights do not necessarily revolve around bygone issues of childhood, many do, and others carry within them echoes of old patterns and habits that surround the current words and tones siblings use. Does the rage among brothers generated by a business argument also reflect one brother's long-standing belief that the others have never taken his views seriously? Is the shouting match between sisters about how often each visits their mother in her nursing home also an expression of deep-seated tensions about who takes more responsibility in the family and who has a right to make decisions?

It is important to distinguish the underlying issues from the immediate ones in order to set those issues aside for the time being. The first order of business is to deal with the *specifics* of the fight itself. At another time, perhaps, in a calmer atmosphere, the sib might want to initiate a discussion of those basic, long-standing disagreements. The point for now, however, is to try to prevent every fight from turning into *the* fight, the one that flashes back and churns up layers of old emotions and resentments. By recognizing early angers and irritations beneath later ones, a sibling can best confine a fight to the present.

Once the old issues have been isolated and set aside, talk about the fight itself can begin. If the fight has been very intense, it may be a good idea to let some time go by first, for cooling off—but not indefinitely. If the conflict is important, it should be faced.

When that facing does take place, it should begin with safety. That means dealing at the start with the least controversial aspects of the fight, those that will not quickly arouse the strongest emotions. Such a starting point may be ways of speaking, rather than a review of what was said. (Experts also advise using "I" words instead of "you" words, as in "I felt hurt," not "You acted like a bitch.") For example, the sister attempting to settle the nursing home quarrel might say, "I didn't mean to snap at you, but I was upset," steering clear of the actual subject of conflict, the sisters' visits to their mother. Only after each sister begins to feel safe again with the other can the discussion move to the details of the argument.

With the discussion under way, a sibling who truly wants to resolve a conflict has a right to state her position and hold her ground. Simply giving in for the sake of peace might bring about that peace but leave behind a residue of resentment (unless the feeling is that the other is right—in which case an apology would be in order). The respondents who stood their ground were the ones most likely to feel they had satisfactorily resolved their problems with their siblings. They had functioned as active partners in the process.

Active, of course, does not mean being one-sided. Siblings learn from their earliest play together how to empathize, how to put themselves in the place of another. These are the qualities they particularly need to call on at times of conflict. Listening so the other knows she's being heard, responding so he knows he is being respected, go a long way toward reaching resolution.

Resolution need not necessarily bring agreement. But it does need to bring to all participants a feeling that their viewpoints are recognized as valid and that each has a right to hold and exercise that viewpoint. The sisters may resolve their immediate battle by agreeing to a visiting schedule that each feels she can meet. That done, eventually they may tackle the deeper issues and also agree that one has no right to tell another what to do but the other has no right to shirk family responsibilities.

In some situations, when a break has been large and deep, a letter may better serve to reopen contact than an attempt at discussion. Writing offers a way to organize thoughts and present ideas that might be too difficult to say in person. But again, a letter should not accuse; it should state one sib's position while acknowledging the other's. And its motives should be sincere.

Sincerity was a concern of the brilliant nuclear physicist mentioned in Chapter Seven, who had been "shamelessly" favored over his brother and repeated the favoritism with his son. His brother, understandably, has been resentful, and the physicist, in an attempt at reconciliation, wrote him a long letter. Furious at receiving no response, he was ready to "write off" the brother, until he began to think more carefully about how sincere his letter was.

"Here I was," he said, "worshiped as the family genius, and what did I do? I wrote my brother one of my long, analytic, literary letters— reverting to the very thing he resented about me. I had to ask myself what my motives were. Did I *want* this to fail? That way, I tried, he thwarted it, and I remain superior, as always. This resonates to childhood—I want to make up, but I want the applause."

Perhaps when the physicist stops seeking applause and writes an honest letter, his brother will respond with a letter or phone call of his own. Or perhaps not. Some relationships like theirs, based on years of unhappiness, may remain limited, although it doesn't hurt for the one who wants to improve matters to keep trying.

Other circumstances may create limitations of their own. Some siblings may be most comfortable settling individual conflicts without ever delving into the weightier underlying issues between them. They may be more willing to limit their relationship in that sense than to open up sensitive, more threatening areas for investigation. In other situations, limitations come not from the sibs but from their spouses. If spouses do not get along, sibs may agree to see less of each other and their families than they would like. Sometimes if there are strong disagreements between a sibling and a brother's or sister's spouse, the sibs may want to arrange means of spending time alone with each other, away from their families. It's an arrangement less satisfactory than family togetherness, but far more satisfactory than sibling separateness.

Most limited are those sibling attachments that become cut off, like that of my friend and her sister or Chuck and Sandy in Chapter Eleven. So much bad history has come between this brother and sister that on the few occasions when they do see each other, they have little to say. Some day, Sandy says, she would like "to sit down with Chuck over a cup of coffee and ask some hard questions." Yet if that day ever comes, it would be better for her, and for anyone who is estranged from a sibling, to reach out gently. A sib seeking reconciliation after a long period of coldness might call a brother, write a letter, or, if possible, invite him for a cup of coffee, but *not* ask the hard questions right away. She should begin with the easy ones, starting, as in all resolutions of sibling fights, in the safe places, and moving only gradually, and only when there is some understanding on both sides, into the darker areas of the conflict.

BANISHING THE GHOSTS

"History," said Selma Fraiberg in discussing the impact of the past on the present, "is not destiny." The images of parents and siblings and the patterns of family behavior that become imprinted on our minds in childhood shape many of our adult responses to the people and events we encounter. But what Fraiberg is saying is that they need not determine our lives. We can be aware of what was hurtful in the past and build on what was beneficial, relating to spouses or children, colleagues or friends, in ways that are under our control. In other words, we can banish the harmful ghosts that haunt us not only from the nursery but from every corner of our existence.

Banishment begins with awareness, and awareness begins when people consciously think about the images and patterns that influence them. Is there, for example, a pattern of favoritism in a mother's family that she may be repeating with her own children—like the nuclear physicist who favors his son just as his father had favored him? Is a father especially harsh with his oldest daughter and protective of his younger son because as secondborn he constantly felt himself put down by his oldest sister?

What of present patterns? Does a woman persistently find herself attracted to autocratic, opinionated men, although she insists that she wants to marry someone who is gentle and sweet? And does she have an autocratic, opinionated older brother of whom she is critical but whom she also idolizes? Does a man become irrationally impatient and irritable with employees who hesitate in making decisions or turn to him for advice? And does he have a younger brother who leans on him for all decisions and refuses to make a move without consulting him first?

By recognizing old sibling patterns and images, we may recognize ourselves replicating those patterns with a lover, a friend, a coworker. By paying attention to the roles we continue to play with brothers and sisters, we can notice ourselves reproducing those roles with a child, a spouse, an employer.

Awareness can lead to control over harmful patterns of behavior. The way to begin gaining that control is to consciously separate the images of the past from the reality of the present and to respond to the present on its own terms. The nurse who treated her youngest son as she would have liked to treat her youngest brother learned to separate the emotions connected with her brother from her feelings toward her son. She also learned that no matter how indulgent she was of her son, she could not undo in that way her domination of her brother years earlier.

Once the images have been separated from the reality, they need to be kept separate by monitoring one's own behavior and reactions. Most of us slip back into old habits easily; change requires practice and vigilance. The bank officer may find many similarities between her older colleague and her older brother. But each time she catches herself reacting to her colleague as she might to her brother— whether now or when she was five or ten or fifteen years old—she needs to stop short and remind herself yet one more time that there is a real person here, separate and distinct from her brother. Punishing him for the brother who doesn't take her seriously will not change her brother, and it might make her colleague very angry. It would be far better to discuss her complaints with him, colleague to colleague, and shove the ghost of her brother out of her office completely.

Sometimes, putting aside old images and consciously changing behavior patterns outside the family can alter the patterns within. A woman who both mothers her younger brother and fights with him may marry a man younger than she whom she identifies in some way with her brother. But because the man is gentler or easier to get along with, or unburdened by emotions she connects with her brother, the woman is able to find a more equal relationship with him that includes some mothering but little fighting. Through her loving relationship with her husband she learns to give up some of her anger at her brother and enjoy warmer ties with him. Her sibling transference has transferred itself from brother to husband and back again to brother.

But more often the flow of change moves in the other direction, and it is the roots that feed the branches. By acknowledging competition and jealousy within oneself, by recognizing similarities and drawing closer to sibs, by resolving conflicts with them, brothers and sisters begin to change the internal images each carries of the other. At peace with one another, they become freer to relate to others as individuals and not as shadows of old history. And unencumbered by either excessive anger or excessive idealism, they are able to balance the seesaws of affection and rivalry, of cooperation and competition, for themselves and in the outside world—in love and family life, at work, and among friends.

I had thought to conclude this book with a long story that had a happy ending, some convoluted Shakespearean comedy that manages to wrap up perfectly in the end. There were stories along those lines among the people I interviewed. There were, for example, two sisters who had fought all their lives until they married two brothers who had fought all their lives. With marriage and new interests to share, the fighting stopped all around, and sisters and brothers emerged as one another's best friends. There were other brothers or sisters who had lost touch over the years and somehow found their way back.

But sifting through transcripts and tapes of interviews, I realized that for most people happy endings didn't come as culminations of elaborate Shakespearean dramas. They came in more modest ways, in small scenes that were part of a larger, ever-changing whole. They came at unexpected moments, in flashes of insight that became turning points in the lives of siblings. They came simply, and left behind a recognition of what a sibling attachment meant, no matter how imperfect the ties or mixed the feelings connected to it.

Here, then, are three scenes, three slices of sibling life, three happy endings that were also beginnings.

SCENE 1: The living room of a cozy apartment in Portland, Oregon. A woman, in her mid-forties, is visiting her older sister. Both look serious, intense. They have been in strong disagreement for many months about the younger woman's religious plans. Reared as Roman Catholics, they had both remained devoted to the Church for years. But some time ago, the younger woman had met and married a Jewish man. Although never asked by her husband to give up her religion, she had become increasingly interested in the idea of converting.

She had discussed her thoughts with her older sister, who had adamantly disapproved. Their parents, both dead, would have seen such an act as a betrayal of their faith, the sister argued. Conversion would set the woman apart from everyone in the family, including the sister. Why couldn't the woman celebrate her husband's holidays with him and their own holidays with the family, without going through such a formal break?

The younger woman had tried to explain her own thoughts, sick at heart at her sister's unhappiness but clear about her feelings. Then they had stopped discussing the subject, each feeling she had made her point.

Now, visiting her older sister, the younger says, "Well, it's over."

The older, recognizing the "it" to mean the religious issue and taking the "over" to mean her sister has dropped the idea of conversion, says joyfully, "Oh, I'm so glad you've put that behind you, and we can just go on as before."

"You don't understand," the younger says, her voice trembling. "It's over. I've done it. The conversion is complete."

"Oh," the older cries. Her eyes brim with tears as she excuses herself and leaves the room. A few minutes later she returns, smiling, her face composed and two glasses of champagne in her hands.

"Mazel tov," she says, using the traditional Jewish greeting for good luck. "It's not what I wanted, but now that it's done, I wish you only the best. We're still sisters, and that's all that matters."

To me, in describing the scene, the older sister says, "I realized at that moment how much I love and need my sister. We will never resolve this difference between us, but we find our way around it because there is so much else in our lives together. We have children of the same age, we share a lifetime of history and experience. I could never give her up."

SCENE 2: The dining room of a glass-walled house in Sacramento, California. Three grown children, two brothers and a sister, ranging in age from early to middle thirties, are seated around the table, having dinner with their parents. The two brothers, the oldest and youngest in the family, recently opened a travel agency together, and the oldest is engaged to be married. The sister, the middle child, has begun a new job handling public relations for a local business firm.

"Why do we have to have this discussion about stuff that happened ages ago?" the older brother is asking.

"It hurt so much and it influenced my life is why," the sister replies. "In every job I've had, I've created my family again. I surround myself with men who are funny, charming, and charismatic like the two of you. And then I'm never heard, just the way I was never heard here at home. I'm an outsider, alone again. I've got to understand it, so I can stop doing it on this job."

"Can we help it that we're funny, charming, and charismatic?" the older brother asks, grinning.

"You can help it that I have felt and still feel so left out of your club," the sister answers in a voice that makes both her brothers listen without interruption. "Do you know what it's like always to be on the outside?" she continues. "I would rush home from school when we were kids, dying to be with the two of you, and you'd just ignore me. You were always together, and I didn't exist. If you let me in, it was to hit me or laugh at me. I never counted, I could never be heard."

The sister is weeping. "I loved you so much, and you didn't want any part of me. And now you're still shutting me out. You call each other all the time. You talk about your work. But nobody asks me about work or calls me, unless it's to arrange about Mom's birthday or Father's Day or something."

The younger brother looks at her, his eyes watering. "Don't you know how much I love you, Trish?" he asks softly. "So many times I've wanted a big sister to talk to, but you always seemed so self-sufficient, I didn't think you cared about me or Doug."

"I was self-sufficient," Trish says, "because I had to be. I had no one to rely on, and you never gave me a chance." She reaches over to touch her younger brother's hand. "But I'm sorry if I wasn't there for you, Brian. I thought I was unwanted."

The older brother, Doug, gets up from his seat and walks over to put his arm around his sister. "I'm the one who's sorry, Trish," he says. "I'm the eldest. I should have understood. I do now. Do you think we can try again as grown-ups?"

"They became a family that night," says the father who describes the scene to me. "It was so painful to hear my grown children cry, to see Trish open up old wounds. My wife and I made a lot of mistakes as parents, but I think our family's going to be all right."

SCENE 3: A posh private club, somewhere in the Northeast. Four elderly siblings, two brothers and two sisters, have gathered for the first time in years. They live miles apart, one brother with his son and daughter-in-law, another with his wife in a retirement community, and each sister, widowed, alone. The sisters write to each other and the others regularly and phone occasionally. The brothers had a falling-out decades earlier, after their mother's death, and although they patched it up, their contact has remained patchy, sporadic. But they have come together now at the posh private club for a party given in honor of the eldest's eightieth birthday by his son and daughter-in-law.

The daughter-in-law, who later describes the scene to me, notices them milling around, mingling with the guests, somewhat shy and awkward with each other. Within a short time, however, they have disappeared from the crowd, all four of them, and she sees them standing in a corner, talking animatedly to each other. As she watches they join hands and begin, slowly, to move around in a circle. They seem to be chanting something, and the daughter-in-law edges closer to listen without being seen. They are chanting, she hears, some childhood song on the order of "Ring Around the Rosie," but a song that includes each of their names. They are singing their song and laughing softly while they circle round, holding hands.

Decades and distances have slipped away as the four elderly people chant and move together to the rhythms of a sibling dance they have known all their lives.

SUMMARY OF SURVEY FINDINGS ABOUT SIBLINGS

Number in sample: 272
Age range: 19–71 (average age: 37.1)

SISTERS AND BROTHERS

Sisters had the closest relationship of any sibling combination on all measures of closeness. Overall, 61 percent of women reported feeling "close" or "very close" to their sisters compared to 48 percent of men in regard to their brothers and 46 percent of men and women in relation to their opposite-sex siblings.

But women more frequently indicated that they had not spoken to their sisters out of anger than did men in relation to their brothers or respondents to their opposite-sex siblings (30 percent of sisters compared to 21 percent of brothers and 17 percent of opposite-sex siblings).

Brothers showed the greatest degree of competitiveness. Men reported comparing themselves to their brothers in significantly greater numbers than did women to their sisters or subjects to their opposite-sex siblings. Example: 33 percent of men compared their finances with their brothers' finances as opposed to 23 percent of women who compared their finances to those of their sisters.

382APPENDIX A

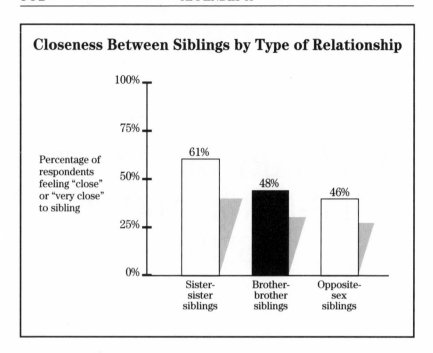

Closeness Between Siblings by Type of Relationship

Percentage of respondents feeling "close" or "very close" to sibling

- Sister-sister siblings: 61%
- Brother-brother siblings: 48%
- Opposite-sex siblings: 46%

CLOSENESS AND DISTANCE

Most respondents saw themselves as "close" (31 percent) and "somewhat close" (31 percent) to siblings. Fewer saw themselves as "very close" (21 percent), and only a small number (17 percent) as "not close at all" to siblings. More than 75 percent responded "No" when asked if there had been times when they have not spoken to siblings out of anger.

Age difference had a significant effect on closeness between siblings. The greater the age difference, the less likely sibs were to be close. Example: 55 percent of subjects felt "close" or "very close" to a sibling between one and four years older, but 38 percent felt "close" or "very close" to sibs five or more years older.

Geographic distance did not interfere with feelings of closeness. Of respondents who lived within one hundred miles of a sibling, 84 percent rated themselves "very close," "close," or "somewhat close," and almost as many—81 percent—who lived at a greater distance described themselves in the same way.

Subjects who felt close to their siblings tended to have parents who felt close to their siblings.

Subjects who felt close to their siblings were more likely to feel close to their parents than subjects who did not feel close to siblings.

Example: 83 percent of those who described themselves as "close" or "very close" to a sibling also described themselves as "close" or "very close" to their mothers. Of those who were "somewhat close" or "not close at all" to a sibling, only 60 percent were "close" or "very close" to their mothers.

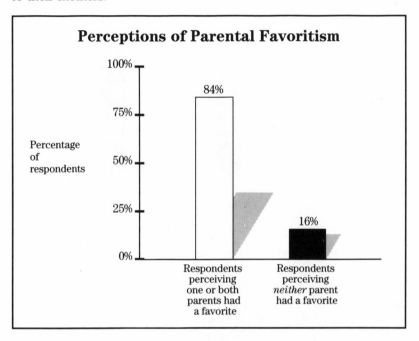

FAVORITISM

The vast majority of respondents—84 percent—perceived that there had been favoritism in their families. About 16 percent felt that neither parent had a favorite. Of those who saw favoritism, slightly less than half viewed themselves as the favorite of either father, mother, or both. A little more than half regarded a sibling as the favorite of either father, mother, or both.

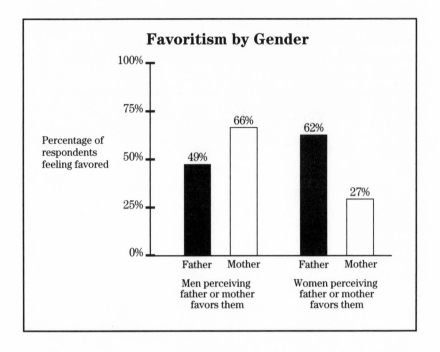

Favoritism by Gender

Cross-sex favoritism emerged as a powerful family force. Men were more likely than women to feel favored by mothers. When respondents perceived their mother had a favorite, 66 percent of the men and only 27 percent of the women felt favored by her. In contrast, women were more likely than men to feel favored by fathers. When respondents perceived that their father had a favorite, 62 percent of the women compared to 49 percent of the men felt favored by him. When they did not choose themselves as favorites, both women and men most often chose a brother as their mother's favorite and a sister as their father's favorite.

Favorites were more likely than nonfavorites to feel secure, but they also felt more guilty than nonfavorites because of their status. Nonfavorites reported feeling more resentful and jealous than favorites, but also more independent as a result of not being favored.

ELDERS AND YOUNGERS

Younger siblings reported comparing themselves to older ones in significantly greater numbers (47 percent) than elders compared themselves to youngers (31 percent).

A significantly larger number of elder siblings (58 percent) perceived younger ones as coming to them for advice than did youngers (47 percent) think of elders as coming to them for advice. This despite the fact that the majority of all subjects said that they did not seek the advice of their siblings.

Comparable numbers of elder and younger siblings indicated that they looked to each other for approval, although youngers speak more openly of wanting approval from their older sibs.

MARRIAGE

Respondents tended to regard a brother's or sister's spouse as improving relationships among siblings. In contrast to popular belief, sisters-in-law more than brothers-in-law were seen as helping sib relationships.

CONFLICT

Care of parents and problems connected to parents ranked highest as causes of sibling conflict.

Financial matters ranked second in sibling problems.

Alcohol and drug abuse ranked third.

Talking to siblings and standing up for what you believe came across as more effective in settling problems than keeping feelings to oneself. Eighty-seven percent of those who had talked to a sibling and 51 percent who had stood their ground indicated that the problem had been resolved satisfactorily.

THE SIBLING QUESTIONNAIRE

Please fill in (or check) your responses to the following. Do not write your name. This is a study of relationships among brothers and sisters. Answers will be kept confidential and entered into a computer for analysis. If questions do not apply to you, leave blank.

A. Sex:_____male _____female   Age:_____years

   Education: _____years   Occupation:_____

   Marital status: _____single _____married _____divorced

   _____separated _____widowed

   Number of brothers:_____   Number of sisters:_____

   Religion:_____   Race:_____

B. FATHER: If your father is living, please fill in all questions below. If your father has died, please fill in questions 4–9 below.

   1. How old is your father? _____years

   2. How far away does your father live? _____miles (approx.)

   3. How often do you see your father or talk to him by phone?

   _____never _____few times a year _____monthly

   _____weekly _____daily

4. What is/was his occupation?_____

   Years of education?_____

5. How close are/were you to your father?

   _____very close _____close _____somewhat close

   _____not close at all

6. Were you your father's favorite child? _____Yes _____No

7. If not, which brother or sister was your father's favorite?

   (DO NOT NAME THE SIBLING, just indicate the sex and current

   age of sibling.)

   _____male _____female; Age:_____years

   OR _____no favorite

8. If you think your father had a favorite son or daughter, or you

   were the favorite, how does this make you feel? (Check all the

   responses that apply to you.)

   _____resentful _____secure _____jealous _____guilty

   _____independent _____capable _____no effect

9. How close is/was your father to his brothers and sisters?

   _____very close _____close _____somewhat close

   _____not close at all _____not applicable

C. MOTHER: If your mother is living, please fill in all questions below. If
   your mother has died, please fill in questions 4–9, then
   continue to question 10.

   1. How old is your mother? _____years

   2. How far away does your mother live? _____miles (approx.)

   3. How often do you see your mother or talk to her by phone?

      _____never _____few times a year _____monthly

      _____weekly _____daily

4. What is/was her occupation? _____

   Years of education?_____

5. How close are/were you to your mother?

   _____very close _____close _____somewhat close

   _____not close at all

6. Were you your mother's favorite child? _____Yes _____No

7. If not, which brother or sister was your mother's favorite?
   (DO NOT NAME THE SIBLING, just indicate the sex and current age of sibling.)

   _____male _____female; Age: _____years

   OR _____no favorite

8. If you think your mother had a favorite son or daughter, or you
   were the favorite, how does this make you feel? (Check all the
   responses that apply to you.)

   _____resentful _____secure _____jealous _____guilty

   _____independent _____capable _____no effect

9. How close is/was your mother to her brothers and sisters?

   _____very close _____close _____somewhat close

   _____not close at all _____not applicable

10. *If one or both of your parents are alive,* who among the broth-
    ers and sisters assumes the most responsibility for their care
    and well-being? Again, indicate sex and age of sibling:

    _____male _____female; Age: _____years

    _____I assume responsibility OR _____equally shared

    _____not applicable

11. Were your parents ever divorced or separated?

    _____divorced _____separated _____neither

    If so, how old were you at the time? _____years

12. How many close friends (not family) do you have?

_____none _____1 _____2–3 _____4–5

_____6 or more

D. BROTHERS AND SISTERS: Please answer the questions in section D for ONE of your brothers or sisters. If you have more than one sibling, fill out separate forms for each one.

1. If this is a   brother   OR a   sister   (circle one)

2. How old is he/she? _____years

3. Is this brother or sister _____full _____step _____half

_____adopted?

4. What is his/her occupation?_____

Years of education?_____

5. How far away does he/she live? _____miles (approx.)

6. How often do you see this brother or sister or talk to him/her on the phone?

_____never _____few times a year _____monthly

_____weekly _____daily

7. How close are you to him/her?

_____very close _____close _____somewhat close

_____not close at all

8. How much . . . (Check best answer)

	Not at all	Some	Very much
a. Do you seek his/her approval?	____	____	____
b. Do you share your inner feelings with him/her?	____	____	____
c. Does he/she understand what you are really like?	____	____	____

	Not at all	Some	Very much
d. Did you go to him/her for advice this past year?	——	——	——
e. Did he/she come to you for advice this past year?	——	——	——
f. If you succeed in something, do you tell him/her?	——	——	——
g. If you fail in something, do you tell him/her?	——	——	——
h. Do habits or behavior of this sibling that annoyed you in childhood still bother you today?	——	——	——

9. Do you compare yourself to this sibling in terms of (check all items that apply):

_____success or failure of children _____achievements

_____finances _____education _____occupation?

_____I don't compare

10a. (IF THIS SIBLING IS MARRIED) Has your sibling's spouse made your relationship with this sibling _____better

_____same _____worse?

b. If there has been a change (better or worse), could you say more about it?

_____

_____

_____

c. (IF YOU ARE MARRIED) If you have problems with your spouse, do you confide them to this sib?

_____Yes _____No

11. Have there been periods of time when you and this sibling have not spoken to one another out of anger?

_____Yes _____No

If yes, could you say more about it?

_____

_____

12. Is there anything else you would like to say about your relationship with this brother or sister? (If you need more space, please use Part F.)

_____

_____

_____

E. COPING WITH PROBLEMS:

1. Please give a general description of an important problem you have had that involves a brother or a sister.

_____

_____

_____

2. What did you do to handle this problem?

_____

_____

_____

3. Thinking about the situation you just described, please check the "Yes" or "No" column for each of the following items depending on whether that item applied to you in handling or coping with the problem.

                                                    No   Yes

a. Talked to my brother(s) or sister(s) to find out more about the situation.   _____   _____

	No	Yes

b. Had fantasies or wishes about things I
might have said or done. _____ _____

c. Felt that time would make a difference,
and the only thing to do was to wait. _____ _____

d. Kept my feelings to myself. _____ _____

e. Bargained or compromised to get
something positive from the situation. _____ _____

f. Avoided being with my brother(s) or
sister(s). _____ _____

g. Made light of the situation; refused to
get too serious about it. _____ _____

h. Stood my ground and fought for what I
wanted. _____ _____

i. Put the problem aside and did not let it
interfere with my relationship with
brother(s) or sister(s). _____ _____

4. Finally, how was the problem resolved?

_____satisfactorily _____unsatisfactorily _____not yet resolved

F. Please use this space for anything else you might wish to say about
your relationship with your brothers or sisters or about influences
that may have led you to be or not to be close to one another.

_____

_____

_____

NOTES

INTRODUCTION

Page

xi   About 80 percent: U.S. Dept. of Commerce, Bureau of the Census, series P-20, no. 450, "Marital Status and Living Arrangements: March 1990," p. 45. Judy Dunn gives the same figure for Europe in *Sisters and Brothers: The Developing Child* (Cambridge, Mass.: Harvard Univ. Press, 1985), 4.

xii   His followers: For attitudes of Freud and his followers toward siblings, see Alice B. Colonna and Lottie M. Newman, "Psychoanalytic Literature on Siblings," *The Psychoanalytic Study of the Child*, vol. 38 (New Haven: Yale Univ. Press, 1983), 285–309.

xii   Not until the 1970s: Sporadic works appeared earlier, but the first major book to describe sibling influences on each other was *The Sibling* by Brian Sutton-Smith and B. G. Rosenberg (New York: Holt, Rinehart and Winston, 1970). Pioneering books of the early 1980s include Stephen P. Bank and Michael D. Kahn, *The Sibling Bond* (New York: Basic Books, 1982); Judy Dunn and Carol Kendrick, *Siblings: Love, Envy, and Understanding* (Cambridge, Mass.: Harvard Univ. Press, 1982); and Michael E. Lamb and Brian Sutton-Smith, eds., *Sibling Relationships: Their Nature and Significance Across the Lifespan* (Hillsdale, N.J.: Lawrence Erlbaum, 1982). Also, in 1983, *The Psychoanalytic Study of the Child* devoted an entire section to "The Sibling Experience."

xiv   developing the questionnaire: Questions constructed by other researchers were revised and included in two parts of the questionnaire: In section D, a few of the measures of closeness were based on a questionnaire by Dale A. Blythe, John P. Hill, and Karen S. Thiel, in "Early Adolescents' Significant Others: Grade and Gender Differences in Perceived Relationships with Familial and Nonfamilial Adults and Young People," *Journal of Youth*

393

and Adolescence 11, no. 6 (1982): 425–50. In section E, the nine choices for coping with conflict were based on the Ways of Coping Questionnaire by Susan Folkman and Richard R. Lazarus, published in "If It Changes It Must Be a Process: A Study of Emotion and Coping During Three Stages of a College Exam," *Journal of Personality and Social Psychology* 48 (1985): 150–70.

xv   all social classes: Social class was measured according to the standardized system of August B. Hollingshead and Fritz C. Redlich, published in *Social Class and Mental Illness* (New York: John Wiley, 1958).

PROLOGUE

7   more time alone together: See Dunn, *Sisters and Brothers*, Introduction.

7   Studies of empathy: Dunn and Kendrick studied the effects of the birth of a sibling on forty firstborn children in Cambridge, England. They discuss the older children's empathy in *Siblings*, chap. 6.

8   "we" and not just "I": For a discussion of "we-ness," see John A. Lindon, "A Psychoanalytic View of the Family: A Study of Family Member Interactions," *The Psychoanalytic Forum* 13 (1969): 38–41.

10   siblinglike fashion: Christianity and Judaism have also been portrayed as rivalrous siblings. See Yosef Hayim Yerushalmi, *Freud's Moses* (New Haven: Yale Univ. Press, 1991), 92–93.

10   "the pain of jealousy": Luise Eichenbaum and Susie Orbach, *Between Women: Love, Envy, and Competition in Women's Friendships* (New York: Penguin Books, 1989), 15.

10   "there was a relief": Ibid., 16.

11   Two psychologists: Helgola G. Ross and Joel I. Milgram, "Important Variables in Adult Sibling Relationships: A Qualitative Study," in Lamb and Sutton-Smith, *Sibling Relationships*, 225–49.

12   ". . . equivalent to admitting maladjustment": Ibid., 236.

12   Peter B. Neubauer: Interview with author, 6 May 1989.

CHAPTER ONE

21   Thomas J. Bouchard, Jr.: Since 1979 Bouchard has headed the Minnesota Center for Twin and Adoption Research. For an over-

view of the Minnesota studies and others, see Constance Holden, "The Genetics of Personality," *Science* 237 (7 Aug. 1987): 598–601.

21   *different from* rather than *similar to:* The seminal article on environmentally caused differences among siblings is Robert Plomin and Denise Daniels, "Why Are Children in the Same Family So Different from One Another?" *Behavioral and Brain Sciences* 10 (1987): 1–60.

21   than any two people . . . : Sandra Scarr and Susan Grajek, "Similarities and Differences Among Siblings," in Lamb and Sutton-Smith, *Sibling Relationships*, 361. Sandra Scarr writes, "Upper middle-class brothers who attend the same school and whose parents . . . use similar child-rearing practices on them are little more similar in personality measures than they are to working class or farm boys, whose lives are totally different."

22   study of shyness: Jerome Kagan, J. Steven Reznick, and Nancy Snidman, "Biological Bases of Childhood Shyness," *Science* 240 (8 Apr. 1988): 167–71.

23   "nonshared environment": Plomin and Daniels, "Why Are Children in the Same Family So Different?", 4.

28   "different as day . . .": Frances Fuchs Schachter and Richard K. Stone, "Comparing and Contrasting Siblings: Defining the Self," in *Practical Concerns About Siblings: Bridging the Research-Practice Gap*, ed. Frances Fuchs Schachter and Richard K. Stone (New York: Haworth Press, 1987), 55–75.

29   "Cain complex": Ibid., 60.

30   "de-identification": Ibid., 56.

33   each role gets preempted: James H. S. Bossard and Eleanor Stoker Boll, *The Large Family System: An Original Study in the Sociology of Family Behavior* (Philadelphia: Univ. of Pennsylvania Press, 1956; Westport, Conn.: Greenwood Press, 1975). On roles, see pp. 210–21.

33   a newspaper article reports: "Brothers Wield Power in Starkly Different Worlds," *The New York Times*, 11 Oct. 1987.

34   even before birth: For how parents project their inner views onto their children, see James L. Framo, *Explorations in Marital and Family Therapy* (New York: Springer, 1982), 28–29.

37   "We just sorta' echo . . .": Sam Shepard, *True West*, act 2, sc. 7, in *Sam Shepard: Seven Plays* (New York: Bantam Books, 1981), 39.

CHAPTER TWO

42   as early as the 1870s: Sir Francis Galton noted the dispropor-
tionate number of firstborns and onlies among prominent English scientists in *English Men of Science: Their Nature and
Nurture* (London: Macmillan, 1874). Almost a century later, Ir-
ving Harris compared the ordinal positions of famous men in
history in *The Promised Seed: A Comparative Study of First
and Later Sons* (Glencoe, Ill.: Free Press, 1964), which became
the basis for many other studies.

42   firstborn personality: See Lucille K. Forer with Henry Still, *The
Birth Order Factor* (New York: David McKay, 1976), and Kevin
Leman, *The Birth Order Book: Why You Are the Way You Are*
(Old Tappan, N.J.: Fleming H. Revell, 1985).

43   firstborns compared to only children: R. B. Zajonc and Gregory
B. Markus, "Birth Order and Intellectual Development," *Psychological Review* 82, no. 1 (1975): 74–98.

43   Two Swiss researchers: Cécile Ernst and Jules Angst, *Birth Order: Its Influence on Personality* (Berlin: Springer-Verlag, 1983).

43   "power interactions": Ibid., 240.

44   "my golden Sigi": Biographical information from Ernest Jones,
The Life and Work of Sigmund Freud, vol. 1 (New York: Basic
Books, 1953).

44   "ill wishes . . .": Letter to Wilhelm Fliess, 3 Oct. 1897, in *The
Complete Letters of Sigmund Freud to Wilhelm Fliess 1887–
1904*, translated and edited by Jeffrey Moussaieff Masson (Cambridge, Mass.: Harvard Univ. Press, Belknap Press, 1985), 268.

44   "A small child . . .": Sigmund Freud, *Introductory Lectures on
Psychoanalysis*, 1916–17, translated and edited by James
Strachey (New York: W. W. Norton, 1966; Liveright, 1977), 204.

45   small animals or vermin: Ibid., 153.

45   "if one comes upon a wish . . .": Ibid., 205.

45   "family complex": Ibid., 333–35.

45   "substitute for the baby . . .": Ibid., 334.

46   comfort baby sibs: Judy Dunn and Carol Kendrick, "The Speech
of Two- and Three-Year-Olds to Infant Siblings: 'Baby Talk' and
the Context of Communication," *Journal of Child Language* 9
(1982): 579–95.

46   elder sisters reward youngers: Brenda K. Bryant, "Sibling Relationships in Middle Childhood," in Lamb and Sutton-Smith, *Sibling Relationships*, 87–121.

46   Louise J. Kaplan: Interview with author, 10 Oct. 1988.

47   "How does your brother . . .": Sutton-Smith and Rosenberg, *The Sibling*, 39–68.

49   younger siblings become more sexually active: Joseph Lee Rodgers and David C. Rowe, "Influence of Siblings on Adolescent Sexual Behavior," *Developmental Psychology* 24, no. 5 (1988): 722–28.

49   older children sacrifice themselves: Bossard and Boll, *The Large Family System*, 158–61.

49   most often confided: Sander Morris Latts, "The Four-Child Equisexed Intact Family: Its Organization and Interactional Patterns" (Ph.D. diss., Univ. of Minnesota, 1966).

49   younger sibs more affected: See Sutton-Smith and Rosenberg, *The Sibling*, 63.

50   Peter B. Neubauer: Interview with author, 6 May 1989.

52   "the need to be responsible . . .": Philip Roth, *The Counterlife* (New York: Farrar Straus Giroux, 1986), 80.

CHAPTER THREE

64   Peter B. Neubauer: Interview with author, 6 May 1989.

64   analysis of Grimm's: Sutton-Smith and Rosenberg, *The Sibling*, 3.

64   feelings of younger children: Bruno Bettelheim, *The Uses of Enchantment: The Meaning and Importance of Fairy Tales* (New York: Random House, Vintage Books, 1977).

64   labels laterborn children: See Ernst and Angst, *Birth Order*, 85, for a table comparing traits ascribed to firstborns and laterborns.

65   Frank J. Sulloway: He presented his findings at a meeting of the American Association for the Advancement of Science in Feb. 1990. See Daniel Goleman, "The Link Between Birth Order and Innovation," *The New York Times*, 8 May 1990, Science section.

66   "Do you think it gives me . . .": Quoted in Paul Roazen, *Freud and His Followers* (New York: New York Univ. Press, reprint, 1984), 179.

66   "Sooner or later . . .": Alfred Adler, *Understanding Human Nature*, 1927, translated by W. Béran Wolfe (New York: Fawcett Premier Books, 1957), 65.

66   "but . . . usually the smallest . . .": Ibid., 123.

66 "what a child *feels* . . .": Ibid., 124.

67 criticisms and disparagements: Judy Dunn and Robert Plomin, *Separate Lives: Why Siblings Are So Different* (New York: Basic Books, 1990). "The results of studies of the sibling relationship," they write, "suggest that children (especially those that are laterborn) who receive more negative treatment from their siblings than they mete out suffer from poor self-esteem . . ." (169).

67 "It is terrible . . ." Stanislaus Joyce, *My Brother's Keeper*, ed. Richard Ellmann (London: Faber and Faber, 1958; Faber Paperback, 1982), 17.

68 Babies placed in playrooms: This according to a study by psychologist Robert B. Stewart, noted in "Siblings' Motherly Concern," *Psychology Today*, March 1984, 8. Observations of very young children in residential nurseries comforting their siblings are described by John Bowlby, *Attachment and Loss*, vol. 2, *Separation Anxiety and Anger* (New York: Basic Books, 1973), 16.

68 Jennifer: Martin Leichtman, "The Influence of an Older Sibling on the Separation-Individuation Process," *Psychoanalytic Study of the Child* 40 (1985): 111–61.

68 system stays balanced: Sutton-Smith and Rosenberg, *The Sibling*, 54–55.

73 Children in the middle: For an engaging discussion of middle children, see Trish Hall, "As Middle Children Become Rarer, Society May Miss Their Influence," *The Wall Street Journal*, 21 Aug. 1986.

74 other children coveted the middle: See Bossard and Boll, *Large Family System*, 209.

74 Levy experiments: David Levy, *Studies in Sibling Rivalry* (New York: American Orthopsychiatric Association, 1937), 205–14.

74 "When the sister sees . . .": Ibid., 209.

77 "the sacrificed child": Dennis E. McGuire and Patrick Tolan, "Clinical Interventions with Large Family Systems: Balancing Interests Through Siblings," in *Siblings in Therapy*, ed. Michael D. Kahn and Karen Gail Lewis (New York: W. W. Norton, 1988), 129.

78 bitter literary wars: The competition between Thomas and Heinrich is described in Nigel Hamilton, "A Case of Literary Fratricide: The *Brüderzwist* Between Heinrich and Thomas Mann," in *Blood Brothers: Siblings as Writers*, ed. Norman Kiell (New York: International Universities Press, 1983), 49–72.

78   "What? How? . . .": Ibid., 70.

79   Therapists see people: See Karen Gail Lewis, "Symptoms as Sibling Messages," in Kahn and Lewis, *Siblings in Therapy*, 264.

CHAPTER FOUR

80   "I can see . . .": Judith Rossner, *His Little Women* (New York: Summit Books, 1990), 240.

80   "I just wish . . .": Louisa May Alcott, *Little Women* (New York: Bantam Books, 1983), 190.

80   "She'll go and fall . . .": Ibid., 191.

81   two identical faces: The image is presented by Aristophanes in Plato, *The Symposium*, translated by Walter Hamilton (New York: Penguin Books, 1986), 59–65.

81   Here is Doug: Doug and Mike are the real names of the Starn twins, photographers who work together. Quotes are from "Doug and Mike, Mike and Doug," produced and directed by filmmaker Cindy Kleine, shown on public television's "Point of View" series, 19 Sept. 1989.

82   "Most mothers . . .": Jane Smiley, "Ordinary Love," in *Ordinary Love and Good Will* (New York: Alfred A. Knopf, 1989; Ballantine Books, 1991), 16.

82   "I always wanted . . .": "Doug and Mike, Mike and Doug."

82   two halves of a whole: For twins' self-views, see Jules Glenn, "Twins in the Theater: A Study of Plays by Peter and Anthony Shaffer," in Kiell, *Blood Brothers*, 280–81.

84   "looking into a mirror": Birgitta Ralston, in the catalogue to her photography show "Sisters," quoted in *The Radcliffe Quarterly* (Mar. 1990), 10.

85   "twinning": Moisy Shopper, "Twinning Reaction in Non-Twin Siblings," *Journal of the American Academy of Child Psychiatry* 13, no. 2 (1974): 391–18.

85   "split" their parents: Frances Fuchs Schachter, "Sibling Deidentification and Split-Parent Identification: A Family Tetrad," in Lamb and Sutton-Smith, *Sibling Relationships*, 123–51.

86   homosexuality as psychological: Freud's views are quoted in Colonna and Newman, "Psychoanalytic Literature," 288.

86   experts have suggested: See Walter Toman, *Family Constellation: Its Effects on Personality and Social Behavior* (New York: Springer, 1976), chap. 6.

87 "Kiss her . . .": In Jane Dunn, *A Very Close Conspiracy: Vanessa Bell and Virginia Woolf* (Boston: Little, Brown, 1990), 115.

94 "the isolate": Bossard and Boll, *The Large Family System*, 215.

98 Chodorow's theory: Nancy J. Chodorow, *The Reproduction of Mothering: Psychoanalysis and the Sociology of Gender* (Berkeley: Univ. of California Press, 1978).

99 "When a man has a brother . . .": John Bowers, "Brotherly Strife," *The New York Times Magazine*, 12 Aug. 1984, About Men.

99 my study and others: One of the earliest to show closeness of sisters was Bert N. Adams, *Kinship in an Urban Setting* (Chicago: Markham, 1968).

99 does not eliminate aggressiveness: This finding corresponds to themes of conflict found more often in women's fantasies about sisters than in men's about brothers in a projective test given by Victoria H. Bedford and described in "A Comparison of Thematic Apperceptions of Sibling Affiliation, Conflict, and Separation at Two Periods of Adulthood," *International Journal of Aging and Human Development* 28, no. 1 (1989): 53–66.

100 "No one can make me madder": Bowers, "Brotherly Strife."

100 study of college students: Michael Eben Shulman, "On Being a Brother: Constructions of the Sibling Experience" (Ph.D. diss., Univ. of Michigan, 1987), 132–37.

101 "I know how he saw me . . .": Ibid., 135.

CHAPTER FIVE

105 "Give me sons . . .": Gen. 30:1. This is often translated as "Give me children . . . ," but the biblical listings of the birth of sons and not daughters and the overall emphasis on sons make it most likely that Rachel was crying for sons.

105 In most cultures: For discussions of various cultures, see Monica McGoldrick, John K. Pearce, and Joseph Giordano, eds., *Ethnicity and Family Therapy* (New York: Guilford Press, 1982).

105 they often abort pregnancies: Nicholas D. Kristof, "Stark Data on Women: 100 Million Are Missing," *The New York Times*, 5 Nov. 1991, Science section.

106 Clarence Thomas: Karen Tumulty, "Sister of High Court Nominee Traveled Different Road," *Los Angeles Times*, 5 July 1991, sec. A.

106   public family battle: Sallie Bingham, *Passion and Prejudice: A Family Memoir* (New York: Alfred A. Knopf, 1989).

106   a child of each sex: Jay D. Teachman and Paul Schollaert, "Gender of Children and Birth Timing," *Demography* 26, no. 3 (Aug. 1989): 411–23. Findings also show that parents with two boys or two girls are quicker to have a third child than are those with one of each sex.

106   girls' self-esteem: Carol Gilligan, Nona P. Lyons, and Trudy J. Hanmer, eds., *Making Connections: The Relational Worlds of Adolescent Girls at Emma Willard School* (Cambridge, Mass.: Harvard Univ. Press, 1990). Gilligan studied a small group of girls at a private school. A much broader survey of three thousand children conducted by the American Association of University Women was reported by Suzanne Daley, "Little Girls Lose Their Self-Esteem . . . ," *The New York Times*, 9 Jan. 1991, sec. B.

108   "the pull of sexual attraction": Freud, *Introductory Lectures*, 333.

109   penis envy: Sigmund Freud, "Some Psychical Consequences of the Anatomical Distinction Between the Sexes," 1925, in *The Standard Edition of the Complete Psychological Works of Sigmund Freud*, ed. James Strachey (London: Hogarth Press and the Institute of Psycho-Analysis, 1961), vol. 19, 243–58. Louise J. Kaplan elaborates on later views of penis envy, particularly those of Karen Horney, in *Female Perversions: The Temptations of Emma Bovary* (New York: Doubleday, 1991), 78–105, 186–93.

110   Louise J. Kaplan: Interview with author, 28 Oct. 1988.

112   Alexander Levay: Interview with author, 10 July 1989.

113   "What law, you ask . . ." Sophocles, *Antigone*, in *The Complete Plays of Sophocles*, translated by Sir Richard Claverhouse Jebb (New York: Bantam Books, Bantam Classics, 1982), 137. It should be remembered, however, that Socrates was portraying sisterly devotion from a male viewpoint.

113   Persian king Darius: The story, told by Herodotus, is cited in S. D. Goitein, *A Mediterranean Society*, vol. 3. (Berkeley: Univ. of California Press, 1978).

113   "To be happy . . .": Henri Troyat, *Chekhov*, translated by Michael Henry Heim (New York: Dutton, 1955), 155.

113   two of Jacob's sons: Simeon and Levi in Genesis 34.

114   gentler form of protection: In Thomas S. Weisner, "Sibling Interdependence and Child Caretaking: A Cultural View," in Lamb and Sutton-Smith, *Sibling Relationships*, 321.

121   college-aged brothers: Shulman, *Being a Brother*, 137–40.

121   "Troublesome": Carol Elizabeth Holden, "On Being a Sister: Constructions of the Sibling Experience" (Ph.D. diss., Univ. of Michigan, 1986), 152. Findings are summarized on pp. 148–52.

124   reports Louise J. Kaplan: Interview with author, 28 Oct. 1988.

124   more "masculine" interests: Sutton-Smith and Rosenberg take that position in *The Sibling*, 22–23.

124   emphasize feminine interests: This follows the de-identification theory of Schachter and Stone.

124   A boy with two older sisters: Brian Sutton-Smith, "Birth Order and Sibling Status Effects," in Lamb and Sutton-Smith, *Sibling Relationships*, 160.

CHAPTER SIX

129   divorce began to outstrip death: Frank F. Furstenberg, Jr., and Graham B. Spanier, *Recycling the Family: Remarriage After Divorce* (Newbury Park, Calif.: Sage Publications, 1987), 39.

129   5.3 million stepfamilies: Unpublished figures according to the Dept. of Commerce, U.S. Bureau of the Census. Reported by Arthur J. Norton and Louisa F. Miller in "Marriage, Divorce, and Remarriage in the 1990s," presented at American Public Health Association Meetings, Nov. 1991.

129   Stepfamily Association: Headquarters are at #212 Lincoln Center, 215 South Centennial Mall, Lincoln, NE 68508.

129   children as source of conflict: Marilyn Ihinger-Tallman, "Sibling and Stepsibling Bonding in Stepfamilies," in *Remarriage and Stepparenting: Current Research and Theory*, ed. Kay Pasley and Marilyn Ihinger-Tallman (New York: Guilford Press, 1987), 178.

130   compressed . . . and blurred together: Emily B. Visher and John S. Visher, *Stepfamilies: Myths and Realities* (Secaucus, N.J.: Citadel Press, 1979). See p. 215.

136   "Go to the Science Fair . . .": Delia Ephron, *Funny Sauce* (New York: Viking, 1986), 118.

137   Judith Wallerstein: The sense of loss and reactions at different ages are based on Judith S. Wallerstein and Sandra Blakeslee, *Second Chances: Men, Women and Children a Decade After Divorce* (New York: Ticknor and Fields, 1989).

137   about 90 percent of children: Figure given by E. Mavis Hetherington, Margaret Stanley-Hagan, and Edward R. Anderson in

"Marital Transitions: A Child's Perspective," *American Psychologist* 44, no. 2 (Feb. 1989): 305.

138   E. Mavis Hetherington: Her findings are based on a six-year study of divorced parents and their children, and described in E. Mavis Hetherington, "Coping with Family Transitions: Winners, Losers, and Survivors," *Child Development* 60 (1989): 1–14.

138   single-parent homes: Ibid., 5.

139   boy-girl differences: Ibid., 6–7, and Hetherington, Stanley-Hagan, and Anderson, "Marital Transitions," 305–6.

140   75 percent of women . . . : Hetherington, "Coping," 1.

140   more difficulty adjusting to remarriage: Hetherington, Stanley-Hagan, and Anderson, "Marital Transitions," 303.

142   Instant family life: For this and other difficulties, see Elinor B. Rosenberg and Fady Hajal, "Stepsibling Relationships in Remarried Families," *Social Casework: The Journal of Contemporary Social Work* 66 (May 1985): 287–92.

142   women's living standards: Lenore Weitzman of Harvard University found that the standard of living of women with minor children declined by 73 percent after divorce, whereas their husband's rose by 42 percent. See Lenore J. Weitzman, *The Divorce Revolution: The Unexpected Social and Economic Consequences for Women and Children in America* (New York: Free Press, 1985). Others have placed the decline lower, but with women still disadvantaged.

143   ambiguity of the relationship: See Andrew Cherlin, "Remarriage as an Incomplete Institution," *American Journal of Sociology* 86 (1980): 636–40.

144   Incest between stepfathers and stepdaughters: Theories about its causes are based on David Finkelhor, *Sexually Victimized Children* (New York: Free Press, 1979), 88–89.

144   children between nine and fifteen: Hetherington, "Coping," 7.

145   divorce rate among the remarried: Furstenberg and Spanier suggest that it is about 5 percent higher than among the first-married in *Recycling the Family*, 45.

148   a new baby is a boon: Lucille Duberman, *The Reconstituted Family: A Study of Remarried Couples and Their Children* (Chicago: Nelson-Hall, 1975).

150   adopting a stepchild: For pros and cons, see Visher and Visher, *Stepfamilies*, 18–22.

151   Delaware Family Study: Leslie M. Stein and Janet L. Hoopes, *Identity Formation in the Adopted Adolescent: The Delaware*

Family Study (New York: Child Welfare League of America, 1985).

152   nonadopted children with adopted siblings: Two case studies are in Theodore J. Jacobs, "On Having an Adopted Sibling: Some Psychoanalytic Observations," *International Review of Psycho-Analysis* 15 (1988): 25–35.

CHAPTER SEVEN

160   "goodness of fit": Stella Chess and Alexander Thomas, *Know Your Child: An Authoritative Guide for Today's Parents* (New York: Basic Books, 1987). See chaps. 3–4.

161   until their children reach adolescence: Terri Apter, *Altered Loves: Mothers and Daughter During Adolescence* (New York: St. Martin's Press, 1990).

161   favoritism in adult life: Ross and Milgram, "Adult Sibling Relationships," in Lamb and Sutton-Smith, *Sibling Relationships*, 234.

161   daughters rather than sons: Joan Aldous, Elisabeth Klaus, and David M. Klein, "The Understanding Heart: Aging Parents and Their Favorite Children," *Child Development* 56 (1985): 303–16.

161   children monitor parents: See Dunn and Plomin, *Separate Lives*, chap. 4.

172   Joseph as best loved: The Joseph story is in Genesis 37–50.

172   ". . . the indisputable favorite . . .": Jones, *Life and Work*, vol. 1, 5.

172   "Almost every discouragement . . .": Alfred Adler, *What Life Should Mean to You*, ed. Alan Porter (Boston: Little, Brown, 1931), 142, 143.

174   Cain murders Abel: Genesis 4:8.

175   "Survivor guilt": Interview with Peter B. Neubauer, 6 May 1989.

CHAPTER EIGHT

178   biblical scapegoat: Lev. 16:8–10.

181   "My mother and I watched . . .": Norman Maclean, "A River Runs Through It," in *A River Runs Through It and Other Stories* (Chicago: Univ. of Chicago Press, 1976), 7.

181   "my Denny, poor Betty . . .": Monica McGoldrick, "Irish Families," in McGoldrick, Pearce, and Giordano, *Ethnicity and Family Therapy*, 323.

181 families as systems: For overviews of family systems theory and the place of scapegoating in it, see Philip J. Guerin, Jr., ed., *Family Therapy: Theory and Practice* (New York: Gardner Press, 1976).

183 a woman who sought counseling: From an interview with Dr. Herman Roiphe.

184 In the family systems framework: On children collaborating in their own scapegoating, see James L. Framo, *Explorations in Marital and Family Therapy: Selected Papers* (New York: Springer, 1982), 28–35.

184 differences school-age children perceive: Dunn and Plomin, *Separate Lives*, chap. 4.

186 "angels" versus "devils": Schachter and Stone, "Comparing and Contrasting Siblings," 64–67.

196 "sibling subsystem": Salvador Minuchin, *Families and Family Therapy* (Cambridge, Mass.: Harvard Univ. Press, 1974), 59.

198 As an illness, anorexia: Ibid., chap. 12.

CHAPTER NINE

199 "I know you've got a secret . . .": Shepard, *Buried Child*, act 2, in *Seven Plays*, 122.

199 "We had enough boys . . .": Ibid., 123.

199 "No! Don't listen . . .": Ibid., 122.

199 "I'm not listening . . .": Ibid., 123.

201 roles of children of alcoholics: Commonly used labels and descriptions are given in Charles Deutsch, *Broken Bottles Broken Dreams: Understanding and Helping the Children of Alcoholics* (New York: Teachers College Press, 1982).

202 unchangeableness of roles: Deutsch writes, "Given over to an exaggerated and rigid identification of self with role, so protected by it and at least nominally rewarded for it, children have great difficulty operating outside it." *Broken Bottles*, 57.

203 rigid disciplining: Rosalie C. Jesse, "Children of Alcoholics: Their Sibling World," in Kahn and Lewis, *Siblings in Therapy*, 235. The descriptions that follow of sons and daughters of alcoholics are based on Jesse and on discussions with Dr. Samuel C. Klagsbrun.

205 sexual abuse by fathers: A strong connection between alcoholism and incest is made by Karin C. Meiselman in *Incest: A Psy-*

chological Study of Causes and Effects with Treatment Recom-mendations (San Francisco: Jossey-Bass, 1978), 93–94.

216   "I had already heard more . . .": Maclean, "A River," 23.

216   "I knew there were others . . .": Ibid., 28–29.

217   study of adult heroin addicts: James F. Maddux and David P. Desmond, "Heroin Addicts and Nonaddicted Brothers," *American Journal of Drug and Alcohol Abuse* 10, no. 2 (1984): 237–48.

217   search for drug-addicted brother: Jonathan Dahl, "Missing in America," *The Wall Street Journal*, 18 Mar. 1991, sec. A.

218   five times more prevalent: Meiselman cites this figure from other studies, although she says, "The question of whether brother-sister incest is more common than father-daughter remains unresolved." *Incest*, 77.

218   a 1978 survey: David Finkelhor, "Sex Among Siblings: A Survey on Prevalence, Variety, and Effects," *Archives of Sexual Behavior* 9, no. 3 (1980): 171–94.

219   sibling incest is brushed off: Psychoanalysts in particular often do not regard sibling incest as necessarily traumatic. Analyst Henri Parens, for example, writes that both fantasies and "actual enactments" of sibling incest can be "adaptive" because they move patients away from incestuous fantasies about parents and "pave the way to their normal attachment to peers." In "Siblings in Early Childhood: Some Direct Observational Findings," *Psychoanalytic Quarterly* 8, no. 1 (1988): 38.

219   rarely is incest mutual: Bank and Kahn, *The Sibling Bond*, 171.

219   women were junior partners: Finkelhor, "Sex Among Siblings," 178.

220   even nonhuman primates: See Stephen J. Suomi, "Sibling Relationships in Nonhuman Primates," in Lamb and Sutton-Smith, *Sibling Relationships*, 329–56. In most species, when opposite-sex siblings enter adolescence they have nothing more to do with each other, whereas same-sex siblings often remain in close contact throughout life.

220   children on kibbutzim: Joseph Shepher, "Mate Selection Among Second Generation Kibbutz Adolescents and Adults: Incest Avoidance and Negative Imprinting," *Archives of Sexual Behavior* 1, no. 4 (1971): 293–307.

220   why do we have such a strong taboo?: Freud's Oedipal theory posits powerful incestuous attractions among family members. If such attraction did not exist, he wrote, "it would not be clear why such severe prohibitions were called for . . . ," *Introductory Lectures*, 210. In *Totem and Taboo* (1913), he portrayed a

time at the dawn of human society when a primal horde of men murdered their father in order to have sexual relations with their mother and sisters, but then, torn with guilt, established taboos against such relations.

220   the pharaohs of ancient Egypt: Ray H. Bixler, "Sibling Incest in the Royal Families of Egypt, Peru, and Hawaii," *Journal of Sex Research* 18, no. 3 (Aug., 1982): 264–81.

220   Cleopatra married and murdered: Ibid., 272.

220   the romantic poets: For an analysis of them, see Luciano P. R. Santiago, *The Children of Oedipus: Brother-Sister Incest in Psychiatry, Literature, History and Mythology* (Roslyn Heights, N.Y.: Libra, 1973). See also James B. Twitchell, *Forbidden Partners: The Incest Taboo in Modern Culture* (New York: Columbia Univ. Press, 1987).

221   "I have never ceased . . .": Quoted in Margot Strickland, *The Byron Women* (New York: St. Martin's Press, 1974), 27.

221   Byron's home: Twitchell, *Forbidden Partners*, 4–7.

221   parental neglect and abandonment: Bank and Kahn discuss these as major causes of sibling incest, in *The Sibling Bond*, 176–77.

221   Alexander Levay: Interview with author, 10 July 1989.

222   Holly Smith study: Holly Smith with Edie Israel, "Sibling Incest: A Study of the Dynamics of Twenty-five Cases," in *Child Abuse and Neglect* 11 (1987): 101–8.

226   women report incidents: Meiselman outlines reasons why women report incest more often than men, in *Incest*, 71–72.

226   the greater the age difference: Finkelhor, "Sex Among Siblings," 178.

226   consequences of incest: Meiselman, *Incest*, 274–79.

CHAPTER TEN

234   "Actually it hardly matters . . .": Helen Featherstone, *A Difference in the Family: Life with a Disabled Child* (New York: Basic Books, 1980), 3–4.

235   The more alike a child: Well children's identification with the medically ill is discussed in David W. Adams and Eleanor Deveau, "When a Brother or Sister Is Dying of Cancer: The Vulnerability of the Adolescent Sibling," *Death Studies* 11 (1987): 279–95.

235   "Whenever I see something . . .": Frances Kaplan Grossman, *Brothers and Sisters of Retarded Children* (Syracuse, N.Y.: Syracuse Univ. Press, 1972), 111.

237 burden of responsibilities: Ibid., 178-80.

237 siblings had been institutionalized: Ibid., 165-73. Grossman takes a strong position against institutionalizing if the family can get help in caring for the child at home. Normal siblings, she says, "often cope more adaptively . . . and experience less guilt and discomfort" when a retarded sib is kept at home. 173.

238 retarded sibs who are older: Ibid., 110.

239 fantasy of the perfect child: Emmett Wilson, Jr., "Stendhal as a Replacement Child: The Theme of the Dead Child in Stendhal's Writings," *Psychoanalytic Inquiry* 8, no. 1 (1988): 128.

239 "the ghost . . .": Ibid., 129. Wilson attributes the phrase to J. H. Kennell and M. Klaus, "Helping Parents After the Birth of a Baby with a Malformation," in *Frontiers of Infant Psychiatry*, vol. 2, ed. J. Call, E. Galenson, and R. Tyson (New York: Basic Books, 1984), 397-403.

240 "It's be quiet . . .": Sue Miller, *Family Pictures* (New York: Harper and Row, 1990), 366.

240 marital difficulties: See Francine Klagsbrun, *Married People: Staying Together in the Age of Divorce* (New York: Bantam Books, 1985), chap. 9.

240 children become fearful and anxious: Especially if a sib is critically ill with cancer or another terminal illness. See Helen Rosen, *Unspoken Grief: Coping with Childhood Sibling Loss* (Lexington, Mass.: D.C. Heath, 1986), 52-53.

240 little information: Grossman, *Brothers and Sisters*, 118-24.

240 "I once thought . . .": Margaret Moorman, "A Sister's Need," *The New York Times Magazine*, 11 Sept. 1988, 44.

241 Siblings and Adult Children Network: Located at 2101 Wilson Blvd., Suite 302, Arlington, VA 22201.

241 Other organizations: Sibling Information Network, a clearinghouse for sibling support groups, is located at 991 Main Street, Suite 3A, East Hartford, CT 06108. Siblings for Significant Change, an advocacy group, is at 105 East 22nd Street, Room 710, New York, NY 10010.

242 more tolerant: Grossman, *Brothers and Sisters*, 116.

242 helping professions: Bernard Farber and William C. Jenne, "Interaction with Retarded Siblings and the Life Goals of Children," *Marriage and Family Living* 25 (Feb. 1963): 96-98. Farber, a sociologist, pioneered in studying siblings of the retarded.

245 replacement child: Wilson, "Stendhal as a Replacement Child," 124–29.

245 Anna O.: Josef Breuer's treatment of Anna O. greatly influenced Freud's own thinking.

245 study of the case: George H. Pollock, "Bertha Pappenheim's Pathological Mourning: Possible Effects of Childhood Sibling Loss," *Journal of the American Psychoanalytic Association* 20 (1972): 476–93.

247 "the germ of self-reproaches . . .": Freud, letter to Fliess, 3 Oct. 1897, in Masson, *Letters to Fliess*, 268.

247 "The wrong one died": Irvin D. Yalom, "The Wrong One Died," in *Love's Executioner and Other Tales of Psychotherapy* (New York: Basic Books, 1989), 118–43.

248 Antoine de Saint-Exupéry: Francine Klagsbrun, *Too Young to Die: Youth and Suicide* (Boston: Houghton Mifflin, 1976; rev. ed. Pocket Books, 1985), 75–77.

248 teenagers may become withdrawn: See David Balk, "Adolescents' Grief Reactions and Self-Concept Perceptions Following Sibling Death: A Study of Thirty-three Teenagers," *Journal of Youth and Adolescence* 12, no. 2 (1983).

249 "Be kind to your parents . . .": Daniel B. Gordon, "Wake," in *Death and the College Student: A Collection of Brief Essays on Death and Suicide by Harvard Youth*, ed. Edwin S. Shneidman (New York: Behavioral Publications, 1972), 82, 90.

251 "When a sibling dies . . .": Barbara Lazear Ascher, "A Brother's Death," *The New York Times Magazine* 19 Nov. 1989, "Hers."

CHAPTER ELEVEN

256 more among themselves: Richard B. Felson, "Aggression and Violence Between Siblings," *Social Psychology Quarterly* 46, no. 4 (1983): 271–85.

257 only children: Toni Falbo, "Only Children in America," in Lamb and Sutton-Smith, *Sibling Relationships*, 296. Falbo writes that only children "acquire a more trusting style of interaction," whereas children with siblings "expect competition from others."

257 fights between siblings to fights between friends: Marcela Raffaelli, "Sibling Conflict in Early Adolescence," (Ph.D. diss., Univ. of Chicago, 1990).

258 parental intervention: Richard B. Felson and Natalie Russo take this position in "Parental Punishment and Sibling Aggression," *Social Psychology Quarterly* 51, no. 1 (1988): 11–18. Chess and Thomas advise parents to "tell their children . . . to settle their own quarrels," *Know Your Child*, 317.

261   highly intense children: Chess and Thomas, *Know Your Child*, 32, 316.

262   one child rejected another: Dunn and Kendrick, *Siblings*, chap. 8.

264   "It is not the practice . . ." Genesis 29:26.

265   second most difficult relationship: Evelyn Millis Duvall reached this conclusion in *In-Laws: Pro and Con* (New York: Association Press, 1954).

270   Daughters outnumber sons: "Mothers Bearing a Second Burden," *The New York Times*, 13 May 1991, sec. A.

270   A woman might spend seventeen years . . . : Steven K. Wisensale and Michael D. Allison, "An Analysis of 1987 State Family Leave Legislation: Implications for Caregivers of the Elderly," *Gerontologist* 28, no. 6 (Dec. 1988): 779–85.

270   those who had always been rivalrous: Ross and Milgram, "Adult Sibling Relationships," 242.

272   Koch family: The squabbling is over Koch industries, a multibillion-dollar oil company. See Robert Tomsho, "Blood Feud," *The Wall Street Journal*, 9 Aug. 1989, sec. A.

272   "Didn't I think I deserved it?": Philip Roth, *Patrimony: A True Story* (New York: Simon and Schuster, 1991), 105.

275   "emotional cutoff": Murray Bowen, *Family Therapy in Clinical Practice* (New York: Jason Aronson, 1978), 382–84.

CHAPTER TWELVE

284   Five types of relationships: Deborah T. Gold, "Sibling Relationships in Old Age: A Typology," *International Journal of Aging and Human Development* 28, no. 1 (1989): 37–51.

285   "enmeshment" versus "disengagement": Minuchin, *Families and Family Therapy*, 54.

287   people who cut themselves off: Bowen, *Family Therapy*, 383.

288   ethnicity is part of our identity: For the importance of ethnicity in defining identity, see Monica McGoldrick, "Ethnicity and Family Therapy: An Overview," in McGoldrick, Pearce, and Giordano, *Ethnicity and Family Therapy*, 3–28.

290   girls in Irish-American families: McGoldrick, "Irish Families," 321–25.

290   black extended families: William C. Hays and Charles H. Mindel, "Extended Kinship Relations in Black and White Families," *Journal of Marriage and the Family* (Feb. 1973): 51–57. See also Paulette Moore Hines and Nancy Boyd-Franklin, "Black Families," in McGoldrick, Pearce, and Giordano, *Ethnicity and Family Therapy*, 88–91.

290   "I felt as though . . .": Brent Staples, "A Brother's Murder," *The New York Times Magazine*, 30 Mar. 1986, About Men.

290   the dominant American culture: See David McGill and John K. Pearce, "British Families," in McGoldrick, Pearce, and Giordano, *Ethnicity and Family Therapy*, 457–79.

291   "Oh, what can you do . . .": John Cheever, "Goodbye, My Brother," in *The Stories of John Cheever* (New York: Alfred A. Knopf, 1978), 21.

291   Attachment theory: John Bowlby, founder of the theory, presents his ideas in the three-volume *Attachment and Loss* (New York: Basic Books, 1969–80). For an overview of the work of theorist Mary Salter Ainsworth, see Mary D. Salter Ainsworth, "Attachment: Retrospect and Prospect," in *The Place of Attachment in Human Behavior*, ed. Colin Murray Parkes and Joan Stevenson-Hinde (London: Tavistock, 1982), 3–30.

292   "good enough" mothers: Donald W. Winnicott, *The Maturational Process and the Facilitating Environment: Studies in the Theory of Emotional Development* (New York: International Universities Press, 1965).

292   preschool children with infant siblings: Michael E. Lamb, "The Development of Sibling Relationships in Infancy: A Short-term Longitudinal Study," *Child Development* 49 (1978): 1189–96.

292   when firstborn children showed affection: Dunn and Kendrick, *Siblings*, chap. 8; Judy Dunn, "Sibling Relationships in Early Childhood," *Child Development* 54 (1983): 787–811.

293   older siblings were happiest: Dunn and Kendrick, *Siblings*, chap. 8.

293   best age spacing: Typical of advocates of at least three years is Burton L. White, *The First Three Years of Life* (New York: Prentice Hall, revised, 1991). T. Berry Brazelton suggests at least two years in *What Every Baby Knows* (New York: Addison-Wesley, 1987).

293   research of Margaret Mahler: Her studies on separation and individuation in infancy have shaped the way we look at child development. See Margaret Mahler, Fred Pine, and Anni Bergman, *The Psychological Birth of the Human Infant* (New York: Basic Books, 1975).

294   less than two: Psychologist Jeannie Kidwell presented this position at the 1985 annual meeting of the American Association for the Advancement of Science. Daniel Goleman, "Spacing of Siblings Strongly Linked to Success in Life," *The New York Times*, 28 May 1985, Science section.

294   Ask schoolchildren: Wyndol Furman and Duane Buhrmester, "Children's Perceptions of the Qualities of Sibling Relationships," *Child Development* 56 (1985): 448–61.

296   the "cliques": Bossard and Boll also found that siblings paired off. *The Large Family System*, 190–93.

296   "in a different voice": Carol Gilligan, *In a Different Voice: Psychological Theory and Women's Development* (Cambridge, Mass.: Harvard Univ. Press, 1982).

296   elderly fare better: Victor Cicirelli, "Feelings of Attachment to Siblings and Well-being in Later Life," *Psychology and Aging* 4, no. 2 (1989): 211–16.

298   "Hansels and Gretels": Bank and Kahn, *The Sibling Bond*, chap. 5.

298   never competed: Eileen Simpson, *Orphans: Real and Imaginary* (New York: Weidenfeld and Nicolson, 1987), 150. Simpson compares her reactions to those of a group of children known as the Terezín orphans. Though not siblings, they spent the first three years of their life together in the concentration camp of Terezín after the Nazis murdered their parents. Even after their liberation, they remained totally devoted to each other and uninterested in pleasing adults.

299   "My brother's fear and pain . . .": Richard Rhodes, *A Hole in the World: An American Boyhood* (New York: Simon and Schuster, 1990), 253.

299   "I also had a self . . .": Simpson, *Orphans*, 98.

300   "It was the strongest love . . .": Susan Cheever, *Home Before Dark: A Biographical Memoir of John Cheever by His Daughter* (Boston: Houghton Mifflin, 1984), 8.

300   "ungainly": Ibid.

300   "psychologically incestuous": Quoted in Scott Donaldson, *John Cheever: A Biography* (New York: Random House, 1988), 249.

Donaldson is also the source for the biographical information here.

301   such examples among the nuns: Simpson, wondering what models the Terezín orphans had, concludes that the women who looked after them in the camp must have been fiercely protective in spite of their own enfeebled state.

304   For more than forty years: George E. Vaillant, *Adaptation to Life* (Boston: Little, Brown, 1977).

304   being close to one's siblings: George E. Vaillant and Caroline O. Vaillant, "Natural History of Male Psychological Health, XII: A 45-Year Study of Predictors of Successful Aging at Age 65," *American Journal of Psychiatry* 147, no. 1 (Jan. 1990): 31–37.

CHAPTER THIRTEEN

306   three groups: Described in Mary Main and Nancy Kaplan, "Security in Infancy, Childhood, and Adulthood: A Move to the Level of Representation," *Monographs of the Society for Research in Child Development* 50, nos. 1–2 (1985): 66–104.

311   "I did my best to suppress . . .": Philip Roth, *The Facts: A Novelist's Autobiography* (New York: Farrar, Straus and Giroux, 1988), 99.

311   "wear out their lives": John Cheever, "The Brothers," in *The Best Short Stories 1938*, ed. Edward J. O'Brien (Boston: Houghton Mifflin, 1938), 86–99.

312   "necessary loss": Judith Viorst, *Necessary Losses: The Loves, Illusions, Dependencies and Impossible Expectations that All of Us Have to Give Up in Order to Grow* (New York: Simon and Schuster, 1986).

313   people in long marriages: Klagsbrun, *Married People.*

313   among working-class families: Mirra Komarovsky, *Blue Collar Marriage* (New York: Random House, Vintage Books, 1967).

315   "In their death . . .": George Eliot, *The Mill on the Floss* (New York: Bantam Books, Bantam Classics, 1987), 472.

316   Divorce undoes: Sources indicating that siblings grow closer after a divorce are cited in Ann Goetting, "The Developmental Tasks of Siblingship over the Life Cycle," *Journal of Marriage and the Family* 48 (Nov. 1986): 709.

319   a projective test: Bedford, "A Comparison of Thematic Apperceptions," 53–66.

320   "To my brother . . .": Roth, *The Facts.*

321   of the rich and famous: Holly Hall, "Fame in the Family," *Psychology Today* (Apr. 1988): 63.

322   "emotional turmoil": Bedford, "A Comparison of Thematic Apperceptions," 63.

323   only 10 percent: Gold gives these percentages in "Siblings in Old Age: Something Special," *Canadian Journal on Aging* 6, no. 3 (1987): 205.

324   53 percent: Ibid., 203.

324   When asked why: Ibid., 204–9.

324   "symbolic representations": Victor G. Cicirelli, "Interpersonal Relationships Among Elderly Siblings," in Kahn and Lewis, *Siblings in Therapy*, 440.

325   only children did not fare as well: Vaillant, "Natural History of Male Psychological Health," 34.

325   the hierarchy of care: Cicirelli, "Interpersonal Relationships," 445.

325   Why the reluctance?: Gold, "Siblings in Old Age," 212.

CHAPTER FOURTEEN

330   "The nature and quality": Sigmund Freud, "Some Reflections on Schoolboy Psychology," 1914, in *Standard Edition*, vol. 13, 243.

331   "Until the end of my third year . . .": Sigmund Freud, "The Interpretation of Dreams," 1900, in *Standard Edition*, vol. 5, 424.

331   "intimate friend and hated enemy": Ibid., 483.

331   "revenants . . .": Ibid., 485.

331   "how we all invent . . ." Janet Malcolm, *Psychoanalysis: The Impossible Profession* (New York: Alfred A. Knopf, 1981), 6.

331   "We must grope around . . .": Ibid.

332   A female patient: In Rosemary H. Balsam, "On Being Good: The Internalized Sibling with Examples from Late Adolescent Analyses," *Psychoanalytic Inquiry* 8, no. 1 (1988): 80.

332   Jerry, a forty-year-old: Herbert M. Rabin, "Peers and Siblings: Their Neglect in Analytic Group Psychotherapy," *International Journal of Group Psychotherapy* 39, no. 2 (Apr. 1989): 213–14.

332 group unity and collaboration: In Sigmund Freud, "Group Psychology and the Analysis of the Ego," 1921, *Standard Edition*, vol. 18, pp. 67–143.

333 "remembers nothing": Sigmund Freud, "Recollection, Repetition and Working Through," 1914, in *Collected Papers*, vol. 2, authorized translation under the supervision of Joan Riviere (New York: Basic Books, 1959), 369.

333 death instinct . . . discounted: See Roazen, *Freud and His Followers*, 327.

334 "strange paradox": From a discussion with Martin Bergmann, 10 Oct. 1991. He develops these ideas in *The Anatomy of Loving: The Story of Man's Quest to Know What Love Is* (New York: Columbia Univ. Press, 1987).

336 "complementary": Toman, *Family Constellation*, chap. 6.

337 contradictory and inconclusive: See Stephen B. Gold and Judith E. Dobson, "Birth Order, Marital Quality, and Stability: A Path Analysis of Toman's Theory," *Individual Psychology* 44, no. 3 (Sept. 1988): 355–64.

337 Lou Andreas-Salomé: Cited in Judith F. Lasky and Susan F. Mulliken, "Sibling Relationships and Mature Love," in Judith F. Lasky and Helen W. Silverman, *Love: Psychoanalytic Perspectives* (New York: New York Univ. Press, 1988), p. 90.

338 Alexander Levay: Interview with author, 10 July 1989.

338 Ms. L.: The case is described in Lasky and Mulliken, "Sibling Relationships," 86–87.

343 anticipation of a second child: Janice Abarbanel presents this theory and the cases of Ms. C. and Ms. B. in "The Revival of the Sibling Experience During the Mother's Second Pregnancy," in *Psychoanalytic Study of the Child* 38 (1983): 353–79.

345 "The multigenerational process": Bowen, *Family Therapy*, 206.

346 "Ghosts in the nursery": Selma Fraiberg, Edna Adelson, and Vivian Shapiro. "Ghosts in the Nursery," *Journal of the American Academy of Child Psychiatry* 14 (1975): 387.

346 family environment: See Paula Bernstein, *Family Ties: Corporate Bonds* (New York: Doubleday, 1985).

347 banking loan officer: Joan Rachel Goldberg, "Family Ties Can Strangle Professional Relations," *American Banker*, 10 Oct. 1985.

348   Leonard Nimoy: Aljean Harmetz, "Leonard Nimoy at the Controls," *The New York Times*, 30 Oct. 1988, "Arts & Leisure."

349   "all sorts of incompetencies": Interview with Theodore Cohn, 15 Jan. 1989.

349   "Dandelion Seed . . .": Interview with John F. Goodson, 8 Feb. 1989.

351   "I grieve for you": 2 Samuel 1:26.

CHAPTER FIFTEEN

353   theory of mind: For an excellent explanation of this concept, see Uta Frith, *Autism: Explaining the Enigma* (Cambridge, Mass.: Basil Blackwell, 1989), chap. 10.

354   pretend play in sibling relations: Naomi Jane Dale, "Early Pretend Play Within the Family" (Ph.D. diss., Univ. of Cambridge, 1983).

357   development of the fetus: Natalie Angier, "One Argument That Competition Has Its Beginnings in the Embryo," *The New York Times*, 12 Feb. 1991, Science section.

358   "Your new beau": Deborah Tannen, *You Just Don't Understand: Women and Men in Conversation* (New York: William Morrow, 1990), 173.

359   siblings don't have such conversations: Ross and Milgram, "Adult Sibling Relationships," 236.

366   "No whim . . .": Vaillant, *Adaptation to Life*, 369.

371   Ways of Coping Questionnaire: Folkman and Lazarus, "If It Changes, It Must Be a Process."

374   "History is not destiny": Fraiberg, "Ghosts," 389.

Suggested Readings

Adams, Bert N. *Kinship in an Urban Setting.* Chicago: Markham, 1968.

Adler, Alfred. *Understanding Human Nature.* 1927. Translated by W. Béran Wolfe. New York: Fawcett Premier Books, 1957.

———. *What Life Should Mean to You.* Edited by Alan Porter. Boston: Little, Brown, 1931.

Alcott, Louisa May. *Little Women.* New York: Bantam Books, 1983.

Arnstein, Helene S. *Brothers and Sisters/Sisters and Brothers.* New York: E. P. Dutton, 1979.

Bank, Stephen P., and Michael D. Kahn. *The Sibling Bond.* New York: Basic Books, 1982.

Bennett, Arnold. *The Old Wives' Tale.* 1908. New York: Heritage Press, 1940.

Bettelheim, Bruno. *The Uses of Enchantment: The Meaning and Importance of Fairy Tales.* New York: Random House, Vintage Books, 1977.

Bossard, James H. S., and Eleanor Stoker Boll. *The Large Family System: An Original Study in the Sociology of Family Behavior.* Philadelphia: University of Pennsylvania Press, 1956; Westport, Conn.: Greenwood Press, 1975.

Bowen, Murray. *Family Therapy in Clinical Practice.* New York: Jason Aronson, 1978.

Bowlby, John. *Attachment and Loss.* 3 vols. New York: Basic Books, 1969–80.

Cheever, John. "The Brothers." In *The Best Short Stories 1938.* Edited by Edward J. O'Brien. Boston: Houghton Mifflin, 1938.

———. "Goodbye, My Brother." In *The Stories of John Cheever.* New York: Alfred A. Knopf, 1978.

Chess, Stella, and Alexander Thomas. *Know Your Child: An Authoritative Guide for Today's Parents.* New York: Basic Books, 1987.

417

Chodorow, Nancy. *The Reproduction of Mothering: Psychoanalysis and the Sociology of Gender.* Berkeley: University of California Press, 1978.

Downing, Christine. *Psyche's Sisters.* San Francisco: Harper and Row, 1988.

Dunn, Jane. *A Very Close Conspiracy: Vanessa Bell and Virginia Woolf.* Boston: Little, Brown, 1990.

Dunn, Judy. *Sisters and Brothers: The Developing Child.* Cambridge, Mass.: Harvard University Press, 1985.

Dunn, Judy, and Carol Kendrick. *Siblings: Love, Envy, and Understanding.* Cambridge, Mass.: Harvard University Press, 1982.

Dunn, Judy, and Robert Plomin. *Separate Lives: Why Siblings Are So Different.* New York: Basic Books, 1990.

Eichenbaum, Luise, and Susie Orbach. *Between Women: Love, Envy, and Competition in Women's Friendships.* New York: Penguin Books, 1989.

Eliot, George. *The Mill on the Floss.* 1860. New York: Bantam Books, Bantam Classics, 1987.

Ernst, Cécile, and Jules Angst. *Birth Order: Its Influence on Personality.* Berlin: Springer-Verlag, 1983.

Falbo, Toni, ed. *The Single-Child Family.* New York: Guilford Press, 1984.

Featherstone, Helen. *A Difference in the Family: Life with a Disabled Child.* New York: Basic Books, 1980.

Fishel, Elizabeth. *Sisters: Love and Rivalry Inside the Family and Beyond.* New York: William Morrow, 1979.

Forer, Lucille K., with Henry Still. *The Birth Order Factor.* New York: David McKay, 1976.

Fraiberg, Selma, Edna Adelson, and Vivian Shapiro. "Ghosts in the Nursery." *Journal of the American Academy of Child Psychiatry* 14 (1975): 387–421.

Franks, Lucinda. *Wild Apples.* New York: Random House, 1991.

Freud, Sigmund. *The Complete Letters of Sigmund Freud to Wilhelm Fliess 1887–1904.* Translated and edited by Jeffrey Moussaieff Masson. Cambridge, Mass.: Harvard University Press, Belknap Press, 1985.

————. "The Interpretation of Dreams." 1900. In the *Standard Edition of the Complete Psychological Works of Sigmund Freud,* vol. 5. Edited by James Strachey. London: Hogarth Press and the Institute of Psycho-Analysis, 1953.

————. *Introductory Lectures on Psychoanalysis.* 1916–17. Translated and edited by James Strachey. New York: W. W. Norton, 1966; Liveright, 1977.

———. "Recollection, Repetition and Working Through." 1914. In *Collected Papers of Sigmund Freud.* Authorized translation under the supervision of Joan Riviere. New York: Basic Books, 1959.

———. "Some Reflections on Schoolboy Psychology." 1914. In *Standard Edition.* Vol. 13. Edited by James Strachey. London: Hogarth Press and the Institute of Psycho-Analysis, 1953.

Gilligan, Carol. *In a Different Voice: Psychological Theory and Women's Development.* Cambridge, Mass.: Harvard University Press, 1982.

Grossman, Frances Kaplan. *Brothers and Sisters of Retarded Children.* Syracuse, N.Y.: Syracuse University Press, 1972.

Guerin, Philip J., Jr., ed. *Family Therapy: Theory and Practice.* New York: Gardner Press, 1976.

Hetherington, E. Mavis. "Coping with Family Transitions: Winners, Losers, and Survivors," *Child Development* 60 (1989): 1–14.

Joyce, Stanislaus. *My Brother's Keeper.* Edited by Richard Ellmann. London: Faber and Faber, 1958; Faber Paperback, 1982.

Kahn, Michael D., and Karen Gail Lewis, eds. *Siblings in Therapy.* New York: W. W. Norton, 1988.

Kiell, Norman, ed. *Blood Brothers: Siblings as Writers.* New York: International Universities Press, 1983.

Lamb, Michael E., and Brian Sutton-Smith, eds. *Sibling Relationships: Their Nature and Significance Across the Lifespan.* Hillsdale, N.J.: Lawrence Erlbaum, 1982.

McGoldrick, Monica, John K. Pearce, and Joseph Giordano, eds. *Ethnicity and Family Therapy.* New York: Guilford Press, 1982.

Maclean, Norman. "A River Runs Through It." In *A River Runs Through It and Other Stories.* Chicago: University of Chicago Press, 1976.

Mann, Thomas. *Joseph and His Brothers.* New York: Alfred A. Knopf, 1948.

Meiselman, Karin C. *Incest: A Psychological Study of Causes and Effects with Treatment Recommendations.* San Francisco: Jossey-Bass, 1978.

Miller, Sue. *Family Pictures.* New York: Harper and Row, 1990.

Minuchin, Salvador. *Families and Family Therapy.* Cambridge, Mass.: Harvard University Press, 1974.

Neubauer, Peter B. "Rivalry, Envy, and Jealousy." *The Psychoanalytic Study of the Child* 37 (1982): 121–42.

Plomin, Robert, and Denise Daniels. "Why Are Children in the Same Family So Different from One Another?" *Behavioral and Brain Science* 10 (1987): 1–60.

Rhodes, Richard. *A Hole in the World*. New York: Simon and Schuster, 1990.

Roazen, Paul. *Freud and His Followers*. New York: New York University Press, reprint, 1984.

Rosen, Helen. *Unspoken Grief: Coping with Childhood Sibling Loss*. Lexington, Mass.: D. C. Heath, Lexington Books, 1986.

Rossner, Judith. *His Little Women*. New York: Summit Books, 1990.

Roth, Philip. *The Counterlife*. New York: Farrar, Straus and Giroux, 1986.

———. *The Facts: A Novelist's Autobiography*. New York: Farrar, Straus and Giroux, 1988.

———. *Patrimony: A True Story*. New York: Simon and Schuster, 1991.

Schachter, Frances Fuchs, and Richard K. Stone, eds. *Practical Concerns About Siblings: Bridging the Research-Practice Gap*. New York: Haworth Press, 1987.

Shepard, Sam. *Buried Child*. In *Seven Plays*. New York: Bantam Books, 1981.

———. *True West*. In *Seven Plays*. New York: Bantam Books, 1981.

Simpson, Eileen. *Orphans: Real and Imaginary*. New York: Weidenfeld and Nicolson, 1987.

Sophocles. *Antigone*. In *The Complete Plays of Sophocles*. Translated by Sir Richard Claverhouse Jebb. New York: Bantam Books, Bantam Classics, 1982.

Sutton-Smith, Brian, and B. G. Rosenberg. *The Sibling*. New York: Holt, Rinehart, and Winston, 1970.

Toman, Walter. *Family Constellation: Its Effect on Personality and Social Behavior*. New York: Springer, 1976.

Twitchell, James B. *Forbidden Partners: The Incest Taboo in Modern Culture*. New York: Columbia University Press, 1987.

Visher, Emily B., and John S. Visher. *Stepfamilies: Myths and Realities*. Secaucus, N.J.: Citadel Press, 1987.

Wallerstein, Judith S., and Sandra Blakeslee. *Second Chances: Men, Women, and Children a Decade After Divorce*. New York: Ticknor and Fields, 1989.

INDEX

Abarbanel, Janice, 343–44
Adaptation to Life (Vaillant), 365
Adler, Alfred, 66, 172
Adolescence/adolescents
closeness and, 302–4
sibling death and reactions of, 247–50
Adoption
Delaware Family Study, 151–53
stepsiblings and, 150
Age spacing, closeness and, 293–94, 295–96
Aging parents
closeness and, 322–23
fights over, 269–71
AIDS, 250–51
Alcoholism and drug abuse
case study of, 207–15
daughters of alcoholic fathers, impact on, 204–5
daughters of alcoholic mothers, impact on, 205–6
middle siblings, impact on, 203
older siblings, impact on, 202–3
reactions of siblings, 206–7
roles siblings play, 201–2
in siblings, 215–18
sons of alcoholic fathers, impact on, 206
sons of alcoholic mothers, impact on, 206
younger siblings, impact on, 203–4
Alcott, Louisa May, 80
Andreas-Salomé, Lou, 337
Angst, Jules, 43–44
Anna O., 245–46
Antigone, 113
Approval from siblings, 10–11
Apter, Terri, 161
Ascher, Barbara Lazear, 251

Attachment theory, 291–96
memories of closeness and attachments in adult life, 305–25
Authority, firstborns and, 48–49

Bank, Stephen, 219, 298
Bedford, Victoria, 319–20, 321–22
Behavioral geneticists, work by, 20–21
Behavior patterns, repetitive. *See* Transference
Bergmann, Martin, 334
Bettelheim, Bruno, 64
Between Women (Eichenbaum and Orbach), 10
Bible, The,
birthright, 78
closeness of brothers and sisters in, 113–14
favoritism in, 105, 172, 173–74
friendships in, 351
laterborns in, 64
sibling fighting in, 264–65
Bingham, Sallie, 106
Birth order. *See also under position*, *e.g.*, Firstborns
accuracy of theories regarding, 43–44
closeness and, 294–96
marriage and, 336–37
opposite-sex siblings and closeness and, 112–21
personality and, 42–43
perspectives based on, 42
power interactions and, 43, 44, 46–48
reversals and reactions by stepsiblings, 140–41
Blue Collar Marriage (Komarovsky), 313
Boll, Eleanor, 33, 49, 74, 94, 296
Bonding
importance of, 354–56

421

Only children, xii, 257, 322, 343
Opposite-sex siblings, relationships between
  birth order and closeness and, 112–21
  case study of older brother/younger sister, 116–21
  case study of older sister/younger brother, 121–24
  favoritism and, 103–11
  problems when there are several, 124–26
  sexuality and, 111–12, 125–26
Orbach, Susie, 10
Ordinary Love (Smiley), 82
Orphanhood, closeness and, 298, 299
Orphans (Simpson), 298

Pappenheim, Bertha, 245–46
Parents
  case studies of parental influence, 23–27, 30–31
  closeness and influence of, 291–92, 297–302
  comparisons/labeling made by, 34–36
  favoritism and, 14
  favoritism (gender) and, 103–11
  favoritism (personal) and, 157–77
  fights after death of, 273–74
  fights and interference from, 258
  fights and parental conflicts, 261
  fights and parental undermining, 260–61
  fights over aging, 269–71, 322–23
  firstborns and relations with, 47
  lastborns and relations with, 76–77
  laterborns and relations with, 65, 67
  need to talk with, about sibling conflicts, 366–70
  personality differences and influence of, 21–22
  rivalry and influence of, 12–14
  scapegoating by, 178–95
  sibling views of, 7–8
  splitting of, by same-sex siblings, 85–86
Past, creation of a common, 8–9
Patrimony (Roth), 272
"Peanuts," 122
Personality
  of firstborns, 42–43
  of laterborn children, 43
Personality differences, parental influences on, 21–22
Plato, 81
Poe, Edgar Allan, 220
Pollock, George, 245
Possessions, fights over, 273–74

Power interactions, 13
  birth order and, 43–44, 46–48
  firstborns and, 46–47
  intensity of, between firstborns and secondborns, 73
  laterborns and, 72
Pretend play, importance of, 354–55

Raffaelli, Marcela, 257–58
Recognition and approval, need for, 71–72
Remarriages, stepsiblings and
  problems created with the breakup of, 145–46
  reactions to, 139–45
Rhodes, Richard, 299
Rivalry. *See* Competition/rivalry
"River Runs Through It, A," (Maclean), 180, 216
Role assumption
  defining, 30
  laterborns wanting to be like firstborns, 68–69, 71, 77–79
  limitations of, 36–37
  melding of, 37–39
Rosenberg, B. G., 47, 68
Ross, Helgola G., 11, 12, 161, 270, 321, 359
Rossner, Judith, 80
Roth, Philip, 52, 272, 311, 320

Saint-Exupéry, Antoine de, 248
Same-sex siblings, relationships between
  among sisters versus among brothers, 96–102
  closeness and, 97, 99–102
  comparisons and competition and, 97–99
  emotional differences and, 98–100
  identical twins and, 81–83
  identity and, 81–84
  rivalry and, 84–85
  sexuality and, 86–87
  splitting of parents and, 85–86
  twinning and, 85
Scapegoat/scapegoating
  case studies of, 187–95, 197–98
  causes for, 180–81, 182
  description of, 178–79
  displacement and, 182–84
  effects of, 179–80
  in family system terms, 181–82
  fights and impact of parental, 259–60
  by parents, 178–95
  reasons why children conform to, 184–86
  by siblings, 195–98

Twins, identical
   identity formation and, 81–83
   temperament in, 21

Understanding Human Nature (Adler), 66

Vaillant, George, 304, 325, 365–66
Viorst, Judith, 312

Wallerstein, Judith, 137

Winnicott, Donald, 292
Woolf, Virginia, 87
Wordsworth, William, 220
Work situations, transference and, 346–49

Yalom, Irvin, 247
You Just Don't Understand (Tannen), 358
Younger siblings. *See* Lastborn siblings; Laterborn siblings

About the Author

Francine Klagsbrun has written more than a dozen books for adults and young people, including *Married People, Voices of Wisdom,* and *Too Young to Die,* and was the editor of the bestselling *Free to Be . . . You and Me.* Her articles have appeared in many national publications, including the *New York Times, Newsweek, Ms.,* and *McCall's,* and she lectures widely on family and social issues. She lives in New York City with her husband and daughter.